Czech Yearbook
of International Law®

Czech Yearbook
of International Law®

Volume X

2019

State Sovereignty

Editors

Alexander J. Bělohlávek
Professor
at the VŠB TU
in Ostrava
Czech Republic

Naděžda Rozehnalová
Professor
at the Masaryk University
in Brno
Czech Republic

Questions About This Publication

www.czechyearbook.org; www.lexlata.pro; editor@lexlata.pro

LEX LATA

Printed in the EU.
ISBN/EAN: 978-90-824603-9-1
ISSN: 2157-2976

Lex Lata B.V.
Mauritskade 45-B
2514 HG – THE HAGUE
The Netherlands

———————————

The title Czech Yearbook of International Law® as well as the logo appearing on the cover are protected by EU trademark law.

Typeset by Lex Lata B.V.

„We regret to announce the death of our most reputable colleague Prof. Nikolay Natov from Bulgaria. We are thankful for his efforts invested in our common project. His personality and wisdom will be deeply missed by the whole editorial team."

Czech Yearbook of International Law®

Address for correspondence & manuscripts

Czech Yearbook of International Law®

Jana Zajíce 32, Praha 7, 170 00, Czech Republic

editor@lexlata.pro

Editorial support:

Tereza Tolarová, Jan Šamlot, Lenka Němečková,
Karel Nohava, Kim Mašek

Czech Yearbook of International Law®

Impressum

Institutions Participating in the CYIL Project

Academic Institutions within Czech Republic

Masaryk University (Brno)
Faculty of Law, Department of International and European Law
[*Masarykova univerzita v Brně, Právnická fakulta,
Katedra mezinárodního a evropského práva*]

University of West Bohemia in Pilsen
Faculty of Law, Department of Constitutional Law & Department
of International Law
[*Západočeská univerzita v Plzni, Právnická fakulta,
Katedra ústavního práva & Katedra mezinárodního práva*]

VŠB – TU Ostrava
Faculty of Economics, Department of Law
[*VŠB – TU Ostrava, Ekonomická fakulta, Katedra práva*]

Charles University in Prague
Faculty of Law, Department of Commercial Law, Department of
European Law & Centre for Comparative Law
[*Univerzita Karlova v Praze, Právnická fakulta,
Katedra obchodního práva, katedra evropského práva & Centrum
právní komparatistiky, PrF UK*]

University College of International and Public Relations Prague
[*Vysoká škola mezinárodních a veřejných vztahů Praha*]

**Institute of State and Law of the Academy of Sciences of the Czech
Republic, v.v.i.**
[*Ústav státu a práva Akademie věd ČR, v.v.i.*]

University of Finance and Administration, Czech Republic
[*Vysoká škola finanční a správní, a.s., Praha, Česká republika*]

Non-academic Institutions in the Czech Republic

Office of the Government of the Czech Republic
Department of Legislation, Prague
[*Úřad vlády ČR, Legislativní odbor, Praha*]

Arbitration Court attached to the Economic Chamber of the Czech Republic and Agricultural Chamber of the Czech Republic, Prague
[*Rozhodčí soud při Hospodářské komoře České republiky a Agrární komoře České republiky*]

International Arbitration Court of the Czech Commodity Exchange, Prague
[*Mezinárodní rozhodčí soud při Českomoravské komoditní burze, Praha*]

ICC National Committee Czech Republic, Prague
[*ICC Národní výbor Česká republika, Praha*]

Institutions outside the Czech Republic Participating in the CYIL Project

Austria

University of Vienna [*Universität Wien*]
Department of European, International and Comparative Law, Section for International Law and International Relations

Poland

Jagiellonian University in Krakow [*Uniwersytet Jagielloński v Krakowie*]
Faculty of Law and Administration, Department of Private International Law

Slovakia

Slovak Academy of Sciences, Institute of State and Law
[*Slovenská akadémia vied, Ústav štátu a práva*], Bratislava

University of Matej Bel in Banská Bystrica
[*Univerzita Mateja Bela v Banskej Bystrici*],
Faculty of Political Sciences and International Relations, Department of International Affairs and Diplomacy

Trnava University in Trnava [*Trnavská Univerzita v Trnave*],
Faculty of Law, Department of Labour Law and Social Security Law

Proofreading and translation support provided by:
SPĚVÁČEK překladatelská agentura, s.r.o., Prague, Czech
Republic and Pamela Lewis, USA.

Contents

BIBLIOGRAPHY, CURRENT EVENTS, CYIL & CYArb® PRESENTATIONS, IMPORTANT WEB SITES

Alexander J. Bělohlávek

All contributions in this book are subject to academic review.

List of Abbreviations

ADR	Alternative Dispute Resolution
AFSJ	Area of freedom, security and justice
ASEAN	Association of South East Asian Nations
CAATSA	Countering America's Adversaries Through Sanctions Act
CCI	The Chamber of Commerce and Industry
CCP	Civil Procedure Code of the Republic of Kazakhstan
CCR	Constitutional Court of Romania
CEDAM	The Community Economic Development Association of Michigan
CEDH	Cour Européenne des Droits de l'Homme
CFIUS	The Committee on Foreign Investment in the United States
CFSP	Common foreign and security policy
CIS	Commonwealth of Independent States
CJEU	Court of Justice of the European Union
CLOUD Act	Clarifying Lawful Overseas Use of Data Act
CNRS	Centre national de la recherche scientifique
COCON	Working Group on Consular Cooperation
COM	Communication from the Commission to the European Parliament and the Council
CPC	Code of Civil Procedure
CSCE	Conference on Security and Co-operation in Europe
CSDP	Common Security and Defence Policy
ČSOB	Checho-Slovak Commercial Bank (Československá obchodní banka)
ČSR	Czechoslovakia (Československá

	republika)
DCFR	Draft Common Frame of Reference
EAS	Ellinika Amyntika Systimata
EC	European Commission
ECHR	European Court of Human Rights
ECJ	European Court of Justice
ECLI	European Case Law Indentifier
ECT	Energy Charter Treaty
EEAS	European External Action Service
EEC	European Economic Community
EPPO	European Public Prosecutor's Office
EU	European Union
FYROM	Former Yugoslav Republic of Macedonia
GDP	The Gross Domestic Product
GWh	Gigawatt hour
HUF	Hungarian Forint
ICC	International Chamber of Commerce
ICJ	The International Court of Justice
ICSID	The International Centre for Settlement of Investment Disputes
IDRL	International Disaster Response Law
ILC	International Law Commission
INCOTERMS	International Commercial Terms
IT	Information Technology
JSC	The Joint Stock Company
MGIMO	Moscow State Institute of International Relations
New York Convention	Convention in the Recognition and Enforcement of Foreign Arbitral Awards, New York, 1958
NGO	Non-governmental Organization
OFAC	Office of Foreign Assets Control
PCIJ	Permanent Court of International Justice
PECL	Principles of European Contract Law
R2P	The Responsibility to Protect
RANEPA	Russian Presidential Academy of National Economy and Public Administration
RFBR	Russian Foundation for Basic Research
SDN list	Specially Designated Nationals And Blocked Persons List
SR	Slovak Republic (Slovenská republika)
SSI List	Sectoral Sanctions Identification List

SSR	The Soviet Socialist Republic
TEU	Treaty on the European Union
TFEU	Treaty on the Functioning of the European Union
TLD	Top Level National Domains
UCP	Uniform Customs and Practice for Documentary Credits
UK	United Kingdom
UN	United Nations
UN Charter	Charter of the United Nations
UN GA	United Nations General Assembly
UN OCHA	United Nations Office for the Coordination of Humanitarian Affairs
UN SC	United Nations Security Council
UNCITRAL	United Nations Commission on International Trade Law
UNCITRAL Model Law	Model law on International Commercial Arbitration as adopted by the United Nations Commission on International Trade Law on 21 June 1985, with amendments on 7 July 2006
UNCTAD	United Nations Conference on Trade and Development
UNIDROIT	International Institute for the Unification of Private Law
URC	Uniform Rules for Collections
US	United States of America
USSR	Union of Soviet Socialist Republics
VCCR	Vienna Convention on Consular Relations
Venice Council	European Commission for Democracy through Law
Vienna Convention	Convention of 24 April 1963 on Consular Relations
.com	Commercial
.int	International
.org	Organization
.ru	Country code top-level domain for the Russian Federation
.su	Country code top-level domain for the SSSR
.рф	Cyrillic country code top-level domain for the Russian Federation

Articles

Antonov Jaroslav Valerievich

The Sanctions against Russia

Key words:
*International sanctions |
tacit consent | international
legal practice | generally
recognized principles and
norms of international law
| international treaty | local
norms | customary law |
law of bubbles | sanctions
from hell | purpose of
sanctions | efficiency of
sanctions | fragmentation
and contextualization of
international legal norms*

Abstract | *Sanctions are one of the key and most controversial issues of international politics, as well as in the theory and practice of international law. The international legal regulation of sanctions is general and is mainly of a recommendatory nature. International legal practices play a special role in the understanding of sanctions. A common practice is for States to introduce unilateral political measures with the tacit consent of the international community. This article considers the sanctions by the European Union and the United States of America against Russia from the position of international law based on the analysis of opinions of scholars, and the analysis of international legal documents regulating the European Union and US sanctions against Russia. The author formulates perspectives of the application of sanctions to evaluate their efficiency. The conclusion summarizes modern problems of. international law, including the objective fragmentation and contextualization of international legal norms, and sets out recommendations for improving the international legal regulation of sanctions.*

Antonov Jaroslav Valerievich is the Head of the Center for Development of E-democracy Mechanisms at the North-West Institute of Management of the Russian Presidential Academy of National Economy and Public Administration. He is a practicing lawyer and an associate professor in the Department of Constitutional and Administrative Law at the North-west Institute of Management of the Russian Presidential Academy of National Economy and Public Administration. He holds a PhD in law and has authored more than 80 papers in international, constitutional, electoral and informational law and more than 60 papers on the legal aspects of e-democracy, e-voting, e-governance, e-government and e-justice, e-arbitration, and e-mediation.
Email contact: antonovjv@gmail.com

| | |

I.   Introduction

1.01. Sanctions in modern international law are one of the most often applied measures of international legal response when compared with other measures.[1] At the same time, there is little or no international legal regulation of sanctions. There is also no common definition of sanctions in the theory and practice of international law.[2]

1.02. The issue of an accurate assessment of sanctions and countermeasures in the conflict between Russia, the European Union and the United States of America is highly politicized and ambiguous, since there is an obvious State monopolization of the information released in the context of what is known as information sovereignty.[3]

1.03. Nevertheless, even the limited freely available information available is sufficient to note the growing dynamics of the degradation of international law. The principle of information sovereignty, formulated both in theory and in practice of international law, essentially contradicts the principle of the freedom of information dissemination. In the modern era of the development of international law, the degradation of civil rights and freedoms occurs when the concept of State sovereignty and national interests, including in the field of local and international security, prevails over individual civil rights. This is especially true regarding the right to freedom of opinion, the right to freedom of the media, the right to freedom of information dissemination. The opposition of the largest States in terms of sanctions proves this assumption.

1.04. I begin with a few my research hypotheses, which will be validated in the subsequent article. These are:

1) There is an objective fragmentation of international law when there are conflicting international norms and customs recognized by a States as a law, if these norms and customs allow the realization of that state's interests.

2) In international political practice, the 'law of the strong' approach dominates, and the assessment of the international act committed by a State directly depends on its political, economic and military power.

---

[1]   I. I. LUKASHUK, INTERNATIONAL LAW: A PARTICULAR PART. Moscow. Walters Kluwer (2005).
[2]   JEREMY FARRALL, MATAM. UNITED NATIONS SANCTIONS AND THE RULE OF LAW, Cambridge, UK: Cambridge University Press (2007).
[3]   JAROSLAV V. ANTONOV, CONDUCT OF ELECTRONIC ARBITRATION, Czech Yearbook of International Law, Volume VII, Lex Lata BV, Hague 3-26 (2018).

II.   The Concept of Sanctions in International Law

1.05.   Sanctions are generally considered to be part of a system of law that ensures compliance with legal norms. Law is as a coercive order, an organization of force, a system of norms providing by sanction.[4]

1.06.   The question of sanctions in international law is extremely controversial and there is no common definition of sanctions. In general, sanctions are coercive measures applied by an international organization to an offender in order to induce them to fulfill obligations arising from the legal relationship of responsibility.[5]

1.07.   Leading Soviet and Russian professor Grygory Tunkin asserts that the basis for the application of sanctions is a refusal to stop illegal actions and fulfill the legal demands of the injured subjects. Sanctions consist of compensation of damage, which is accompanied by coercive measures in the event of failure by the State of this duty. Regarding international crimes, new phenomena emerge regarding sanctions. Sanctions in this case are not limited to compensation for damage, but also include measures that are preventative in nature.[6]

1.08.   International sanctions are political and economic decisions that are part of diplomatic efforts by countries, multilateral or regional organizations against States or organizations either to protect national security interests, or to protect international law, and defend against threats to international peace and security.[7]

1.09.   Sanctions are a means to change a perceived illegal attitude through international public law, and a means of restoring the situation previous to some drastic event. They are a means of compensation for the damage caused by some entity subject to international law, and a means of punishing the carelessness or indifference with regard to the exercise of a legal right, or in terms of individuals, namely, the rehabilitation of the person to whom the criminal sanctions of international law are applied.[8]

1.10.   Abi-Saab defines sanctions as 'coercive measures taken in execution of a decision of a competent social organ, i.e., an

---

[4]   HANS KELSEN, GENERAL THEORY OF LAW AND STATE (1945).

[5]   I. I. LUKASHUK, INTERNATIONAL LAW: A PARTICULAR PART. Moscow. Walters Kluwer (2005).

[6]   GRIGORY I. TUNKIN, THE THEORY OF INTERNATIONAL LAW 430, 478-499 (1970).

[7]   GARY HUFBAUER, ECONOMIC SANCTIONS RECONSIDERED. Washington, DC: Peterson Institute for International Economics 5 (2007); DAVID CORTRIGHT, THE SANCTIONS DECADE: ASSESSING UN STRATEGIES IN THE 1990S. LOPEZ, GEORGE A. BOULDER, Colo.: Lynne Rienner Publishers 1 (2000).

[8]   DANIEL STEFAN PARASCHIV, THE SYSTEM OF SANCTIONS IN THE PUBLIC INTERNATIONAL LAW, Publishign House CH Beck, Bucharest 17 (2012).

organ legally empowered to act in the name of the society or community that is governed by the legal system.'[9]

1.11. Josef Kunz notes that legal sanctions constitute the reaction of the legal community against a delict.[10] The historical process after the First World War was to replace the single sanctions of States with collective measures of a collective security system.[11] There is a visible problem of applying unilateral sanctions by major world States. B. Ferencz notes that the unilateral use of force in order to achieve national goals has proven to be a destructive force and futility.[12]

1.12. Even as early as 1920, Ronald F. Roxburgh considered international sanction through pressure and strength and balance of power helps to ensure the supremacy of law.

1.13. If the strength of one warring state and its allies is immeasurably greater than the strength of the opposing state and its allies, the rules of law will probably secure general observance by all. The strong party will conform with them because the demands of necessity will not be exacting enough to make it worth while to incur the displeasure of neutral states; the weak party will conform for fear of adding a neutral to the number of its foes. [13]

1.14. In general, sanctions have to be adopted in accordance with the constituent instrument of the international organization. Although there is no scholarly agreement on the exact scope of the substantive limits, legal limitations flow from *ius cogens* obligations and the principle of proportionality.[14]

1.15. The International Law Commission has stated that the term 'sanctions' is used to refer to measures taken by international organizations, especially on the basis of Chapter VII of the UN Charter.[15]

1.16. In general, there is a problem in international law regarding the procedure for the application of sanctions. This is actively

---

[9] VERA GOWLLAND-DEBBAS, ED. UNITED NATIONS SANCTIONS AND INTERNATIONAL LAW: COLLOQUIUM ON UNITED NATIONS SANCTIONS AND INTERNATIONAL LAW 1999, Genève. The Hague: Kluwer Law International (2001).

[10] Available at: https://www.jstor.org/stable/2195251?seq=1#page_scan_tab_contents (accessed on 31 December 2018).

[11] Josef L. Kunz, *Sanctions In International Law*, 54(2) THE AMERICAN JOURNAL OF INTERNATIONAL LAW 324, 324-347(1960).

[12] Ben Ferencz, *Enforcing International Law*. 1 L 18 (1983).

[13] Ronald F. ROXBURGH, *The Sanction Of International Law*, 14(1/2) THE AMERICAN JOURNAL OF INTERNATIONAL LAW 26, 26-37 (1920), available at: https://www.jstor.org/stable/pdf/2187838.pdf (accessed on 31 December 2018).

[14] Natalia CHIRTOACĂ & Dumitrița FLOREA, *The USV Annals of Economics and Public Administration*, 13(1) 17 (2013), available at: http://www.seap.usv.ro/annals/ojs/index.php/annals/article/viewFile/513/569 (accessed on 31 December 2018).

[15] I. I. LUKASHUK, INTERNATIONAL LAW: A PARTICULAR PART. Moscow. Walters Kluwer (2005).

used by interested States, often abusing their rights and their sovereignty.[16]

1.17. The main problem in the application of sanctions, contributing to the growth of arbitrariness, is the ability to assess the presence or absence of elements of an offense in the acts of the State.[17]

1.18. Sanctions can be a powerful tool for influencing other States. At the same time, it is necessary to take into account the mechanism for the formation of customary international law. Thus, the tacit consent of other States to unlawful acts of an economically and politically strong State in order to preserve good relations with that State and/or receive hidden preferences often contributes to the creation of customs, which may be illegal in a legal way. Such examples are known in the history of international law.[18]

1.19. As an example, we can mention the case of US intervention in Panama in 1989 on the basis of the protection of US citizens in Panama. The 29 December of 1989 year at the 44th session of the UN General Assembly adopted resolution No. 44/240 about armed intervention in Panama.[19]

1.20. In international practice, there are cases of separation of multinational states on the basis of the generally accepted principle of equal rights and self-determination of peoples.[20] As a result of this practice, a new international law is created and the unlawful political act that was not protested by the world community is essentially transforming into a legal one.

1.21. The UN adopted a resolution to limit the application of the principle of equal rights and self-determination of peoples for the separation of multinational states.[21] But the contemporary concept of principle of equal rights and self-determination of peoples is far from perfect because there is no in international law legal a generally accepted legal procedure for the separation of states in accordance with the principle of equal rights and self-determination of peoples.

1.22. Therefore, it is almost impossible to give a correct international legal assessment of the procedure for the separation of states at the present stage. Thus, all the legitimacy or illegitimacy of the separation of the state is based on a set of unilateral political acts of recognition of new states by the states constituting the international community.

---

[16] I. I. LUKASHUK, INTERNATIONAL LAW: A PARTICULAR PART. Moscow. Walters Kluwer (2005).
[17] I. I. LUKASHUK, INTERNATIONAL LAW: A PARTICULAR PART. Moscow. Walters Kluwer (2005).
[18] I. I. LUKASHUK, INTERNATIONAL LAW: A PARTICULAR PART. Moscow. Walters Kluwer (2005).
[19] Available at: https://undocs.org/en/A/RES/44/240 (accessed on 31 December 2018).
[20] I. I. LUKASHUK, INTERNATIONAL LAW: A PARTICULAR PART. Moscow. Walters Kluwer (2005).
[21] Available at: http://www.un.org/en/ga/search/view_doc.asp?symbol=A/RES/2625(XXV) (accessed on 31 December 2018).

III.   European Union Sanctions against Russia

1.23. The declared reasons for the imposition of sanctions against Russia are the highly politicized topic of the joining of Crimea and Sevastopol to Russia (in the EU documents, the joining of Crimea and Sevastopol to Russia is called an 'illegal annexation'),[22] as well as accusing Russia of violating the territorial integrity, sovereignty and independence of Ukraine.

1.24. The initial list of persons to whom the individual EU sanctions were imposed was approved by Council Regulation EC №269 / 2014, 17 March 2014[23] and then repeatedly extended.[24]

1.25. On 31 July 2014, the EU Council imposed sectoral sanctions against three industries of Russia: military-industrial, banking and oil. The goal of sectoral sanctions was 'to increase the cost of Russia's actions to undermine Ukraine's territorial integrity, sovereignty and independence' and 'promote a peaceful settlement of the crisis.'[25]

1.26. Regulation №833/2014 firstly, imposed an embargo on the supply of arms and dual-use goods to Russia. Secondly, it banned five Russian State-staked banks - VTB, VEB, Gazprombank, Rosselkhozbank, Sberbank - from accessing EU borrowing on the long-term market for 90 days. Thirdly, it placed an embargo on the supply of equipment to Russia for deepwater exploration and production of oil in the Arctic, or any shale oil projects. The bodies of the Member States responsible for the application of sectoral sanctions did leave the right to authorize the execution of relevant transactions concluded before August 1, 2014.

1.27. According to the MGIMO associate professor Ivan Gudkov, in order to protect the EU economic operators from civil liability to Russian counterparties for non-fulfillment of transactions caused by the introduced sectoral sanctions, Article 11 of Regulation No. 833/2044 established a ban on satisfying the corresponding claims of Russian counterparties.[26]

---

[22] See for example: http://www.consilium.europa.eu/en/press/press-releases/2018/06/18/illegal-annexation-of-crimea-and-sevastopol-eu-extends-sanctions-by-one-year/pdf (accessed on 31 December 2018).

[23] COUNCIL REGULATION (EU) NO 269/2014 OF 17 MARCH 2014 CONCERNING RESTRICTIVE MEASURES IN RESPECT OF ACTIONS UNDERMINING OR THREATENING THE TERRITORIAL INTEGRITY, SOVEREIGNTY AND INDEPENDENCE OF UKRAINE, available at: https://eur-lex.europa.eu/legal-content/EN/TXT/PDF/?uri=CELEX:32014R0269&from=GA (accessed on 31 December 2018).

[24] Available at: http://www.alleuropa.mgimo.ru/sanktsii-es-v-otnoshenii-rossii-neeffektivnostj-i-nezakonnostj-1 (accessed on 31 December 2018).

[25] COUNCIL REGULATION (EU) NO. 833/2014 OF 31 JULY 2014 CONCERNING RESTRICTIVE MEASURES IN VIEW OF RUSSIA'S ACTIONS DESTABILISING THE SITUATION IN UKRAINE, OJ L 229/1, available at: https://publications.europa.eu/en/publication-detail/-/publication/65b043ca-18c2-11e4-933d-01aa75ed71a1/language-en (accessed on 31 December 2018).

[26] Available at: http://www.alleuropa.mgimo.ru/sanktsii-es-v-otnoshenii-rossii-neeffektivnostj-i-

1.28. As Gudkov notes, Article 11 of Regulation No. 833/2044 laid the burden of proving the inapplicability of sanctions to specific transactions on plaintiffs, which contradicts the general principle of law, according to which the burden of proving a particular circumstance must be borne by a party referring to it in support of its interest.[27] It is obvious that such provisions represent a tough administrative interference in civil-law relations, the legitimacy of which has been questioned.[28]

1.29. This assertion is debatable. For the satisfaction of a legitimate interest, the plaintiff whose rights have been violated usually refers to the court, and then the plaintiff must prove their claim.

1.30. If the plaintiff's rights to enforce the contract are violated by law, the plaintiff must challenge the law, and not file claims against the defendant on the basis that the defendant complied with the provisions of the law and in the process violated the rights and legitimate interests of the plaintiff. The defendant cannot and should not be responsible for the laws adopted in the State that result in the failure to fulfill an obligation under the contract in connection with the execution of the law.

1.31. The defendant in this case has no legal interest or standing to challenge the law and should not be required to prove lack of liability for simply complying with the law. Otherwise, each defendant who did not fulfill their obligations by virtue of the law would have to present evidence of their lack of liability in a trial. It should also be noted that the fact of the adoption of the new law is a universally recognized circumstance excluding the responsibility of the party for failure to fulfill the obligation under the contract, also known as force majeure.[29]

1.32. Therefore, the reference to general principles of law in this case is not correct.

1.33. On 8 September 2014, the Council of the European Union adopted a new package of sectorial and individual sanctions, published and enacted on 12 September 2014. The second package of sectorial sanctions, according to the chairmen of the European Commission and the European Council, was designed to 'increase the effectiveness of measures already taken' and to reinforce the principle that EU sanctions are aimed at changing Russia's position regarding actions in Ukraine.[30]

---

nezakonnostj-1 (accessed on 31 December 2018).
[27] Available at: https://eur-lex.europa.eu/legal-content/EN/TXT/?uri=OJ:JOL_2014_229_R_0001 (accessed on 31 December 2018).
[28] Available at: http://www.alleuropa.mgimo.ru/sanktsii-es-v-otnoshenii-rossii-neeffektivnostj-i-nezakonnostj-1 (accessed on 31 December 2018).
[29] Available at: http://opil.ouplaw.com/view/10.1093/law:epil/9780199231690/law-9780199231690-e1042 (accessed on 31 December 2018).
[30] Available at: http://www.alleuropa.mgimo.ru/sanktsii-es-v-otnoshenii-rossii-neeffektivnostj-i-

Czech Yearbook of International Law®

1.34. The reason for the adoption of a new package of sanctions, as the chairman of the European Council stated, was the condemnation of 'the increased inflow of fighters and weapons from the territory of the Russian Federation into Eastern Ukraine and the aggression by Russian armed forces on Ukrainian territory'.[31]

1.35. This package extended restrictions on access to the EU financing market for three key Russian oil companies (Rosneft, Transneft, Gazprom Neft) and three defense companies (Oboronprom, UAC, Uralvagonzavod), and the period of allowable borrowing was reduced from 90 to 30 days. In addition, new restrictions were introduced in the oil sector: EU companies were prohibited from providing services for the exploration and production of deep-sea, Arctic and shale oil.

1.36. Unlike individual sanctions, the EU's sectorial sanctions directly affected the interests of key sectors of the Russian economy. It is quite natural that it was the sectorial sanctions of the EU that aroused a response from Russia.

1.37. On 6 August 2014, less than a week after the adoption of Regulation No. 833/2014, the President of Russia signed the Decree 'On the application of certain special economic measures to ensure the security of the Russian Federation.' The decree became the basis for the imposition by the Russian government of an embargo on the import of a number of food products from countries using 'economic sanctions against Russian legal entities and (or) individuals.'

1.38. European States such as Italy, Hungary, Greece, France, Cyprus and Slovakia are among the EU states most skeptical about the sanctions and have called for review of sanctions.[32]

1.39. At present, European Union sanctions are planned to be extended until February 2019.[33] Thus, the conflict between the European Union and the Russian Federation will continue to develope while the current foreign policy of the European Union and the Russian Federation is maintained.

IV. United States Sanctions against Russia

1.40. US sanctions against Russia developed in a specific chronological order.

---

nezakonnostj-1 (accessed on 31 December 2018)
[31] Statement by the President of the European Council H.V. Rompuy on further restrictive measures against Russia 08 September 2014, available at: http://www.consilium.europa.eu/uedocs/cms_data/docs/pressdata/en/ec/144839.pdf (accessed on 31 December 2018)
[32] Available at: https://uk.reuters.com/article/uk-ukraine-crisis-eu-idUKKCN0WG1B4 (accessed on 31 December 2018).
[33] Available at: https://www.rt.com/business/431841-russia-eu-sanctions-economy/ (accessed on 31 December 2018).

IV.1. Restrictions on US Corporations

1.41. There are general restrictions that were placed on US corporations and individuals conducting business with Crimea. It was articulated in Executive Order 13685 of 19 December 2014 entitled 'Blocking Property of Certain Persons and Prohibiting Certain Transactions with Respect to the Crimea Region of Ukraine'.[34]

IV.2. Sectoral Sanctions – Sectorial Sanctions Identification List

1.42. In July of 2014 limited sectoral sanctions were introduced against several banks (Gazprombank, Vneshtorgbank, Russian Agricultural Bank and Vnesheconomobank) and two energy companies (Rosneft and Novatek). Since then the list has continued to expand. These companies are not subject to an asset freeze, but US persons are unable to enter into certain transactions with them. These companies appear on a new Sectoral Sanctions Identification List (SSI List) and are not in the Specially Designated Nationals list. Russia's largest company - the United Shipbuilding Corporation has been added to the SDN list.[35]

1.43. On 6 March 2014, the US President signed Executive Order 13660 placing sanctions on any individual or entity responsible for or complicit in actions that undermine the democratic process or threaten the peace, security and stability of Ukraine.[36] This was expanded on 17 March 2014 and 20 March 2014 by Executive Orders 13661 and 13662 enabling the targeting of Russian entities and individuals, including Russian officials, persons businessmen, banks and commercial organizations.[37]

1.44. These three executive orders were implemented by Regulation (31 CFR part 589).[38] In July 2015, Office of Foreign Assets Control (herinafter - OFAC) designated five Crimean port operators and one sea ferry operator pursuant to Executive Order 13685. The seaports affected are at Kerch, Sevastopol,

---

[34] Available at: https://www.treasury.gov/resource-center/sanctions/Programs/Documents/ukraine_eo4.pdf (accessed on 31 December 2018).
[35] Available at: https://www.treasury.gov/resource-center/faqs/Sanctions/Pages/faq_other.aspx#ukraine (accessed on 31 December 2018).
[36] Available at: https://www.state.gov/e/eb/tfs/spi/ukrainerussia/ (accessed on 31 December 2018); https://www.treasury.gov/resource-center/sanctions/Programs/Documents/ukraine_eo.pdf (accessed on 31 December 2018).
[37] Available at: https://www.treasury.gov/resource-center/sanctions/Programs/Documents/ukraine_eo2.pdf (accessed on 31 December 2018); https://www.treasury.gov/resource-center/sanctions/Programs/Documents/ukraine_eo3.pdf (accessed on 31 December 2018).
[38] Available at: https://www.treasury.gov/resource-center/sanctions/Programs/Documents/31cfr589.pdf (accessed on 31 December 2018).

Feodosia, Evpatoria and Yalta.[39] The US has extended its targeted sanctions against senior Russian officials, businessmen and organizations until 6 March 2017.[40]

1.45. On 27 October 2017, the US Department of State issued public guidance on the implementation of Section 231 of 'Countering America's Adversaries Through Sanctions Act' (hereinafter - CAATSA) accompanied by list of entities considered to be operating in Russia's defence or intelligence sectors. [41] Under this legislation, the President of the USA also may impose sanctions against individuals that engage in 'significant' transactions with entities on this list. [42]

1.46. On 2 August 2017, the US President signed into law the 'Countering America's Adversaries Through Sanctions Act' (CAATSA). The Act expands and codifies sanctions against Russia. It opens up designations for entities and persons operating in (or providing support to) certain sectors of Russian economy, specifically railway, financial services, mining, energy, metals, defence and related material. It also reduces tenors for transactions listed under Directive 1 E.O. 13622 from 30 to 14 days and under Directive 2 from 90 to 60 days respectively.[43]

1.47. On 6 April 2018, a number of Russian individuals and entities have been added to OFAC's SDN List: senior Russian officials, businessmen and organizations.[44] OFAC has also issued General License 12C,[45] General License 13C,[46] General License 14,[47] General License 15[48] and General License 16,[49] authorising certain transactions with a number of Russian entities to allow for continued maintenance and wind down activities.

1.48. On 16 August 2018, the US Department of State made a determination that will trigger sanctions under the 'Chemical

---

[39] Available at: https://www.treasury.gov/resource-center/sanctions/Programs/Documents/ukraine_eo4.pdf (accessed on 31 December 2018).
[40] Available at: https://www.skuld.com/topics/legal/sanctions/russia/insight-russia-sanctions/#chapter-2 (accessed on 31 December 2018).
[41] Available at: https://www.state.gov/t/isn/caatsa/275118.htm (accessed on 31 December 2018).
[42] Available at: https://www.skuld.com/topics/legal/sanctions/russia/insight-russia-sanctions/#chapter-2 (accessed 31 December 2018).
[43] Available at: https://www.skuld.com/topics/legal/sanctions/russia/insight-russia-sanctions/#chapter-2 (accessed on 31 December 2018).
[44] Available at: https://www.treasury.gov/resource-center/sanctions/OFAC-Enforcement/Pages/20180406.aspx (accessed on 31 December 2018).
[45] Available at: https://www.treasury.gov/resource-center/sanctions/Programs/Documents/ukraine_gl12c.pdf (accessed on 31 December 2018).
[46] Available at: https://www.treasury.gov/resource-center/sanctions/Programs/Documents/ukraine_gl13c.pdf (accessed on 31 December 2018).
[47] Available at: https://www.treasury.gov/resource-center/sanctions/Programs/Documents/ukraine_gl14.pdf (accessed on 31 December 2018).
[48] Available at: https://www.treasury.gov/resource-center/sanctions/Programs/Documents/ukraine_gl15.pdf (accessed on 31 December 2018).
[49] Available at: https://www.treasury.gov/resource-center/sanctions/Programs/Documents/ukraine_gl16.pdf (accessed on 31 December 2018).

and Biological Weapons Control and Warfare Elimination Act'. The first round of sanctions took effect on 27 August 2018 and introduced a ban on exports to Russia of security-sensitive products and technology, with an exemption permitted for existing contracts and termination of related export licenses. On 27 August 2018, the Department of State published a Notice bringing mandatory sanctions under the Chemical and Biological Weapons Control and Warfare Act into force.

V.   Efficiency of Applying Sanctions against Russia

1.49.   There are some aspects of efficiency of applying sanctions.[50] Scholarly literature examines the impact of economic sanctions on poverty and economic growth.[51]

1.50.   Scholar Christine Lumen considers the following purpose of economic sanctions:
- Deterrence;
- Compliance (Coercion);
- Destabilization (Subversion);
- Signaling;
- Symbolic tool.

1.51.   Sanctions should be considered based on the purpose of their application. But do sanctions fulfil this purpose? This issue is debatable. The evaluation of efficiency depends on what the objectives of sanctions are.[52]

1.52.   Sanctions may be aimed at enforcing compliance with international law. This may include requirements to change political behavior in a certain way (to leave the territory, transfer suspects, to cease active military actions) or to encourage compromise between the parties to the conflict. Also, sanctions can be taken in order to contain the conflict. The arms embargo is typical for this purpose. Sanctions can also be developed to express outrage, but without a clear political goal.[53]

1.53.   The Hungarian Foreign Minister Mr. Szijjártó note that "The sanctions policy has proven to be a mistaken and unsuccessful

---

[50] DURSUN PEKSEN SOCIO-ECONOMIC AND POLITICAL CONSEQUENCES OF ECONOMIC SANCTIONS FOR TARGET AND THIRD-PARTY COUNTRIES, available at: https://www.ohchr.org/Documents/Events/Seminars/CoercitiveMeasures/DursunPeksen.pdf (accessed on 31 December 2018).

[51] DYLAN O'DRISCOLL IMPACT OF ECONOMIC SANCTIONS ON POVERTY AND ECONOMIC GROWTH (2017), available at: http://gsdrc.org/wp-content/uploads/2017/06/136-Impact-of-economic-sanctions-on-poverty-and-economic-growth.pdf (accessed on 31 December 2018).

[52] Simon Chesterman & Bernard Pouligny, *Are Sanctions Meant To Work? The Politics of Creating and Implementing Sanctions through the United Nations*, 9 Global Governance 503, 503-518 (2003), available at: https://papers.ssrn.com/sol3/papers.cfm?abstract_id=1119103 (accessed on 31 December 2018).

[53] Simon Chesterman & Bernard Pouligny, *Are Sanctions Meant To Work? The Politics of Creating and Implementing Sanctions through the United Nations*, 9 Global Governance 503, 503-518 (2003), available at: https://papers.ssrn.com/sol3/papers.cfm?abstract_id=1119103 (accessed on 31 December 2018).

response, which has caused major damage to Europe while failing to realise the set goals, such as the enforcement of the Minsk Agreements. Conflicts of a non-economic nature must be handled via non-economic means. Maintaining the sanctions is causing losses for Europe; the Russian economy has already acclimatised itself to them".[54]

1.54. Considering that the sanctions against Russia have been enacted since 2014 and new measures are being taken, and the desired purpose for the European Union and the United States regarding the conflict in Ukraine as a whole has not been reached, it can be concluded that the sanctions are not efficient.

1.55. I think in this situation sanctions can provoke conflict and create unavoidable obstacles to dialogue and consensus so far.[55]

1.56. Despite the generally anti-Russian scientific research the scholars Andreas Beyer and Benno Zogg note that «Sanctions have largely failed to thwart Russian aggression in Ukraine since 2014".[56]

1.57. And Andreas Beyer and Benno Zogg highlight some key points about sanctions against Russia: «Since their adoption in 2014, the EU, the US and other Western states regularly extended sanctions against Russia without a clear strategy or assessment of whether they are succeeding.

1.58. The Russian population bears the costs of sanctions, not the oligarchic elite. This inner circle now depends even more on state support. Russians perceive sanctions as humiliating; they have thus stirred nationalist sentiment and helped boost Putin's popularity.

1.59. Hence, sanctioning states should abandon the current approach of only lifting sanctions for Moscow's full compliance with the Minsk agreements. Europe should allow for a gradual easing of sanctions, which enables and requires Russia to make first de-escalatory steps in Ukraine".[57]

1.60. So, I think that none of these typical purposes of sanctions were achieved. On the contrary, sanctions provoke conflict and create unavoidable obstacles to dialogue and consensus so far.

1.61. In my opinion the efficiency of sanctions should be measured, including in the context of compliance with generally recognized

---

[54] Available at: https://eu-brusszel.mfa.gov.hu/eng/news/the-sanctions-against-russia-have-failed-from-both-a-political-and-economic-perspective (accessed on 31 December 2018).
[55] Available at: https://www.nytimes.com/2014/08/22/opinion/when-sanctions-lead-to-war.html (accessed on 31 December 2018).
[56] Andreas Beyer, Benno Zogg, *Time to Ease Sanctions on Russia*, 6(4) POLICY PERSPECTIVES (2018)., available at: http://www.css.ethz.ch/content/dam/ethz/special-interest/gess/cis/center-for-securities-studies/pdfs/PP6-4_2018.pdf (accessed on 31 December 2018).
[57] Andreas Beyer, Benno Zogg, *Time to Ease Sanctions on Russia*, 6(4) POLICY PERSPECTIVES (2018)., available at: http://www.css.ethz.ch/content/dam/ethz/special-interest/gess/cis/center-for-securities-studies/pdfs/PP6-4_2018.pdf (accessed on 31 December 2018).

principles and norms of international law. In this case, sanctions should be consistent with the principle of international cooperation established in Article 1, paragraph 3, of the UN Charter.[58]

VI.   Perspectives on the Application of Sanctions against Russia

1.62.   Considering the prospects for applying sanctions against Russia, it should be noted that the conflict is escalating now, and the US plans to introduce new so-called sanctions 'from hell'.[59]

1.63.   The new draft sanctions showed an extremely negative trend expressed in the personalization of sanctions in order to increase US pressure on Russia. In fact, sanctions are imposed on persons holding public office in Russia, including affecting the President of the Russian Federation V.V. Putin. Thus, the person occupying the highest State post and acting in the interests of the entire Russian people is subject to political and economic pressure.

1.64.   The Presidential elections in the Russian Federation received various assessments, but were generally recognized by international observers as free and fair.

1.65.   Viktor Guminsky, the head of the special observing mission from the Commonwealth of Independent States (CIS) state that the recent presidential election held in Russia was free, legitimate and competitive.[60]

1.66.   Li Yongquan, the director of the Institute of Russian, Eastern European and Central Asian Studies of the Chinese Academy of Social Sciences and an election observer from China noted that «Legally and organization-wise, the presidential election was conducted very well. The strongest impression is that Russian voters are very mature".[61]

1.67.   The conclusions of Organization for Security and Cooperation (hereinafter – OSCE) about overly controlled environment on presidential election[62] is debatable in the context of sanctions against the Russian Federation. In my opinion, the state should independently ensure not only transparency, but also the security of the elections. In assessing justice and freedom

---

[58]   Available at: http://www.un.org/en/sections/un-charter/chapter-i/index.html (accessed on 31 December 2018).

[59]   Available at: https://www.reuters.com/article/us-usa-russia-sanctions/us-senators-introduce-russia-sanctions-bill-from-hell-idUSKBN1KN22Q (accessed on 31 December 2018).

[60]   Available at: https://sputniknews.com/russia-elections-2018-news/201803191062686896-international-observers-election/ (accessed on 31 December 2018).

[61]   Available at: https://sputniknews.com/russia-elections-2018-news/201803191062686896-international-observers-election/ (accessed on 31 December 2018).

[62]   Available at: https://www.osce.org/odihr/elections/375661 (accessed on 31 December 2018).

of elections, it is necessary to take into account, including the current international situation. Otherwise, the free choice of citizens may be influenced by the states concerned.

1.68. Thus, in my opinion the personalization of responsibility destroys the whole foundation of modern international law, the subjects of which are States, and those who occupy State posts express solely the will of the State on behalf of and in the interests of the population.

1.69. In my opinion in accordance with the generally recognized principles and norms of international law, the prosecution of individuals and legal entities by imposing sanctions whose guilt has not been proved cannot be justified.

1.70. In fact, this violates the entire theoretical concept of such subjects of law as legal entities and the state.[63] Legal entities as well as States are governed by specific people, but they bear responsibility independently as subjects of law. In my opinion sanctions should be directed to the State as a subject of public law, and not to specific individuals that represent the State.

1.71. Moreover, the adoption of such a document is a violation of the fundamental principle of State sovereignty. The State cannot conduct an independent domestic and foreign policy when the official representing the State is under economic or political influence. In the current form, such sanctions are discrediting democracy and show disrespect for the choice of the population in free elections.

1.72. If current dynamics continue, I think that international law will become the 'law of bubbles' in the next 10 years, when each State will have its own bubble of laws as large as its economic and military power. In my opinion this essentially means that the international assessment of the legitimacy of the actions of State in the international arena directly depends on the political, economic and military power of the State.

VII.   Conclusion

1.73. In conclusion, it should be noted that the concept of sanctions in international law requires consolidation in acts of international law, because at present the practice of applying sanctions by individual States is becoming an international custom due to the tacit consent of other States.

1.74. Sanctions are applied only by an authorized international body or organization and this is noted both in the writings of scholars and in international acts. In this case, sanctions should have

---

63   I. I. LUKASHUK, INTERNATIONAL LAW: A PARTICULAR PART. Moscow. Walters Kluwer (2005).

been introduced with the approval of the UN Security Council. It is a function of the Security Council of United Nations to call on Members to apply economic sanctions and other measures not involving the use of force to prevent or stop aggression.[64]

1.75. On the official website of the UN Security Council there are no resolutions for the period 2013-2018 years regarding the commission of international offences, acts of aggression and annexation of the Russian Federation against Ukraine.[65]

1.76. Based on the above theoretical provisions, the so-called 'sanctions' against Russia are not Sanctions in the traditional sense. What are being called 'sanctions' can be primarily assessed as unilateral political measures that pursue the specific geopolitical interests of the European Union and the United States of America.

1.77. Currently, guided by the principles of customary law, a State may, at its discretion, impose sanctions on another State due to the fact that it violates the rules of international law, in the opinion of the former State. At the same time, the fact of violation of international law does not need to be confirmed in international courts or organizations, or to involve other States in support of their position.

1.78. In this case, the former State acts in the sole judge and the executioner. In fact, the adoption and securing of a sanctions depends on the economic, political and military might of the that State. At the same time, the sanctioned State is compelled to choose the forms and methods of defense independently, because other States are afraid to act in wanting to maintain good relations with the sanctioning State even at the cost of ignoring the violations of international law. However, in the future such a situation may have the opposite effect and the tables could turn if the sanctioned State gains greater political, military and economic power than the sanctioning State. The conflict between such States is not resolved by means of such sanctions, but is repeated.

1.79. Undoubtedly, this practice contributes to the escalation of conflict on the one hand, and on the other, generates the disintegration of general international law into constantly changing contextual norms.

1.80. In this sense, there is a breakdown and fragmentation of international law, when international treaties and international customs exist in different political dimensions.

---

[64] Charter of United Nations, available at: http://www.un.org/en/sc/about/functions.shtml (accessed on 31 December 2018).

[65] Available at: http://www.un.org/en/sc/documents/resolutions/ (accessed on 31 December 2018).

1.81. International treaties are recognized as long as the State has an interest in observing them. The interest in observing the provisions of a treaty does not drive international customs, when the wrongful acts of the State, with the tacit consent of other States, become international custom. This raises the fundamental question of the existence of international law precisely as a real law, and not as a collection of political declarations.

1.82. The responsibility of the State and the highest officials expressing the will of the people must be divided in order to ensure the principle of State sovereignty and independence of the State. At present, there is a practice of abuse of international law, when sanctions apply to the State, to its associated legal entities, and to senior State officials.

1.83. Sanctions should be precisely the consequence of the commission of an international offense, and not an arbitrary political act. In this sense, the following principles of the application of sanctions as a measure of international responsibility are quite justified:

1) Sanctions are applied only as a result of the commission of an international offense by the State. The establishment of the fact of committing an offense must be confirmed by a competent international organization, which includes representatives of the State accused of committing an offense. Such an organization may be the International Court of Justice, or an international organization whose decisions are recognized by States as mandatory.

2) The subjects of sanctions are the States acting on the basis of the decision of the competent organization.

3) Sanctions cannot be applied to officials of the State that committed the offense. The State should be held accountable.

Summaries

FRA   [*Les sanctions à l'encontre de la Russie*]
Les sanctions sont l'un des sujets les plus controversés de la politique internationale, tout comme de la théorie et de la pratique du droit international. Les textes du droit international se prononcent sur les sanctions en termes généraux et contiennent avant tout des recommandations. Les usages du droit international jouent un rôle spécifique dans l'analyse des sanctions. Il est

Czech Yearbook of International Law®

de pratique commune pour les États d'appliquer des mesures politiques unilatérales avec l'accord tacite de la communauté internationale. Le présent article se propose d'examiner, dans la perspective du droit international, les sanctions mises en place par l'Union européenne et par les États-Unis contre la Russie, en se fondant sur les points de vue des théoriciens et sur l'analyse des textes du droit international relatifs à ces sanctions. L'auteur réfléchit sur les perspectives de l'application de ces sanctions puis évalue leur efficacité. En conclusion, il passe en revue les problèmes actuels du droit international, y compris la fragmentation objective et la contextualisation de ses normes, et propose des recommandations pour améliorer la réglementation des sanctions dans le cadre du droit international.

CZE [*Sankce proti Rusku*]

Sankce jsou jedním z klíčových a nejvíce kontroverzních témat mezinárodní politiky, jakož i teorie a praxe mezinárodního práva. Úprava sankcí v mezinárodním právu je obecná a převážně doporučujícího charakteru. Pro účely porozumění sankcím hrají zvláštní roli zvyklosti mezinárodního práva. Běžnou praxí států je zavádět jednostranná politická opatření s tichým souhlasem mezinárodní komunity. Tento článek posuzuje sankce Evropské unie a Spojených států amerických vůči Rusku z hlediska mezinárodního práva na základě analýzy stanovisek teoretiků a analýzy dokumentů mezinárodního práva upravujících sankce Evropské unie a Spojených států vůči Rusku. Autor uvádí vyhlídky aplikace sankcí za účelem zhodnocení jejich účinnosti. V závěru autor shrnuje moderní problémy mezinárodního práva, včetně objektivní fragmentace a kontextualizace norem mezinárodního práva, a předkládá doporučení ke zlepšení mezinárodněprávní regulace sankcí.

POL [*Sankcje wobec Rosji*]

Sankcje to jeden z kluczowych i najbardziej kontrowersyjnych tematów w polityce międzynarodowej oraz teorii i praktyki prawa międzynarodowego. Artykuł analizuje sankcje nałożone przez Unię Europejską i Stany Zjednoczone Ameryki na Rosję w świetle prawa międzynarodowego, na podstawie analizy stanowisk teoretyków i analizy dokumentów prawa międzynarodowego

Czech Yearbook of International Law®

regulujących sankcje Unii Europejskiej i Stanów Zjednoczonych w stosunku do Rosji.

DEU   [*Sanktionen gegen Russland*]

Sanktionen sind ein höchst kontroverses Schlüsselthema der internationalen Politik ebenso wie der Theorie und Praxis des Völkerrechts. Dieser Beitrag beurteilt die Sanktionen seitens der Europäischen Union und der Vereinigten Staaten von Amerika gegen Russland aus Sicht des internationalen Rechts, auf der Basis einer Analyse der Stellungnahmen diverser Theoretiker und der völkerrechtlichen Dokumente, in denen diese Sanktionen der EU und USA gegen Russland geregelt sind.

RUS   [*Санкции против России*]

Санкции являются одним из ключевых и наиболее дискуссионных вопросов международной политики, а также теории и практики международного права. В статье предпринята попытка рассмотрения санкций Европейского союза и Соединенных штатов Америки против России с позиции международного права на основе анализа мнений ученых, анализа международно-правовых документов, регламентирующих санкции Европейского союза и США против России.

ESP   [*Sanciones contra Rusia*]

Las sanciones constituyen uno de los temas esenciales y a la vez más controvertidos de la política internacional, así como de la teoría y la práctica del derecho internacional. El presente artículo examina las sanciones de la Unión Europea y los Estados Unidos de América contra Rusia desde el punto de vista del derecho internacional basándose en el análisis de opiniones teóricas y en el análisis de documentos del derecho internacional que regulan las sanciones de la Unión Europea y los Estados Unidos contra Rusia.

| | |

Bibliography

JAROSLAV V. ANTONOV, CONDUCT OF ELECTRONIC ARBITRATION, Czech Yearbook of International Law, Volume VII, Lex Lata BV, Hague (2018).

Andreas Beyer, Benno Zogg, *Time to Ease Sanctions on Russia*, 6(4) POLICY PERSPECTIVES (2018).

Simon Chesterman & Bernard Pouligny, *Are Sanctions Meant To Work?*

The Politics of Creating and Implementing Sanctions through the United Nations, 9 Global Governance 503 (2003).

Natalia CHIRTOACĂ & Dumitrița FLOREA, 13(1) *The USV Annals of Economics and Public Administration* 17 (2013).

DAVID CORTRIGHT, THE SANCTIONS DECADE: ASSESSING UN STRATEGIES IN THE 1990S. LOPEZ, GEORGE A. BOULDER, Colo.: Lynne Rienner Publishers (2000).

JEREMY FARRALL, MATAM. UNITED NATIONS SANCTIONS AND THE RULE OF LAW, Cambridge, UK: Cambridge University Press (2007).

Ben Ferencz, *Enforcing International Law*. 1 L 18 (1983).

VERA GOWLLAND-DEBBAS, ED. UNITED NATIONS SANCTIONS AND INTERNATIONAL LAW: COLLOQUIUM ON UNITED NATIONS SANCTIONS AND INTERNATIONAL LAW 1999, Genève. The Hague: Kluwer Law International (2001).

GARY HUFBAUER, ECONOMIC SANCTIONS RECONSIDERED. Washington, DC: Peterson Institute for International Economics (2007).

HANS KELSEN, GENERAL THEORY OF LAW AND STATE (1945).

Josef L. Kunz, *Sanctions In International Law*, 54(2) THE AMERICAN JOURNAL OF INTERNATIONAL LAW (1960).

I. I. LUKASHUK, INTERNATIONAL LAW: A PARTICULAR PART. Moscow. Walters Kluwer (2005).

Ronald F. ROXBURGH, *The Sanction Of International Law*, 14(1/2) THE AMERICAN JOURNAL OF INTERNATIONAL LAW 26 (1920).

DANIEL STEFAN PARASCHIV, THE SYSTEM OF SANCTIONS IN THE PUBLIC INTERNATIONAL LAW, Publishing House CH Beck, Bucharest (2012).

GRIGORY I. TUNKIN, THE THEORY OF INTERNATIONAL LAW (1970).

Czech Yearbook of International Law®

Adrienn Becánics

State Sovereignty and the Right to Consular Protection of the European Union

Key words:
EU citizenship | diplomatic protection | consular assistance | EU Law | international law | state sovereignty

Abstract | *In order to define the legal scope of the provision of consular protection within the EU, it is necessary to analyse international law rules that might touch upon the legal regulation of the consular relationships. There are no international law rules reserving consular protection to the full discretion of the States. Therefore it is necessary to determine the relationship between International and EU law rules in the scope of consular protection. In addition, it is necessary to analyse what power is given to the EU by the Member States in the context of consular protection and what power remains in the discretion of the States. This article will analyse legal instruments and 'soft law' acts in connection with the right to consular protection, its extraterritorial character and the supranational legal order, which has partially overcome the internal public law of the Member States.*

Adrienn Becánics is an assistant lecturer with the Department of European and International Law, Faculty of Law, at the University of Debrecen. She graduated from the Faculty of Law, University of Debrecen and lectures in International Law and European Law at the Faculty of Law, University of Debrecen. Her focus is on diplomatic and consular law, particularly the consular protection of European citizens in third countries.
E-mail: adrienn.becanics@ law.unideb.hu

| | |

Czech Yearbook of International Law®

I.   Introduction: Sovereignty as an Essential Characteristic of States[*]

2.01.   The fundamental principle of State sovereignty has a variety of meanings, but in its most common usage, it is the term for the totality of international rights and duties recognized by international law.[1] The whole of international law and the freedom of choice of the political, social, economic and cultural system of a State rest on such sovereignty.[2] From that aspect, it is sufficient to say that a State's sovereignty extends to the area of its foreign policy, and that there is no rule of customary international law to prevent a State from choosing and conducting a foreign policy in co-ordination with that of another State.[3] Sovereignty is therefore an essential and inseparable characteristic of the State.[4]

2.02.   Under current international law, sovereignty is defined as follows: Sovereignty in the sense of contemporary public international law denotes the basic international legal status of a state that is not subject, within its territorial jurisdiction, to the governmental, executive, legislative, or judicial jurisdiction of a foreign state or to foreign law other than public international law.[5] It is also defined as the 'ultimate authority, held by a person or institution, against which there is no appeal.'[6]

2.03.   In other words, sovereignty is the ultimate power, authority and/or jurisdiction over a people and a territory. No other person, group, or State can tell a sovereign entity what to do on its land. A sovereign entity can decide and administer its own laws free of external influences while at the same time following the limitations of international law. Such sovereignty has two sides: the internal and the external. The internal side of sovereignty investigates internal control and authority and external sovereignty - explores the independent conduct of foreign relations. These are the prime features of the State.[7]

---

*   This paper and the associated research was supported by the ÚNKP-17-3 New National Excellence Program of the Ministry of Human Capacities.
1   THE CREATION OF STATES IN THE INTERNATIONAL LAW, Oxford: Clarendon, 33 (James Crawford ed., 2006).
2   Military and paramilitary activities in and against Nicaragua (Nicaragua/United States of America), Judgement, I.C.J. Reports 1986, paragraph 263.
3   Military and paramilitary activities in and against Nicaragua (Nicaragua/United States of America), Judgement, I.C.J. Reports 1986, paragraph 265.
4   BENOYTOSH BHATTACHARYYA, A FIRST COURSE OF POLITICAL SCIENCE WITH CONSTITUTIONS OF INDIAN REPUBLIC AND PAKISTAN, Calcutta 89- 103 (1949).
5   Helmut Steinberger, *'Sovereignty',* in ENCYCLOPAEDIA OF PUBLIC INTERNATIONAL LAW, vol. 10/12, 414 (Rudolf Bernhard ed., 1987).
6   World Encyclopaedia, Oxford University Press, sovereignty (2008).
7   SATOW'S DIPLOMATIC PRACTICE, Oxford, 4.30 (Sir Ivor Roberts ed., 2017).

Czech Yearbook of International Law®

It denotes the competence and ultimate authority of a State to control matters within its territory and the people within it. Territorial jurisdiction confers the power to regulate and adjudicate on acts within its territory. Control over its people confers the power to grant or withdraw nationality and to regulate the admission of alien immigrants to the country.[8] Nevertheless, internal sovereignty of a democratic State will be conducted under the rule of law. The rule of law includes that the rules are set out in a constitution or in recorded practice. In a broader sense it implies transparency, equality, and the freedom of the individual.[9] External sovereignty implies a State's independence from all other States, with the capacity and power to conduct its own affairs within the international community. It is to be emphasized that sovereignty under international law does not imply supremacy over legal persons, but is qualified by the principles of equality between States and non-intervention in the internal affairs of other States.[10]

2.04.   The abovementioned nature of a sovereign state does not stay in the exclusive competence of the States in all circumstances. Therefore, when a State joins in an international organization, it has to deal with sharing the authority on sovereign power and decision-making mechanisms.

II.   Diplomatic and Consular Protection in Connection with the Sovereignty of States

2.05.   Before dealing with this aspect of States' sovereignty, adequate attention should be devoted to the special feature of diplomatic and consular protection, since they have a close bond with both sides of the internal and external sovereignty of States. The concepts of diplomatic and consular protection are mainly derived from international law and provisions of customary origin binding all States. As a matter of fact, consular assistance originates in the traditional relationship between the legal principles of territoriality and personhood, which are bound up with the sovereignty of States. The relationships between States and their citizens that reside within their territories are regulated by the national law of States. The tension with this relationship starts when citizens leave the territory of their own State and come under the jurisdiction of a foreign State. Consular assistance usually emerges in situations when a citizen transfers

---

[8]   *Ibid.*, at 4.31.
[9]   *Ibid.*, at 4.37.
[10]   *Ibid.*, at 4.38.

their place of residence to another State, and the authority that both States can claim to exercise is limited by the obligation to respect the sovereignty of another State. The State of citizenship is limited by the duty to respect the territorial jurisdiction of the State of residence, while the authority of she State of residence is limited by the personhood relationship between the citizen and the State.[11] One of the main features of consular assistance is that it usually appears in these types of situations.

2.06. This feature was based upon a legal doctrine called 'extraterritoriality'. According to this doctrine, the citizens or protected persons of the State enjoy exemption from the local jurisdiction and they remained under the laws and administration of their own State.[12] If a person finds themselves in a situation of distress, the consular authority of the sending State will provide assistance. International law specifies these functions,[13] but the list is not exhaustive, because it regards the national administrative law of the sending State.[14] It is also worth mentioning that the functions of the consular offices can only be practiced within the limits imposed by the laws and regulations of the receiving State.[15] For instance, they have a particular role in assisting nationals in finding lawyers, visiting prisons and contracting local authorities, but they are unable to intervene in the judicial process of the receiving State.[16] On the other hand, the Vienna Convention on Consular Relations imposes an obligation on the receiving State to allow and facilitate the exercise of these consular functions.[17]

2.07. In light of the above-mentioned characteristic of consular protection, it seems obvious that the consular protection is closely connected with the question of sovereignty, from the point of the sending and receiving State as well. In this manner, beyond the rules of international law, the legal systems of the sending and the receiving State play an important role in

---

[11]   Stefano Battini, *International Administrative Law today: the Case of Consular Assistance and diplomatic Protection, in* EUROPEAN CITIZENSHIP AND CONSULAR PROTECTION NEW TRENDS IN EUROPEAN LAW AND NATIONAL LAW, Napoli: editoriale Scientifica 57-58 (Sebastiano Faro, Mario P. Chiti, Erich Schweighofer eds., 2012).

[12]   Luke T. LEE, John QUIGLEY, CONSULAR LAW AND PRACTICE, Oxford: Oxford University Press 47 (2008).

[13]   See Vienna Convention on Consular Relations (Adopted at Vienna on 24 April 1963, entered into force on 19 March 1967) 596 UNTS 261 Article 5.

[14]   Stefano Battini, *International Administrative Law today: the Case of Consular Assistance and diplomatic Protection, in* EUROPEAN CITIZENSHIP AND CONSULAR PROTECTION NEW TRENDS IN EUROPEAN LAW AND NATIONAL LAW, Napoli: editoriale Scientifica 59-60 (Sebastiano Faro, Mario P. Chiti, Erich Schweighofer eds., 2012).

[15]   See Vienna Convention on Consular Relations (Adopted at Vienna on 24 April 1963, entered into force on 19 March 1967) 596 UNTS 261 Article 5.

[16]   MALCOLM .N. SHAW, INTERNATIONAL LAW, Cambridge 688 (2003).

[17]   See Vienna Convention Chapter II, Section I, in particular Article 28: 'The receiving State shall accord full facilities for the performance of the functions of the consular post.'

ensuring consular protection. Hence, consular protection could not be defined as a preserved decision of one State, and it could not ensure this kind of protection without the cooperation of another State or States. Although diplomatic protection has different features, legal scholars have often confused diplomatic protection and consular assistance.[18] The diplomatic actions open to a State is limited by the restrictions imposed on countermeasures by international law. The traditional view maintains that the State of nationality acts on its own behalf and has discretion in the exercise of this right, and it has the complete freedom of action with respect to international rules.[19] While the principle of non-intervention does limit the scope of consular protection it has no presence in diplomatic protection since it is not an internal affair but an international dispute.[20] The discretionary nature of the State's right to exercise diplomatic protection is affirmed by draft Article 2 of the UN Report of the International Court of Justice in the Barcelona Traction case.[21] It is also worth mentioning that contemporary developments which grant individuals direct access to international judicial bodies to assert claims against both foreign States and their State of nationality lend a new approach to this question.[22] The ILC Draft Article 19 establishes a 'Recommended practice' declaring that a State entitled to exercise diplomatic protection 'should [...] give due consideration to the possibility of diplomatic protection...' [23] Therefore, the State has a wide scope of discretion on the decision whether to exercise an action in defence of the legitimate interest of the individual.

2.08.   Contrary to diplomatic protection, consular protection may be conceived as an individual right, there is no international law rule reserving consular protection to the State's full discretion.[24] Consular law and also a fundamental right to consular protection[25] exist in about one third of the EU Member States.

---

[18]   FIRST REPORT ON DIPLOMATIC PROTECTION, John R. Dugard, 7 March and 20 April 2000, U.N. Doc. A/CN.4/506 and Add. 1, paragraph 43.
[19]   See the case of Mavrommatis Palestine Concessions (Grecee/United Kingdom) P.C.I.J. Series A, No.2 (1924).
[20]   ANNEMARIEA VERMEER-KÜNZLI, THE PROTECTION OF INDIVIDUALS BY MEANS OF DIPLOMATIC PROTECTION, Leiden: PrintPartners Ipskamp 80 (2007).
[21]   Case concerning the Barcelona Traction Light and Power Company Limited (Belgium/ Spain), Second Phase, Judgement, I.C.J. Reports 1970, p 44.
[22]   FIRST REPORT ON DIPLOMATIC PROTECTION, John R. Dugard, 7 March and 20 April 2000, U.N. Doc. A/CN.4/506 and Add. 1, paragraph 61.
[23]   Draft Articles on Diplomatic Protection with commentaries, ILC, A/61/10, 2006, Article 19.
[24]   EVA-MARIA POPTCHEVA, MULTILEVEL CITIZENSHIP, THE RIGHT TO CONSULAR PROTECTION OT EU CITIZENS ABROAD, Brussels: P.I.E. Peter Lang, 51-52 (2014).
[25]   A fundamental right to consular protection is granted by Bulgaria, Estonia, Hungary, Latvia, Lithuania, Poland and Romania. See Sebastian Faro, Mandalina B. Morau, *Comparative analysis of legislation and practice on consular protection and assistance of the 27 EU countries*, Table 9, *in* EUROPEAN CITIZENSHIP AND CONSULAR PROTECTION NEW TRENDS IN EUROPEAN LAW AND NATIONAL LAW, Napoli: editoriale

Otherwise, a consular policy is implemented.[26] Despite those ten Member States that provide consular protection as a matter of policy, judicial review of the refusal may be sought by the person affected. According to the Austrian Federal Constitution, the Austrian Administrative Court is 'competent to secure the legality of all acts of the public administration...'[27] and renders judgments on complaints which allege the illegality of decisions of administrative authorities.'[28] This clearly supports the view that the liability of States on consular protection is not a sovereign decision of the States, but rather a concrete obligation.

III. Membership in the EU from the Perspective of Consular Protection

2.09. 'The institutional view of organizations of states result in an actual, as opposed to a formal, qualification of the principle of sovereign equality. Thus an organization may adopt majority voting and also have a system weighed voting; and may be permitted to take decisions, and even to make binding rules, without the express consent of all or any of the member states.[29]'

2.10. It can be said that on joining the organization each member consented in advance to the institutional aspects of that organization, and thus in a formal way the principle that obligations can only arise from the consent of States and the principle of sovereign equality are satisfied. In practice, the European Communities, while permitting integration which radically affects domestic jurisdiction for special purposes, has been careful not to jar the delicate treaty structures by a too-ready assumption of implied powers. If an organization encroaches on the domestic jurisdiction of members to a substantial degree the structure may approximate a federation, and not only the area of competence of members but their very personality will be in issue. The line is not easy to draw, but the following criteria could provide some support: the obligatory nature of membership; majority decision-making; the determination of jurisdiction by the organization of jurisdiction by the organization itself, and

Scientifica 216 (Sebastiano Faro, Mario P. Chiti, Erich Schweighofer, eds., 2012).
[26]   Erich Schweighofer, *The Protection of Union citizens in third countries: Aspects of international and European Law*, in EUROPEAN CITIZENSHIP AND CONSULAR PROTECTION NEW TRENDS IN EUROPEAN LAW AND NATIONAL LAW, Napoli: editoriale Scientifica 75 (Sebastiano Faro, Mario P. Chiti, Erich Schweighofer, eds., 2012).
[27]   Article 129 of the Austrian Federal Constitution.
[28]   Article 130 paragraph 1 of the Austrian Federal Constitution.
[29]   IAN BROWNLIE, PRINCIPLES OF PUBLIC INTERNATIONAL LAW, Oxford: Oxford University Press, 291-292 (7th ed., 2008).

the binding quality of decisions of the organization apart from the consent of member States.[30]

2.11. In the foregoing paragraphs the abovementioned criteria will be analysed from the perspective of decision-making of consular protection in the European Union.

2.12. The European Union is more than a classic intergovernmental organization and less than a federative State. The EU is a specific complex organism, which disposes of independent decision-making tools and its own power mechanisms.[31] The Treaties on the European Union (TEU) and Treaties on the Functioning of the European Union (TFEU) represented a compromise between the supranational institutions and resting control with the governments of Member States. Due to its extraterritorial character, the provision of consular protection to unrepresented Union citizens links together obligations under both EU law and rules of general and specific public international law. The obligations under European Union law come up against the limits drawn by public international law, interposing itself often between international and national law.[32] With regard to this aspect, it should be noted that the European Union is itself a product of international law, and a product of the relationship between sovereign States with the purpose of creating rights and obligations.[33] Nonetheless, its different character from other traditional international organizations is beyond question. The Court of Justice in its leading case *van Gend & Loos* concluded that the European Economic Community (EEC) Treaty went over the traditional arrangements between International Law actors implying solely obligations between the member States. The Community involved the citizens as new actors with an active roll as addresses of the Community provisions, and established institutions with sovereign rights whose exercise affects not only Member States but also their citizens.[34] The Court also stated that the Community constitutes a new legal order of international law for the benefit of which the States

---

[30] IAN BROWNLIE, PRINCIPLES OF PUBLIC INTERNATIONAL LAW, Oxford: Oxford University Press, 291-292 (7th ed., 2008).
[31] ONDREJ HAMULÁK, NATIONAL SOVEREIGNTY IN THE EUROPEAN UNION, VIEW FROM THE CZECH PERSPECTIVE, Springer 1 (2016).
[32] See Sir Daniel Bethlehem, *International Law, European Community Law, National Law: Three Systems in Search of a Framework, Systematic Relativity in the Interaction of law in the European Union, in* INTERNATIONAL LAW ASPECTS OF THE EUROPEAN UNION, The Hague/London/Boston 172 (Martti Koskenniemi ed., 1998).
[33] *Ibid.*, at 178.
[34] Judgement of the Court of Justice of 05 February 1963 in the case 26/62, *NV Algemene Transport en Expeditie Onderneming van Gend & Loos* v. *Netherlands Inland Revenue Administration* (van Gend en Loos) ECR 1963, p. 00001.

have limited their sovereign rights within limited fields.[35] One of these fields is consular protection which has to be extended by the Member States to all European citizens in the territory of a third country.

2.13. Article 23 TFEU and Article 46 EU Charter of Fundamental Rights provide:

> Every citizen of the Union shall, in the territory of a third country in which the Member State of which he is a national is not represented, be entitled to protection by the diplomatic or consular authorities of any Member State, on the same conditions as the nationals of that State. Member States shall adopt the necessary provisions and start the international negotiations required to secure this protection.

2.14. First of all, one must determine whether or not Article 23 TFEU establishes a true individual right to diplomatic and consular protection and what kind of relationship may exist between the national and EU citizenship with regard to this subject.

2.15. As for the latter, citizenship is traditionally conceived as a genuine bond between States and its nationals. EU citizenship is the only instrument in international law which has a significant impact on this special relationship. It differs from double citizenship, which entails being a citizen of two States at the same time.[36] EU citizenship does not replace national citizenship, but complements it and has a remarkable effect on it. Before EU citizenship Member States had an absolute sovereign decision on the acquisition and loss of citizenship. In the case *Micheletti*, the European Court of Justice (ECJ) clarified that although the citizenship remains a discretionary power of national authorities, it must be exercised in conformity with the fundamental freedoms protected by EU law.[37] In another substantial case the Court held that the Member States must have due regard to EU citizenship, which is intended to be 'the fundamental status of nationals of the Member States.'[38] The connection between the national and Union citizenship is also clarified in Article 20 (1) of TFEU:[39] '[...]Citizenship of the Union shall be additional to

---

[35] Eva-Maria Poptcheva, Multilevel Citizenship, The Right to Consular Protection of EU citizens abroad, Brussels: P.I.E. Peter Lang 52-55 (2014).

[36] Giacinto Della Cananea, *The European Union and consular protection- A new public law, in* European citizenship and consular protection new trends in European Law and National Law, Napoli: editoriale Scientifica 48-53 (Sebastiano Faro, Mario P. Chiti, Erich Schweighofer, eds., 2012).

[37] ECJ, Case C-369/96, Micheletti and others v Delegación del Gobierno en Cantabria, ECR 1992 p. I-4239 § 10.

[38] ECJ, Case C-184/99, Grzelczyk, C-184/99, ECR 2001 p. I-6193, § 31.

[39] Consolidated versions of the Treaty on European Union and the Treaty on the Functioning of the European Union 2012/C 326/01, Article 20 (1).

and not replace national citizenship.' Therefore on one hand, European citizenship cannot be equalled to citizenship, and individual nationals of EU Member States consider themselves nationals of a certain State. On the other hand, EU citizenship has been a 'stimulation of European identity'[40] and it gives a number of rights in addition to the citizenship of a Member State.[41]

IV.   The Role the EU Legal System Plays in the Decision Making of Consular Protection

2.16.   Until the Treaty of Lisbon the European Community did not have the competence to act and only Member States had adopted decisions with international agreements among themselves within the confines of their internal sovereign competence. Nevertheless, the Council of the European Union had the competence to establish a new working group on consular cooperation (COCON) to adopt guidelines on protection of unrepresented European Community nationals. The contents of the very first guidelines were never published in any official journal and only operated on a soft law basis to the Member States, while remaining unknown to most European citizens. Pressure by the European Commission on the Council led to the approval of EC Decision 95/553/EC.[42] The Decision is an act *sui generis*, but is still an Act of an EC body signed by the then President of the Council and not by the Representatives of the Governments of the Member States with unanimous consent.[43] The legal basis of this decision was Article 20 of the EC Treaty, added by the Treaty on European Union of 1992 as Article 8C. The intergovernmental nature of the area transpires in it: 'Member States shall establish the necessary rules among themselves and start the international negotiations required to secure this protection.' The binding provisions of the Decision 95/553/EC on the protection of EU citizens had to wait seven

---

[40]   Ad hoc Committee on 'A People's Europe', 'Adonnino Report A People's Europe', Luxembourg, 1985, prepared according to the mandate issued by the Fontainebleau European Council of 25 and 26 June 1984, in Bulletin of the European Communities Supplement, 7/85, p.7, available at: http://aei.pitt.edu/992/1/andonnino_report_peoples_europe.pdf (accessed on 7 February 2018).

[41]   Anna Maria Helene, Vermeer- Künzli, The Protection of Individuals by means of Diplomatic Protection, Diplomatic Protection as a Human Rights Instrument, PrintPartners Ipskamp, 94 (2007).

[42]   Decision of the Representatives of the Governments of the Member States meeting within the Council of 19 December 1995 regarding protection for citizens of the European Union by diplomatic and consular representations, OJ L 314, 28/12/1995, p73.

[43]   Alessandro Ianniello-Saliceti, *The long road to the protection of EU citizens abroad*, in European Citizenship and Consular Protection New Trends in European Law and National Law, Napoli: editoriale Scientifica 7 (Sebastiano Faro, Mario P. Chiti, Erich Schweighofer, eds., 2012).

years for ratification procedures, and entered into force only in 2002. Another decision with links to consular assistance was established in the same format of the Representatives of the EU Member States gathered in the Council in 1996. This decision on the delivery of the emergency travel document[44] was entered into force in 2002 after waiting six years to be ratified.

2.17. In light of the above, one must observe that this legal basis of adopting Community decisions in the field of consular protection was an intergovernmental *sui generis* decision without involving the EU. The reason why Member States felt the danger of delegating competence to the Union could be explained by the fact that the Community measures were seen by some Member States as a too dangerous step for their sovereignty,[45] since their traditional prerogative would have been given to the EU.[46]

2.18. The system of consular protection was a relatively marginal question in the shadow of the central questions of European citizenship, such as European Parliament voting rights. However, this issue has become a priority for Member States, in the ten years following adoption. Events such as the terrorist attacks of September 2001, the Bali bombings in October 2002, or the crisis in Lebanon in July 2006 catapulted this neglected area to the top of the political schedule.[47] Member States had to choose between maintaining their prerogatives or reinforcing EU cooperation by endowing the Council with express legislative power to adopt Directives establishing the coordination measures on consular assistance. That was an urgent question since the broadening of the EU to include Member States which are not represented in numerous third countries. This was the case in December 2004, when the tsunami hit South East Asia, where a significant number of EU citizens found themselves without representation in the countries affected by the disaster. In Thailand, for example seventeen Member States are represented whereas only six are represented in Sri Lanka and three in Brunei.[48]

---

[44] 96/409/CSFP: Decision of the Representatives of the Governments of the Member States, meeting within the Council of 25 June 1996 on the establishment of an emergency travel document. OJ L 168, 06.07.1996 (ETD) Annex II. 4.

[45] Consular and Diplomatic Protection. Legal Framework in the EU Member States. CARE (Citizens Consular Assistance Regulation in Europe) 2010 (CARE Final Report) available at: http://www.careproject.eu/images/stories/ConsularAndDiplomaticProtection.pdf (accessed on 29 June 2018).

[46] Madalina Bianca Morau, *Protection of EU citizens abroad: A legal assessment of the EU citizen's consular and diplomatic protection*, 3(2) PERSPECTIVES ON FEDERALISM 91-92 (2011).

[47] Ana Mar Fernandez, *Consular Affairs in an Integrated Europe*, in Consular Affairs and Diplomacy, Leiden: Martinus Nijhoff Publishers 102 (Jan Melissen ed., 2011).

[48] European Commission, 'Green Paper on Diplomatic and Consular Protection', 28 November 2006 (COM (2006) 712 final.

V.   The New Legal System

2.19.   As a result of these new challenges, various non-binding guidelines have been adopted under the aegis of the COCON Council working group. Additionally, the provisions of consular protection have been put on a new legal platform with the entry into force of the Treaty of Lisbon on 1 December 2009 amending the Treaty on European Union and the Treaty establishing the European Community.[49] The new second paragraph of the Article 23 TFEU allows the enactment of directives by the Council in order to facilitate the consular protection: 'The Council, acting in accordance with a special legislative procedure and after consulting the European Parliament, may adopt directives establishing the coordination and cooperation measures necessary to facilitate such protection.'[50] It seems clear that the Lisbon Treaty has brought a significant change to the legal framework of consular protection: instead of the previous intergovernmental *sui generis* decision making, the EU had a sufficient competence in the legislative procedure.[51]

2.20.   After consulting the European Parliament, the Council acts by qualified majority (Article 16(3) TEU). The replacement of unanimous decision-making with qualified majority voting and the involvement of the European Parliament limit the long defended sovereignty of the Member States. Nonetheless, the wording of the Article 23 TFEU indicate only a coordinative and cooperative role to the EU and do not authorize the Council to harmonise the national law and practice on the consular protection of citizens.[52] The aim was to establish a sufficient individual right which was confirmed by Article 46 of the Charter of Fundamental Rights of the EU.[53] Article 23 TFEU ensures the possibility for the protection of EU citizens regardless of which Member States have representation in the affected third country. Basically, EU law did not create a new right, since consular assistance already exists in Member States, which now they have to afford to the nationals of the other Member States.[54] By the abolition of these pillars, consular protection of

---

[49]   The Treaty of Lisbon was signed on 13 December 2007 by the heads of State or Government of the EU Member States. Published in the Official Journal of the European Communities C 306 of 17 December 2007.

[50]   Article 23 paragraph 2 TFEU.

[51]   Madalina Bianca Morau: *Protection of EU citizens abroad: A legal assesment of the EU citizen's consular and diplomatic protection*, 3(2) PERSPECTIVES ON FEDERALISM 91-92 (2011).

[52]   *Ibid.*, at 92.

[53]   *'Every citizen of the Union shall, in the territory of a third country in which the Member State of which he or she is a national is not represented, be entitled to protection by the diplomatic or consular authorities of any Member State, on the same conditions as the nationals of that Member State.'*

[54]   Imola Schiffner, *Protection of European Citizens in Third States Under Article 23 TFEU, in* HUNGARIAN YEARBOOK OF INTERNATIONAL LAW AND EUROPEAN LAW 2013, Budapest: Eleven International Publishing 384 (Szabó Marcel, Petra Lea Láncos, Réka Varga eds., 2014).

EU citizens was placed under the scope of the EU institutions and the Court of Justice of the EU. The Treaty of Lisbon also established the European External Action Service (EEAS) and the EU Delegations as a diplomatic mission of the integration in third countries which cooperate with diplomatic and consular missions of Member States.[55] Although the pillar structure of the EU was abandoned, there are institutional provision links to consular protection which belongs to common foreign and security policy (CFSP)[56] and therefore are still under specific competency and decision-making rules.[57]

2.21. The special legislative procedure on consular protection is regulated in Article 289 TFEU. The Directive needed to be proposed by the European Commission according to Article 17 paragraph 2 TEU.[58] In the decision-making mechanism, the Council of the European Union adopts the directives after consulting the European Parliament.[59] By the authorization of Article 23 of TFEU, the European Commission in its Working Programme for 2011 presented a proposal on a directive for the end of 2011.[60] On the 14 December 2011 the Commission submitted the proposal[61] for this Council directive on consular protection for citizens of the Union abroad.[62] On the 25 October 2012, the European Parliament adopted its amendments to the proposal.[63] Two main novelties proposed by the Parliament related to the sovereignty of the Member States. Firstly, the Parliament would create a competence for the European Union External Action (EEAS) to provide consular protection itself. Second was the replacement of the soft law origin Lead State Concept by coordination and consular protection provided by Union delegations, whose leadership role was in the voluntary hand of the Member States.

---

[55] Treaty of Lisbon, point 30) on the new Article 188 Q on delegations.

[56] See Consolidated version of the Treaty on European Union (TEU). OJ C 326, 10.2012. Title V. especially Article 22 and Articles 29-31.

[57] Erzsébet Csatlós, *Europeanisation of Consular Protection for EU Citizens in Third States*, 2017(2) JOGELMÉLETI SZEMLE 15 (2017).

[58] 'Union legislative acts may only be adopted on the basis of a Commission proposal, except where the Treaties provide otherwise. Other acts shall be adopted on the basis of a Commission proposal where the Treaties so provide.'

[59] 'In the specific cases provided for by the Treaties, the adoption of a regulation, directive or decision by the European Parliament with the participation of the Council, or by the latter with the participation of the European Parliament, shall constitute a special legislative procedure.'

[60] European Commission, Communication to the European Parliament, the Council, the European Economic and Social Committee of the Regions, Commission Work Programme 2011, Annex II: Indicative list of possible initiatives under consideration, 27 October 2010, COM(2010)623 final.

[61] European Commission, Proposal for a Council Directive on consular protection for citizens of the Union abroad of 14 December 2011, COM(2011)881 final.

[62] EVA-MARIA POPTCHEVA, MULTILEVEL CITIZENSHIP, THE RIGHT TO CONSULAR PROTECTION OF EU CITIZENS ABROAD, Brussels: P.I.E. Peter Lang 235 (2014).

[63] European Parliament, Legislative resolution of 25.10.2012 on the proposal for a Council directive on consular protection for citizens of the Union abroad (COM(2011)0881 – C7-0017/2012 – 2011/0432 (CNS)).

VI.   Council Directive 2015/637 of 20 April 2015

2.22.   The 2015/637/ EU on the coordination and cooperation measures aim was to lay down the cooperation and coordination measures necessary to further facilitate consular protection for unrepresented citizens of the Union.[64] This Directive stated that it does not affect consular relations between Member States and third countries, such as their rights and obligations arising from international customs and agreements, and in particular from the Convention of 24 April 1963 on Consular Relations (the Vienna Convention). The Directive should not prevent the Member State which is not represented in a third country from delivering consular protection to one of its nationals.[65] This statement strengthens the attitude of the Member States as they do not want to endow their prerogative act to another Member State. Article 3 of the Directive stated that the 'requested Member State shall relinquish the case as soon as the Member State of nationality confirms that it is providing consular protection to the unrepresented citizen.' The limitation of the scope of consular protection by the EU Member State is obvious. Therefore, the supranational law of the EU does not oblige the Member State to pass over its prerogative to another Member State.

2.23.   Another significant Article of the Directive links to the cooperation of Member States' authorities with one another and with the Union, in particular the Commission and the EEAS, in a spirit of mutual respect and solidarity.[66] In third countries the Union is represented by the Union delegations, which, in close cooperation with the diplomatic and consular missions of the Member States, contribute to the implementation of the right of Union citizens to consular protection, as specified further in Article 35 of the Treaty on the European Union. 'This Directive fully recognizes, and further enhances, the contribution already provided by the EEAS and by Union delegations, in particular during crisis situations, in accordance with Council Decision 2010/427/EU (2), in particular Article 5(10) thereof.'[67] The interesting point about the role of Union delegation in Article 11 is that the predestination of the suggestion of the European Parliament would create a competence for the Union delegation

---

[64]   Council Directive 2015/637 of 20 April 2015 on the coordination and cooperation measures to facilitate consular protection for unrepresented citizens of the Union in third countries and repealing Decision 95/553/EC. OJ L 106, 24 April 2015. (Consular Directive).

[65]   Consular Directive preamble (11).

[66]   Consular Directive preamble (16).

[67]   Consular Directive preamble (17).

to provide consular protection itself. It was based on the fact that the Union has more external delegations than any other Member States. It is contemplated in the abovementioned Article to clearly reject this proposal and that the delegations shall only cooperate and coordinate with Member States' embassies. It is obvious that Member States abstain from the possibility of creating European consulates. Reasons for this could be found not only in the sovereignty of Member States, but in the general provisions of international law. Firstly, there is a lack of a genuine link between the European Union and European citizens, since the Union is not a State and therefore has no nationals. Secondly, the new Union model of citizenship cannot be effective if the third countries oppose this model, since Article 8 of the Vienna Convention on Consular Relations (VCCR)[68] gives them the choice.[69]

2.24. In this context it should be pointed out that some problems appear in the scope of the international regulation of consular protection. According to Article 8 of the 1963 Vienna Convention on Consular Relations, if a State intends to provide consular assistance in the receiving State on behalf of a third State, appropriate notification must be given to the receiving State, which has the right to object.[70]

2.25. The substantial article of the VCCR expressly allows the possibility that nationals of one State are represented by a consular officer of another State. According to Lee, a consul may sometimes act for nationals of a third State, the possibility of which is sometimes assured in treaties. In the absence of these kind of treaties, consuls may not practice assistance without the consent of the receiving State.[71] In this regard one can admit that the consular protection of the Union citizens does not affect only the Member States' sovereignty, but the sovereignty of the receiving third States as well.

2.26. With respect to the legal force of the Directive compared with the previous Decisions, it should be noted that the Member States shall bring into force the laws, regulations and administrative

---

[68] Vienna Convention on Consular Relations (adopted 24 April 1963, entered into force 19 March 1967) 596 UNTS 261, 172 states parties. Article 8: 'Upon appropriate notification to the receiving State, a consular post of the sending State may, unless the receiving State objects, exercise consular functions in the receiving State on behalf of a third State.'
[69] Mario P. Chiti, Madalina Morau, *The right to consular protection before and after Lisbon in European Citizenship and consular protection, in* EUROPEAN CITIZENSHIP AND CONSULAR PROTECTION NEW TRENDS IN EUROPEAN LAW AND NATIONAL LAW, Napoli: editoriale Scientifica, 34 (Sebastiano Faro, Mario P. Chiti, Erich Schweighofer eds., 2012).
[70] Erzsébet Csatlós, *Europeanisation of Consular Protection for EU Citizens in Third States,* 2017(2). JOGELMÉLETI SZEMLE 15 (2017).
[71] LUKE T. LEE, JOHN QUIGLEY, CONSULAR LAW AND PRACTICE, Oxford: Oxford University Press 55-58 (3rd ed., 2008).

provisions necessary to comply with this Directive by 1 May 2018.[72] It makes evident that the legislative acts of the Union on the field of consular protection have been invigorated in the last decade and the supranational decision-making made an improvement on the representation of Union citizens abroad.

VII.   Closing remarks

2.27.   The expansion of EU competence leads in a straightforward way to the strengthening of European citizenship in connection with third States and the European consciousness by virtue of the transfer of competences from the national to the European level. With this cooperation between Member States, the protection of the citizens beyond the boarders of the Union is maximized and gives an essential content to European citizenship. Thus, by deputing competence to the EEAS, the Union delegation, and the Lead States with respect to consular protection, the new Directive becomes a milestone not only in the field of protection, but in the history of Union citizenship as well. Despite the fact that a relevant prerogative and the sovereignty of the States is in question, Member States tend to broaden the sense of security of Union citizens in third States while empowering the institutions of the Union to lead the cooperation of consular protection. There is no competence to consolidate the protection, but the right to seek consular protection from the embassy or consulate of any Member State is a manifestation of the mutual solidarity and cooperation between the Union.

| | |

Summaries

FRA   [*La souveraineté de l'État et le droit à la protection consulaire par l'Union européenne*]
Afin de définir le cadre juridique de la protection consulaire au sein de l'Union européenne, il convient d'analyser les normes du droit international potentiellement applicables aux relations consulaires. Il n'existe pas de norme du droit international selon laquelle la protection consulaire serait réservée au seul libre arbitre des États. Partant, il est nécessaire de définir la relation qui existe entre les normes du droit international et les normes du droit de l'Union dans le domaine de la protection consulaire.

---

[72]   Consular Directive Article 17.

Il convient ensuite d'examiner le pouvoir délégué à l'Union par les États membres en ce qui concerne la protection consulaire, ainsi que le pouvoir résiduel exercé par les États membres individuels selon leur libre arbitre. Le présent article se consacre à l'analyse des instruments juridiques et des actes du « droit mou » relatifs au droit à la protection consulaire, de leur caractère extraterritorial et de certains aspects de l'ordre juridique supranational, qui a absorbé une partie du droit public national des États membres.

CZE [*Státní svrchovanost a právo na konzulární ochranu Evropské unie*]

Pro potřeby definování právního rámce poskytování konzulární ochrany v rámci Evropské unie je nezbytné analyzovat normy mezinárodního práva, které se mohou právní úpravy konzulárních vztahů dotýkat. Neexistují žádné normy mezinárodního práva, které by konzulární ochranu vyhrazovaly plně jednotlivým státům a jejich volnému uvážení. Je proto nezbytné definovat vztah mezi normami mezinárodního práva a normami unijního práva v oblasti konzulární ochrany. Dále je nutno analyzovat pravomoc, která je Evropské unii svěřována členskými státy v kontextu konzulární ochrany, a zbytkovou pravomoc vykonávanou jednotlivými státy v rámci jejich volného uvážení. Tento článek se zabývá rozborem právních nástrojů a aktů „soft law" v souvislosti s právem na konzulární ochranu, dále analýzou jeho extrateritoriální povahy a nadnárodního právního řádu, kterým bylo částečně překonáno vnitrostátní veřejné právo členských států.

| | |

POL [*Suwerenność państwowa i prawo do ochrony konsularnej Unii Europejskiej*]

Artykuł analizuje relację między normami prawa międzynarodowego i normami prawa unijnego w zakresie ochrony konsularnej w związku z suwerennością państw członkowskich. Celem artykułu jest szczegółowe omówienie instrumentów prawnych i aktów „soft law" w związku z prawem do ochrony konsularnej, charakteru ekstraterytorialnego tego prawa i ponadnarodowego porządku prawnego, który częściowo zastępuje krajowe prawo publiczne kraju członkowskiego.

DEU   [*Staatshoheit und Recht auf konsularischen Schutz der Europäischen Union*]
Dieser Artikel analysiert die Beziehung zwischen den Normen des internationalen Rechts und den Normen des Unionsrechts im Bereich konsularischer Schutz im Kontext mit der Souveränität der Mitgliedsstaaten. Zweck dieses Beitrags ist eine eingehende Abhandlung der juristischen Instrumente und der Rechtsakte des „Soft Law" im Zusammenhang mit dem Recht auf konsularischen Schutz, dessen extraterritorialen Charakters und der supranationalen Rechtsordnung, die das innerstaatliche öffentliche Recht der Mitgliedsstaaten zu Teilen abgelöst hat.

RUS   [*Государственный суверенитет и право на консульскую защиту Европейского союза*]
В статье анализируется связь между нормами международного права и нормами права ЕС в области консульской защиты в отношении суверенитета государств-членов. Целью данной статьи является подробное обсуждение правовых инструментов и актов «soft law» в свете права на консульскую защиту, его экстерриториального характера и транснационального права, которое частично заменило национальное публичное право государств-членов.

ESP   [*La soberanía del Estado y el derecho a la protección consular de la Unión Europea*]
El presente artículo analiza la relación entre las normas del derecho internacional y las normas del derecho comunitario en el ámbito de la protección consular con respecto a la soberanía de los Estados miembros. El texto se pone como objetivo examinar minuciosamente los instrumentos jurídicos y los actos "soft law" en relación con el derecho a la protección consular; su carácter extraterritorial; y el ordenamiento jurídico supranacional que ha superado parcialmente el derecho público interno de los Estados miembros.

| | |

Bibliography

Stefano Battini, *International Administrative Law today: the Case of Consular Assistance and diplomatic Protection, in* European citizenship and consular protection new trends in European Law and National Law., editoriale Scientifica, Napoli (Sebastiano Faro, Mario P. Chiti, Erich Schweighofer eds., 2012).

Sir Daniel Bethlehem, *International Law, European Community Law, National Law: Three Systems in Search of a Framework, Systematic Relativity in the Interaction of law in the European Union,* in INTERNATIONAL LAW ASPECTS OF THE EUROPEAN UNION, The Hague/London/Boston (Martti Koskenniemi ed., 1998).

Helmut Steinberger, *'Sovereignty',* in ENCYCLOPAEDIA OF PUBLIC INTERNATIONAL LAW, vol. 10/12 (Rudolf Bernhard ed., 1987).

BENOYTOSH BHATTACHARYYA, A FIRST COURSE OF POLITICAL SCIENCE WITH CONSTITUTIONS OF INDIAN REPUBLIC AND PAKISTAN, Calcutta (1949).

IAN BROWNLIE, PRINCIPLES OF PUBLIC INTERNATIONAL LAW, Oxford: Oxford University Press (7th ed, 2008).

Giacinto Della Cananea, *The European Union and consular protection- A new public law,* in EUROPEAN CITIZENSHIP AND CONSULAR PROTECTION NEW TRENDS IN EUROPEAN LAW AND NATIONAL LAW, Napoli: editoriale Scientifica (Sebastiano Faro, Mario P. Chiti, Erich Schweighofer, eds., 2012).

Mario P. Chiti, Madalina Morau, *The right to consular protection before and after Lisbon in European Citizenship and consular protection,* in EUROPEAN CITIZENSHIP AND CONSULAR PROTECTION NEW TRENDS IN EUROPEAN LAW AND NATIONAL LAW, Napoli: editoriale Scientifica (Sebastiano Faro, Mario P. Chiti, Erich Schweighofer eds., 2012).

THE CREATION OF STATES IN THE INTERNATIONAL LAW, Oxford: Clarendon (James Crawford ed., 2006).

Erzsébet Csatlós, *Europeanisation of Consular Protection for EU Citizens in Third States,* 2017(2) JOGELMÉLETI SZEMLE (2017).

Sebastian Faro, Mandalina B. Morau, *Comparative analysis of legislation and practice on consular protection and assistance of the 27 EU countries,* Table 9, in EUROPEAN CITIZENSHIP AND CONSULAR PROTECTION NEW TRENDS IN EUROPEAN LAW AND NATIONAL LAW, Napoli: editoriale Scientifica (Sebastiano Faro, Mario P. Chiti, Erich Schweighofer, eds., 2012).

Ana Mar Fernandez, *Consular Affairs in an Integrated Europe,* in Consular Affairs and Diplomacy, Leiden: Martinus Nijhoff Publishers 102 (Jan Melissen ed., 2011).

ONDREJ HAMULÁK, NATIONAL SOVEREIGNTY IN THE EUROPEAN UNION, VIEW FROM THE CZECH PERSPECTIVE, Springer (2016).

Alessandro Ianniello-Saliceti, *The long road to the protection of EU citizens abroad,* in EUROPEAN CITIZENSHIP AND CONSULAR PROTECTION NEW TRENDS IN EUROPEAN LAW AND NATIONAL LAW, Napoli: editoriale Scientifica (Sebastiano Faro, Mario P. Chiti, Erich Schweighofer, eds., 2012).

LUKE T. LEE, JOHN QUIGLEY, CONSULAR LAW AND PRACTICE, Oxford: Oxford University Press (3rd ed., 2008).

Madalina Bianca Morau, *Protection of EU citizens abroad: A legal assessment of the EU citizen's consular and diplomatic protection*, 3(2) PERSPECTIVES ON FEDERALISM (2011).

EVA-MARIA POPTCHEVA, MULTILEVEL CITIZENSHIP, THE RIGHT TO CONSULAR PROTECTION OT EU CITIZENS ABROAD, Brussels: P.I.E. Peter Lang (2014).

SATOW'S DIPLOMATIC PRACTICE, Oxford, 4.30 (Sir Ivor Roberts ed., 2017).

Imola Schiffner, *Protection of European Citizens in Third States Under Article 23 TFEU, in* HUNGARIAN YEARBOOK OF INTERNATIONAL LAW AND EUROPEAN LAW 2013, Budapest: Eleven International Publishing (Szabó Marcel, Petra Lea Láncos, Réka Varga eds., 2014).

Erich Schweighofer, *The Protection of Union citizens in third countries: Aspects of international and European Law*, in EUROPEAN CITIZENSHIP AND CONSULAR PROTECTION NEW TRENDS IN EUROPEAN LAW AND NATIONAL LAW, Napoli: editoriale Scientifica (Sebastiano Faro, Mario P. Chiti, Erich Schweighofer, eds., 2012).

MALCOLM .N. SHAW, INTERNATIONAL LAW, Cambridge 688 (2003).

ANNA MARIA HELENE VERMEER-KÜNZLI, THE PROTECTION OF INDIVIDUALS BY MEANS OF DIPLOMATIC PROTECTION, DIPLOMATIC PROTECTION AS A HUMAN RIGHTS INSTRUMENT, PrintPartners Ipskamp (2007).

ANNEMARIA VERMEER-KÜNZLI, THE PROTECTION OF INDIVIDUALS BY MEANS OF DIPLOMATIC PROTECTION, Leiden: PrintPartners Ipskamp (2007).

World Encyclopaedia, Oxford University Press, sovereignty (2008).

Czech Yearbook of International Law®

Alexander J. Bělohlávek

ORCID iD 0000-0001-5310-5269
https://orcid.org/0000-0001-5310-5269

Key Words:
*Court jurisdiction |
international jurisdiction |
supremacy | sovereignty |
territoriality | principle of
territoriality | international
agreement/treaty |
exterritoriality | presumption
of exteritoriality | personality
| principle of personality |
passive personality | principle
of passive personality |
universality | principle of
universality | internationally
criminal offences | aircraft
hijackings | human rights
| terrorism | legalization
of proceeds from crime |
money laundering | source/
main criminal offence | close
connection | subsidiarity
of court jurisdiction |
competition | diplomatic
protection | interference |
prohibition of interference
(non-interference) | forum
non conveniens | recognition
of a decision | enforcement
of a decision | ordre public |
public policy | reservation of
public policy*

Court Jurisdiction as an Expression of Sovereignty, and a State's Own Assessment of Court Jurisdiction as a Material Expression of State Sovereignty

Abstract | *Decisions on court jurisdiction are a material expression of State sovereignty. Opinions are divided as to whether civil court jurisdiction is regulated under international law. The author believes that this area is subject to the same principles that govern any other area of court jurisdiction. The fundamental premise is the principle of territoriality, which can also be interpreted conversely, i.e. as a presumption against exterritoriality. The principle of territoriality may not apply in exceptional situations, which are provided for by an international agreement or treaty. It may also be excluded by the principle of personality, or as a result of the international criminality of the act. The author maintains that any exceptions to the principle of territoriality must be minimized, and that the principle of personality, similarly to the principle of passive personality, should apply only if jurisdiction is refused primarily by, the state in which the act was committed, and secondarily by the state in*

Alexander J. Bělohlávek,
Univ. Professor, Prof.
zw., Dr. iur., Mgr., Dipl.
Ing. oec (MB), prof.
hon., Dr. h. c. Lawyer
(Managing Partner of
Law Offices Bělohlávek),
Dept. of Law, Faculty
of Economics, Ostrava,
Czech Republic; Faculty of
Law and Administration
Collegium Humanum
University (Poland), Dept.
of Int. law, Faculty of law,
West Bohemia University,
Pilsen, Czech Republic,
Dept. of Int. and European
Law, Faculty of Law,
Masaryk University, Brno,
Czech Republic (visiting).
Vice-President of the
International Arbitration
Court at the Czech
Commodity Exchange,
Arbitrator in Prague, Paris
(ICC), Vienna (VIAC),
Moscow, Vilnius, Warsaw,
Minsk, Almaty, Kiev,
Bucharest, Ljubljana, Sofia,

which the offender has their residence, and only in absolutely exceptional cases. Court jurisdiction in internationally criminal acts is another exception to the presumption of exterritoriality. Prosecution of the legalization of proceeds from crime is difficult. The author opines that it is principally inadmissible to prosecute the legalization of proceeds from crime in a State in which the primary criminal offence was not committed, and at the same time, (i) the source/main criminal offence is not criminal in both of these states, or (ii) the source criminal offence is not an international criminal offence. Conversely, if neither of these presumptions is met, any prosecution of the legalization of proceeds from the criminal activity would constitute inadmissible interference with the court jurisdiction of another State and the violation of the sovereignty of another State. This would be true, for instance, if the State in which such legalization is allegedly being committed has classified the source/main offence as criminal, as opposed to the State in which the source/main offence was committed.

Kuala Lumpur, Harbin (China), Shenzhen (China) etc., Arbitrator pursuant to UNCITRAL Rules. Member of ASA, DIS, ArbAut etc. Immediately past president of the WJA – the World Jurist Association, Washington D.C./USA. E-mail: office@ablegal.cz

| | |

I. Assessment of One's Own Jurisdiction as a Component and Expression of Sovereignty

I.1. Court Jurisdiction from Perspective of International Law

3.01. Decisions on the international jurisdiction of a State's own courts are an important component of the exercise of judicial power. This is because the public power of the State is one of the fundamental components of State power. The exercise of judicial power is viewed by international law as court jurisdiction. It constitutes one of the three components of State power, which is the central manifestation of State sovereignty, on which the judiciary is based.[1] Court jurisdiction can also be characterized as the authority of a sovereign entity of international law to

---

[1] MALCOLM N. SHAW, INTERNATIONAL LAW, Cambridge: Cambridge University Press 572 (5th ed. 2003); John Raymond, *Exercise of Concurrent International Jurisdiction: "Move with Circumspection Appropriate"*, VIII(4) BOSTON COLLEGE INDUSTRIAL AND COMMERCIAL LAW REVIEW 673 (1967); OPPENHEIM'S INTERNATIONAL LAW, Oxford: Oxford University Press 457 (Watts Jennings eds., 9th ed. 1996); IAN BROWNLIE, PRINCIPLES OF PUBLIC INTERNATIONAL LAW, Oxford: Oxford University Press 299 (7th ed. 2008).

Czech Yearbook of International Law®

assert its own power and influence on individuals or entities and things in a recognized manner.

I.2.   Civil Court Jurisdiction from the Perspective of International Law

3.02. Judiciary in civil matters and the issue of jurisdiction in civil proceedings are indeed an area to which public international law pays the least attention. Consequently, the issue merits a special brief note in the introduction to this article. Legal professionals and academics differ on a number of issues, including the extent and the manner whereby international law actually interferes with decisions on jurisdiction. Some authors believe that this area is entirely ignored by public international law.[2] However, the Spanish Supreme Court in *Harry Winston Inc.* v. *Tuduri* formulated a contrary conclusion. The Court held that court jurisdiction in civil matters is absolute and undisputable. It is based on the principle of State sovereignty, i.e. on international law as well. Hence, Spanish courts ought to have jurisdiction in all matters in which a lawsuit was filed with them.[3] Both of these lines of thought would result in the non-existence of any limits to court jurisdiction in civil matters. Hence, both lines of thought, as presented above, have the same result, namely the absence of any limits to court jurisdiction in civil proceedings.

3.03. On the other hand, Ian Brownlie has arrived at a contrary conclusion. He claims that there is no major difference between civil court jurisdiction, on the one hand, and criminal jurisdiction, on the other hand in relation to foreigners, or, as the case may be, that there is no difference between the rules of public international law regulating these two domains. In support of his conclusion, Brownlie argues that the exercise of civil court jurisdiction is backed substantially by sanctions laid down by criminal law.[4] This opinion appears very difficult to justify and, as such, has been severely criticized by experts.[5]

3.04. The actual qualities of the relationship between civil court jurisdiction and public international law are to be found

---

[2]   PETER MALNCZUK, AKEHURST'S MODERN INTRODUCTION TO INTERNATIONAL LAW, London: Routledge 110 (7th ed. 1997); Derek Bowet, *Jurisdiction: Changing Patterns of Authority over Activities and Resource*, 53(1) BRITISH YEARBOOK OF INTERNATIONAL LAW 3-4 (1983); MALCOLM N. SHAW, INTERNATIONAL LAW, Cambridge: Cambridge University Press 579 (5th ed. 2003); JOHN G. COLLIER, CONFLICT OF LAWS. Cambridge: CUP, Cambridge Studies in International and Comparative Law 390 (3rd ed. 2001).

[3]   See INTERNATIONAL LAW REPORTS, Vol. 34, London: Butterworths 49-50 (Elihu Lauterpacht ed. 1967); Michael Akehurst, *Jurisdiction in International Law*, 46 Brit. Y. B. Int'l L. 172 (1972-1973).

[4]   IAN BROWNLIE, PRINCIPLES OF PUBLIC INTERNATIONAL LAW, Oxford: Oxford University Press 300 (7th ed. 2008).

[5]   Michael Akehurst, *Jurisdiction in International Law*, 46 Brit. Y. B. Int'l L. 170 (1972-1973).

somewhere between these two extremes. It is clear that the considerations of the Spanish Supreme Court must be supplemented by the fact that other States are also endowed with identical State sovereignty, and all other States derive their court jurisdiction in civil matters from such sovereignty. The unilateral and unlimited exercise of court jurisdiction in civil matters could therefore interfere with the State sovereignty of another State.[6] However, a closer examination of the basis of the jurisdiction vested in the civil courts of various States has revealed that the States base their jurisdiction on a number of varying circumstances, and that, in a number of instances, no actual connection need exist to a particular dispute or any other matter that is the subject matter of the proceedings, or any act of a civil court. For instance, some *common law* countries allow court jurisdiction to be established merely by the fact that the respondent was served with the complaint, also known as the petition opening the proceedings, in the given State. Hence, a brief and random presence in the territory of the State during which the individual or entity is served is enough.[7] Michael Akehurst states that despite the above, States seldom complain about the application of these or similar rules regulating the determination of jurisdiction in civil matters.[8] It is clear that Akehurst somewhat less critically defends the *common law* approach in this regard. Conversely, I claim that similar situations are unfortunately by no means exceptional, and result in fundamental excesses as regards the rights of the parties and access to court.

3.05.   In any case, however, the exercise of court jurisdiction in civil matters may clearly have effects in the sphere of public international law, although there are principally no rules of public international law that would regulate these issues. The abovementioned limitations must be interpreted more as a voluntary self-limitation of the State, as a courtesy towards other States.[9]

II.   Premises and Limits of Court Jurisdiction

3.06.   Generally speaking, the court jurisdiction of a State is an expression of the State's sovereign nature, but nonetheless, it

---

[6]   Michael Akehurst, *Jurisdiction in International Law*, 46 Brit. Y. B. Int'l L. 176 (1972-1973).
[7]   MALCOLM N. SHAW, INTERNATIONAL LAW, Cambridge University Press, Cambridge 651-652 (5th ed. 2003).
[8]   Michael Akehurst, *Jurisdiction in International Law*, 46 Brit. Y. B. Int'l L. 170 (1972-1973).
[9]   Donald E. Childress, *Jurisdiction, Limits Under International Law.* 2016, *in* ENCYCLOPEDIA OF PRIVATE INTERNATIONAL LAW. Edward Elgar Publishing 1052 (J. BASEDOW, eds. 2017).

Czech Yearbook of International Law®

is not unlimited. It can only be implemented within the limits defined by international law. It is by no means exceptional that two or more States may assert their court jurisdiction in the same case, and this phenomenon is mostly acceptable, and sometimes and to some extent even considered practical.[10]

3.07.   In order to assess the limits of court jurisdiction, it is necessary to factor in the differences between justice in (i) criminal, (ii) civil, and (iii) administrative matters. Although the fundamental principles applicable to the limits of court jurisdiction in relation to these types of justice are mutually intertwined, there are significant differences, which will be elaborated on or factored in below.

III.   The Principle of Territoriality

III.1.   The Premises of Principle of Territoriality

3.08.   The basic principle for the exercise of the State's jurisdiction is the principle of territoriality.[11] This doctrinal basis has been articulated in the decision of the Permanent Court of International Justice in the *Lotus* case.[12] The Permanent Court of International Justice has held that the State court's jurisdiction is principally connected to the territory of the State, and exterritorial impact is only possible by virtue of a permissive rule of international law.[13] We may also paraphrase this principle as a presumption against exterritoriality.[14] This principle mirrors another principle articulated in the decision made in the *Lotus* case. Within the boundaries of its own territory, a State is only

---

[10]   OPPENHEIM'S INTERNATIONAL LAW, Oxford: Oxford University Press 456-457 (Watts Jennings eds., 9th ed. 1996); IAN BROWNLIE, PRINCIPLES OF PUBLIC INTERNATIONAL LAW, Oxford: Oxford University Press 312 (7th ed. 2008); Michael Akehurst, *Jurisdiction in International Law*, 46 Brit. Y. B. Int'l L. 152 (1972-1973).

[11]   IAN BROWNLIE, PRINCIPLES OF PUBLIC INTERNATIONAL LAW, Oxford: Oxford University Press 299 (7th ed. 2008); John Raymond, *Exercise of Concurrent International Jurisdiction: "Move with Circumspection Appropriate"*, VIII(4) BOSTON COLLEGE INDUSTRIAL AND COMMERCIAL LAW REVIEW 673 (1967); Michael Akehurst, *Jurisdiction in International Law*, 46 Brit. Y. B. Int'l L. 152 (1972-1973).

[12]   Judgment of Permanent Court of International Justice of 7 September 1927 in *Lotus* (*France* v. *Turkey*), C.P.J.I Recueil, 1927, Series A.

[13]   In the English version of the judgment (cit.:)

Now the first and foremost restriction imposed by international law upon a State is that, failing the existence of a permissive rule to the contrary, it may not exercise its power in any form in the territory of another State. In this sense, jurisdiction is certainly territorial; it cannot be exercised by a State outside its territory, except by virtue of a permissive rule derived from international custom or from a convention.

The case concerned court jurisdiction in criminal matters. The conclusions, though, may be applied more generally to jurisdiction as such.

[14]   CEDRIC RYNGAERT, CONCEPT OF JURISDICTION IN INTERNATIONAL LAW, Oxford: Oxford University Press 9 (2015); Maggie Gardner, *Retiring Forum Non* Conveniens, 91(2) NYU Law Review 435 (2017).

limited in its court jurisdiction if any such limitation is explicitly stipulated by a rule of international law.[15] It has also been held that, under certain factual circumstances, jurisdiction may be vested with the courts of two or more States. However, the Permanent Court of International Justice has offered no solution to such jurisdictional competition.

III.2.   Exceptions to Principle of Territoriality

3.09.   There are several exceptions to the above-mentioned principle in which court jurisdiction may be asserted exterritorialy.

III.2.1. An Exception Based on International Agreement or Treaty

3.10.   The extension of court jurisdiction contained in an international agreement or treaty has become more and more frequent and is welcome and fully approved by international law. States provide for borderline situations and for the possibilities of other States to assert their court jurisdiction in contested or otherwise expressly prohibited cases (for instance, in a part of the State's territory). A number of international treaties of this kind have been enacted to counter international organized crime and terrorism.[16]

3.11.   However, these cases usually give rise to no problems in interpretation or conflicts. Moreover, international agreements usually set forth mechanisms for the resolution of such conflicts

---

[15]   In the English version of the judgment (cit.:)

[I]t does not, however, follow that international law prohibits a State from exercising jurisdiction in its own territory, in respect of any case that relates to acts that have taken place abroad, and in which it cannot rely on some permissive rule of international law. Such a view would only be tenable if international law contained a general prohibition against States extending the application of their laws and the jurisdiction of their courts to persons, property and acts outside their territory, and if, as an exception to this general prohibition, it allowed States to do so in certain specific cases. But this is certainly not the case under international law as it stands at present. Far from laying down a general prohibition to the effect that States may not extend the application of their laws and the jurisdiction of their courts to persons, property and acts outside their territory, it leaves them in this respect a wide measure of discretion, which is only limited in certain cases by prohibitive rules; as regards other cases, every State remains free to adopt the principles that it regards as best and most suitable. This discretion left to States by international law explains the great variety of rules that they have been able to adopt without objections or complaints on the part of other States; it is in order to remedy the difficulties resulting from such variety that efforts have been made for many years past, both in Europe and America, to prepare conventions, the effect of which would be precisely to limit the discretion at present left to States in this respect by international law, thus making good the existing lacunae in respect of jurisdiction or removing the conflicting jurisdictions arising from the diversity of principles adopted by the various States. In these circumstances, all that can be required of a State is that it should not overstep the limits that international law places upon its jurisdiction; within these limits, its title to exercise jurisdiction rests in its sovereignty.

[16]   For example International Convention Against Taking of Hostages of 17 December 1979, Montreal Convention for Suppression of Unlawful Acts Against Safety of Civil Aviation of 23 September 1971, et al.

arising within the framework of the subjective and objective scope of the respective international agreement.

III.2.2. An Exception Resulting from Application of the Principle of Personality

3.12. Apart from the principle of territoriality, international law also recognizes the principle of personality, which allows the assertion of court jurisdiction over a State's own nationals if the relevant act occurred abroad.[17]

3.13. A related principle is the principle of passive personality. This principle enables a State to assert court jurisdiction in cases where a criminal offence committed by a foreigner abroad has adverse consequences for a citizen of the given State, especially if it was committed against the citizen.[18]

3.14. But exceptions resulting from the principle of personality or passive personality are not globally accepted. These approaches are generally recognized especially in the common law countries. I argue that, conversely, any exceptions to the principle of territoriality must be minimized. Likewise, the principle of personality, similarly to the principle of passive personality, should apply if, and only if jurisdiction is refused primarily by the State in which the offence was committed, and secondarily, the State in which the offender has their residence, and only in absolutely exceptional cases.

III.2.3. An Exception Resulting from International Criminality of Offence and Legalization of Proceeds from Crime

3.15. Another exception to the presumption of exterritoriality is court jurisdiction in matters concerning selected criminal offences classified as internationally criminal offences with adverse consequences for the entire international community. This exception is also designated as the principle of universality. Such criminal offences include piracy, war crimes, certain grave violations of human rights, aircraft hijackings and terrorism.[19]

---

[17] IAN BROWNLIE, PRINCIPLES OF PUBLIC INTERNATIONAL LAW, Oxford: Oxford University Press 303 (7th ed. 2008); MALCOLM D. EVANS, INTERNATIONAL LAW, Oxford: Oxford University Press 345-347 (2nd ed. 2010); MALCOLM N. SHAW, INTERNATIONAL LAW, Cambridge University Press, Cambridge 584 (5th ed. 2003); OPPENHEIM'S INTERNATIONAL LAW, Oxford: Oxford University Press 462 (Watts Jennings eds., 9th ed. 1996).

[18] IAN BROWNLIE, PRINCIPLES OF PUBLIC INTERNATIONAL LAW, Oxford: Oxford University Press 304 (7th ed. 2008); MALCOLM D. EVANS, INTERNATIONAL LAW, Oxford: Oxford University Press 351-352 (2nd ed. 2010); MALCOLM N. SHAW, INTERNATIONAL LAW, Cambridge University Press, Cambridge 589 (5th ed. 2003).

[19] MALCOLM D. EVANS, INTERNATIONAL LAW, Oxford: Oxford University Press 348-349 (2nd ed. 2010); MALCOLM N. SHAW, INTERNATIONAL LAW, Cambridge University Press, Cambridge 584 (5th

3.16. Another category which legitimizes the exercise of court jurisdiction by some State includes criminal offences that seriously disrupt internal affairs. Such criminal offences include offences that jeopardize a State's political and military security, counterfeiting of the State's currency, violation of the regulation of immigration, and endangerment of public health.[20]

3.17. Another category includes criminal offences committed during the preparation for or participation in other criminal offences committed in a State that asserts its court jurisdiction.[21]

3.18. However, the extent of the international criminality of selected offences is by no means settled and uniformly defined, and ongoing intensive globalization has brought about a number of other acts that could fall within this category. Consequently, certain offences, such as the legalization of proceeds from crime, also known as money laundering, are intensively discussed. The major problem to be resolved is the determination of the law according to which the criminality of the primary offence should be assessed, i.e. the offence that generated the proceeds that are being legalized. I believe that it is principally prohibited to prosecute the legalization of proceeds from crime in a State in which the primary criminal offence (source of the proceeds) was not committed, and at the same time, (i) the source/main criminal offence is not criminal in both of these States, or (ii) the source/main criminal offence is not an internationally criminal offence. Conversely, if neither of these presumptions is met, any prosecution of the legalization of proceeds from the criminal activity would constitute inadmissible interference with the court jurisdiction of another State, and the violation of the sovereignty of another state. This would be true, for instance, if the state in which such *legalization* is allegedly being committed has classified the source/main offence as criminal, as opposed to the State in which the source/main offence was committed.

IV. The Principle of Subsidiarity of Court Jurisdiction and Requirement of Close Connection between State and Case

3.19. The principle of subsidiarity of court jurisdiction, which is very close to the requirement of a close connection between the

---

ed. 2003); OPPENHEIM'S INTERNATIONAL LAW, Oxford: Oxford University Press 592 (Watts Jennings eds., 9th ed. 1996); OPPENHEIM'S INTERNATIONAL LAW, Oxford: Oxford University Press 469-470 (Watts Jennings eds., 9th ed. 1996).

[20] OPPENHEIM'S INTERNATIONAL LAW, Oxford: Oxford University Press 469-471 (Watts Jennings eds., 9th ed. 1996).

[21] OPPENHEIM'S INTERNATIONAL LAW, Oxford: Oxford University Press 460, 468 (Watts Jennings eds., 9th ed. 1996).

Court Jurisdiction as an Expression of Sovereignty, and a State's Own Assessment ...

Czech Yearbook of International Law®

State and the respective case, is a significant limitation of court jurisdiction of a more general nature. The assertion of court jurisdiction with respect to criminal offences committed by foreigners where the elements of such offences are predominantly concentrated in the territory of a foreign State may interfere with the sovereignty of another state and a breach the sovereign equality of States.[22] The principle of subsidiarity is based on the general requirement of a certain quality and proximity of the connection between the State and the respective case in which that State asserts its court jurisdiction.[23]

3.20.   In compliance with the principle of subsidiarity, States are not allowed to assert their court jurisdiction if it could involve unreasonable interference with the sovereignty of another State that has closer connections to the case.[24]

3.21.   The U.S. Supreme Court refers to the existence of this rule as a customary component of public international law. The Court has employed this principle, inter alia, in *Empagran s.a.* v. *f. Hoffmann-Laroche, Ltd.*, in its deliberations on whether to issue a decision concerning issues related to the protection of competition in which U.S. courts are vested with jurisdiction according to national laws, but at the same time, the case has a closer connection to another State.[25]

---

[22]   IAN BROWNLIE, PRINCIPLES OF PUBLIC INTERNATIONAL LAW, Oxford: Oxford University Press 308, 311 (7th ed. 2008); Lotika Sarkar, *Proper Law of Crime in International Law*, 11(2) ICLQ, Cambridge: CUP 469 (1962); Hans Kelsen, *Principle of Sovereign Equality of States as Basis for International Organization*, 53(2) YALE LAW JOURNAL 207 (1944); OPPENHEIM'S INTERNATIONAL LAW, Oxford: Oxford University Press 476 (Watts Jennings eds., 9th ed. 1996); Sovereign equality is one of the fundamental principles and normative rules of public international law. This customary part of international law is also expressed in the Montevideo Convention of 1933, Article 4, which reads as follows: 'States are juridically equal, enjoy the same rights, and have equal capacity in their exercise. The rights of each do not depend upon the power that it possesses to assure its exercise, but upon the simple fact of its existence as a person under international law.'

[23]   Lotika Sarkar, *Proper Law of Crime in International Law*, 11(2) ICLQ, Cambridge: CUP 467 (1962); IAN BROWNLIE, PRINCIPLES OF PUBLIC INTERNATIONAL LAW, Oxford: Oxford University Press 300 (7th ed. 2008); OPPENHEIM'S INTERNATIONAL LAW, Oxford: Oxford University Press 457-458, 469 (Watts Jennings eds., 9th ed. 1996);

[24]   CEDRIC RYNGAERT, CONCEPT OF JURISDICTION IN INTERNATIONAL LAW, Oxford: Oxford University Press 14 (2015); Ryngaert, C.M.J. (2015); RESEARCH HANDBOOK ON JURISDICTION AND IMMUNITIES IN INTERNATIONAL LAW 30 (Alexander Orakhelashvili ed. 2015); OPPENHEIM, INTERNATIONAL LAW, Section 128 (Elihu Lauterpacht 8th ed. 1955); Frederick Mann, *Anglo-American Conflict of International Jurisdiction*, 13 Int'l & Comp. L.Q. 1460 (1964).
The close connection of the respondent to the forum in civil litigation is also emphasized in Regulation EU 1215/2012 on jurisdiction and the recognition and enforcement of judgments in civil and commercial matters (Brussels I bis Regulation): see Recital 16 and provisions regarding special jurisdiction contained in the entire Regulation.

[25]   Decision of the U.S. Supreme Court in *EMPAGRAN S.A.* v. *F. HOFFMANN-LAROCHE, LTD.*, 542 U.S. 155 (2004) (cit.:)

First, this Court ordinarily construes ambiguous statutes to avoid unreasonable interference with other nations' sovereign authority. This rule of construction reflects customary international law principles and cautions courts to assume that legislators take account of other nations' legitimate sovereign interests when writing American laws. It thereby helps the potentially conflicting laws of different nations work together in harmony.
The preceding era was characterized by a very broad exercise of prescriptive and court

3.22. A similar approach appears in other recent rulings issued by the U.S. appellate courts.[26] In their deliberations on whether or not the exercise of court jurisdiction exceeds the principle of subsidiarity, the U.S. courts provide an answer to the question of whether the interests and the connection of the case to the U.S. are sufficiently strong compared to the interests and connections of other States, to justify the exercise of exterritorial court jurisdiction. In this connection, the courts examined a number of factors. Although such factors are created with due regard for the specifics of the protection of competition, they may also principally be adopted and used in other areas of law. They include the evaluation of (i) the intensity of the conflict with the legal system and rules/standards of another State, (ii) the nationality of the parties and the principal place of business of corporations, (iii) the likelihood of accomplishing compliance with the law in the enforcement of the law by each of the States involved, (iv) the comparison of the effects of the unlawful conduct in the given States, (v) the degree of the express intention to impair the U.S. market by acts committed abroad, (vi) the predictability of such effects, and (vii) the place of the unlawful act or its individual elements.[27]

3.23. A mostly analogous principle of subsidiarity is extensively applied in criminal matters with an international overlap through the discretion of law enforcement authorities, which is based directly on statute (e.g. Belgium,[28] Spain[29] and Switzerland[30]) or

---

jurisdiction by the U.S., especially in the area of protection of competition. Such approach was sharply and undoubtedly correctly criticized in the international community, primarily by European states and the EU. Gradually, the U.S. courts have also started to consider the issue of interference with the court jurisdiction of other States and the latest developments, conversely, point towards the application of the principle of subsidiarity of court jurisdiction, see also MALCOLM D. EVANS, INTERNATIONAL LAW, Oxford: Oxford University Press 355-356 (2nd ed. 2010).

[26] See also: *Timberlane Lumber Company et al.*, Plaintiffs-appellants, v. *Bank of America National Trust and Savings Association, Etal.*, Defendants-appellees, 749 F.2d 1378 (9th Cir. 1984) (cit.:)

the problem [of extraterritorial jurisdiction] should be approached in three parts: Does the alleged restraint affect, or was it intended to affect, the foreign commerce of the United States? Is it of such a type and magnitude so as to be cognizable as a violation of the Sherman Act? *As a matter of international comity and fairness, should the extraterritorial jurisdiction of the United States be asserted to cover it?* (emphasis by the Author of this Article). *Mannington Mills, Inc.*, Appellant, v. *Congoleum Corporation*, Appellee, 595 F.2d 1287 (3rd Cir. 1979).

[27] *Timberlane Lumber Company, et al.*, Plaintiffs-appellants, v. *Bank of America National Trust and Savings Association, Etal.*, Defendants-appellees, 749 F.2d 1378 (9th Cir. 1984).

[28] Article 12bis of the Belgian Code of Criminal Procedure requires the public prosecutor to determine how effectively the proceedings can be conducted in a different court jurisdiction.

[29] Article 23(4) of the Spanish Basic Act on Judiciary.

[30] Article 264m(2)(a) of the Swiss Code of Criminal Procedure.

Court Jurisdiction as an Expression of Sovereignty, and a State's Own Assessment ...

Czech Yearbook of International Law®

on conclusions made by jurisprudence (e.g. Germany,[31] United Kingdom,[32] Denmark,[33] Norway[34] and Sweden[35]).

V. The Principle of Non-interference

3.24.   A related obligation resulting from international law is the prohibition of interference with the affairs of other States, i.e. their internal court jurisdiction. Honoring the prohibition of interference is a prerequisite for the exterritorial exercise of court jurisdiction in compliance with international law.[36] However, the principle of non-interference is based on a very high limit of the intensity with which the affairs of another State are interfered with. The interference must be forcible, authoritarian and considerably intensive. Transgression of the limit of court jurisdiction in a relatively common criminal, civil or administrative case does not represent interference with the sovereignty of the State with a closer connection to the given case, the intensity of which would be sufficient to constitute a violation of the prohibition of interference.[37]

VI. Forum Non Conveniens

3.25.   The doctrine of *forum non conveniens* may also be considered an expression of the limitation of court jurisdiction. The doctrine is based on the Anglo-American legal tradition, and its essence is close to the requirement of a close connection of the State to the case.

3.26.   This doctrine stipulates that the courts, especially in the United Kingdom and in the U.S., are free to refuse, at their own discretion, their international jurisdiction if they conclude that there is another, more convenient forum to resolve the dispute.[38]

---

[31]   Decision of the German Supreme Court, Case No. 150s99/94 of 13 July 1994, also confirmed by a decision of the Regional Court in Salzburg of 31 May 1995.

[32]   Decision of the Federal Public Prosecutor of 2 October 2005, Case No. JZ 311.

[33]   REDRESS/FIDH. *Extraterritorial Jurisdiction in European Union: Study of Laws and Practice in 27 Member States of European Union,* 2010, p. 262.

[34]   REDRESS/FIDH. *Extraterritorial Jurisdiction in European Union: Study of Laws and Practice in 27 Member States of European Union,* 2010, p. 111.

[35]   REDRESS/FIDH. *Extraterritorial Jurisdiction in European Union: Study of Laws and Practice In 27 Member States of European Union,* 2010, p. 246.

[36]   IAN BROWNLIE, PRINCIPLES OF PUBLIC INTERNATIONAL LAW, Oxford: Oxford University Press 311-312 (7th ed. 2008).

[37]   OPPENHEIM'S INTERNATIONAL LAW, Oxford: Oxford University Press 434 (Watts Jennings eds., 9th ed. 1996).

[38]   CEDRIC RYNGAERT, CONCEPT OF JURISDICTION IN INTERNATIONAL LAW, Oxford: Oxford University Press 9 (2015); Maggie Gardner, *Retiring Forum Non* Conveniens, 91(2) NYU Law Review 391 (2017); Decision of U.S. Supreme Court in *Sinochem Int'l Co.* v. *Malay. Int'l Shipping Corp.,* 549 U.S. 422, 425 (2007). (cit.):

> [A] federal court has discretion to dismiss on forum non conveniens grounds "when an alternative forum has jurisdiction to hear [the] case, and ... trial in the chosen forum would

The doctrine has a discretionary nature and, as such, represents an expression of the reflection of certain circumstances. Regard should be given in the exercise of court jurisdiction, but it does not represent a binding limit for the application thereof.

VII. Redress Available to Individuals against the Transgression of Limits of Court Jurisdiction by a State

3.27.   The exercise of court jurisdiction outside the limits thereof may cause a number of serious problems to the respondent, but essentially also to other persons or entities involved in the proceedings. Such problems may include linguistic complications relating to the person's defense, defense in a foreign legal environment associated with higher costs, the need to travel, and more. All of the above entail potentially high costs and, moreover, depend on specific circumstances. Redress against such transgressions of the limits of court jurisdiction that would be available to individuals exist, but are very limited.

VII.1. Diplomatic Protection

3.28.   Diplomatic protection is an instrument of last resort that should also be available if the limits of court jurisdiction are transgressed by a foreign State vis-à-vis a citizen/national, after all remedies in the respective foreign State are exhausted.[39] But it is an instrument that some States (such as the Czech Republic) employ rarely and exceptionally.

3.29.   Moreover, a State has no legal obligation to provide diplomatic protection. Current experience in this area shows that, in view of the approach and unwillingness to employ this instrument exhibited by certain States, it is de facto only a theoretical possibility, although it may still be considered an existing and living instrument that would merit more authority, considering the excessive approach of certain States in forcing their own court jurisdiction. Indeed, the basic principle still applies, i.e. a State which fails to protect its own sovereignty, fails to protect itself and de facto relinquishes its sovereignty voluntarily.

---

establish ... oppressiveness and vexation to a defendant ... out of all proportion to the plaintiff's convenience, or ... the chosen forum [is] inappropriate because of considerations affecting the court's own administrative and legal problems.

[39]   IAN BROWNLIE, PRINCIPLES OF PUBLIC INTERNATIONAL LAW, Oxford: Oxford University Press 492 (7th ed. 2008).

VII.2. A Defense Using a System of Protection of Fundamental Rights

3.30. The right to a fair trial/due process is a broadly acknowledged component of fundamental human rights. It is also expressed in Article 6 of the European Convention for the Protection of Human Rights and Fundamental Freedoms, and once all national remedies have been exhausted, the protection of this right can be sought by filing an application with the European Court of Human Rights.[40] However, an analysis of the likelihood of the application being successful if the applicant complains about transgressions in the sense of the exterritorial application of court jurisdiction would exceed the scope of this paper.

VII.3. A Defense at the Stage of Recognition and Enforcement of a Decision

3.31. Another means of defense available to individuals is the defense against the recognition and enforcement of a decision in their home State. This remedy is only available with respect to the property consequences of the decision, and the necessary prerequisite is that the decision will only be unenforceable in the State in which it was made, especially due to a debtor's lack of assets.

3.32. The grounds for the refusal to recognize the decision could, for instance, also consist of the attraction of jurisdiction by an authority of a foreign State that does not have a sufficiently close connection to the given case (Section 15 of Czech Act No. 91/2012 Coll., on Private International Law).[41] This condition is articulated as follows (cit.):

> [t]he matter falls under the exclusive jurisdiction of Czech courts, or if the proceedings could not have been undertaken by any authority in a foreign state if the provisions pertaining to the jurisdiction of Czech courts had been applied when assessing the jurisdiction of the foreign authority, unless the party to the proceedings, against whom the foreign judgment is made, has voluntarily submitted to the jurisdiction of the foreign authority [...].

---

[40] Article 6 and Article 35 of European Convention for Protection of Human Rights and Fundamental Freedoms of November 4, 1950.
[41] PETR BŘÍZA, ZÁKON O MEZINÁRODNÍM PRÁVU SOUKROMÉM. [Title in Translation: Private International Law Act] 100 – 107 (1st ed. 2014).

3.33. Similar rules have been adopted by a number, if not the majority, of other legal systems, such as the United Kingdom, etc.[42]

3.34. In order to determine whether these grounds for the refusal of a foreign judgment can be applied, it is necessary to apply the law of the State in which the recognition and enforcement of the foreign decision is sought concerning the jurisdiction of the courts of that State from the perspective of the foreign authority that issued the decision. Unless the foreign authority had jurisdiction when applying the law, the recognition of the decision will be denied.

3.35. Another possible reason for refusing recognition is a manifest conflict of the recognition with public policy. This is sometimes referred to as conflict with *ordre public*. It would have to be assessed whether the breach of the limits of court jurisdiction stipulated by public international law suffices to constitute a manifest conflict of the recognition of the decision with public policy. I agree that the reservation of public policy (*ordre public*) can be easily abused. On the other hand, I consider this reservation the only effective remedy to prevent excesses that is recognized by the law. Some experts argue that the reservation of public policy (*ordre public*) is an almost *extinct instrument,* and something that should be almost exterminated in the application of the law. I cannot agree, and I maintain that this instrument is becoming more and more important, especially in the context of globalization.

| | |

Summary

FRA [*La compétence juridictionnelle en tant que manifestation de la souveraineté et l'appréciation de sa propre compétence par la juridiction en tant que manifestation matérielle de la souveraineté de l'État*]

Les décisions sur la compétence juridictionnelle représentent une manifestation matérielle de la souveraineté de l'État. En ce qui concerne la compétence des juridictions civiles, le débat persiste quant à savoir s'il s'agit d'un domaine réglementé par le droit international. L'auteur estime que c'est bien le cas et que les principes applicables à ce domaine ne diffèrent nullement de ceux qui sous-tendent les autres domaines de la

---

[42] DAVID MCCLEAN, KISCH BEEVERS, CONFLICT OF LAWS, London: Sweet & Maxwell 156 (6th ed. 2005); *Emanuel v. Symon*, CA 1908, p. 309.

compétence juridictionnelle. Il s'agit en premier lieu du principe de territorialité, ou, dans une perspective inverse, de l'exclusion de l'exterritorialité. Des dérogations au principe de territorialité peuvent être prévues par un traité international ou découler de l'application du principe de personnalité, ainsi que d'une incrimination internationale d'un acte. L'auteur est d'avis que les dérogations au principe de territorialité doivent rester minimes et le principe de personnalité (y compris le principe de personnalité passive) ne doit s'appliquer que lorsque la compétence est refusée d'abord par l'État où l'infraction a été commise, puis par l'État sur le territoire duquel se trouve l'auteur de l'infraction, et doit être utilisé à titre tout à fait exceptionnel. Une autre dérogation au principe d'exclusion de l'exterritorialité est la compétence juridictionnelle en matière d'infractions frappées d'une incrimination internationale. Dans cette catégorie, les poursuites relatives au blanchiment de capitaux illicites sont particulièrement problématiques. L'auteur estime que les poursuites en matière de blanchiment de capitaux illicites sont inadmissibles lorsqu'elles ont lieu dans un État autre que l'État de l'infraction principale (source des capitaux) et que (i) l'infraction principale n'est pas incriminée dans ces deux États, ou (ii) l'infraction principale n'est pas frappée d'une incrimination internationale. Lorsqu'aucune de ces conditions n'est remplie (par exemple, l'État dans lequel a lieu le blanchiment de capitaux érige l'acte principal en infraction, alors que l'État où a eu lieu cet acte ne le fait pas), toute poursuite du blanchiment de capitaux illicites constituerait une ingérence inadmissible dans le pouvoir juridictionnel d'un autre État (en l'espèce, de l'État d'origine), et, partant, une violation de sa souveraineté.

CZE [*Soudní pravomoc jako projev suverenity a vlastní posouzení soudní pravomoci jako materiální projev státní suverenity*]
Rozhodování o soudní pravomoci je materiálním projevem státní suverenity. Pokud jde o civilní soudní pravomoc, vedou se spory o tom, zda vůbec jde o oblast upravenou mezinárodním právem. Podle autora tomu tak je a platí zde naprosto shodné principy, jako u všech jiných oblastí soudní pravomoci. Základním východiskem je princip teritoriality, kterou lze chápat též obráceně jako presumpci proti exteritorialitě. Výjimky z principu teritoriality mohou existovat na základě mezinárodní smlouvy, v důsledku uplatnění principu personality a v důsledku mezinárodní trestnosti činu. Podle autora výjimky z teritoriálního principu je nutno minimalizovat a princip personality, stejně jako princip pasivní personality mají nastupovat výlučně tehdy, jestliže svou pravomoc odmítají primárně stát místa spáchání

činu, stejně jako sekundárně i stát místa pobytu pachatele, a to jen v naprosto výjimečných případech. Další výjimkou z presumpce exteritoriality je soudní pravomoc ve věcech činů tzv. mezinárodně trestných. Problematické je stíhání legalizace výnosů z trestné činnosti, tj. praní špinavých peněz. Podle autora je zásadně nepřípustné stíhání legalizace výnosu z trestné činnosti ve státě, v němž nebyl spáchán primární trestný čin (zdroj výnosu) a současně (i) zdrojový trestný čin není trestný v obou těchto státech, nebo (ii) zdrojový trestný čin není činem mezinárodně trestným. Naopak není-li splněn ani jeden z těchto předpokladů, například stát, kde má docházet k legalizaci, si zdrojový čin jako trestný vyhodnotí, stát takového zdrojového činu však nikoli, bylo by stíhání legalizace výnosu z trestné činnosti nepřípustným zasahováním do soudní pravomoci jiného státu (zdrojového státu) a tedy porušováním suverenity jiného státu.

| | |

POL   *[Kompetencje sądowe jako przejaw suwerenności i ocena kompetencji sądu jako materialny przejaw suwerenności państwowej]*

Rozstrzyganie w sprawie kompetencji sądowych to materialny przejaw suwerenności. Punkt wyjścia stanowi zasada terytorialności. Wyjątki od zasady terytorialności muszą być minimalizowane, a zasada narodowości podmiotowej i przedmiotowej mogą mieć zastosowanie wyłącznie wtedy, kiedy swoją właściwość odrzucą zarówno państwo miejsca popełnienia czynu, jak i państwo miejsca pobytu sprawcy. Ściganie legalizacji zysków z działalności przestępczej (tzw. pranie brudnych pieniędzy) zdaniem autora jest niemożliwe w państwie, w którym popełniono główne przestępstwo (źródło zysku), a jednocześnie (i) główne przestępstwo nie jest przestępstwem w obu tych krajach lub (ii) główne przestępstwo nie jest czynem karalnym w świetle prawa międzynarodowego. Z kolei jeżeli nie zostanie zaspokojona żadna z tych przesłanek, np. państwo, w którym rzekomo dochodzi do legalizacji uzna czyn główny za przestępstwo, natomiast państwo tego czynu głównego – nie, wówczas ściganie legalizacji zysków z działalności przestępczej stanowiłoby niedopuszczalne naruszanie nadrzędności jurysdykcyjnej, a tym samym suwerenności innego państwa.

DEU [*Richterliche Gewalt als Ausdruck der Souveränität und die gesonderte Beurteilung richterlicher Kompetenzen als materieller Ausdruck der Staatshoheit*]
Entscheidungen über die richterliche Gewalt sind materieller Ausdruck der Souveränität. Ausgangspunkt ist das Territorialitätsprinzip. Ausnahmen von diesem müssen auf das Minimum beschränkt bleiben, und das Prinzip der Personalität kann ebenso wie das Prinzip der passiven Personalität ausschließlich dort zum Tragen kommen, wo primär der Staat des Tatorts sowie sekundär auch der Staat des Aufenthaltsorts des Täters sich ihrer Entscheidungsgewalt entsagen. Nach Auffassung des Autors kommt eine Strafverfolgung wg. der Legalisierung von Einkünften aus krimineller Tätigkeit (sog. Geldwäsche) in einem Staat, in dem die primäre Straftat (als Quelle der Einkünfte) nicht begangen wurde, nicht in Frage, wenn zugleich (i) die Ursprungsstraftat nicht in beiden Staaten strafbar ist, oder (ii) die Ursprungsstraftat kein internationales Verbrechen ist. Umgekehrt gilt, dass wenn keine dieser Voraussetzungen erfüllt ist – Beispiel: der Staat, in dem die Legalisierung erfolgen soll, wertet die Ausgangstat als Straftat, der Staat, in dem sie stattfand, aber nicht – die Strafverfolgung der Legalisierung von Einkünften aus krimineller Tätigkeit eine unzulässige Verletzung der richterlichen Hoheitsgewalt und damit der Souveränität eines anderen Staates darstellt.

RUS [*Судебное правомочие как выражение суверенитета и собственная оценка судебного правомочия как материальное выражение суверенитета государства*]
Принятие решения о судебном правомочии является материальным выражением суверенитета. Отправной точкой является принцип территориальности. Исключения из территориального принципа должны быть минимальными, а принцип персональности, впрочем, как и пассивный принцип персональности, должен возникать в исключительных случаях, т. е., если от своего правомочия отказывается как государство, в котором произошло преступление (первично), так и государство, в котором находится место проживания преступника (вторично). По мнению автора, наказание легализации доходов, полученных преступным путем (так называемое отмывание денег), исключается в государстве, в котором первичное преступление (источник дохода) не было совершено, и в то же время (i) первичное преступное действие не является наказуемым в обоих этих государствах или (ii) первичное преступное действие не является действием, наказуемым

Czech Yearbook of International Law®

в международном масштабе. Наоборот, если не будет выполнена ни одна из этих предпосылок, — например, государство, в котором происходит легализация, оценит первичное действие как преступное, а государство такого первичного действия так не считает, — то наказание легализации доходов, полученных преступным путем, было бы недопустимым нарушением юрисдикционного суверенитета, а следовательно, и суверенитета другого государства.

ESP [***La jurisdicción como expresión de soberanía y la propia decisión sobre la jurisdicción como una expresión material de la soberanía***]

La decisión sobre la jurisdicción constituye una expresión material de la soberanía. El principio de territorialidad sirve como punto de partida. Las excepciones del principio territorial tienen que ser mínimas pudiendo recurrirse al principio de personalidad, así como al principio de personalidad pasiva solo de modo exclusivo, en caso de que la jurisdicción es rechazada tanto primariamente por el Estado de la comisión del delito como, de modo secundario, por el Estado donde reside su autor. La persecución de la legalización del producto del delito (llamada también lavado de capitales) queda descartada, según la opinión del autor, en el Estado donde no fue cometido el delito primario (la fuente del producto) y, a la vez, (i) el delito originario no es delictivo en ambos Estados, o bien, (ii) el delito originario no es delictivo a nivel internacional. Si, al contrario, no se cumple ninguno de estos presupuestos, por ejemplo, el Estado en el que supuestamente se produce la legalización clasifica el acto originario como delictivo, sin embargo, el Estado del acto originario no lo califica como tal, la persecución de la legalización del producto del delito constituiría una violación de la soberanía jurisdiccional, y por ello, también de la soberanía de otro Estado.

| | |

Bibliography

Michael Akehurst, *Jurisdiction in International Law*, 46 Brit. Y. B. Int'l L. (1972-1973).

Derek Bowet, *Jurisdiction: Changing Patterns of Authority over Activities and Resource*, 53(1) BRITISH YEARBOOK OF INTERNATIONAL LAW (1983).

IAN BROWNLIE, PRINCIPLES OF PUBLIC INTERNATIONAL LAW, Oxford: Oxford University Press (7th ed. 2008).

PETR BŘÍZA, ZÁKON O MEZINÁRODNÍM PRÁVU SOUKROMÉM. [Title in Translation: Private International Law Act] (1st ed. 2014).

Donald E. Childress, *Jurisdiction, Limits Under International Law*. 2016, *in* ENCYCLOPEDIA OF PRIVATE INTERNATIONAL LAW, Edward Elgar Publishing (J. BASEDOW, eds. 2017).

JOHN G. COLLIER, CONFLICT OF LAWS. Cambridge: CUP, Cambridge Studies in International and Comparative Law (3rd ed. 2001).

MALCOLM D. EVANS, INTERNATIONAL LAW, Oxford: Oxford University Press (2nd ed. 2010).

Maggie Gardner, *Retiring Forum Non* Conveniens, 91(2) NYU Law Review (2017).

OPPENHEIM'S INTERNATIONAL LAW, Oxford: Oxford University Press (Watts Jennings eds., 9th ed. 1996).

Hans Kelsen, *Principle of Sovereign Equality of States as Basis for International Organization*, 53(2) YALE LAW JOURNAL (1944).

OPPENHEIM'S INTERNATIONAL LAW, Section 128 (Elihu Lauterpacht 8th ed. 1955).

INTERNATIONAL LAW REPORTS, Vol. 34, London: Butterworths (Elihu Lauterpacht ed. 1967).

Frederick Mann, *Anglo-American Conflict of International Jurisdiction*, 13 Int'l & Comp. L.Q. (1964).

DAVID MCCLEAN, KISCH BEEVERS, CONFLICT OF LAWS, London: Sweet & Maxwell (6th ed. 2005).

PETER MALNCZUK, AKEHURST'S MODERN INTRODUCTION TO INTERNATIONAL LAW, London: Routledge (7th ed. 1997).

RESEARCH HANDBOOK ON JURISDICTION AND IMMUNITIES IN INTERNATIONAL LAW (Alexander Orakhelashvili ed. 2015).

John Raymond, *Exercise of Concurrent International Jurisdiction: "Move with Circumspection Appropriate"*, VIII(4) BOSTON COLLEGE INDUSTRIAL AND COMMERCIAL LAW REVIEW (1967).

CEDRIC RYNGAERT, CONCEPT OF JURISDICTION IN INTERNATIONAL LAW, Oxford: Oxford University Press (2015).

Lotika Sarkar, *Proper Law of Crime in International Law*, 11(2) ICLQ, Cambridge: CUP (1962).

MALCOLM N. SHAW, INTERNATIONAL LAW, Cambridge University Press, Cambridge (5th ed. 2003).

Fabrizio Di Benedetto

Defining the Notion of 'National Security' under Article 4(2) TEU. What is Really Left of Member States' Sovereignty?

Key words:
national security | Member States | sovereignty | national identity | Article 4(2) TEU | internal security | external security | national security organization | police | armed forces | defense | EU law

Abstract | *The notion of national security under EU law is ill-defined and often used as a catch-all category, covering a wide range of security-related issues. However, after the Lisbon Treaty, EU Treaties expressly include the concept of 'national security' under Article 4(2) TEU, a rule most commonly known as the 'identity clause,' which refers to national security as a 'sole competence' of Member States. The present article identifies what falls within this concept and how Member States can legitimately use such a competence. The analysis proposed here does not aim to say something particularly new. By contrast, it construes a comprehensive notion of national security so as to give the reader an overview of the main aspects that fall within this framework. In doing so, this work takes into consideration not only what Member States have not conferred to the EU with regard to the protection of their internal and external security (although not without the control of the ECJ), but also the limits that EU law encounters when it touches upon issues that are traditionally linked to internal and external security. Indeed, although the EU is entitled to intervene in some of these areas, an intimate core of security issues remains under the exclusive competence (i.e., the sovereignty) of its Members.*

Fabrizio Di Benedetto obtained his PhD in European Union Law at Università degli Studi di Milano (2016). Since 2015, he has worked in the financial sector as an antitrust and State aid adviser. His main research activities focus on the control of foreign direct investment for security reasons.
E-mail: fabrizio.dibenedetto@alice.it

I. Introduction

4.01. The European integration process has shown that the European Union (EU) is more than a traditional international organization, given that EU law aims at creating 'an ever closer union among the peoples of Europe'[1] and 'constitutes a new legal order of international law for the benefit of which the *States have limited their sovereign rights*.'[2] Indeed, sovereignty[3] can be limited by the autonomous decision of a State to participate in international organizations[4] like the EU.

4.02. However, also a supranational legal order like that established by EU Treaties, whose rules enjoy primacy over national laws,[5] recognizes that there are fields where Member States still maintain their sovereignty, especially regarding the protection of what is often referred to as "national security". This includes the possibility not only to solely define their security concerns, although not without the control of EU institutions,[6] but also to unilaterally adopt acts on how to protect such a legitimate interest.[7] In particular, according to Article 4(2) of the Treaty on the EU (TEU)

> The Union shall respect the equality of Member States before the Treaties as well as their national identities, inherent in their fundamental structures, political and constitutional, inclusive of regional and local self-government. It shall respect their essential State functions, including ensuring the territorial integrity of the State, maintaining law and order and safeguarding national security. In particular, *national security remains the sole responsibility of each Member State*.[8]

---

[1]   ECJ Judgment of 16 June 2005, C-105/03, *Pupino* [2005] ECLI:EU:C:2005:386, p. 36.

[2]   ECJ Judgment of 5 February 1963, Case 26-62, *van Gend & Loos* [1963] ECLI:EU:C:1963:1 (section B) (emphasis added).

[3]   With regard to the concept of sovereignty, see Hans Kelsen, La dottrina pura del diritto, Torino: Einaudi 322 (1966).

[4]   *Ibid.*, at 377.

[5]   ECJ Judgment of 15 July 1964, Case 6-64, *Costa* v. *ENEL* [1964] ECLI:EU:C:1964:66.

[6]   This is generally true for all the security concerns of Member States. In this regard, see ECJ Judgment of 14 March 2000, C-54/99, *Association Eglise de scientologie de Paris* [2000] ECLI:EU:C:2000:124, p. 17.

[7]   By contrast, in a context like the internal market where EU enjoys a shared competence, Member States remain free to solely 'decide on the degree of protection' they intend to afford to public order and public security (*i.e.*, internal and external security, as well as the security of supply of fundamental goods), but 'in so far as there are no [EU] harmonising measures providing for measures necessary to ensure the protection of those interests' (ECJ Judgment of 26 March 2009, C-326/07, *Commission* v. *Italy* [2009] ECLI:EU:C:2009:193, p. 42 and 41). However, the EU's power to adopt harmonized rules does not mean that it has a general power to regulate all the aspects that could potentially fall under the internal market (ECJ Judgment of 5 October 2000, C-376/98, *Germany v. European Parliament and Council* [2000] ECLI:EU:C:2000:544, p. 83), especially where the EU legislative power touches upon issues of national security that are at the core of Member States' sovereignty (in this regard, see paragraph IV on Article 346 TFEU).

[8]   Emphasis added. In general, on Article 4(2) TEU's identity clause, see Barbara Guastaferro, Beyond

4.03. This provision was inserted in the text of EU Treaties only in 2009, with the entry of the Lisbon Treaty. The text of Article 4(2) TEU originates from that of Article I-5(1) of the Treaty establishing a Constitution for Europe (Constitutional Treaty), which stated

> The Union shall respect the equality of Member States before the constitution as well as their national identities, inherent in their fundamental structures, political and constitutional, inclusive of regional and local self-government. It shall *respect their essential State functions*, including ensuring the *territorial integrity of the State, maintaining law and order and safeguarding national security*.[9]

4.04. Notwithstanding the similarities between the two texts of these provisions, they have a fundamental difference. In fact, while Article I-5(1) of the Constitutional Treaty did not define an exclusive competence of Member States over national security,[10] Article 4(2) TEU expressively declares that the protection of national security falls within the exclusive competence of Member States. In other words, the EU Treaty acknowledges the existence of an area of Member States' sovereignty that, according to the texts of both the TEU and the Constitutional Treaty, should include matters of internal and external security that are generally considered as not conferred to the EU. According to a well-established EU Court of Justice (ECJ) case law, internal security may be affected by, *inter alia*, 'a direct threat to the peace of mind and physical security of the population of the Member State concerned', while external security may be affected by, *inter alia*, 'the risk of a serious disturbance to the foreign relations of that Member State or to the peaceful coexistence of nations.'[11]

4.05. In this regard, it must be noted that the reference contained in Article 4(2) TEU to an exclusive competence of Member States seems to be redundant. Indeed, according to the principle of

---

THE EXCEPTIONALISM OF CONSTITUTIONAL CONFLICTS: THE ORDINARY FUNCTIONS OF THE IDENTITY CLAUSE, New York: Jean Monnet Working Paper 01/12 (2012). Moreover, on the identity clause from a national sovereignty perspective see Theodore Konstadinides, *Dealing With Parallel Universes: Antinomies of Sovereignty and the Protection of National Identity in European Judicial Discourse*, 34(1) YEARBOOK OF EUROPEAN LAW, 127 – 169 (2015), and Mary Dobbs, *Sovereignty, Article 4(2) TEU and the Respect of National Identities: Swinging the Balance of Power in Favour of the Member States?* 33(1) YEARBOOK OF EUROPEAN LAW, 298 – 334 (2014). Furthermore, on the notion of national security before the Lisbon Treaty, see Steve Peers, *National Security and European Law*, 16(1) YEARBOOK OF EUROPEAN LAW, 363 – 404 (1997).

[9] Emphasis added.

[10] Antonio Cantaro, *Il rispetto delle funzioni essenziali dello Stato, in* L'ORDINAMENTO EUROPEO. VOL. 1: I PRINCIPI DELL'UNIONE, Milano: Giuffrè 507, 516 (Stelio Mangiameli ed., 2006).

[11] ECJ Judgment 2 May 2018, C-331/16 and C-366/16, *K. and H.F.* [2018] ECLI:EU:C:2018:296, p. 42.

conferral enshrined in Article 4(1) TEU and in Article 5(2) TEU,[12] Member States have the power to transfer a portion of their sovereignty to the EU and there should be no need to specify that something not conferred to the EU remains under the sole responsibility of its Members. However, as will be discussed below, EU law often touches upon areas linked to internal and external security. Moreover, in any case, the exercise of Member States' exclusive competences cannot jeopardize the application of EU law, and the ECJ is always entitled to intervene in order to ensure the uniform application of EU rules.[13]

4.06. Given the intrusiveness of EU law in the fields of internal and external security where, by contrast, Member States have always advocated for a broad interpretation of their competences,[14] during the drafting of the Lisbon Treaty, the United Kingdom[15] requested the inclusion of national security as the exclusive competence of Member States in order to encompass in the EU Treaties a general clause to limit the expansion of EU law over the sovereign spheres of its Members. Obviously, because of the inclusion of the expression 'national security' within EU Treaties, such a concept must be autonomously interpreted as a notion of EU law.

II. An Autonomous Notion of National Security under EU Law

4.07. To better understand the meaning of national security as encompassed in Article 4(2) TEU, one should first refer to the working documents of the European Convention, the assembly responsible for drafting the Constitutional Treaty. In 2002, Working Group V focusing on 'Complementary Competences' (Working Group V) was in charge of the revision of the then Article 6(3) TEU as amended by the Treaty of Nice.[16] They

---

[12] Article 4(1) TEU: 'In accordance with Article 5, competences not conferred upon the Union in the Treaties remain with the Member States.' Article 5(2) TEU: 'Under the principle of conferral, the Union shall act only within the limits of the competences conferred upon it by the Member States in the Treaties to attain the objectives set out therein. Competences not conferred upon the Union in the Treaties remain with the Member States.'

[13] In this regard, see ECJ Judgment of 2 March 2010, C-135/08, *Rottman* [2010] ECLI:EU:C:2010:104, p. 41, and GIACOMO DI FEDERICO, L'IDENTITÀ NAZIONALE DEGLI STATI MEMBRI NEL DIRITTO DELL'UNIONE EUROPEA. NATURA E PORTATA DELL'ART. 4, PAR. 2, TUE, Napoli: Editoriale Scientifica 159 (2017), with reference to ECJ Judgment of 2 February 1989, 186/87, *Cowan* [1989] ECLI:EU:C:1989:47, and ECJ Judgment of 7 July 1992, C-369/90, *Micheletti* [1992] ECLI:EU:C:1992:295. For similar considerations, see ECJ Judgment of 4 June 2013, C-300/11, *ZZ* [2013] ECLI:EU:C:2013:363, p. 38.

[14] This is an approach that Member States have also adopted in recent cases. See Opinion of Advocate General Kokott of 20 July 2017, C-187/16, *Commission v. Austria* [2017] ECLI:EU:C:2017:578, recently confirmed by the ECJ Judgment of 20 March 2018, C-187/16, *Commission v. Austria* [2018] ECLI:EU:C:2018:194.

[15] GIACOMO DI FEDERICO, *supra* note 13, at 158.

[16] Article 6(3) TEU as amended by the Treaty of Nice (2001), 'The Union shall respect the national identities

recommended that the European Convention make the provisions contained in Article 6(3) TEU, on the duty of the EU to respect the national identity of Member States, more transparent, by clarifying the essential elements of national identity that, in particular, comprised

> fundamental structures and essential functions of the Member States notably their political and constitutional structure, including regional and local self-government; their choices regarding language; national citizenship; territory; legal status of churches and religious societies; *national defence and the organisation of armed forces.*[17]

4.08.   As is clear from the aforementioned texts of Article I-5(1) and Article 4(2), this recommendation was taken into account in drafting both the Constitutional Treaty and the EU Treaties currently in force.

4.09.   The notion of national security under Article 4(2) TEU can also be inferred by ECJ case law. Indeed, in the *J.N. case*, Advocate General Sharpston analyzed the scope of applying Article 4(2) TEU along with Article 72 of the Treaty on the Functioning of the EU (TFEU).[18] The latter provision states that the Treaty rules on the Area of Freedom Security and Justice (AFSJ) 'shall not affect the exercise of the responsibilities incumbent upon Member States with regard to the maintenance of law and order and the safeguarding of internal security'. In this regard, it must be noted that the notion of internal security and that of public order are not clearly distinguished by EU case law.[19] According to Advocate General Sharpston, Article 4(2) TEU and Article 72 TFEU originate from the same principle, *i.e.*, the need to designate to Member States the possibility '*to combat threats to their national security or their public order effectively*'.[20] More generally, according to Advocate General Ruiz-Jarabo Colomer, Member States have not only 'a considerable degree of latitude to oversee the *maintenance of law and order* in their territories', but also wide discretion regarding 'the *division of powers* between the various *security forces and bodies*'.[21]

---

of its Member States.'

[17]   Emphasis added.

[18]   View of Advocate General Sharpston of 26 January 2016, C-601/15 PPU, *J.N.* [2016] ECLI:EU:C:2016:85, p. 137.

[19]   Opinion of Advocate General Bot of 8 June 2010, C-145/09, *Tsakouridis* [2010] ECLI:EU:C:2010:322, p. 65.

[20]   View of Advocate General Sharpston, *supra* note 18 (emphasis added).

[21]   Opinion of Advocate General Ruiz-Jarabo Colomer of 10 December 2002, C-103/01, *Commission* v. *Germany* [2002] ECLI:EU:C:2002:738, p. 38 (emphasis added).

4.10. From the above analysis, it follows that the concept of national security should include both police and military operations (*i.e.*, internal and external security operations), and organizations (*i.e.*, internal and external security organizations), in order to protect their own security.

4.11. Traditionally, Member States have widely interpreted their powers over internal and external security. However, the notion of national security, which represents the exclusive competence of Member States, is narrower than that advocated by Member States. Indeed, according to the ECJ's settled case law, although it is for Member States to take the appropriate measures to ensure their internal and external security, these fields are not entirely excluded from the application of EU law.[22] Thus, EU law affects Member States' measures taken for internal and external security concerns. As it will be argued below, both Treaty rules and EU secondary acts often touch upon issues of internal and external security operations and organization, reducing Member States' room for *manoeuvre* in these fields. In fact, EU lawmakers and the ECJ have the power to adopt secondary acts or intervene over different aspects of Member States' internal and external security to promote EU objectives and the uniform application of EU law, with particular attention to the free movement of people, the internal market and the enjoyment of EU social rights.

4.12. Thus, the analysis proposed here will better define the notion of national security under EU law, to understand what is really left to Member States and especially how Member States can legitimately use this sole competence. In this regard, the following discussion will also identify the watershed between what is encompassed within the exclusive competence of Member States over national security, on the one hand, and what are the security-related fields where the EU is entitled to intervene, on the other (see paragraph III regarding national security operations, and paragraph IV regarding national security organization).

4.13. Thus, Article 4(2) TEU is interpreted here as a specular rule to Article 3 TFEU on the EU's exclusive competences, although such an interpretation is still debated.[23] Therefore, the notion of national security will be construed as both referring to areas of

---

[22] ECJ Judgement of 15 December 2009, C-387/05, *Commission* v. *Italy* [2009] ECLI:EU:C:2009:781, p. 45, and ECJ Judgment of 11 March 2003, C-186/01, *Dory* [2003] ECLI:EU:C:2003:146, pp. 29 – 30. Regarding this last case, see Panos Koutrakos, *How Far is Far Enough? EC Law and the Organisation of the Armed Forces after Dory*, 66(5) MODERN LAW REVIEW 759 – 768 (2003). With reference to Member States' power over internal security and public order, see also ECJ Judgment of 9 December 1997, C-265/95, *Commission* v. *France* [1997] ECLI:EU:C:1997:595, p. 33.

[23] In this regard, see GIACOMO DI FEDERICO, *supra* note 13, at 63 – 65.

internal and external security where Member States remain free to take appropriate measures and where, thus, they have not conferred any power to the EU, and by subtraction in respect to the EU's intervention in areas linked to internal and external security. Differently put, after establishing the limits of the EU's intervention, the remaining aspects will come under the sole responsibility of Member States over national security by virtue of Article 4(2) TEU. In this regard, there are Treaty rules that limit the EU's ability to intervene in areas linked to internal and external security, which can be used to identify the content of the notion of national security under Article 4(2) TEU. These provisions include Article 346 and Article 347 TFEU, often referred to as wholly exceptional clauses under EU Treaties, which recognize that Member States retain the right to derogate to the entire body of EU law.[24]

III.   Member States' Exclusive Competence over National Security Operations

4.14.   As already said, Member States are substantially free to adopt measures for the protection of their internal and external security. Indeed, Member States have not conferred to the EU their powers to regulate and conduct police and military operations for combatting and preventing internal or external threats (*e.g.*, checks on persons to prevent threats within their territory, arrests of people, operations to prevent or respond to an internal or external attack). In this regard, it must be noted that today the boundaries between external and internal and military and police measures are blurred.

4.15.   Member States' competence over internal and external security operations is also expressively recognized by Treaty rules. On the one hand, Article 72 TFEU clearly states that Member States remain responsible for the protection of their internal security, notwithstanding the establishment of the AFSJ and the abolition of internal (*i.e.*, intra-EU) borders' control on persons. On the other, Article 347 TFEU recognizes the power of Member States to adopt measures for internal and external security concerns. These include 'in the event of serious internal disturbances affecting the maintenance of law and order,' as well as 'in the event of war, serious international tension constituting a threat of war, or in order to carry out obligations it has accepted for the purpose of maintaining peace and international security'. This

---

[24]   For a similar approach, see *ibid.*, at 70, 156 – 159. In general, on wholly exceptional clauses under EU Treaties, see Panos Koutrakos, *The Notion of Necessity in the Law of the European Union*, 41 NETHERLANDS YEARBOOK OF INTERNATIONAL LAW 193 – 218 (2011).

Treaty rule only requires Member States to 'consult each other with a view to taking together the steps needed to prevent the functioning of the internal market being affected by measures' adopted for security concerns.[25] In fact, the establishment of an area without restrictions to the free movement of natural and legal persons, services and capitals (*i.e.*, the internal market) can be negatively affected by measures taken under Article 347.

4.16. In this respect, if the European Commission (Commission) believes that an action adopted by a Member State by virtue of Article 347 TFEU violates EU law, the EU executive branch has the ability to sue the State concerned before the ECJ by virtue of an ordinary infringement procedure *ex* Article 258 TFEU. Moreover, the Commission, as well as any Member State may also, in the light of Article 348(2) TFEU, 'bring the matter directly before the Court of Justice if it considers that another Member State is making *improper use of the powers provided for in Articles 346 and 347*. The Court of Justice shall give its ruling in camera.'[26] Moreover, Article 348(1) TFEU provides that the Commission – before bringing the matter to the ECJ *ex* Article 348(2) – and the Member State concerned shall examine how to adjust the measures adopted in the light of Article 347 and 346 where such measures 'have the effect of distorting the conditions of competition in the internal market'. Thus, the Treaty provides two different means for the Commission and for the ECJ to intervene in cases where Member States abuse of their power under Article 347 TFEU.[27] They may bring an ordinary and a special infringement procedure. In particular, the latter encompassed under Article 348(2) TFEU seems to be provided for under urgent situations,[28] where *prima facie* the invocation of Article 347 by the Member State concerned seems to be reasonable.

4.17. In other words, according to Article 348(2) TFEU, the ECJ is entitled to sanction any abuse of Article 347 by Member States[29]

---

[25] Article 347 TFEU on which see Ivana Palandri, *Art. 347 TFUE*, in Commentario breve ai Trattati dell'Unione europea Padova: CEDAM 1548 – 1549 (Fausto Pocar, Maria Caterina Baruffi eds., 2014). The fact that Articles 72 and 347 TFEU refer to an exclusive responsibility of Member States is confirmed by the Explanations Relating to the Charter of Fundamental Rights [2007] OJ C 303/02, according to which Member States 'take action in the areas of national defence in the event of war and of the maintenance of law and order, in accordance with their responsibilities recognised in Article 4(1) of the Treaty on European Union and in Articles 72 and 347 of the Treaty on the Functioning of the European Union' (Explanation on Article 52, paragraph 5). In this regard, see also View of Advocate General Sharpston, *supra* note 18, at 65.

[26] Emphasis added.

[27] Martin Trybus, *The EC Treaty as an Instrument of European Defence Integration: Judicial Scrutiny of Defence and Security Exceptions*, 39(6) Common Market Law Review 1347, 1360 – 1361 (2002).

[28] *Ibid.*, at 1361.

[29] With regard to both the notion of improper use under Article 347 TFEU and the situations that fall within the scope of this Treaty provision, see Opinion of Advocate General Jacobs of 6 April 1995, C-120/94, *FYROM* [1995] ECLI:EU:C:1995:109, pp. 61 – 72.

Defining the Notion of 'National Security' under Article 4(2) TEU.

Czech Yearbook of International Law®

in the context of an urgent and in camera procedure. For example, where the adoption of measures according to Article 347 TFEU leads to disproportionate and unnecessary restrictions to the internal market or to trade with third countries[30] – which represents the external dimension of the internal market – the ECJ can sanction such national measures representing an abuse of the power granted to Member States by Article 347. Indeed, as argued by Advocate General Jacobs in the *Former Yugoslav Republic of Macedonia* case (*FYROM* case), with regard to national foreign policy measures adopted under Article 347 TFEU for potential external threats and affecting trade with a third country, '[i]f a Member State considers, rightly or wrongly, that the attitude of a third State threatens its vital interests, its territorial integrity or its very existence, then *it is for the Member State to determine how to respond to that perceived threat*.'[31] This can also be true for a threat that an external observer would define as unlikely,[32] provided both that such a threat is genuinely (*i.e.*, not wholly unreasonably)[33] perceived by the Member State and its population[34] – also considering the broader context in which the Member State concerned acts[35] – and it is not a way to hide for example protectionist objectives to the benefit of the national economy.[36] In this regard, '*there are no judicial criteria by which such matters may be measured* [because the] decision to take such action is essentially of a political nature;'[37] and '[t]he sole limit placed on the autonomy of the Member States is that they may not make improper use of their powers,'[38] which the ECJ is entitled to assess in the light of the proportionality principle.[39]

4.18.   Given the above considerations, it follows that when a Member State carries out police and military operations, in light of Article 347 TFEU, aimed at defending its population and territory in case of exceptional circumstances for their security, in a proportionate manner, against an effective or a genuinely perceived threat within their borders or coming from abroad

---

[30]   Ivana Palandri, *Art. 348 TFUE*, in Commentario breve ai Trattati dell'Unione europea Padova: CEDAM 1549, 1551 (Fausto Pocar, Maria Caterina Baruffi eds., 2014). In particular, with regard to the relation between Article 347 TFEU and trade with third countries see Nicholas Emiliou, *Strategic Export Controls, National Security and the Common Commercial Policy*, 55(1) European Foreign Affairs Review 55 – 78 (1996).

[31]   Opinion of Advocate General Jacobs, *supra* note 29, at 65 (emphasis added).

[32]   *Ibid.*, at 58.

[33]   *Ibid.*, at 56.

[34]   *Ibid.*, at 58.

[35]   *Ibid.*, at 57 and 59.

[36]   *Ibid.*, at 67.

[37]   *Ibid.*, at 65 (emphasis added).

[38]   *Ibid.*, at 67.

[39]   *Ibid.*, at 70 – 72.

(this could be particularly the case of Member States at the EU's external borders), or to prevent such a threat,[40] it is doubtful that these measures could amount to an abuse under Article 347 TFEU, although there could be for example some negative impact for the internal market. For the purposes of the present article, the just-mentioned measures fall under the legitimate use of the exclusive competence of Member States regarding their national security *ex* Article 4(2) TEU.[41]

4.19. Finally, as already said, the ECJ is entitled to judge Member States' initiatives under Article 347 TFEU in order to distinguish between proper use and improper use (*i.e.*, abuse) of this Treaty provision. In fact, what *prima facie* seems to constitute a national security operation can be the source of an abuse, for example because of its unnecessary effects on the internal market or disproportionate duration; thus, such a measure cannot be considered a legitimate national security operation. Indeed, as is clear from ECJ case law, measures adopted by Member States by virtue of Article 347 TFEU must be temporary; once the crisis that justified the adoption of emergency measures ceases to exist, the application of such measures must be stopped.[42] Therefore, the adoption of proportionate measures of limited duration, and whose genuine objective is the protection of national security in cases of effectively or genuinely perceived threats (which, for example, can include strong limits to the freedoms of movement for the strictly necessary period of time), represent the legitimate use of the exclusive competence of Member States on national security *ex* Article 347 TFEU read in conjunction with Article 4(2) TEU. In this respect, EU law cannot prevent Member States from adopting such measures that are inherent in their intimate sovereign spheres.

4.20. With specific regard to police operations, which are however less urgent than those under Article 347, where police operations correspond to measures of border control, Treaty provisions on the AFSJ – which provide for the abolition of border control on persons – as well as the Schengen's *acquis* apply. Moreover, the adoption of rules governing these police operations do not fall within the exclusive competence of Member States, but rather within the matters conferred to the EU (*i.e.*, shared competence over the AFSJ), thus the EU is entitled to intervene in this regard.

---

[40] Opinion of Advocate General Cosmas of 23 March 2000, C-423/98, *Albore* [2000] ECLI:EU:C:2000:158, p. 31.

[41] According to Martin Trybus, *supra* note 27, at 1362, Article 347 is very close to the notion of national security and, thus, to the sovereignty of Member States. For a partially different view, see Panos Koutrakos, *Is Article 297 EC a 'Reserve of Sovereignty'?* 37(6) COMMON MARKET LAW REVIEW 1339 – 1362 (2000).

[42] Opinion of Advocate General Cosmas, *supra* note 40, at 32.

Indeed, in this field, EU institutions have adopted common rules based on Article 77 TFEU aiming to provide Members States with necessary procedures and conditions regarding the temporary re-establishment of their border controls between them to prevent serious threats to public order and security, although such a re-establishment cannot exceed two years.[43] Thus, although the re-establishment of borders' control for internal security reasons remains a prerogative of Member States, it could be reasonably argued that Member States have substantially conferred to the EU a shared competence over the regulation of such measures. However, this is without prejudice to Member States' power to adopt police actions under Article 72 TFEU, in cases of public order and internal security concerns.[44]

4.21.   In other words, under ECJ case law there is a clear distinction between genuine police actions that represent the proper use of Article 72 TFEU, and those that are assimilated to general measures of border control, also in cases where they are conducted kilometers away from the border. In fact,

> the exercise of police powers may not, in particular, be considered equivalent to the exercise of border checks when the police measures *do not have border control as an objective*, are based on general *police information and experience* regarding possible threats to public security and aim, in particular, to combat cross-border crime, are devised and executed in a manner clearly *distinct from systematic checks* on persons at the external borders and are carried out on the basis of *spot-checks*.[45]

4.22.   Therefore, similar to what was previously stated with regard to Article 347 TFEU, Member States can legitimately use their competence under Article 72 TFEU to combat or prevent risks for the internal security in a proportionate manner such as adopting spot-checks at the borders, so that they do not abuse their powers imposing, for example, wide border checks like those adopted at the external borders with third countries. Indeed,

---

[43]   Article 25 of the Regulation (EU) 2016/399 of the European Parliament and of the Council of 9 March 2016 on a Union Code on the rules governing the movement of persons across borders (Schengen Borders Code) [2016] OJ L 77/01. Regarding the fact that EU rules on borders' control limit Member States' prerogatives, see Steve Peers, *supra* note 8, at 388-389. However, with regard to the re-establishment of borders' control in case of foreseeable events, the Schengen Borders Code does not impose a specific time limit, although Member States are required to use their prerogatives in line with the general principle of proportionality.

[44]   *Ibid.*, Article 27(4).

[45]   ECJ Judgment of 21 June 2017, C-9/16, *A* [2017] ECLI:EU:C:2017:483, p. 35 (emphasis added). The case concerned a Member State's measure adopted within an area of 30 kilometers from that Member State's land border. The ECJ gave its judgment interpreting the then provision which is now encompassed under Article 23 of the Regulation 2016/399 (*supra* note 43) which is a specification of Article 72 TFEU.

systematic checks at the borders serve to control the movement of persons, rather than the need to protect the country's security. Thus, the just-described police operations should be considered as a legitimate use of the powers recognized by Member States under the notion of national security *ex* Article 72 TFEU read in conjunction with Article 4(2) TEU.

4.23. Moreover, regarding genuine police operations adopted by Member States, Article 276 TFEU states that

> [i]n exercising its powers regarding the provisions of Chapters 4 [*i.e.*, judicial cooperation in criminal matters] and 5 [*i.e.*, police cooperation] of Title V of Part Three relating to the area of freedom, security and justice, *the Court of Justice of the European Union shall have no jurisdiction to review the validity or proportionality of operations* carried out by the police or other law-enforcement services of a Member State or the exercise of the responsibilities incumbent upon Member States with regard to the maintenance of law and order and the safeguarding of internal security.[46]

4.24. Therefore, the substantive power of ECJ review 'is expressly excluded [...] so far as concerns the validity or proportionality of operations carried out by the police or other law enforcement services'.[47] This Treaty provision highlights the limits of the jurisdiction of the ECJ in the context of the judicial and police cooperation within the AFSJ, with reference to Member States' measures that correspond to those to which Article 72 refers. In other words, the ECJ is not entitled to judge such the validity and proportionality of police operations, even in exercising its jurisdiction in the field of AFSJ.

4.25. Finally, as a corollary to the exclusive competence of Member States over national security operations, according to Article 346(1)(a) TFEU[48] Member States are free to refuse to share information when its disclosure would be contrary to their essential security interests.[49] By way of analogy, similar provisions

---

[46] Italics added.

[47] Opinion of Advocate General Kokott of 11 November 2004, C-105/03, *Pupino* [2004] ECLI:EU:C:2004:712, p. 31. In general, on Article 276 TFEU (then Article 35(5) of the TEU) see also, Opinion of Advocate General Mengozzi of 26 October 2006, C-354/04 P and C-355/04 P, *Gestoras Pro Amnistía* and *Segi* [2006] ECLI:EU:C:2006:667.

[48] '[N]o Member State shall be obliged to supply information the disclosure of which it considers contrary to the essential interests of its security.' On Article 346 TFEU see Ivana Palandri, *Art. 346 TFUE*, in COMMENTARIO BREVE AI TRATTATI DELL'UNIONE EUROPEA Padova: CEDAM 1546-1548 (Fausto Pocar, Maria Caterina Baruffi eds., 2014).

[49] According to the ECJ case law, also Article 346 TFEU must be interpreted narrowly, as other security derogations under EU Treaties (ECJ Judgment *Commission* v. *Italy*, *supra* note 22, p. 45).

are also included in EU secondary acts, such as Article 30(2) of the Directive 2004/38/EC on the right of citizens of the Union and their family members to move and reside freely within the territory of the Member States (Directive 2004/38).[50] Article 30(2) of the Directive 2004/38, indeed, provides an exception, for reasons linked to 'interests of State security', to the general rule according to which 'a Union citizen who is the subject of a measure restricting his freedom of movement and of residence on public policy, public security or public health grounds should be informed, precisely and in full, of the grounds for such a measure.'[51]

4.26. In this regard, as argued by Advocate General Bot in the *ZZ* case, both Article 346(1)(a) TFEU and Article 30(2) of Directive 2004/38 can be considered as specifications of Article 4(2) TEU.[52] It follows that no one has the right to obtain information from a Member State if the latter believes that such a supply of information would jeopardize national security. However, according to the ECJ, Article 30(2) of Directive 2004/38 must be interpreted as allowing a Member State to refuse to give information to a person whose admission in its territory has been prohibited, to the extent that such a refusal of information 'is limited to that which is strictly necessary' and provided that the person concerned 'is informed, in any event, of the essence of those grounds in a manner which takes due account of the necessary confidentiality of the evidence.'[53] Similarly, regarding Article 346(1)(a) TFEU, Advocate General Kokott argued that 'a measure is appropriate for ensuring attainment of the objective pursued [by Article 346(1)(a) TFEU] only if it genuinely reflects a concern to attain it in a consistent and systematic manner.'[54]

4.27. Thus, Member States' exclusive competence with regard to national security operations under Article 4(2) TEU covers both police and military operations for internal and external security threats, although the regulation of the temporary re-establishment of borders' control for internal security reasons should rather fall under the shared competence over the AFSJ. However, in order not to negatively affect the free movement of people under the AFSJ and the internal market, the exercise of police and military powers must meet two criteria. First, police

---

[50] Directive 2004/38/EC of the European Parliament and of the Council of 29 April 2004 on the right of citizens of the Union and their family members to move and reside freely within the territory of the Member States amending Regulation (EEC) No 1612/68 and repealing Directives 64/221/EEC, 68/360/EEC, 72/194/EEC, 73/148/EEC, 75/34/EEC, 75/35/EEC, 90/364/EEC, 90/365/EEC and 93/96/EEC [2004] OJ L 158/77.

[51] Opinion of Advocate General Bot, of 12 September 2012, C-300/11, *ZZ* [2012] ECLI:EU:C:2012:563, p. 55.

[52] *Ibid.*, at 66-67.

[53] ECJ Judgment *ZZ, supra* note 13, at 69.

[54] Opinion of Advocate General Kokott, *supra* note 14, at 71.

Czech Yearbook of International Law®

and military measures must be genuinely linked to a necessity of national security, such as internal and external security measures that contrast or prevent effective or genuinely perceived threats. Second, they must be conducted in a way, and for the duration strictly necessary to protect internal and external security (*i.e.*, in a proportionate manner). By contrast, Member States have no right under Article 4(2) TEU to adopt non-genuine and non-proportionate measures, which represent an abuse of the power recognized to Member States by this Treaty rule, which can be sanctioned by the ECJ, especially to ensure the effectiveness of the free movement of people and the internal market, including its external dimension.

IV. Member States' Exclusive Competence over National Security Organization

4.28. The organization of police and military forces, as already argued, generally falls within those areas of internal and external security where Member States have a great discretion. However, as will be shown below, not all the aspects of these matters fall within the exclusive competence of Member States.

4.29. Regarding the organization of military forces, before the Lisbon Treaty, in the *Dory* case the ECJ clearly recognized that the decision of a Member State to 'ensure its defence in part by compulsory military service' is the expression of 'a choice of military organisation to which [EU] law is consequently not applicable,'[55] even though the compulsory military service at issue was reserved only for men, thus ignoring the principle of sex equality enshrined in the social provisions of the EU Treaties and in other EU secondary rules. Indeed, this was 'an inevitable consequence of the choice made by the Member State regarding military organisation,'[56] which – moreover – was included within the constitution of the Member State concerned. Therefore, it could be argued that decisions on whether and how to establish a compulsory military service, as part of the fundamental or constitutional choices of military organization, should fall within Member States' exclusive competence over national security, which is now encompassed under Article 4(2) TEU.

4.30. The same could be said with regard to the organization of police forces. Indeed, as stressed by Advocate General Ruiz-Jarabo Colomer in his already mentioned Opinion, EU Treaties

---

[55] ECJ Judgment *Dory*, *supra* note 22, at 39.
[56] *Ibid.*, at 41. In this regard, it must be noted that, in their observations to the ECJ, the Commission and some Member States argued that compulsory military service does not constitute an employment relationship (*ibid.*, at 26 – 28). However, in its decision the ECJ did not really take into account this argument.

recognize the existence of a wide discretion of Member States not only over the organization of their armed forces, but also of their forces for the maintenance of law and order. In particular, Member States retain great discretion in defining 'the division of powers between the various security forces and bodies'.[57] Therefore, these decisions regarding the organization of police and military forces should be included among the fundamental choices of internal and external security organization to which EU law is not applicable, therefore falling within the exclusive competence of Member States over national security by virtue of Article 4(2) TEU.

4.31. The fact that the fundamental choices of military and police organization lie within the sovereign sphere of Member States is also confirmed by the intergovernmental nature of the Treaty provisions that aim at establishing closer cooperation in the field of security matters. Indeed, according to Article 42(2) TEU, the Common Security and Defence Policy (CSDP) includes 'the progressive framing of a common Union defence policy' that 'will lead to a *common defence, when the European Council, acting unanimously, so decides*. It shall in that case recommend to the Member States the adoption of such a decision *in accordance with their respective constitutional requirements*'.[58] Thus, an EU army could be established only 'through a super-governmental, integrationist, pro-federal project',[59] whose start is in the hands of the Member States and conditioned on its compatibility with their constitutional rules. Similarly, the establishment of stronger cooperation in internal security within the AFSJ is completely within the discretion of Member States. In fact, as stated by Article 73 TFEU, they have the sole responsibility to organize between themselves some 'forms of cooperation and coordination as they deem appropriate between the competent departments of their administrations responsible for safeguarding national security'. Finally, again in the context of AFSJ, according to Article 86(4) TFEU, Member States retain the power to veto the extension of the powers of the European Public Prosecutor's Office 'to include serious crime having a cross-border dimension and amending accordingly paragraph 2 as regards the perpetrators of, and accomplices in, serious crimes affecting more than one Member State'. Indeed, on this matter the European Council 'shall act unanimously

---

[57] Opinion of Advocate General Ruiz-Jarabo Colomer, *supra* note 21, at 38.
[58] Emphasis added.
[59] Luigi Lonardo, *Integration in European Defence: Some Legal Considerations*, 2(3) EUROPEAN PAPERS 887, 892 (2017).

Czech Yearbook of International Law®

after obtaining the consent of the European Parliament and after consulting the Commission.'

4.32. However, Member States' competence over their national security organization has not prevented the EU from adopting, on the basis of Articles 53, 62 and 114 TFEU on the harmonization for the internal market, secondary rules like Directive 2009/81/EC on the coordination of procedures for the award of certain works contracts, supply contracts and service contracts by contracting authorities or entities in the fields of defense and security (Directive 2009/81).[60] That was not an easy task, given that Member States have tried for a long time to keep rules on the award of public contracts in defense and security under their discretion. Nevertheless, they still retain the power to derogate from EU procedures for the purchase of military goods and services in some particular circumstances. This is recognized by recital 16 of the Directive 2009/81 that is related to Article 346(1)(a) and (b) TFEU[61]. This recital states that

> the award of contracts which fall within the field of application of this Directive can be exempted from the latter where this is justified on grounds of public security or necessary for the protection of *essential security interests* of a Member State. This can be the case for contracts in the fields of both *defence and security which necessitate such extremely demanding security of supply requirements or which are so confidential and/or important for national sovereignty* that even the specific provisions of this Directive are not sufficient to safeguard Member States' *essential security interests, the definition of which is the sole responsibility of Member States.*[62]

---

[60] Directive 2009/81/EC of the European Parliament and of the Council of 13 July 2009 on the coordination of procedures for the award of certain works contracts, supply contracts and service contracts by contracting authorities or entities in the fields of defence and security, and amending Directives 2004/17/EC and 2004/18/EC [2009] OJ L 216/76. Regarding the scope of Article 346 TFEU I benefited the reading of Martin Trybus, BUYING DEFENCE AND SECURITY IN EUROPE, Oxford-New York: Cambridge University Press 112 (2014), 82 – 87, 278 – 283 and 303 – 305.

[61] According to the Commission, the confidentiality of information in cases related to weapons should be assessed in light of Article 346(1)(b) and not in that of Article 346(1)(a). See Commission, 'Interpretative communication on the application of Article 296 of the Treaty in the field of defence procurement' COM (2006) 779 final, 7 December 2006, section 1. In general, on Article 346(1)(b) TFEU see Martin Trybus, *Case C-337/05, Commission v. Italy (Agusta and Agusta Bell Helicopters), judgment of the Court (Grand Chamber) of 8 April 2008, and Case C-157/06, Commission v. Italy, judgment of the Court (Second Chamber) of 2 October 2008*, 46(3) COMMON MARKET LAW REVIEW 973 – 990 (2009).

[62] Emphasis added. A similar interpretation of Article 346(1)(b) was offered in the Opinion of Advocate General Ruiz-Jarabo Colomer of 10 February 2009, C-284/05, *Commission v. Finland* [2009] ECLI:EU:C:2009:67 (pp. 116-117):

> [e]ach Member State must define the essential interests of its security, identify and classify threats damaging to its security and, ultimately, assess whether it is appropriate to implement any of the restrictions referred to in Article [346 TFEU], by balancing rights which, because they

Czech Yearbook of International Law®

4.33. Put differently, Member States can exclude the application of Directive 2009/81 where a contract in the fields of defense or security is characterized by a high degree of confidentiality or importance, so that it falls within the sovereign spheres of Member States, the exclusive competence over national security *ex* Article 4(2) TEU, which is – indeed – recalled in recital 1 of the Directive.

4.34. As just said, the same principle encompassed under recital 16 of Directive 2009/81, which recognizes the right of Member States to protect the confidentiality of information regarding their essential security interests, can be found in the aforementioned Article 346(1)(a) TFEU, which, according to Advocate General Bot, is a specification of Article 4(2) TEU.[63] In this respect, as stated by Advocate General Kokott in her already mentioned Opinion, this Treaty provision allows 'certain derogations from the procurement procedures prescribed by EU law,' not only in the field of military production but in all those related to security issues,[64] that may be actually 'justified by the fact that a Member State does not wish simply to disclose security-related information to foreign undertakings or undertakings controlled by foreign nationals, in particular undertakings or persons from non-member countries.'[65] In this regard, Member States can set aside EU secondary rules on tender procedures, as well as Treaty rules on the internal market – based on principles such as non-discrimination, transparency and competition – only when such a decision 'genuinely reflects a concern to attain [the objective of Article 346 TFEU] in a consistent and systematic manner.'[66] Thus, only certain public contracts in the fields of defense and security that are genuinely and strictly connected to the very core of Member States' essential interest of national security should fall within the exclusive competence of Member States under Article 4(2) TEU, providing room for Member States to adopt awarding rules that depart from secondary and primary EU rules. However, Member States must use their exclusive competence in a proportionate manner, as also confirmed

---

concern the very essence of a State's sovereignty, do not fall within the scope of Community law. The classification of an autonomous concept such as 'essential interests of its security' [does not] come within the Community sphere. As Community law currently stands, that concept is, by definition, exclusively a matter for the Member States. [Author's note: the addition in square brackets was necessary due to a translation error from Spanish to English.]

[63] Opinion of Advocate General Bot, *supra* note 51, at 66 – 67.
[64] It must be noted that the scope of Article 346(1)(a) TFEU is very broad and it is not limited to information regarding weapons. Indeed, in the case to which the Opinion of Advocate General Kokott (*supra* note 14) refers, the government of Austria used Article 346(1)(a) in order to derogate from the EU public tender rules in the field of the services related to the printing of official documents.
[65] Opinion of Advocate General Kokott, *supra* note 14, at 70.
[66] *Ibid.*, at 71.

by recital 17 of the Directive 2009/81. In this regard, it must be noted that the ECJ is always entitled to intervene over the exercise of national exclusive competences. In all other cases, EU secondary rules on public tenders apply, including those that provide the necessary procedures and means to protect the confidentiality of information and the security of supply.

4.35. In other words, given that Article 346 does not represent an automatic exclusion from EU law and its invocation (although legitimate) is not enough to identify an area of Member States' sovereignty, it is necessary to find the right borderline between the internal market and Member States' exclusive competence over national security on a case-by-case basis. However, in this regard, it can reasonably be argued that where the mere application of free movement principles to specific public contracts in security and defense fields would be incompatible with the very core of Member States' essential security interests, EU Members are and will be always entitled to entirely exclude these specific contracts from the internal market by means of Article 346 (*e.g.*, because internal market rules would impose the disclosure of very confidential information of national security to foreign persons). Thus, such specific public contracts fall under Member States' exclusive competence over the fundamental choices of national security organization. Putting it differently, Member States have a permanent right to keep under their sovereign sphere the awarding rules of such public contracts, enjoying the maximum level of discretion (*e.g.*, directly and continuously awarding a certain contract to a national historical operator to protect very confidential information). Differently saying, Article 346 represents a persistent limitation to EU law and, thus, to the EU legislative power, although in exceptional cases. This could be the case of contracts that must remain secret, which are mentioned under recital 20 of the Directive 2009/81. Secret contracts could be those linked to the core activities of intelligence services, which indeed enjoy an explicit exclusion from the scope of Directive 2009/81 in Article 13(b). In fact, because of their very inner nature, such public contracts systematically fall under Article 346(1)(a), allowing a permanent derogation from the entire body of EU law and not only from the mentioned Directive. Such an enduring limitation to EU law, and to the EU legislative power, is doomed to persist until there won't be a consensus among Member States to stop from invoking Article 346, which basically would correspond to a common political will to transform the EU into a federal or *quasi*-federal State, which is very unlikely at the present.

4.36. The same limited interpretation of Member States' freedom of action also applies to Article 346(1)(b) TFEU,[67] according to which

> [t]he production of and trade in arms, munitions and war material are subject to special treatment [...] by virtue of which the provisions of the Treaty do not preclude the Member States taking, in relation to those particular activities, such measures as they consider necessary for the protection of the essential interests of their security. The arms, munitions and war material covered by that regime are set out on the list drawn up by the Council on 15 April 1958 and mentioned in [Article 346(2) TFEU].[68]

4.37. Indeed, although this regime 'is intended to preserve the freedom of action of the Member States in certain matters affecting national defence and security,' as it 'confers on the Member States a particularly wide discretion in assessing the needs receiving such protection,'[69] in exercising such a discretion, Member States must try not to 'adversely affect the conditions of competition in the common market regarding products which are not intended for specifically military purposes,' as well as 'products which are on the Council's list of 15 April 1958 but are capable of being put to civilian use as well (products called mixed use [products]) or products covered by the said list but intended for export.'[70] For example, a Member State is free to adopt measures of economic support in favor of a single undertaking within the framework of its sole competence over economic policy, if such supporting measures are necessary to ensure the production of military goods included in the Council's list of 1958, and affect neither civil/dual-use items nor exports of military goods within the aforementioned list, so that their effects on intra-EU trade are absent or limited to the strictly necessary (*i.e.*, proportionate). Indeed, the Commission considers economic support measures like the ones just described not only as falling outside the scope of State aid rules,[71] but also as not representing an abuse of Article 346 TFEU, which could be investigated by the Commission under the aforementioned Article 348(1) TFEU.

---

[67]   '[A]ny Member State may take such measures as it considers necessary for the protection of the essential interests of its security which are connected with the production of or trade in arms, munitions and war material; such measures shall not adversely affect the conditions of competition in the internal market regarding products which are not intended for specifically military purposes.'

[68]   EU Tribunal Judgment of 30 September 2003, T-26/01, *Fiocchi munizioni* [2003] ECLI:EU:T:2003:248, p. 57.

[69]   *Ibid.*, at 58.

[70]   *Ibid.*, at 63.

[71]   European Commission Decision of 20 November 2017, State aid implemented by the Hellenic Republic for Hellenic Defence System S.A. (EAS – Ellinika Amyntika Systimata), C(2017) 7361 final.

Czech Yearbook of International Law®

4.38. Thus, State aid rules cannot preclude Member States to adopt measures that are necessary and proportionate to protect their very essential security interest. Such measures represent the legitimate use of Member States' exclusive competence over national security organization by virtue of Article 4(2) TEU. In this regard, possible future EU initiatives to sustain investment in the defense sector would be adopted under Article 6 TFEU (*i.e.*, supporting competences), thus basically without prejudice to Member States' competences. By contrast, where such a genuine link between a Member State's decision and an essential security interest does not exist, the situation falls entirely within the scope of EU law, providing room to the Commission to intervene *ex* Article 108 TFEU or Article 348(1) TFEU. Moreover, as already said, the ECJ is entitled to assess whether Member States properly use their power under Article 346 TFEU. This is to avoid abusive conduct by Member States to the detriment of competition within the internal market, such as economic supporting measures that are necessary for the production of an item encompassed under the 1958 list, but that also favor the export activities of the beneficiary undertaking.

4.39. Furthermore, with regard to the recruitment policy of police and military bodies, although Member States have the responsibility to make decisions on the organization of their armed forces, '[i]t does not follow [...] that such decisions must fall entirely outside the scope of [EU] law.'[72] Indeed, according to well-established ECJ case law, the social provisions of the Treaty, which include the principle of equal treatment for men and women, also apply to 'employment in the public service.'[73] EU rules on the implementation of such a principle[74] are therefore applicable to the access to police and military forces.[75] In other words, notwithstanding the attempts of Member States to consider their 'constitutional rule prohibiting women from performing armed service' to fall within 'matters of defence, which [...] remain within the Member States' sphere of sovereignty,'[76] the ECJ has repeatedly stated that EU law applies both to employment access to, and working conditions within, national security

[72] ECJ Judgment of 26 October 1999, C-273/97, *Sirdar* [1999] ECLI:EU:C:1999:523, p. 15. See also, ECJ Judgment of 11 January 2000, C-285/98, *Kreil* [2002] ECLI:EU:C:2000:2, p. 15.
[73] *Ibid.*, *Kreil*, at 18.
[74] Council Directive 76/207/EEC of 9 February 1976 on the implementation of the principle of equal treatment for men and women as regards access to employment, vocational training and promotion, and working conditions [1976] OJ L 39/40, now replaced by Directive 2006/54/EC of the European Parliament and of the Council of 5 July 2006 on the implementation of the principle of equal opportunities and equal treatment of men and women in matters of employment and occupation [2006] OJ L 204/23.
[75] See ECJ Judgment of 15 May 1986, 222/84, *Johnston* [1986] ECLI:EU:C:1986:206, p. 22, and ECJ Judgment *Sirdar*, *supra* note 72, at 20, and ECJ Judgment *Kreil*, *supra* note 72, at 19.
[76] ECJ Judgment *Kreil*, *supra* note 72, at 12.

Czech Yearbook of International Law®

forces. Thus, Member States have substantially conferred to the EU the power to adopt secondary acts in order to ensure sex equality in the context of the organization of police and military forces. By contrast, as the *Dory* case shows, the principle of gender equality does not apply to decisions that pertain to the fundamental choices of national security organization that come under the exclusive competence of Member States, such as the establishment of compulsory military services reserved to men.

4.40. In this regard, in order to properly understand what comes within the exclusive competence of Member States on the organization of police and military forces, one could try to identify a distinction between 'fundamental' and 'non-fundamental' organization choices. Indeed, the first category should encompass all elements that are essential for the protection of national security, such as the aforementioned decisions on compulsory military service, those on the duties and tasks of police and military forces. This category should also include Member States' decisions regarding the economic measures to sustain their essential military manufacturers, and those concerning the rules for the award of specific public contracts, which basically correspond to those that contain relevant essential security information and those of utmost importance for the national defense, justifying the invocation of Article 346. However, in this last regard, national governments must exercise their competence adopting only strictly proportionate measures so as not to excessively restrict relevant EU rules (*i.e.*, State aid and internal market rules). There is, indeed, a genuine link between the mentioned decisions and the protection of national security, so that they fall within Member States' exclusive competence over national security organization. By contrast, other aspects, such as the adoption of rules on the award of public contracts in the fields of security and defense, to which Article 346 is not applicable, and those on gender requirements for the access to police and military forces, should not form part of the fundamental choices of police and military organizations, thus falling outside Member States' sole responsibility over national security organization *ex* Article 4(2) TEU and, consequently, coming under EU law. In fact, for example, there is not a sufficiently genuine link between the gender of security officers, who have traditionally been men, and the protection of national security. In effect, as argued by Advocate General La Pergola in the *Sirdar* case, already in the early 1980s experimental trials regarding the participation of women within the armed forces showed that '[n]ot only was combat effectiveness not compromised, but the deployment of

Czech Yearbook of International Law®

women, far from undermining military cohesion, in fact even reinforced the *esprit de corps*.'[77] Moreover, the EU secondary rules applicable to the case provide for some derogation from the principle of gender equality, particularly where the total exclusion of women from a specific unit of the army is supported 'by reason of the 'interoperability' rule established for the purpose of ensuring combat effectiveness'.[78] Indeed, where the organization of a certain army branch 'differs fundamentally from that of other units,'[79] the exclusion of women can be justified by deferring to secondary law rules.

V.   Conclusions

4.41.   Member States have an exclusive competence over national security that firstly includes matters that refer to areas where EU law generally does not apply, such as those related to fundamental choices on both the establishment of a compulsory military service, and the division of powers between the various security forces and bodies. The same is true also for police and military actions adopted to protect Member States' internal and external security. However, in this last regard, the legitimate exercise of the sole competence of Member States over national security is limited to the adoption of necessary (*i.e.*, genuine) and proportionate measures for the protection of national security, in order not to unduly limit the free movement of people (*e.g.*, with systematic borders' control) and the internal market. The same principles of necessity and proportionality apply to the exercise of Member States' exclusive competence over other fundamental choices of national security organization (*i.e.*, national procedures for the award of public contracts and national measures of economic sustain, both for the protection of Member States' essential security interests), so as not to disproportionately affect relevant EU rules. Indeed, as argued by Advocate General Kokott in her Opinion regarding Article 346 TFEU, although a Member State is accorded,

> a *wide discretion* in security matters, it is not entirely free, but is *subject to review by the Court*. In particular, it is for that Member State to prove that it is necessary to have recourse to the measures

---

[77]   Opinion of Advocate General La Pergola of 18 May 1999, C-273/97, *Sirdar* [1999] ECLI:EU:C:1999:246, p. 45.

[78]   ECJ Judgment *Sirdar, supra* note 72, at 29. Regarding the distinction between fundamental and non-fundamental choices of national security organization I benefited the reading of Panos Koutrakos, *supra* note 22.

[79]   *Ibid.*, at 30.

taken by it in order to protect its essential national security interests. The Member State concerned must therefore ultimately undergo *a proportionality test*,

which, according to relevant scholarly literature, is not the traditional proportionality test applied to national restrictions on the freedoms of movement within the internal markets. In fact, the assessment applied by the ECJ to national measures adopted under the wholly exceptional clauses of EU Treaties appears to be less strict than that applied in the context of the internal market. In other words, a measure is illegitimate only when it is clear and manifest that it is wholly unreasonable and disproportionate.[80] In any case, as already argued, a proportionality test is applicable also to the exercise of Member States' exclusive competence, so as to avoid violations of EU law.[81]

4.42. Therefore, the exercise of the exclusive competence of EU Members over national security should be given a narrow interpretation. In this regard, a Member State is entirely free to unilaterally act in areas encompassed under national security, provided that national measures do not constitute an abuse of its power. That is to say, such measures must be proportionate and necessary for the achievement of a national security objective without unnecessarily restricting the application of EU law that are eventually relevant. Once a Member State uses its exclusive competence over national security in such a way, it follows that EU rules should not preclude the State from taking such an action.[82]

4.43. A limited interpretation of national security under Article 4(2) TEU is perfectly in line with that which the ECJ gives to the identity clause included in the same Article 4(2) TEU.[83] Indeed, according to the most recent case law on Article 4(2)

---

[80] Opinion of Advocate General Kokott, *supra* note 14, at 54 (emphasis added). Regarding the differences between the tests applied by the ECJ, see: Martin Trybus *supra* note 60; Panos Koutrakos, *The application of EC law to defence-related industries—changing interpretations of Article 296 EC, in* THE OUTER LIMITS OF EUROPEAN UNION LAW, London-New York: Hart Publishing, 307 – 327 (Catherine Barnard, Okeoghene Odudu eds., 2009); and Martin Trybus, *supra* note 27, at 1371 – 1372.

[81] ECJ Judgment *Rottman, supra* note 13, at 59.

[82] For analogous conclusions, see ECJ Judgment *Dory, supra* note 22, at 42.

[83] The first part of Article 4(2) TEU states that

[t]he *Union shall respect* the equality of Member States before the Treaties as well as their *national identities*, inherent in their fundamental structures, political and constitutional, inclusive of regional and local self-government. It shall respect their essential State functions, including ensuring the territorial integrity of the State, maintaining law and order and safeguarding national security (emphasis added).

In this regard, see ECJ Judgment of 28 November 1989, C-379/87, *Groener* [1989] ECLI:EU:C:1989:599, ECJ Judgment of 2 July 1996, C-473/93, *Commission v. Luxemburg* [1996] ECLI:EU:C:1996:263, and ECJ Judgment of 22 December 2010, C-208/09, *Sayn-Wittgenstein* [2010] ECLI:EU:C:2010:806.

TEU, the identity clause refers only to the core of national and constitutional values. In fact, as stated by Advocate General Bot in his Opinion in the *M.A.S. & M.B.* case,[84] only fundamental and overriding constitutional principles fall within the scope of the identity clause under Article 4(2) TEU.[85] In effect, the concept of national identity under Article 4(2) TEU 'should be confined to the hard core of national identity, which arguably include[s] the form of State and government and little more,'[86] such as

> the protection of basic principles of State organization (such as federalism, republican form of government, monarchical form of government, etc.); State sovereignty and the principle of democracy; State symbols (e.g. the flag); State aims; the protection of human dignity, fundamental rights, and the principle of the rule of law (*Rechtsstaat, état de droit*).[87]

4.44. Therefore, in favor of a uniform and coherent interpretation of Article 4(2) TEU, it could be argued that given that its first part – *i.e.*, the identity clause – is interpreted narrowly, the same limited interpretation should be given to its second part, in which national security is described as the sole responsibility of Member States.

4.45. The definition of national security under EU law proposed here is clearly non-exhaustive and needs more specification by the ECJ and scholarly doctrine in order to identify a more comprehensive framework.

4.46. In conclusion, a narrow interpretation of the exclusive competence of Member States on national security is systematically coherent with well-established ECJ case law regarding other Member States' exclusive competences. For

---

[84] Opinion of Advocate General Bot of 18 July 2017, C-42/17, *M.A.S. & M.B.* [2017] ECLI:EU:C:2017:564 with reference to ECJ Judgment of 5 December 2017, C-42/17, *M.A.S. & M.B.* [2017] ECLI:EU:C:2017:936. On this ECJ's decision, in particular for its relations with another ECJ's decision (ECJ Judgment of 8 September 2015, C-105/14, *Taricco* [2015] ECLI:EU:C:2015:555), see Michał Krajewski, *'Conditional' Primacy of EU Law and Its Deliberative Value: An Imperfect Illustration from Taricco II*, European Law Blog, 18 December 2017, available at: http://europeanlawblog.eu/2017/12/18/conditional-primacy-of-eu-law-and-its-deliberative-value-an-imperfect-illustration-from-taricco-ii/ (accessed on 29 June 2018); Michał Krajewski, *A Way Out for the ECJ in Taricco II: Constitutional Identity or a More Careful Proportionality Analysis?* European Law Blog, 23 November 2017, available at: http://europeanlawblog.eu/2017/11/23/a-way-out-for-the-ecj-in-taricco-ii-constitutional-identity-or-a-more-careful-proportionality-analysis/ (accessed on 29 June 2018), and Marco Bassini, Oreste Pollicino, *Defusing the Taricco Bomb through Fostering Constitutional Tolerance: All Roads Lead to Rome*, Verfassungsblog, 5 December 2017, available at: https://verfassungsblog.de/defusing-the-taricco-bomb-through-fostering-constitutional-tolerance-all-roads-lead-to-rome/ (accessed on 29 June 2018).

[85] *Ibid.*, Opinion of Advocate General Bot, at 169 – 187.

[86] Giacomo Di Federico, *Identifying National Identities in the Case Law of the Court of Justice of the European Union*, 19(4) Diritto dell'Unione europea 769, 801 – 802 (2014).

[87] Armin von Bogdandy, Stephan Schill, *Overcoming Absolute Primacy: Respect for National Identity under the Lisbon Treaty*, 48(5) Common Market Law Review 1417, 1432 (2011).

Defining the Notion of 'National Security' under Article 4(2) TEU.

Czech Yearbook of International Law®

example, Article 345 TFEU, on the principle of neutrality of EU law with regard to national systems of property ownership, recognizes 'a Member States' prerogative (that is, the exclusive competence) to choose their system of property ownership.'[88] In other words, EU Treaties do not preclude or impose nationalization or privatization. Consequently, EU institutions have no competence over decisions on public or private ownership of undertakings, which remain under the sole responsibility of Member States. However, 'whilst the Member States may indeed choose their system of property ownership, the consequences resulting from that choice and the conditions under which property is held are not removed from the scope of applicable rules of EU law,'[89] in particular non-discrimination and free movement rules.

4.47.   In short, Member States have strongly limited their sovereignty by joining the EU[90]. The wide jurisdiction of the ECJ can involve sanction of any abuse of the national security competence of Member States. The Commission has broad powers to intervene in order to ensure the effectiveness and uniform application of EU law. Treaty rules provide to the EU the possibility to regulate areas that are strongly tied with national security concerns such as those related to military goods and services,[91] with the aim of strengthening the free movement of people, the internal market and the enjoinment of social rights throughout the EU. All these elements have restricted the freedom that Member States traditionally had with regard to their national security. In this regard, it has been argued that the inclusion of such a matter in the Treaty as a sole competence of Member States represents only a 'cosmetic operation.'[92] This shows the expansionist nature of EU law, which is a feature that persists even in difficult times for the EU integration process such as the current one.

| | |

---

[88]   Opinion of Advocate General Sharpston of 21 December 2016, Opinion procedure 2/15, *EUSFTA* [2016] ECLI:EU:C:2016:992, p. 341.
[89]   *Ibid.*, at 340.
[90]   According to some commentators, EU's decisions taken under Treaty rules on police cooperation and CFSP, could in theory limit the exclusive competence of Member States over national securiy (see Nicholas Grief, *EU law and security*, 32(5) European Law Review 752-765 (2007)). However, such decisions of the EU do not affect the prerogative of Member States to act for the protection of their own internal or external security, but rather these EU acts can require them (by means of the duty of sincere cooperation) to use their police and military forces with the aim of protecting the collective security of the EU and its Member States.
[91]   For the latest developments with regard to the internal market of defense products see Martin Trybus, Luke R.A. Butler, *The internal market and national security: Transposition, impact and reform of the EU directive on Intra-Community Transfers of Defence Products*, 54(2) Common Market Law Review 403 – 441 (2017).
[92]   Giacomo Di Federico, *supra* note 13, at 119.

Summaries

FRA [*Définir la notion de « sécurité nationale » au sens de l'article 4, paragraphe 2, du traité sur l'Union européenne. Que reste-t-il de la souveraineté des États membres ?*]

Le droit de l'UE ne définit pas clairement la notion de « sécurité nationale », qui est par conséquent utilisée comme une catégorie chapeau, couvrant une large gamme de questions ayant trait à la sécurité. Depuis le traité de Lisbonne, le droit de l'UE comprend une référence explicite à la « sécurité nationale », introduite par l'article 4, paragraphe 2, du traité sur l'Union européenne. Cette disposition, connue sous le nom de « clause d'identité », stipule que la sécurité nationale « reste de la seule responsabilité de chaque État membre ». Le présent article définit le contenu et la portée de cette notion, tout en précisant la manière dont les États membres peuvent légitimement exercer cette responsabilité. L'auteur explique la notion complexe de « sécurité nationale » de façon à attirer l'attention à tous ses aspects fondamentaux. L'article se focalise non seulement sur les pouvoirs que les États membres n'ont pas délégués à l'Union européenne, en ce qui concerne la protection de leur sécurité intérieure et extérieure (quoique sous le contrôle de la Cour de justice de l'UE), mais aussi sur les limites auxquelles le droit de l'UE se heurte lorsqu'il touche aux questions qui sont traditionnellement associées à la sécurité intérieure et extérieure. Si l'Union européenne est en droit d'intervenir dans certains de ces domaines, l'essentiel des questions de sécurité relève du pouvoir exclusif des États membres, donc de leur souveraineté.

CZE [*Definování pojmu „národní bezpečnost" ve smyslu článku 4 odst. 2 Smlouvy o Evropské unii. Co skutečně zbylo ze svrchovanosti členských států?*]

Pojem „národní bezpečnost" dle práva EU není jasně definován a je velmi často užíván jako sběrná kategorie pokrývající širokou škálu otázek souvisejících s bezpečností. Po uzavření Lisabonské smlouvy však smlouvy EU výslovně obsahují pojem „národní bezpečnost" dle článku 4 odst. 2 Smlouvy o Evropské unii, normu nejběžněji známou pod označením „klauzule identity", která odkazuje na národní bezpečnost jako „výhradní odpovědnost" členských států. Tento článek vymezuje obsah a rozsah tohoto pojmu a objasňuje způsob, jak mohou členské státy tuto pravomoc právoplatně vykonávat. Předkládaná analýza vykládá komplexní pojem národní bezpečnosti tak, aby čtenáři nabídla přehled hlavních aspektů, které do tohoto rámce spadají. Tato práce současně zohledňuje nejen to, co členské státy nesvěřily Evropské unii, pokud jde o ochranu jejich vnitřní a vnější bezpečnosti (byť nikoli mimo rámec kontroly vykonávané Evropským soudním dvorem), ale i meze, na něž právo EU naráží, když se dotýká otázek, které jsou s vnitřní a vnější bezpečností tradičně spojovány. Přestože je Evropská unie oprávněna v některých těchto oblastech zasahovat, nejniternější jádro bezpečnostních otázek zůstává v rámci výlučné pravomoci (tj. svrchovanosti) jejích členů.

| | |

POL [*Definicja pojęcia „bezpieczeństwo narodowe" w świetle artykułu 4 ust. 2 Traktatu o Unii Europejskiej. Co rzeczywiście pozostało z suwerenności państw członkowskich?*]
Pojęcie „bezpieczeństwa narodowego" w myśl prawa UE nie jest wyraźnie zdefiniowane i bardzo często używa się go jako pewnej kategorii zbiorczej. Po zawarciu Traktatu z Lizbony traktaty UE zaczęły definiować pojęcie „bezpieczeństwa narodowego" w myśl artykułu 4 ust. 2 Traktatu o Unii Europejskiej jako „wyłączną odpowiedzialność" krajów członkowskich. Artykuł przybliża treść i zakres tego pojęcia oraz wyjaśnia sposób, w jaki kraje członkowskie mogą wykonywać te kompetencje w sposób prawomocny. Chociaż Unia Europejska w pewnych obszarach może ingerować w niektórych sprawach bezpieczeństwa wewnętrznego i zewnętrznego, najważniejsze kwestie związane z bezpieczeństwem pozostają wyłącznie w kompetencjach jej członków.

DEU [*Definition des Begriffs der „nationalen Sicherheit" im Sinne des Art. 4 Abs. 2 des EU-Vertrags. Was ist letztlich von der Souveränität der Mitgliedsstaaten geblieben?*]
Der Begriff der „nationalen Sicherheit" ist im EU-Recht nicht klar definiert und wird sehr häufig als eine Art Sammelkategorie gebraucht. Nach dem Abschluss des Vertrags von Lissabon enthalten die EU-Verträge nun aber ausdrücklich den Begriff der „nationalen Sicherheit" im Sinne des Art. 4 (2) EUV als „ausschließliche Verantwortung" der Mitgliedsstaaten. Der vorliegende Beitrag grenzt Inhalt und Umfang dieses Begriffs ab und erklärt, auf welche Weise die Mitgliedsstaaten diese Kompetenz rechtsgültig wahrnehmen können. Zwar ist die Europäische Union in bestimmten Fällen der inneren und äußeren Sicherheit zum Eingriff berechtigt; der allerinnerste

Kern der Sicherheitsfragen verbleibt aber in der ausschließlichen Hoheitsgewalt ihrer Mitglieder.

RUS [***Определение термина «национальная безопасность» в свете пункта 2 статьи 4 Договора о Европейском союзе. Что на самом деле осталось от суверенитета государств-членов?***]

Термин «национальная безопасность» в соответствии с правом ЕС четко не определен и очень часто используется как некая «сборная» категория. Однако после заключения Лиссабонского договора в договорах ЕС содержится термин «национальная безопасность» буквально в соответствии с пунктом 2 стати 4 Договора о Европейском союзе, т. е. как «исключительная ответственность» государств-членов. В этой статье определяется содержание и сфера действия данного термина, а также разъясняется способ, каким государства-члены могут данную компетенцию законным образом реализовывать. Хотя Европейский союз имеет право вмешиваться в некоторые области внутренней и внешней безопасности, суть вопросов безопасности остается в исключительной компетенции его членов.

ESP [***La definición del término "seguridad nacional" en virtud del artículo 4, párrafo 2, del Tratado de la Unión Europea. En realidad, ¿Qué parte de la soberanía de los Estados miembros ha permanecido?***]

La legislación de la UE no define claramente el término de la "seguridad nacional" siendo a menudo utilizado como una categoría de recogida. No obstante, tras la firma del Tratado de Lisboa, los tratados de la UE contienen expresamente el término "seguridad nacional" en virtud del artículo 4, párrafo 2, del Tratado de la Unión Europea como "responsabilidad exclusiva" de los Estados miembros. El presente texto delimita el contenido y la amplitud de dicho término aclarando el modo en el que los Estados miembros pueden ejercer tal potestad legítimamente. A pesar de que en ciertos ámbitos de la seguridad interior y exterior, la Unión Europea posee el derecho a intervenir, la esencia más profunda de las cuestiones de seguridad permanece exclusivamente en el marco de la competencia de sus miembros.

| | |

Czech Yearbook of International Law®

Bibliography

Armin von Bogdandy, Stephan Schill, *Overcoming Absolute Primacy: Respect for National Identity under the Lisbon Treaty*, 48(5) COMMON MARKET LAW REVIEW 1417 (2011).

Antonio Cantaro, *Il rispetto delle funzioni essenziali dello Stato*, in L'ORDINAMENTO EUROPEO. VOL. 1: I PRINCIPI DELL'UNIONE, Milano: Giuffrè 507 (Stelio Mangiameli ed., 2006).

Mary Dobbs, *Sovereignty, Article 4(2) TEU and the Respect of National Identities: Swinging the Balance of Power in Favour of the Member States?* 33(1) YEARBOOK OF EUROPEAN LAW, 298 (2014).

Giacomo Di Federico, *Identifying National Identities in the Case Law of the Court of Justice of the European Union*, 19(4) DIRITTO DELL'UNIONE EUROPEA 769 (2014).

Giacomo Di Federico, L'IDENTITÀ NAZIONALE DEGLI STATI MEMBRI NEL DIRITTO DELL'UNIONE EUROPEA. NATURA E PORTATA DELL'ART. 4, PAR. 2, TUE, Napoli: Editoriale Scientifica 159 (2017).

Nicholas Grief, *EU law and security*, 32(5) EUROPEAN LAW REVIEW 752-765 (2007).

BARBARA GUASTAFERRO, BEYOND THE EXCEPTIONALISM OF CONSTITUTIONAL CONFLICTS: THE ORDINARY FUNCTIONS OF THE IDENTITY CLAUSE, New York: Jean Monnet Working Paper 01/12 (2012).

HANS KELSEN, LA DOTTRINA PURA DEL DIRITTO, Torino: Einaudi 322 (1966).

Theodore Konstadinides, *Dealing With Parallel Universes: Antinomies of Sovereignty and the Protection of National Identity in European Judicial Discourse*, 34(1) YEARBOOK OF EUROPEAN LAW, 127 (2015).

Panos Koutrakos, *How Far is Far Enough? EC Law and the Organisation of the Armed Forces after Dory*, 66(5) MODERN LAW REVIEW 759 – 768 (2003).

Panos Koutrakos, *The Notion of Necessity in the Law of the European Union*, 41 NETHERLANDS YEARBOOK OF INTERNATIONAL LAW 193 – 218 (2011).

Panos Koutrakos, *Is Article 297 EC a 'Reserve of Sovereignty'?* 37(6) COMMON MARKET LAW REVIEW 1339 – 1362 (2000).

Panos Koutrakos, *The application of EC law to defence-related industries—changing interpretations of Article 296 EC*, in THE OUTER LIMITS OF EUROPEAN UNION LAW, London-New York: Hart Publishing, 307 (Catherine Barnard, Okeoghene Odudu eds., 2009).

Luigi Lonardo, *Integration in European Defence: Some Legal Considerations*, 2(3) EUROPEAN PAPERS 887 (2017).

Ivana Palandri, *Art. 348 TFUE*, in COMMENTARIO BREVE AI TRATTATI

DELL'UNIONE EUROPEA Padova: CEDAM 1549, 1551 (Fausto Pocar, Maria Caterina Baruffi eds., 2014).

Martin Trybus, BUYING DEFENCE AND SECURITY IN EUROPE, Oxford-New York: Cambridge University Press 112 (2014).

Martin Trybus, *The EC Treaty as an Instrument of European Defence Integration: Judicial Scrutiny of Defence and Security Exceptions,* 39(6) COMMON MARKET LAW REVIEW 1347 (2002).

Martin Trybus, Luke R.A. Butler, *The internal market and national security: Transposition, impact and reform of the EU directive on Intra-Community Transfers of Defence Products,* 54(2) COMMON MARKET LAW REVIEW 403 (2017).

Adam Giertl

State Sovereignty in the Context of Disaster Response: Its Exercise and Limitations

Key words:
disaster | state sovereignty | humanitarian aid | human rights | humanitarian principles | duty to seek assistance

Czech Yearbook of International Law®

Abstract | Disasters and in particular major natural calamities have a significant influence on the development of various communities. Recently, several such events gained international attention and were subject to a more or less concerted international effort to provide aid to victims of the disasters.[1] It is established that a disaster is defined by the magnitude of the disruption of the functioning of a society. The negative effects of a disaster on society must be at first addressed by the State on the territory of which the disaster took place. For that matter, the event of a disaster and the response to it is frequently perceived as the internal affair of a State. However, emerging international rules of disaster response recognize a situation when the capabilities of States may be exceeded. On the other hand, most states are bound by human rights treaties and related rules. It is established that appropriate assistance to victims of the disaster is part of respecting obligations stemming from international instruments of human rights protection. This article comments on the issue of sovereignty of the State and its relation to the provision of humanitarian aid by the external actors on the territory of the affected State. The article comments on the notion of sovereignty in international disaster response law (IDRL), the role of the affected State and the rules concerning giving consent to external assistance and setting up the conditions of such consent.

JUDr. Adam Giertl is currently affiliated with the Faculty of Law of the Pavol Jozef Šafárik University in Košice, where he works at the Institute of International Law and European Law as researcher and lecturer of International Public Law. He is also a PhD. candidate in the field of International Law. In his research, he focuses on the questions of statehood in international law and regionalism in international law. He currently examines the international legal aspects of disaster response. E-mail: adam.giertl@upjs.sk; giertl.adam@gmail.com

---

[1] Such events were for example disaster caused by the tidal bore in Bangladesh in 1970 or more recently major disasters caused by tsunami in Southeast Asia in 2004, Cyclone Nargis in 2008, earthquake in Haiti in 2010.

Finally, the article briefly addresses the duty of a State to seek external assistance under specific circumstances.

| | |

I.   Introduction

5.01.   There is a broad range of international legal rules that are concerned with the protection of an individual person with specific status or in specific circumstances. Rules of standing international law protect children, people with disabilities, and victims of war.[2] Every human being is legally protected by international rules of human rights protection, whether on an universal or regional level.[3]

5.02.   On the other hand, international public law is firmly anchored on the principles that protect sovereign states – specifically their territorial integrity, political independence and equal sovereignty with other sovereign states.[4] States are the only members of the international community with full legal capacity. Simply put, international public law is still a legal system primarily regulating the legal relationships of States. The protection of individuals is regulated by international treaties that are by definition concluded on a consensual basis by States and between them. Regardless of the theoretical background, the legal protection of individual human beings established by international treaties can be interpreted as a self-imposed

---

[2]   Convention on the Rights of the Child. Adopted and opened for signature, ratification and accession by General Assembly resolution (UN GA Res.) 44/25 of 20 November 1989, entry into force 2 September 1990, available at: http://www.ohchr.org/EN/ProfessionalInterest/Pages/CRC.aspx (accessed on 20 July 2018); Convention on the Rights of Persons with Disabilities, adopted as annex to the UN General Assembly Resolution 61/106, available at: https://www.un.org/development/desa/disabilities/resources/general-assembly/convention-on-the-rights-of-persons-with-disabilities-ares61106.html (accessed on 20 July 2018); See website of International Committee of the Red Cross for the Geneva Conventions of 1949 and additional Protocols (I., II. and III.), available at: https://www.icrc.org/eng/war-and-law/treaties-customary-law/geneva-conventions/overview-geneva-conventions.htm.

[3]   First major instrument stipulating universal character of human rights was Universal Declaration of Human Rights (UN GA Res. 217 (III)) of 1948, available at: http://www.un.org/en/ga/search/view_doc.asp?symbol=A/RES/217(III) (accessed on 20 July 2018). Legally binding treaties that provide for protection of human rights on universal level of international legal regulation are for example International Covenant on Civil and Political Rights, available at: http://www.ohchr.org/en/professionalinterest/pages/ccpr.aspx (accessed on 20 July 2018); and International Covenant of Economic, Social and Cultural Rights, available at: http://www.ohchr.org/EN/ProfessionalInterest/Pages/CESCR.aspx (accessed on 20 July 2018).

[4]   See Article 2 paragraph 1 of United Nations Charter, available at: http://www.un.org/en/sections/un-charter/chapter-i/index.html (accessed on 20 July 2018) and Declaration on Principles of International Law concerning Friendly Relations and Co-operation among States in accordance with the Charter of the United Nations adopted within the UN GA Resolution 2625 (XXV) from 24 October 1970, UN Doc. A/RES/2625 (XXV), available at: http://www.un.org/en/ga/search/view_doc.asp?symbol=A/RES/2625(XXV) (accessed on 20 July 2018).

Czech Yearbook of International Law®

limitation of the powers that States possess by virtue of their sovereignty.[5]

5.03. This article addresses the above-mentioned conflict between sovereignty and the obligation to respect human rights in the context of disasters. International Disaster Law or more precisely International Disaster Response Law (IDRL) is a system of rules that have recently gained much attention. The hallmark of the formation of the specific system of norms is the Draft Articles on the Protection of Persons in the Event of Disasters – the output of work of the International Law Commission (ILC).[6] The individual persons and their needs and rights form the philosophical core of the instruments related to the events of disasters.[7] However, it is a fact that the disasters and their effects take place within the jurisdiction of individual States.

5.04. There are several notions that emphasize the duties of the States towards the subjects on their territory in the event of disasters. These duties are mainly to respect human dignity, maintain human rights, to request external assistance under specific circumstances and others. On the other hand, there is a constant appeal within the IDRL instruments that stresses the respect of sovereignty of States and that every external assistance can be facilitated within the jurisdiction of the State in concern only with its consent and under its supervision.[8]

---

[5] It is a well-established concept of international law that the obligation stemming from the rules of international public law are binding not only *inter partes* but are also effective *erga omnes*. They bind the state to respect such rules *vis-à-vis* the international community as a whole. Due to the growing universalization of international human rights systems after the World War II, the obligation stemming from universal human rights documents are sometimes described as customary and *erga omnes* in nature, because the whole international community is interested in respecting them. See Erika De Wet, *The International Constitutional Order*, 55(1) INTERNATIONAL AND COMPARATIVE LAW QUARTERLY 51, 60-61 (2006); available at:
https://www.eui.eu/Documents/DepartmentsCentres/AcademyofEuropeanLaw/CourseMaterialsHR/HR2009/DeWet/DeWetBackgroundReading2.pdf (accessed on 20 July 2018).

[6] Draft articles on the protection of persons in the event of disasters, 2016. Adopted by the International Law Commission at its sixty-eighth session, in 2016, and submitted to the General Assembly as a part of the Commission's report covering the work of that session (A/71/10), paragraph 48, available at: http://legal.un.org/ilc/texts/instruments/english/draft_articles/6_3_2016.pdf (accessed on 20 July 2018).

[7] See for example Preamble and Article 2 of the Draft Articles on the protection of persons in the event of disasters, 2016; Model Act for the Facilitation and Regulation of International Disaster Relief and Initial Recovery Assistance Pilot Version November 2011, International Federation of Red Cross and Red Crescent Societies, Geneva, 2011, Introduction, at iv., available at:
http://www.ifrc.org/PageFiles/88609/Pilot%20Model%20Act%20on%20IDRL%20(English).pdf (accessed on 20 July 2018).

[8] See Article 2 of Model Act for the Facilitation and Regulation of International Disaster Relief and Initial Recovery Assistance Pilot Version November 2011 (*Supra* note 6); Introduction to the Guidelines for the domestic facilitation and regulation of international disaster relief and initial recovery assistance (IDRL Guidelines), International Federation of Red Cross and Red Crescent Societies, Geneva, 2011, at 13., available at: http://www.ifrc.org/PageFiles/41203/1205600-IDRL%20Guidelines-EN-LR%20(2).pdf (accessed on 20 July 2018); Resolution of the UN General Assembly 46/182 Strengthening of the coordination of the humanitarian emergency assistance of the United Nations, Annex – Guiding Principles, paragraph 3. Un Doc. A/RES/46/182.

5.05. This article argues that during its development the IDRL made the connection between sovereignty and responsibility even stronger. The refusal of the State to provide necessary assistance or its inability to do so might be a subject of international responsibility. The present article analyses several aspects where the notion 'sovereignty comes with responsibility'[9] becomes real in the context of disaster response.[10]

II.   The Notion of Sovereignty in the Context of Disaster Response

5.06. Disaster is defined as a calamitous event or series of events resulting in widespread loss of life, great human suffering and distress, mass displacement, or large-scale material or environmental damage seriously disrupting the functioning of a society.[11] Given this definition, which is cited almost verbatim from the ILC´s Draft Articles on Protection of Persons in the Event of Disasters (Draft Articles), it is clear that not every event generally described as a disaster qualifies as a disaster for the purposes of the IDRL. An international regime can clearly be applied in events that have potential to disrupt the functioning of a society or have already done so. It can be assumed that the purpose of a limited scope of definition is to ensure that international law shall step in only in the most urgent and most serious emergencies.[12] However, the seriousness of the

---

[9] The cited principle can be found for example in the Corfu Channel Case. Judge Alvarez in his individual opinion stated, 'By sovereignty, we understand the whole body of rights and attributes which state possesses in its territory... Sovereignty confers rights upon States and imposes obligations on them.' Individual opinion by Judge Alvarez, at 44, *Corfu Channel (United Kingdom of Great Britain and Northern Ireland v. Albania*, available at: http://www.icj-cij.org/files/case-related/1/001-19490409-JUD-01-01-EN.pdf (accessed on 20 July 2018).

[10] Read also Lucia Bódišová, *Application of the Sovereignty of the States in the Process of Elimination of the Consequences of the Natural and Man-made Disasters* (Slovak: *Uplatňovanie suverenity štátov v procese odstraňovania následkov prírodných a priemyselných katastrof*), in THE PLACE, ROLE AND SIGNIFICANCE OF DOMESTIC LAW IN ENSURING THE PERFORMANCE OF OBLIGATIONS STEMMING FROM INTERNATIONAL LAW AND EUROPEAN LAW – COLLECTION OF SCIENTIFIC RESEARCH PAPERS BY PHD. STUDENTS AND YOUNG RESEARCHERS (Slovak: *Miesto, úloha a význam vnútroštátneho práva pri zabezpečovaní plnenia záväzkov vyplývajúcich z medzinárodného práva a európskeho práva – Zborník vedeckých prác doktorandov a mladých vedeckých pracovníkov*), Košice: Univerzita Pavla Jozefa Šafárika v Košiciach 282, 288 (Dominika Becková, Adam Giertl eds., 2018); available at: https://unibook.upjs.sk/img/cms/2018/pravf/miesto-uloha-a-vyznam-naweb.pdf (accessed on 20 July 2018).

[11] See Draft Articles on the protection of persons in the event of disasters, 2016, Article 3 a) *Supra* note 5.

[12] '...the reference to a 'calamitous' event serves to establish a threshold, by reference to the nature of the event, whereby only extreme events are covered. '(...) for the event, or series of events, to be considered 'calamitous' in the sense required by the draft articles, it has to result in one or more of four possible outcomes: widespread loss of life, great human suffering and distress, mass displacement or large-scale material or environmental damage. Accordingly, a major event such as a serious earthquake, which takes place in the middle of the ocean or in an uninhabited area and which does not result in at least one of the four envisaged outcomes, would not satisfy the threshold requirement ..'
See Draft articles on the protection of persons in the event of disasters, with commentaries 2016, Article 3 paragraph 4, 5, available at: http://legal.un.org/ilc/texts/instruments/english/commentaries/6_3_2016.pdf

disruption can differ from one situation to another. It is more likely that the same event may have radically different impacts on developing countries than on a highly developed nation. The capabilities of States and the general state of society and economic power directly affect how the State handles the crisis induced by the disaster.[13]

5.07.   Regardless of the economic power or political situation, the role of the State is indispensable in an effort to properly respond to the consequences of the disaster. As the United Nations General Assembly (UN GA) Resolution 46/182 states within the Guiding Principles adopted thereof, the sovereignty, territorial integrity and national unity of States has to be fully respected.[14] This notion directly reflects the UN Charter as well as the Declaration on Principles of International Law concerning Friendly Relations and Co-operation among States in accordance with the Charter of the United Nations of 1970.[15] Thus, humanitarian assistance should be provided with the consent of the affected State and in principle based on an appeal by the affected State.[16] Indeed the cited wording of Guiding Principles did not explicitly exclude the possibility of providing humanitarian assistance without the consent of the affected State. The UN GA anticipated the situation when obtaining such consent might be impossible or would be easily delayed. However, the principle is that the assistance should be facilitated upon the request of the affected State.

5.08.   The Draft Articles on Protection of Persons in the Event of Disasters brings a formulation that is more precise. For example, Article 3(c) defines the assisting State as a 'State providing assistance to an affected State with its consent.' A similar wording was adopted with respect to the definition

---

(accessed on 20 July 2018).

[13]   This was reflected for example in UN GA Resolution 42/169 that declared the 90´s as the international decade for natural disaster reduction. The emphasis was put especially on the need to reduce the impact of disasters and improving the capacity of the countries to mitigate the consequences of the disaster in particular with respect of developing countries. See UN GA Resolution 42/169, 169 International decade for natural disaster reduction from 11 December 1987, UN Doc. A/RES/42/.

[14]   See UN GA Resolution 46/182 Strengthening of the coordination of humanitarian emergency assistance of the United Nations from 19 December 1991, Annex: Guiding Principles, paragraph 2. UN Doc. A/RES/46/182.

[15]   *Supra* note 3.

[16]   The principle that the provision of external assistance requires the consent of the affected State is fundamental to international law. Accordingly, paragraph 3 of the guiding principles annexed to General Assembly resolution 46/182 notes that '*humanitarian assistance should be provided with the consent of the affected country and in principle on the basis of an appeal by the affected country*' (emphasis mine). See Draft articles on the protection of persons in the event of disasters, with commentaries 2016, Article 13 paragraph 2 in connection with UN GA Resolution 46/182 Strengthening of the coordination of humanitarian emergency assistance of the United Nations from 19 December 1991, Annex: Guiding Principles, paragraph 3, Ibid. A similar wording is included in other instruments related to IDRL such as IDRL Guidelines. See Introduction to the Guidelines for the domestic facilitation and regulation of international disaster relief and initial recovery assistance, *Ibid.*, at 17.

of the 'other assisting actor' where the consent of the affected State is formulated as a precondition of the operation of an intergovernmental organization, a relevant NGO or another entity within the territory of affected State.[17]

5.09. The Draft Articles stipulate rules specifically regarding the consent of the State in the wording of Article 13. The first paragraph declares rather simply that the 'provision of external assistance requires the consent of the affected state.' This rule is dubbed in the Commentary of the Draft Articles as the core principle regarding the implementation of international relief assistance. The treaty instruments that regulate matters of the IDRL encompass comparable provisions.[18] As was previously noted regarding the UN GA resolution 46/182, it is indeed clear that other relevant UN documents also stipulate respect to the sovereignty of the State and set a condition of the consent of the affected State before international assistance is facilitated.

II.1. The role of the Affected State during the Facilitation of the Assistance

5.10. The role of the affected State is not terminated after it gave consent for international assistance. An affected State is obliged towards persons on its territory to provide protection and relief assistance if a disaster strikes the territory under its jurisdiction.[19] The affected State bears primary responsibility to facilitate assistance and its responsibility still exists when foreign actors facilitate emergency relief on its territory.[20] It is confirmed that the affected State has a primary role in the direction, control, coordination and supervision of relief. Thus, any action of international actors must be carried out under the

---

[17] Draft Articles on protection of persons in the event of disasters; *Ibid.*, Article 3(c) and (d).

[18] See for example Article 4 paragraph 5 of the Tampere Convention on the Provision of Telecommunication Resources for Disaster Mitigation and Relief Operations, available at: http://www.ifrc.org/Docs/idrl/I271EN.pdf (accessed on 20 July 2018). See also Article 3 paragraph 1 of the ASEAN Agreement on disaster management and emergency response, available at: http://agreement.asean.org/media/download/20140119170000.pdf (accessed on 20 July 2018).

[19] Various instruments stress the responsibility of the State to facilitate emergency relief as appropriate. Compare: 'The government of the affected state has the primary responsibility, while National Red Cross or Red Crescent Societies and other domestic civil society actors play a key supporting role.' Model Act for the Facilitation and Regulation of International Disaster Relief and Initial Recovery Assistance, Introduction, at. iv., Ibid., 'Each state has the responsibility first and foremost to take care of the victims of natural disasters and other emergencies occurring on its territory. Hence, the affected state has the primary role in initiation, organization, coordination and implementation of the humanitarian assistance on its territory.' See UN GA Resolution 46/182, *Ibid.*

[20] As the above-mentioned IDRL Guidelines, stipulate: 'Affected States have the primary responsibility to ensure disaster risk reduction, relief and recovery assistance in their territory. National Red Cross and Red Crescent Societies, as auxiliaries to the public authorities in the humanitarian field, and domestic civil society actors play a key supporting role at the domestic level (...). Affected States have the sovereign right to coordinate, regulate and monitor disaster relief and recovery assistance provided by assisting actors on their territory, consistent with international law.' IDRL Guidelines, 2011, *Ibid.*, at 15.

Czech Yearbook of International Law®

supervision of the affected State. The notion of a primary role of the affected State was also reflected in the UN GA resolution 46/182. The primacy of the affected State also emanates from the fact that the State itself is best placed to determine the gravity of the emergency and to formulate appropriate response policies and relief measures. Thus, the position of the affected State in determining needs and coordinating the relief efforts is irreplaceable.[21] As the Commentary of the Draft Articles says, it is essential that the State exercise control over the manner in which relief operations are carried out. These operations shall be carried out in a manner consistent with the international law, be it the rules of a universal international law or specific rules of IDRL.[22] The assisting actor must not violate the natural rights of States. It should not violate its sovereign rights especially those connected to its political independence and territorial integrity. On the other hand, the humanitarian relief is facilitated within the jurisdiction of the affected state and the assisting actor should act in accordance with domestic law. The Draft Article does not stipulate such a duty, because as the Commentary to the Draft Article points out, the legislation of the affected state may not 'in all cases regulate or provide for the primary position of a State in a disaster response situation.'[23] Simply said, the assisting actor should not follow interests other than the one of helping persons in need in accordance with the principles of humanity, neutrality and impartiality. The State shall have discretion in determining the most appropriate form of assistance as the expression of its role in a situation. However, this discretion has to be exercised in good faith.

II.2. Consent with Assistance and Conditions of Assistance

5.11. The wording of the rule stipulated in Article 10 paragraph 2 must be read in connection with another rule formulated in Article 13 that stipulates that the consent to external assistance must not be withheld arbitrarily. There may exist political considerations as to why States refuse offers of assistance, including avoiding foreign influence on domestic matters or the need of government

---

[21] Model Act for the Facilitation and Regulation of International Disaster Relief and Initial Recovery Assistance, *Ibid.*, Article 5(a), (b).
[22] 'An affected State's discretion to determine the most appropriate form of assistance is an aspect of its primary role in the direction, control, coordination and supervision of disaster relief assistance under draft Article 10 paragraph 2. This discretion must be exercised in good faith in accordance with an affected State's international obligations' Draft articles on the protection of persons in the event of disasters, with commentaries 2016, *Ibid.*, Article 13 paragraph 10.
[23] *Ibid.*, Article 10 paragraph 9.

to avoid being perceived as weak.[24] It is an established rule that if humanitarian aid is offered to a State, such a State should in principle not to turn the offer down especially when such an act may worsen the situation of any affected persons.[25] Even when the State fails to respond to such offer in a timely manner, such a failure may be marked as arbitrary.[26] Of course, the arbitrariness of the refusal must always be assessed on a case-by-case basis. However, several general criteria were identified by the ILC to determine whether the refusal is arbitrary. The ILC stated that the refusal of assistance is not arbitrary if:

a) A State is willing, able and has capacity and resources to facilitate the assistance on its own.

b) A State has already accepted sufficient assistance from elsewhere.

c) The relevant offer of assistance is made in violation of the IDRL rules. It must especially respect the notion that the assistance must be provided in accordance with humanitarian principles.[27]

5.12. On the other hand, the Oxford Guidance on the Law Regulating Humanitarian Relief Operations in Situations of Armed Conflict commissioned for publication by the UN Office for the Coordination of Humanitarian Affairs (UN OCHA) set a non-exhaustive list of conditions under which withholding the consent of the affected State shall be deemed arbitrary. It stated that the withholding is arbitrary when there is

a) Withholding consent to humanitarian relief operations in situations where the civilian population is inadequately supplied and the state intends to cause, contribute to, or perpetuate starvation. This would violate the prohibition on starvation of the civilian population as a method of warfare.

b) Withholding consent to medical relief operations, including on the ground that medical supplies, equipment, and personnel could treat wounded

---

[24] See Lucia Bódišová, *Supra* note 10, at 289.
[25] See Adam Giertl, *International Responsibility in the Context of Disaster Response*, In CZECH YEARBOOK OF PUBLIC & PRIVATE INTERNATIONAL LAW, Vol. 8, Prague: Czech Society of International Law 68–69 (2017).
[26] Within the context of armed conflict, the United Nations Security Council (UN SC) formulated a statement with respect to humanitarian assistance during armed conflict. It stated in resolution 2139 (2014) of 22 February that it condemned all cases of denial of humanitarian access and recalled that 'arbitrary denial of humanitarian access and depriving civilians of objects indispensable to their survival, including willfully impeding relief supply and access, can constitute a violation of international humanitarian law'. Similar approach may be adopted with respect to humanitarian aid denial in the event of a disaster, when the denial of emergency assistance may lead to the emergence of responsibility of the State. See Draft Articles on the protection of persons in the event of disasters, with commentaries 2016, *Ibid.*, Article 13 paragraph 6.
[27] *Ibid.*, Article 13 paragraph 8.

enemy combatants. The wounded and sick – including enemy combatants – must receive, to the fullest extent practicable and with the least possible delay, the medical care required by their condition. No distinction may be made on any grounds other than medical ones.

c) Withholding consent to medical relief operations as they might assist wounded and sick enemy combatants would violate this rule. Moreover, the same medical supplies, equipment, and personnel are also likely to be necessary for the civilian population, which would also be denied the medical relief to which it is entitled.

d) Withholding consent to humanitarian relief operations in order to punish the civilian population for acts for which it is not responsible, such as acts committed by the party to the conflict with effective control over it. This would violate the prohibition on collective punishment.

e) Selective withholding of consent to humanitarian relief operations with the intent or effect of discriminating against a particular group or section of the civilian population. For example, systematically rejecting offers to conduct humanitarian relief operations in areas populated by ethnic groups perceived as favoring the enemy. This would violate the prohibition on discrimination.

f) Withholding of consent to humanitarian relief operations that violate fundamental human rights as applicable in situations of armed conflict. This includes withholding consent in circumstances where doing so would violate the rights to bodily integrity, or prevent the satisfaction of the minimum core of relevant economic, cultural, and social rights, such as the rights to an adequate standard of living, and to essential health and medical services.[28]

5.13.   It must be stated that the abovementioned signs of arbitrariness are applicable in armed conflict. The situation of armed conflict is indeed different from disaster and there are specific applicable rules, but as humanitarian law provides guidance for the IDRL, the above-mentioned criteria may serve as valuable lead to determine when the conduct or non-conduct of the State is arbitrary. For the establishment of good faith in mutual

---

[28]   Oxford Guidance on the Law Relating to Humanitarian Relief Operations in Situations of Armed Conflict Commissioned by the United Nations Office for the Coordination of Humanitarian Affairs, Oxford Institute for Ethics, Law and Armed Conflict, 2013, paragraph 51, at 23–24, available at: https://www.unocha.org/sites/unocha/files/Oxford%20Guidance%20pdf.pdf (accessed on 20 July 2018).

relations of the affected State and the subject offering assistance, the affected State may formulate the criteria when consent shall be withheld. By so doing, the affected State shall avoid the appearance that its denial of giving consent will be considered arbitrary. Indeed, the core principle is that the withholding of consent must not lead to a breach of a State's international obligations, such as those that stem from the international human rights instruments and others.[29]

5.14. As already mentioned, the State has a primary role in the direction, coordination and supervision of the provided assistance. This prerogative of the State is closely connected with its right to set out the conditions of the provision of external assistance. Such conditions have to be in accordance with the applicable rules of international law and domestic law. This rule, which found its place in Article 14 of the Draft Article reflects the wording of the above-mentioned Article 10 and further details its provisions.[30] The setting of such conditions shall be guided by the needs of the affected persons and the quality of the assistance. The Draft Articles specifically state that a State shall indicate the scope and the type of sought assistance. The rule does not establish a duty to impose conditions, but if the State decides to impose them, it may announce these conditions in advance and in relation to specific forms of assistance provided by particular actors. All set conditions must be in accordance with the legal principles that are inherent to IDRL such as humanitarian principles, sovereignty and with the other obligations of the affected persons or entities under international law. The requirement of compliance with national law serves to emphasize the role of national law, and therefore pointing out the primary role of the State and its sovereignty with respect to adopting and enforcing the particular legislation. The right of a State to legislate on matters it deems necessary is the exercise of its sovereign rights and external actors acting within the jurisdiction of the affected State shall act in compliance with its laws. On the other hand this rule requires no specific legislation to be adopted prior the setting of conditions. It simply states that the conditions must respect any relevant domestic legislation. In addition,

[29] 'An affected State's discretion to determine the most appropriate form of assistance is an aspect of its primary role in the direction, control, coordination and supervision of disaster relief (...). This discretion must be exercised in good faith in accordance with an affected State's international obligations. The Commission encourages affected States to give reasons where consent to assistance is withheld. The provision of reasons is fundamental to establishing the good faith of an affected State's decision to withhold consent. The absence of reasons may act to support an inference that the withholding of consent is arbitrary.' Draft articles on the protection of persons in the event of disasters, with commentaries 2016, *Ibid.*, Article 13 paragraph 10.
[30] 'The affected State may place conditions on the provision of external assistance. Such conditions shall be in accordance with the present draft articles, applicable rules of international law, and the national law of the affected State.' Draft articles on the protection of persons in the event of disasters, 2016, Article 14.

the assisting actor must act in accordance with the domestic law of the affected State at all times during the facilitation of any assistance. However, it is not explicitly stated in the Draft Articles, but there are specific IDRL treaties providing for such obligations.[31] The compliance of the actions of foreign actors on the territory of the State with the domestic law stems from the principle of respect for sovereignty and is inherent for universal international law as well as for the other specific fields of international law (e.g. law of diplomatic relations). The State is entitled to deny unwanted or unneeded assistance. However, this right must be interpreted in the context of arbitrary withholding of consent with external assistance. If the affected State made a decision to set the conditions of external relief, the aim of such conditions must be to ensure meeting the needs of affected persons as appropriate. In this respect, the Draft Article clearly states that conditions – if adopted – must take into account the needs of persons and the quality of assistance. No other aspects may be invoked by the affected State.

III.   Duty to Seek Assistance

5.15.   Situations may occur when the capacity of the State to react in a proper manner is exceeded by the magnitude of the disaster and such a State is unable to respond and provide the required assistance. In such cases, the Draft Articles foresee a rule setting out an obligation of the State to seek external assistance.[32] Earlier, the situation where there are relevant offers of external assistance and IDRL rules stipulate the duty of the affected State not to turn them down arbitrarily was discussed... However, the IDRL also provides a framework for a situation when the State is unable to provide assistance on its own due to the magnitude of a calamitous event. In such cases, the State is obliged – for the sake of meeting the needs and protecting the rights of people affected by the disasters – to seek external assistance. The rule is not a prohibition, but it establishes the duty to act. The failure to act accordingly may lead to the responsibility of the State either to other States or to persons affected by the disaster who are at the time of the disaster or afterwards residing within its jurisdiction.

5.16.   It must be noted that in the event of disaster many human rights are negatively affected such as the right to life, right to adequate food and access to water, right to adequate shelter, sanitation,

---

[31]   See for example Article 13 paragraph 2 of the ASEAN Agreement on disaster management and emergency response, *Ibid.*
[32]   See Adam Giertl, *Supra* note 25, at 70-71.

medical assistance and many more. States are obliged under international human rights instruments not only to respect some human rights but also to carry out measures to ensure the protection of those rights. For example, the right to life is non-derogable even in the event of public emergency that threatens the life of a nation. A natural disaster qualifies as such an emergency.[33] There are several instruments in existence that provide for the duty of a State to carry out measures to protect specific rights of persons in the event of disasters. If a State is unable to provide the required protection, it might be held liable for a breach of certain rights of individuals, if it does not seek external assistance.[34]

5.17. It is not stated when disaster manifestly exceeds the capacity of the State. Such excess must be assessed on a case-by-case basis. The same situation may be handled differently by different States. The management of emergency will depend on the economic strength of a State, its political stability, the functionality of its competent organs, and more. However, the duty to seek external assistance when the disaster has exceeded the response capacity of the State does not preclude that State from also seeking external assistance in a situation when the national capacities are sufficient to handle the situation but the combined effort of domestic and external facilitators may ensure better quality and timeliness of the needed relief.

IV.   Conclusion

5.18. In this article, I put emphasis on three aspects of disaster response: the role of the affected State, the consent and conditions of external assistance and the duty to seek external assistance in order to examine the position of the sovereignty of the State in response to disaster. From this point, I offer a number of conclusions. First, it is the affected State that bears the primary responsibility for providing relief to the victims of disasters that took place on its own territory. For the failure to facilitate relief adequately and in a timely manner, it can be

---

[33] Compare International Covenant on Civil and Political Rights, Article 4, available at: http://www.ohchr.org/en/professionalinterest/pages/ccpr.aspx (accessed on 20 July 2018).

[34] As the ILC comments: 'The Commission considers that the duty to seek assistance in draft Article 11 also derives from an affected State's obligations under international human rights instruments and customary international law. Recourse to international support may be a necessary element in the fulfilment of a State's international obligations towards individuals where the resources of the affected State are inadequate to meet protection needs. While this may occur also in the absence of any disaster, as alluded to in the commentary to draft Article 5, a number of human rights are directly implicated in the context of a disaster, including the right to life, the right to adequate food, the right to health and medical services, the right to safe drinking water, the right to adequate housing, clothing and sanitation and the right to be free from discrimination.' Draft Articles on the protection of persons in the event of disasters, with commentaries 2016, *Ibid.*, Article 11 paragraph 2.

Czech Yearbook of International Law®

held responsible. The IDRL is firmly anchored in principles of sovereign equality of States and non-intervention into internal affairs of the States that are inherent to an international universal. However, sovereignty is connected with the various legal duties to other States and members of international community and to the individuals under that State's jurisdiction as well.

5.19.   Secondly, the previous partial conclusion is reflected in a principle that external assistance is subject to the consent of the affected State and that the affected State is under certain conditions entitled to withhold such consent. However, the right of a State to withhold consent is limited. Such denial must not be based on arbitrary reasons and the State must act in accordance with its international obligations and good will.

5.20.   Thirdly, if a State gives its consent to provide external assistance on its territory it fulfills a primary role in the coordination, direction and supervision of assistance. It is entitled to set conditions of such assistance. However, this right is also limited. In a situation where the magnitude of a disaster manifestly exceeds the capacity of the State to react, the State is obliged to seek external assistance. The IDRL strictly adheres to the notion of sovereignty and its rules put lots of emphasis on a respect for sovereignty. However, IDRL rules also stress the limits of such sovereignty, especially in the cases when individuals are in jeopardy. The emphasis on the needs and rights of the victims of disasters is inherent in all IDRL instruments. The humanitarian aspect is thus stressed as well as consensual nature and spirit of cooperation when the need is at the utmost.

5.21.   However, it remains unclear how compliance with such rules can be enforced, should the State be adamant in its refusal of external assistance. Practice has shown that the implication of R2P principle was not accepted in the context of disaster. On the other hand, measures against the State under Article 41 of the UN Charter may make a bad situation worse. As it appears, collective or individual sanctions without the use of force targeted directly against the leaders of the governing regimes, not affecting the populations of the State, or various retorsions appear to be a possible solution if the question of enforcement arises.

Summaries

FRA [*La souveraineté de l'État dans le contexte des catastrophes : son exercice et ses limitations*]

Les catastrophes de grande ampleur, qu'elles soient d'origine naturelle ou humaine, ont une incidence fondamentale sur le développement des communautés sociales. Tout au long de l'histoire, certains de ces évènements ont attiré une attention internationale et ont fait l'objet d'une aide internationale plus ou moins bien coordonnée, dont le but était d'apporter le secours aux victimes de la catastrophe. Il est entendu, en principe, que l'ampleur d'une catastrophe est définie par son impact sur le fonctionnement de la société en question. Les conséquences négatives d'une catastrophe doivent être prises en charge en premier lieu par l'État sur le territoire duquel la catastrophe s'est produite. Par conséquent, on considère la catastrophe et l'intervention subséquente comme une affaire intérieure de cet État. Depuis récemment toutefois, le système des règles internationales relatives aux interventions en cas de catastrophes connaît des situations où l'intervention dépasse le cadre du pouvoir de l'État. En effet, la plupart des États sont liés par des traités internationaux relatifs aux droits de l'Homme et par des règles y afférentes. Il est constant que l'aide apportée aux victimes des catastrophes tombe sous le coup des instruments assurant la protection internationale des droits de l'Homme. Le présent article réfléchit sur les relations qui peuvent exister entre la souveraineté d'un État et l'aide humanitaire apportée par des acteurs étrangers sur le territoire de cet État. Il examine la question de la souveraineté dans le contexte du droit international des interventions lors de catastrophes (International Disaster Response Law – IDRL), ainsi que le rôle de l'État sinistré, les règles en matière de consentement à l'aide internationale et les conditions d'un tel consentement. En conclusion, l'article se consacre brièvement à l'obligation de l'État de solliciter une aide internationale dans certaines circonstances.

CZE [*Suverenita státu v kontextu reakce na katastrofy: její výkon a omezení*]

Katastrofy a zvlášť velké přírodní pohromy mají zásadní dopad na rozvoj různých společenství. Za dobu historického vývoje některé takové události získaly mezinárodní pozornost a staly se předmětem více méně koordinovaného mezinárodního úsilí o poskytnutí pomoci obětem katastrofy. V zásadě se ustálilo, že katastrofa je definována tím, do jaké míry byly fungování společnosti narušené v důsledku dopadů katastrofy. Negativní důsledky katastrofy na společnost musí být v první řadě řešeny státem, na jehož území ke katastrofě došlo. Vzhledem k tomu pohlížíme na katastrofu, jakož i na reakci na katastrofu jako na vnitřní záležitost státu. Vznikající mezinárodní pravidla reakcí na katastrofu však rozeznávají situace, kdy mohou být způsobilosti státu reagovat překonány. Na druhé straně většina států je nějakým způsobem vázána mezinárodními smlouvami o lidských právech a souvisejícími pravidly. Ustálilo se, že odpovídající pomoc obětím katastrof spadá pod dodržování závazků vyplývajících z mezinárodních nástrojů ochrany lidských práv. Tento článek se vyjadřuje k problematice suverenity státu a jejího vztahu k poskytování humanitární pomoci zahraničními aktéry na území katastrofou zasáhnutého státu. Článek se vyjadřuje k otázce suverenity v mezinárodním právu v důsledku reakce na katastrofy (International Disaster Response Law – IDRL), jakož dále k úloze zasáhnutého státu a k pravidlům týkajícím se udělování souhlasu se zahraniční pomocí a k podmínkám pro udělení takového souhlasu. Nakonec článek stručně komentuje povinnost státu vyhledat zahraniční pomoc za určitých okolností.

POL [*Suwerenność państwa w kontekście reakcji na katastrofy: wykonywanie i ograniczenia*]

Państwa są suwerenne i równe wobec siebie. Ich suwerenność jest nienaruszalna i chroniona przez powszechnie przyjmowane normy prawa międzynarodowego. W związku z konkretnymi wydarzeniami, takimi jak katastrofy, suwerenność państw jest ograniczana do ich zobowiązań wobec jednostek, które podlegają ich jurysdykcji. Chociaż udzielanie pomocy zagranicznej na terenie kraju, w którym wydarzyła się katastrofa, jest uzależnione od jego zgody, istnieją również szczególne obowiązki w sytuacji, kiedy poszkodowane państwo nie jest w stanie udzielić adekwatnej pomocy ofiarom katastrof, np. obowiązek poszukiwania pomocy i obowiązek nieodmawiania celowo udzielenia zgody na pomoc z zagranicy. Poszkodowane państwo ponosi główną odpowiedzialność za udzielenie adekwatnej pomocy ofiarom katastrof.

DEU [*Die Souveränität des Staats im Kontext der Katastrophenbeantwortung: Ausübung und Beschränkung der Staatsgewalt*]

Die Staaten sind souverän und einander ebenbürtig. Ihre Souveränität ist unverletzlich und wird von den allgemein anerkannten Normen des Völkerrechts geschützt. Im Falle besonderer Ereignisse wie z.B. Katastrophen ist die Souveränität des Staats auf dessen Verpflichtungen gegenüber den Einzelnen beschränkt, die seiner Jurisdiktion unterworfen sind. Zwar ist die ausländische Hilfeleistung auf dem Gebiet eines von einer Katastrophe heimgesuchten Staats mit dessen Einverständnis bedingt; es existieren aber besondere Pflichten, falls und soweit ein betroffener Staat nicht in der Lage ist, den Opfern von Katastrophen angemessen Hilfe zu bieten, darunter z.B. die Pflicht, um Hilfe nachzusuchen, oder die Pflicht, die Zustimmung zu ausländischen Hilfsaktionen nicht willkürlich zu verweigern. Der betroffene Staat trägt die primäre Verantwortung für die Erbringung adäquater Hilfeleistungen an Katastrophenopfer.

RUS [*Суверенитет государства в контексте реагирования на катастрофы или бедствия: его реализация и ограничения*]

Государства суверенны и равны друг перед другом. Их суверенитет неприкосновенен и защищён общепринятыми нормами международного права. Во время особых событий, например, во время катастроф или бедствий, суверенитет государств ограничен их обязательствами перед людьми, находящимися под их юрисдикцией. В то время как предоставление иностранной помощи на территории государства, пострадавшего от катастрофы или бедствия, зависит от согласия данного государства, существуют также особые обязательства в том случае, если пострадавшее государство не способно само оказать адекватную помощь жертвам катастрофы или бедствия. Это, например, обязанность обращаться за помощью и обязанность своевольно не отказывать в предоставлении согласия на иностранную помощь. Пострадавшее государство несёт основную ответственность за оказание адекватной помощи жертвам катастрофы или бедствия.

ESP [*La soberanía del Estado en el contexto de la actuación ante desastres: su ejecución y restricción*]

Los Estados son soberanos e iguales unos a los otros. Su soberanía es inviolable y está protegida por normas del derecho internacional aceptadas universalmente. En tiempos de determinados acontecimientos como pueden ser desastres naturales, la soberanía de los Estados queda restringida por sus obligaciones hacia los individuos sometidos a su jurisdicción. Aunque la prestación de la ayuda extranjera en el territorio del Estado afectado por el desastre está condicionada por su consentimiento, existen asimismo obligaciones específicas en caso de que el Estado afectado no tenga capacidad de prestar una ayuda adecuada a las víctimas del desastre como, por ejemplo, la obligación de buscar ayuda y la obligación de no negarse voluntariamente a otorgar el consentimiento con la ayuda extranjera. La principal responsabilidad por la prestación de una ayuda adecuada a las víctimas de los desastres recae en el Estado afectado.

| | |

Bibliography

Lucia Bódišová, *Application of the Sovereignty of the States in the Process of Elimination of the Consequences of the Natural and Man-made Disasters* (Slovak: *Uplatňovanie suverenity štátov v procese odstraňovania následkov prírodných a priemyselných katastrof*), *in* THE PLACE, ROLE AND SIGNIFICANCE OF DOMESTIC LAW IN ENSURING THE PERFORMANCE OF OBLIGATIONS STEMMING FROM INTERNATIONAL LAW AND EUROPEAN LAW – COLLECTION OF SCIENTIFIC RESEARCH PAPERS BY PHD. STUDENTS AND YOUNG RESEARCHERS (Slovak: *Miesto, úloha a význam vnútroštátneho práva pri zabezpečovaní plnenia záväzkov vyplývajúcich z medzinárodného práva a európskeho práva – Zborník vedeckých prác doktorandov a mladých vedeckých pracovníkov*), Košice: Univerzita Pavla Jozefa Šafárika v Košiciach 282 (Dominika Becková, Adam Giertl eds., 2018).

Adam Giertl, *International Responsibility in the Context of Disaster Response, In* CZECH YEARBOOK OF PUBLIC & PRIVATE INTERNATIONAL LAW, Vol. 8, Prague: Czech Society of International Law 68–69 (2017).

Erika De Wet, *The International Constitutional Order*, 55(1) INTERNATIONAL AND COMPARATIVE LAW QUARTERLY (2006).

Pavel Mates | Jan Šmíd

European Clauses in the Constitutions – Are They Really Necessary?

Keywords:
The European Union | legal order of the European Union | sovereignty | constitution | European clause

Abstract | *The existence of the European Union and its legal order has often collided with the traditional concepts of the State and international law until the middle of the 20th century. Most scholars do not attempt to define the Union, but look for the differences between it and the State or other international organizations. Similarly, there are also analogous attempts to identify the characteristics of European Union law.*

These exact ambiguities motivated individual countries to cope with the phenomenon of transferring of the competences to the European level in their national law. While the relationship between national and international law and the related issue of sovereignty has been resolved a relatively long time ago, the establishment of European integration brings a new form of this problem.

In all constitutions of the Member States of the European Union, the relationship to this integration is solved in some form, either by referring to the international organization or institution, without it being specified, or, on the contrary, by expressly discussing that relationship. The reason for the choice is not clear in most cases. An important role in relation to European Union law is played by the constitutional tribunals of the Member States, which are supposed to keep the protection of the national constitutions and also to ensure the obligations of the States resulting from the membership within the European Union and the conformity of the national values with the values of the European Union. The subject, which

PhDr. Mgr. Jan Šmíd, Ph.D., teaches the theory of law, constitutional law and political science at the University of Finance and Administration in Prague. He also teaches political philosophy and the philosophy of law at Jan Evangelista Purkyně University in Ústí nad Labem, and teaches political ideologies at the University of Economics in Prague. He specializes in the above topics, which he has elaborated on in his contributions to several collections of papers and articles published in academic journals.
E-mail: john_smid@yahoo.com

Doc. JUDr. Pavel Mates, CSc., lectures on administrative law at the University of Finance and Administration in Prague and on the theory of law at the Faculty of Socioeconomics at J. E. Purkyně University in Ústí nad Labem. He specializes in the issue of administrative criminal law and the legal regulation of e-government. He has published several monographs and dozens of articles in Czech and foreign journals on these issues. He is a member of the legislative body of the government.
E-mail: pavel.mates@ujep.cz; pmates@mail.vsfs.cz

determines the concrete extent of the delegation of the competences, is, in the final instance, the Court of Justice. Thanks to its case-law, it sometimes makes the boundary determined by the mentioned clauses very obscured and unstable.

The core of this article is devoted to the analysis of so-called integration clauses in the constitutions of the Member States, on the basis of which it can be concluded, that their formulations are various. It deals with the significant aspects within the individual countries, such as the nature of their legal order, the time when the amendment of the constitution was made, and also by a range of other, sometimes also rather subjective circumstances, such as the current political situation in the given country and attitudes of their inhabitants to the integration which caused such a plurality of adjustments.

| | |

I.   The Nature of the Legal Order of the European Community and the European Union

6.01.   The European Union and its legal order traditional fundamentally shook conceptions of the forms of the State and international law that prevailed until the middle of the 20th century. However, current scholarship seems to be circling around a problem in this regard, rather than providing definitions. Thus, we can find out by reading such scholarship that the European Union is a *sui generis* institution. It is neither a State nor a common international organization, but is rather something more difficult to define with existing terminology. According to some visions, it should aim at joining together States and people who do not create the 'State'.[1] Its peculiarity is seen in the fact that it constituted permanent political relations, including strong interactions among its authorities and also among the Member States and subsidies the relations among the national States mutually and also towards integration itself.[2] It simultaneously creates conflicts both paradoxically and logically, because the

---

[1]   Artur Kozak, *Deficyt demokracicji a intergracja europejska* (The Democracy Deficit and European Integration), *in* AKSJOLOGICZNE I PRAKTYCZNE ASPEKTY INTEGRACJI EUROPEJSKIEJ (Axiological and Practical Aspects of European Integration) Wrocław: University of Wrocław Publisher 7 (Ewa Kozerska, Tomasz Scheffler eds., 2007); DAVID BLANCHARD, LA CONSTITUTIONNALISATION DE L'UNION EUROPÉENNE, Rennes: Editions Apogée 40 (2001). Some authors, however, find in the Union certain elements of the confederacy or confederalism and even indicate courageously that it should transform sometime into the federal state. LOUIS FAVOREU AND TEAM, DROIT CONSTITUTIONNEL, Paris: Dalloz 389-390 (2005).

[2]   JANA RESCHOVÁ, EVROPSKÝ KONSTITUCIONALISMUS: ZDROJE, FORMY A TENDENCE (The European Constitutionalism: Sources, Forms and Tendenciess), Prague: Publishing house Oeconomica 53 (2003).

Czech Yearbook of International Law®

institutions of the individual States and supranational ones compete amongst themselves. In effort to find a solution, scholars are formulating another, equally embarrassing thesis regarding the new sovereignty. This concept refers to the relationship of the European Union and its Member States, in which traditional State sovereignties are mingled with the influences of a new system. Under such a system, of sovereignty, some powers are submitted to the European Union and its authorities and carried out by them, while others are performed together and still others remain in the purview of national States.[3]

6.02. Similarly, there is discussion of the characteristics of European law, which is not classified within the sphere of public international law inter alia because it is under the control of its own case-law, even though it is said to it that it is special legal order.[4] The gradual development of European integration has led to some scholars considering the system of European institutions and law as a new form of constitutional law, where the existence of a State is not necessarily required for the existence of constitutional law. The Constitution thus can be also established outside the framework of the State.[5]

6.03. What distinguishes European law from international law is that European law operates in a domestic legal order through its own legal force. Regardless of whether this regulation is based on the monistic or dualistic concept, it 'cut(s) off the umbilical cord' between Community and international law.[6] This indifference leads to the fact that we meet up in the doctrine and case-law with a number of further arguments, each of which bring only new complications. For example, Community law is treated by the national authorities more as international law, regardless the fact that its precedence over laws is accepted concurrently. It is made into the difference between the founding treaties and secondary law, which is denoted in such a way that it approaches the character of State law, built with complicated question marks over the subjectivity of the European Union. At the same time, there are discussions on the topic of whether European Union law is autonomous from the very beginning or is subsequently

3 KAREL KLÍMA, TEORETICKÁ VÝCHODISKA EVROPSKÉ ÚSTAVNOSTI (The Theoretical Basis of the European Constitutionality), *in* Instytucje prawa konstytucyjnego w dobie integracji europejskiej (The Institutions of Constitutional Law in the Era of the European integration), Warsaw: Sejm Publishing 369-370 (2009).
4 For example ECJ Judgement of 30 May 2006, C-459/03, *Commission* v. *Ireland* [2006] ECR I-4635.
5 KAREL KLÍMA, ÚSTAVNÍ PRÁVO (Constitutional Law), Pilsen 108-109 (3rd ed. 2006).
6 Zdeněk Kühn, *Ještě jednou k ústavnímu základu působení komunitárního práva v českém právním řádu* (Once Again to the Constitutional Basis of the Influence of Community Law in Czech Legal Order), 10 PRÁVNÍ ROZHLEDY (Legal Insights) 395 (2004); ECJ judgement of 19 November 1991, C-6/90, *Frankovich and Others* v. *Italy* [1991] ECR I-5357; DENYS SIMON, KOMUNITÁRNÍ PRÁVNÍ ŘÁD (Community Legal Order), Praha (Prague): ASPI 80-81 (2005).

separated from international law and refers to one of its regional subsystems and to what extent these concepts are reflected in the constitutional anchoring of so-called integration standards in the State Constitutions.[7]

6.04.   When reading these usually argumentative and stylistically improved discussions, it is necessary to ask what is their practical significance. Most especially, it is important to ask whether political goals are pursued through them. Their authors do not obviously say, if their purpose is the strengthening or disengaging of integration. It is worth noting that practically everybody speaks about so-called competence loss (*Kompetenzverlust*) in relation to the European Union. However, less discussed is the fact that relevant constitutional articles may also affect the membership or participation in other transnational organizations, respectively in the institutions such as international criminal tribunals. However, these losses are much smaller and usually affect a much narrower spectrum of traditionally approached sovereignty.[8]

6.05.   The attempts of the individual States to cope internally with the transfer of their competences to European-wide institutions are concurrently motivated from several directions. One of them is the establishment of the independent sovereignty of the European Union.[9] The very fact of the transfer of the competences is often understood as the transfer of a part of sovereignty. Given this widespread understanding, there is pressure to clarify the sovereignty of individual national States in the emerging situation of the relationship of two sovereigns.[10] This conflict is already known from the relationship of national and international law. However, with the emergence of transnational European integration, law is confronted with a new form of this problem.

II.   Sovereignty

6.06.   The ambiguity of the term of 'sovereignty' itself is equally important. In the context of European integration, there are

---

[7]   KAREL KLÍMA, *supra* note 5, at 374; JIŘÍ MALENOVSKÝ, MEZINÁRODNÍ PRÁVO VEŘEJNÉ: JEHO OBECNÁ ČÁST A POMĚR K VNITROSTÁTNÍMU PRÁVU, ZVLÁŠTĚ PRÁVU ČESKÉMU (Public International Law: Its General Part and Relation to National Law, Especially to Czech Law), Brno: Doplněk, 404 (2007); ALEKSANDRA KUSTRA, PREPISY I NORMY INTEGRACYJNE W KONSTYTUCJACH WYBRANYCH PAŃSTW CZŁONKOWSKICH UE (Transposing and Integration Standards for the Consulates of the EU Member States), Toruń: Dom Organizatora 280-283 (2009).

[8]   Jiří Malenovský, *O chudokrevnosti' mezinárodních rozměrů české ústavy a možných terapiích* (About the 'Anemia' of the International Dimensions of the Czech Constitution and Possible Therapies), 7 PRÁVNÍK (Lawyer) 554-555 (1997); KAREL KLÍMA, KOMENTÁŘ K ÚSTAVĚ A LISTINĚ (A Commentary on the Constitution and the Charter), Pilsen: Publishing Aleš Čeněk 143-145 (2009).

[9]   KAREL KLÍMA, *supra* note 5, at 110.

[10]   KAREL KLÍMA, *supra* note 5, at 84.

discussions about a new sovereignty, or alternatively about shared sovereignty. In each case, there is a need to clarify this term. It is possible to observe a certain opinion shift from the emphasis on sovereignty as the absolute independence of State power in decision-making.

6.07. In historical-legal and political philosophical literature, the term sovereignty appears quite late. It is important to realize that even the term of the State, seemingly self-evident, is not eternal, but it appears from a certain historical stage at the end of the Middle Ages, and the beginning of modern history.[11] Similarly with it, the associated term of State sovereignty originated in a certain period and it is, to a certain extent, a rather theoretical construct, which was often sketched by theory as a Weberian 'ideal type', whose exact reflection in reality is discovered only very rarely.

6.08. The theory of sovereignty is connected inextricably to the name of Jean Bodin, and refers to State power independent of other powerful institutions, both inside and outside the state. We can characterize it as a kind of power which has the following attributes:

- the highest
- final
- generality of effect
- independent.[12]

6.09. It is obvious, that, especially in the last aspect, we do not meet up with many practical examples of the absolute independence of States. Nevertheless, there are other interpretations of sovereignty which define sovereign State power as independent of one or another power, both at the beginning of the 20th century[13] and at the end of it.[14]

6.10. Despite this, a whole range of the authors stands against these definitions, who are aware of the un-sustainability of such a concept of sovereignty. Georg Jellinek refused to confuse sovereignty with unlimited power. According to him, the State is limited itself by the law and recognition of obligations from international law. A State unbounded by its law was possible, according to him, only in a strict theocracy, where God or a ruler

---

[11] QUENTIN SKINNER, O STÁTĚ (About the State), Prague: Oikomenh (2013).
[12] DAVID MILLER, BLACKWELLOVA ENCYKLOPEDIE POLITICKÉHO MYŠLENÍ (Blackwell´s Encyclopedia of Political Thought), Brno 513-514 (1995).
[13] JIŘÍ PRAŽÁK, ZÁKLADNÍ RYSY VŠEOBECNÉHO PRÁVA STÁTNÍHO (The Basic Features of General State Law), Prague: Jednota právnická (Legal Unity) VII (1900).
[14] VÁCLAV PAVLÍČEK, ÚSTAVNÍ PRÁVO A STÁTOVĚDA: I. DÍL OBECNÁ STÁTOVĚDA (Constitutional Law and State Sciences: 1st part General State Sciences), Prague 67-72 (1998), author is Jiří Grospič.

with divine attributes ruled.[15] (It should be noted, that Jellinek could not know the phenomenon of the totalitarian regimes during writing a work, but it can be assumed, that he would assign them there.) Other authors are inclined to a concept of sovereign as not fully perfect independent or unlimited power, and these authors take the sovereignty of the modern democratic State for a limited one.[16]

6.11.   However, limited sovereignty is not only the result of modern legal and political processes, leading to the emergence of the range of democratic legal States. The power of the State has always been limited by a number of the internal and external factors. Some of them even question the existence of a 'classical' sovereignty, which is often associated for example with the Westphalian system. Nevertheless, not one imparts to the individual States all elements associated with sovereignty, nor that States did not have the absolute power and independence.[17] Some authors even talk about the 'Westphalian myth' or about a hypocritical idea spread by the States themselves that they are absolutely independent in an unlimited way.[18]

6.12.   The term 'sovereignty' has not been clarified even today. Instead of the discussions of the nature of the problem, all discussions are exhausted logically by focusing on the problem, what the term 'sovereignty' actually means. Obviously, since we are discussing an abstract concept in the field of social sciences, it is not possible to assume a consensus or at least a clarification of the majority interpretation in the near future. An interesting observation is made by Raymond Aron.

> "In order to avoid of the formal difficulties resulting from the contradiction between the theory of (absolute) sovereignty and (supra-state) theory of international law, one school of the legal theorists wishes this term to be rather completely eliminated. Personally, I would not be against the fact, if it was *abandoned from the term "sovereignty"* as a consequence of these ambiguities, that it brings with

---

[15]   GEORG JELLINEK, VŠEOBECNÁ STÁTOVĚDA (General State Sciences), Prague 387(1906).

[16]   VLADIMÍR ZOUBEK, PRÁVOVĚDA A STÁTOVĚDA: ÚVOD DO PRÁVNÍHO A STÁTOVĚDNÍHO MYŠLENÍ (Legal Sciences and State Sciences: the Introduction to Legal and State-Sciences Thinking), Pilsen 274 (2010).

[17]   VOJTĚCH BELLING, ZROZENÍ SUVERÉNA: POJEM SUVERENITY A JEHO KRITIKA V MODERNÍ POLITICKÉ A PRÁVNÍ FILOSOFII: SUVERENITA A NORMATIVNÍ KONSTRUKCE REALITY (Birth of the Sovereign: the Term of Sovereignty and Its Critique in Modern Political and Legal Philosophy: Sovereign and Normative Construction of Reality), Brno 29 (2014).

[18]   Luke Glanville, *The Myth of 'Traditional Sovereignty*, 57(1) INTERNATIONAL STUDIES QUARTERLY 79-90 (2013); similarly also the authors Piirimäe Pärtel, Stephen Krasner, *in* SOVEREIGNTY IN FRAGMENTS THE PAST, PRESENT AND FUTURE OF A CONTESTED CONCEPT, Cambridge (Hent Kalmo, Quentin Skinner, ed., 2010).

itself. But the lawyers like to imagine, that once they eliminate the word, they will also remove the facts, that cover the term."[19]

6.13.   Aron´s interpretation of what sovereignty is must be taken seriously, given that it is such a politically exposed and theoretically unclear term. While States have surrendered full sovereignty for a long time, neither the States nor scholarly theories want to abandon the term. Currently, there does not exist a substitute for it, although the ongoing process of transnational integration encourages the coining of such a term. The practice anticipates the theory, and that is also one of the consequences of how the individual States of the European Union cope with incorporating the 'European clause' in various ways.

III.   The Constitutional Solution to the Relationship with the European Union

6.14.   In all constitutions of the Member States of the European Union, the relationship to this integration is solved in some form. This is accomplished with language referring to an international organization or institution without it being specified. An example is Article 10a of the Constitution of the Czech Republic and Article 34 of the Belgian Constitution. It can also be accomplished by naming such an organization explicitly like Article 7(2) of the Constitution of the Slovak Republic and Article 2/A of the Hungarian Constitution.[20] Such implicit or explicit constitutional articles do not make a solution any more clear.[21] Indeed, even where the constitutions speak about the delegation of powers in general, it is possible to encounter various terminology. For example the Danish Constitution in Article 20(1) refers to the delegation on the international authorities. The Constitution of the Kingdom of the Netherlands sets forth in Article 92 that the Treaty or legislation on its legal basis may transfer judicial and administrative powers onto international institutions. The Greek Constitution states in Article 28(2) that constitutional powers may be entrusted to an international organization. The reason for the choice of particular terms cannot be deduced from the texts of the Constitutions, and in

---

[19]   MIROSLAV NOVÁK, ARONOVO POJETÍ SUVERENITY A SCHMITTOVA KRITIKA SVĚTOVÉHO STÁTU (Aron´s Concept of Sovereignty and Schmitt´s Critique of the World State); VOJTĚCH BELLING, LUKÁŠ KOLLERT, SUVERENITA PANOVNÍKA, LIDU A STÁTU V MODERNÍ POLITICKÉ FILOSOFII (Sovereignty of the Ruler, People and State in Modern Political Philosophy), Ústí upon Elbe 158-186 (2017).
[20]   Lithuania even adopted a special constitutional law in 2004 on the membership of the Republic of Lithuania in the European Union.
[21]   ALEKSANDRA KUSTRA, supra note 7, at 36-37.

our opinion, it has no practical importance. In any case, law is given to all Member States for formulating the relationship towards the European Union in the constitutions. All States must respect the primacy of European Union law and adapt National law to it.[22]

6.15. As well as in national law, the constitutional tribunals of the Member States also play an important role in relation to European Union law. Their status is certainly dichotomous and sometimes even nearly schizophrenic. On the one hand, they have to maintain the protection of national constitutions, but at the same time, they have also to ensure that the obligations of the States resulting from the membership in the European Union are secured, and to guarantee conformity of national values with the values of the European Union. Their judicature affected many countries such that, after the Maastricht Treaty, it became necessary to adopt both the integration articles of the constitutions, and also their concrete forms.[23] Due to dynamically developing relationships and tensions with regard to the deepening of integration, it can be justly expected that this role will not diminish in the future.[24]

6.16. At the same time, it is always necessary to keep in mind that the Court of Justice is ultimately the one who determines the specific extent of the transfer. It can for example determine a sometimes subtle boundary between the principles of priority and direct effect, and has frequently been solving very complex problems in relation to directives. Another example is the institution of so-called implicit powers, through which the principle of conferred powers set forth in Article 5 of the Treaty on the European Union is broken. This occurs when the Court of Justice can also discover other powers not explicitly mentioned. Such powers can, however, be reasonably deduced from primary or secondary law. This has happened for example in some areas of the international relations with matters falling

---

[22] Eugeniusz Piontek, *Konstytucje państw członkowskich v porządku prawnym unii europejskiej (Constitutions of the Member States in the Legal Order of the European Union), in* INSTYTUCJE PRAWA KONSTYTUCYJNEGO W DOBIE INTEGRACJI EUROPEJSKIEJ (Institutions of Constitutional Law in the Era of the European Integration), Warsaw: Sejm Publishing 411 (2009).

[23] See for example FRANÇOIS BORELLA, ÉLEMENTS DE DROIT CONSTITUTIONNEL, Paris: Presses de Sciences Po 385 (2008) and next ones.

[24] The following is an example of when the constitutional courts relied on European law. Directive 2006/24/EC, relating to the retention of data, ordering that entities which ensure any public communication network, must store widely operational and location data for up to 12 months and provide the same to the police and intelligence services. This Directive, or its implementation to national legal orders, was declared by the constitutional courts of a number of countries as unconstitutional (e.g. Federal Constitutional Court of Germany in its decision of 2 March 2010 1 of BvR 256/08, 1 BvR 263/08 and 1 BvR 586/08, and the Czech Constitutional Court in its finding of File Number Pl. ÚS 24/10/), and also undoubtedly under their influence, it was annulled by The Court of Justice through the Judgement in the Joined Cases of Number C 293/12 and C594/12.

Czech Yearbook of International Law®

under the sphere of the European Union or international law, or with the fundamental principles of the European Union law or the objectives of the European Union.[25] By this, the boundary determined by the mentioned clauses becomes naturally very obscure and moveable.

IV.   Examples of Integration Clauses

6.17.   The constitutional integration clause, or integration empowerment is factually superfluous. This may seem extreme, but with regard to the nature and principle of the functioning of these formulations, the priority application arises from the European Union law with all its consequences. This is true not because of the fact that the domestic constitution determines it to be this way, but because they are determined by the very nature of this legal order that each country accepts by signing the treaty. This cannot happen to the discrepancy between domestic and European Union law in this sector, because as a consequence of the principle of delegated powers within the meaning of Article 5 of the Treaty on the European Union, certain issues have been excluded from the competence of the national authorities and have been transferred to the European Union.[26]

6.18.   The interesting example of the extent to which explicit constitutional changes were necessary comes from France, which despite belonging to the original European Community for four decades, in 1992 demonstrated formally by a change to its constitution, that it is necessary to distinguish between Community and international law. Similarly, the *Grundgesetz* of Germany was self-sufficient until the Maastricht Treaty, with Article 24(1). According to this, the association may transfer sovereign rights onto international institutions. Only then the need of adoption of the integration clause in the form of Article 23 was found out. In Belgium, the possibility of the transfer of powers to another body of international law was not mentioned in the constitution until 1970, even though in this case, it was

---

[25]   IVO ŠLOSARČÍK, POLITICKÝ A PRÁVNÍ RÁMEC EVROPSKÉ INTEGRACE (Political and Legal Scope of the European Integration), Prague: Wolters Kluwer 138-143 (2010); SACHA PRECHAL, DIRECTIVES IN EC LAW, Oxford: Oxford University Press 180 (2005) and next ones; e.g. the ECJ judgement of 26 October 1999, C-273/97, *Angela Maria Sirdar* v. *The Army Board, Secretary of State for Defence* [1999] ECR I-7403, where The Court deduced its competence there, where it deals with the principle of equal treatment between men and women within the whole area, to which the Community, respectively the European Union law applies. However, in a particular case, it dealt with the service in the army, which is a matter belonging under the scope of domestic law.

[26]   Zdeněk Kühn, Jan Kysela, *Na základě čeho bude působit komunitární právo v českém právním řádu?* (On What Basis Community Law Will Work in Czech Legal Order?), 1 PRÁVNÍ ROZHLEDY (Legal Insights) 23 (2004).

one of the first participants in the gradually emerging integration formations of the European Coal and Steel Community to the European Economic Community. In these cases, the judicature concluded, especially in the Belgium case that Community law is a new legal system, whose primacy is determined by the fact that the performance of some powers were delegated on it through the concluding of relevant treaties. Likewise, the French Court Cassation concluded the primacy of the European Community legal order in 1975. Their argument focused on the one hand on its peculiarity, and on the other hand by the mention about the general applicable primacy of all international treaties, which meet the conditions under Article 55 of the Constitutions.[27]

6.19. The solution, that was chosen by Italy is also interesting. Article 11 of its constitution of 1947, agrees with the limitations of sovereignty on the assumption of equality with other States. Such an equality is needed to build the order that will ensure peace and justice among people. Of course, when the Italian constitution was approved, only the visionaries might have an idea that an integration could exist in the form of the European Communities or even of the European Union. However, nothing new has been added to this article and only thanks to its interpretation made by Italian Constitutional Court, the existence of an autonomous position of Community law, different from both national and international law, was recognized in 1984. In this ruling, the primacy of the Community, and European Union law being prior to national law was also recognized explicitly.

6.20. Most countries, however, considered it necessary to include the integration clauses in their constitutions. Regardless of whether this happened and in what form, the declared purpose is seen in the need for the creation of a *harmonious environment*. This allows European Union law to operate in the territory of the State regardless of whether it is considered to be international law or it is applicable there directly. This again relates to the discussions on the nature of European Union law, because, regardless of its conception, it gets into the national environment. This supports the initial thesis of this article, which asked to what extent these clauses are really necessary.[28] On the other hand, all constitutionalists mention, that it happens to the delegation or conversion of the authorities, competences and powers

---

[27] MARIÁN GIBA, SÚDNA KONTROLA ÚSTAVNOSTI VE FRANCÚZKU (Judicial Supervision of the Constitutionality in France), Bratislava: Wolter Kluwer 179 (2017); ZDENĚK KÜHN, *supra* note, at 396. The difference between these original and explicitly integration articles is seen. In the first ones, it was about sovereignty, whereas in the newer ones, it was about the delegation of the competences, constitutional powers etc. into their constitutions.

[28] JIŘÍ ZEMAN, PŘISTOUPENÍ K EU A NUTNOST PROVÁDĚNÍ ÚSTAVNÍCH ZMĚN (Assession to the European Union and the Need of Making Constitutional Changes), Brno: Masaryk University 61 (2009).

only to a certain set and defined extent. States thus retain their sovereignty, although at the same time, it is considered, that vis-à-vis the integration trends concretely functioning in the European Union, it is not considered to be the sovereignty as it was understood in the first half of the last century. The doctrines such as the new sovereignty are formulated strive to resolve the question of the democratic legitimacy of the European Union, the nature of the supranational legal order, the necessity of constitutional changes and more.[29]

6.21. In Germany, it was made by a change to the *Grundgesetz* in 1992 in the form of the inclusion of Article 23, which adjusted the possibility for the association to transfer 'its sovereign rights by the law and with the consent of the Federal Council' to the European Union while as well it broadly guarantees the rights of the countries. At the same time, a safeguard was also incorporated into the basic law, expressed by the German Constitutional Court, according to which the fundamental rights contained in articles 1-20 and the cooperation of the countries during legislation cannot be thereby affected. This rather reserved attitude was set due to the fact that, according to the statement of the Constitutional Court, the European Union is not a 'State based on the democratic principles'.[30]

6.22. The French Constitution has been gradually changed since 1992. Relatedly, the judicature of *Conseil constitutionnel* concluded in 2004 that certain provisions of the Treaty on the Constitution for Europe were incompatible with the French Constitution. That is why Section XV, titled the European Communities and the European Union was incorporated into it. It is worth noting that the French constituents emphasized in the wordings the fact that the States forming the European Union do not give up sovereignty. Rather, they only decided freely to perform some competences together. France declared furthermore its agreement with the Maastricht Treaty, the Amsterdam Treaty and the Treaty of Lisbon. It also chose to recognize European arrest warrants, declared active and passive voting rights to municipal elections to the citizens of the European Union settled in France, and more. Those obligations and rights are granted largely under the condition of mutuality.[31]

---

[29] For example Francisco Balaguer Callejón, *La fragmentation du pouvoir constituant, in* LE POUVOIR CONSTITUANT AU XXIE SIECLE, not stated: Institut Univesitaire Varenne 23-28 (Francisco Balaguer Callejón, Stéphane Pinon, Alexandre Viala, eds., 2017).

[30] See the judgement of the Federal Constitutional Court of 30 June 2009 – 2 BvE 2/08, 2 BvE 5/08, 2 BvR 1010/08, 2 BvR 1022/08, 2 BvR 1259/08 and 2 BvR 182/09 the Ratification Act to the Treaty of Lisbon.

[31] MARIÁN GIBA, *supra* note 27, at 185-188; THE EUROPEAN CONSTITUTION AND NATIONAL CONSTITUTIONS: RATIFICATION AND BEYOND, The Hague: Kluwer Law International 106-108 (ANNELI ALBI, JACQUES ZILLER eds., 2007).

6.23. The short Article 34 (originally 25a) of the Belgian Constitution introduced in 1970 provides that the exercise of certain powers may be transferred to international institutions by a treaty or by a law. Such treaty or law will then determine with which powers it deals, providing the possibility of accepting further enlarging of the European Union powers in a flexible way.

6.24. Article 9(2) of the Austrian Constitution, which was incorporated into it in 1981, is rather broader, but similar in content. According to it, individual sovereign rights of the Federation may be transferred to international institutions and authorities by law or state treaty. Such a transfer may provide for the functioning of bodies of foreign States within the country and Austrian authorities abroad within international law. Although this regulation appears to be sufficient a later 'European Union clause', was incorporated into the constitution in 1994 as the voluminous section B. under the title of the European Union, when the country became the part of the European Union. It regulated the representation of Austria in the European Parliament, and its participation in the establishment of other bodies of the European Union. It also established an information duty of the Federation towards other countries in case that the intention concerning the European Union would affect the independent competence of the countries. It ensured the influence of both Chambers of the Parliament on the creation of laws of the European Union, and especially insured the cooperation of Austria in the Common Foreign and Security Policy of the European Union, with regard to the country´s statute of neutrality.[32]

6.25. Poland incorporated the integration clause directly into the new constitution of 1997, which was adopted when the country was already preparing intensively for accession to the European Union. Under Article 90 of the Constitution of the Republic of the Poland, the competences of State authorities in certain matters could be delegated to international organizations or international bodies. It could happen by the law, requiring a qualified approval of both Chambers of the Parliament, or by referendum, and a qualified majority is also required for the ratification of such a treaty.[33] Evidently, the constitutionalists

---

[32] More specifically see especially THEO ÖHLINGER, HARALD EBERHARD, VERFASSUNGSRECHT, Wien: Facultas-WUV (2016);
Due to the fact that the whole amendment of the Constitution was adopted by these articles, they had to be approved within the meaning of Article 44(3) of the Constitution by a referendum, which was on 12 June 1994. As in France, the Austrian Constitution declares in its Article 117(2) active and passive voting rights to the municipalities of the citizens of other Member States of the European Union, under the conditions set by the countries.

[33] Compare for example: PODSTAWOWE PROBLEMY STOSOWANIA KONSTYTUCJI

strived for a balanced regulation. On the one side, such a regulation opens the possibility of the expansion of the European Union. At the same time, it is not resigned on the guarantee of the sovereignty of the Republic of Poland. In this situation, Article 91(3) of the Constitution, in which the primacy of European Union law prior to the domestic law is declared expressly, seems to be rather redundant, because this fact already results from the delegation of the competences.[34]

6.26. In the Portuguese Constitution, such clause is contained in Article 7(6), which opens the possibilities for the country to negotiate joint performance powers. These are necessary for the development of reciprocity in the European Union, with respect to the principle of subsidiarity and with regard to the realization of economic and social cohesion. Article 8(4) states expressly that the treaties of the European Union and Acts issued by its authorities are used by Portugal in its legal order with regard to fundamental democratic principles of the State. As was mentioned regarding the previous countries, this is actually redundant, if we do not take into consideration the explicit references about Portugal as the democratic State.

6.27. The Czech Republic has chosen an implicit and cost-effective solution. Its Constitution states that 'the Czech Republic respects its obligations, which result from international law',[35] and that 'certain powers of the authorities of the Czech Republic may be delegated to the international organization or institution by the international treaty'.[36]

6.28. In comparison with the Czech Republic, neighboring Slovakia adopted an amendment to its Constitution 90/2001 Coll. This amendment includes among other things new wording of Article 7, which looks into this issue more extensively and explicitly. While the original wording supposes the possibility to join 'a state alliance with other states', newly added paragraph 2 mentions explicitly the right of entry to the European Communities and the European Union, including the transfer of parts of the performance of its rights. Similarly, attached was the right to join 'the organization of mutual collective security'.

6.29. Both steps were taken before the accession of Slovakia to the European Union and NATO (North Atlantic Treaty Organization) in the same year, 2004. Although it is possible, to

RZECZYPOSPOLITEJ POLSKIEJ. RAPORT WSTĘPNY (Basic Problems of Applying of the Constitution of the Republic of Poland. Preliminary Report), Warsaw: Sejm Publishing House (Kazimierz Działocha ed., 2004); PRAWO UNII EUROPEJSKIEJ. ZAGADNIENIA SYSTEMOWE (European Union Law. System Issues), Warsaw: Publisher Economic Law and Practise (Jan Barcz ed., 2006).

[34] ALEKSANDRA KUSTRA, *supra* note 7, at 279.
[35] Article 1(2) of the Constitution of the Czech Republic.
[36] Article 10a(1) of the Constitution of the Czech Republic.

deduce the right from the original text of Article 7, the need for an amendment arose. It likely emerged due to the cooperating influence of political factors in a bid to secure the political support for the intended integration steps and to eliminate potential objections of insufficient support in the Constitution. Following Article 7, the Slovak Constitutional Court stated for example in its finding III. ÚS 666/2016 Coll. of Resolutions, that

> the origin of the membership of the Slovak Republic in the European Union lies, among other things, also in the voluntary surrender of the part of the sovereignty of the state in favor of the European Union. It deals concurrently also with the part of the sovereignty during generally binding regulation of the social relations.

6.30. The second reason, which also applies in the case of Sweden, was the unwillingness to allow the transfer of competences by a general clause. The European Union is considered to be an unique institution, and is provided a privilege that the Member States are willing to transfer to it a part of their competences to a much greater extent than is customary, and is or would be enabled to any other international organizations.[37] In Sweden, it seemed as necessary to adopt new legal regulation, for the reason that the existing provision of the Constitution concerning the transfer of certain competences to the international organizations did not envisage such a large transfer that the membership in the European Union had required.

6.31. Sweden also adopted the changes in its Constitution through an amendment to the constitution in the context of accession to the European Union. Changes included the section titled The Instrument of Government (SFS nr: 1974:152), namely in Chapter 10, which deals with the relationship with other States and international organizations.

6.32. The authorization in Article 2(3), states that it is possible, in the case of the European Union, to give the valid consent of *Riksdag* (the Parliament of the Swedish Kingdom) with an international treaty dealing with the cooperation within the European Union, without the need of its final version.[38]

6.33. Swedish legal regulation also pursued the objective of limiting the transferring of the competences to the European Union, both in procedural and substantive aspects. The content of a three-fourths majority of *Riksdag* and the procedure corresponding to the Constitutional Act are required for the transfer of the

---

[37] The Constitution of Sweden: The Fundamental Laws and the Riksdag Act. p. 43.

[38] The Instrument of Government (IG) 10:4.

competences. Legislators are materially banned in connection with the integration, from changing the principles of the governmental form in Sweden.[39]

6.34. Danish legal regulation is similar to the Swedish one. It requires in Article 20(2) for transfer of the competences a five-sixths majority. If it is not achieved, it is referred to a referendum. It does not mention either a substantive-legal limitation, or the European Union explicitly.

V. Conclusion

6.35. The reasons why some States chose so-called silent changes of their constitutions and did not expressly reflect on the relation to the European Union and its law, or why other states made a general clause, or why still others opted for detailed regulation, relate mainly to the aspects within the individual countries. Such aspects include the nature of their legal order, the time when the amendment of the constitution was made, and also by a range of other, sometimes also rather subjective circumstances, such as the current political situation in the given country and the attitudes of their inhabitants to the integration. Such varied circumstances caused such a plurality of adjustments, whose rationality in concrete cases would not be easy or possible to detect. Undoubtedly, general evolutionary tendency is in fact the transformation of sovereignty to the transnational entities, in which case it deals with an unfinished process, which cannot anticipate every detail of the development.

| | |

Summaries

FRA　[*Les « clauses européennes » introduites dans les constitutions sont-elles vraiment nécessaires ?*]
　　La naissance de l'Union européenne et de son système juridique a profondément changé la conception traditionnelle de l'État et du droit international, qui prévalait jusqu'à la moitié du XXe siècle. La plupart des auteurs, plutôt que de chercher à définir l'Union, se concentrent sur les différences qui existent entre celle-ci et les États ou les organisations internationales ; ceci s'applique aussi au droit de l'Union. Dans cette situation, les pays membres doivent trouver une solution pour réconcilier leur droit national

---

[39]　The Instrument of Government (IG) 10:5, paragraph one).

et les pouvoirs délégués à l'Union européenne. Si la relation entre le droit national et le droit international et la question y afférente de la souveraineté de l'État font l'objet d'un consensus depuis relativement longtemps, l'intégration européenne nous confronte à une nouvelle réalité. Les constitutions de tous les États membres se prononcent, d'une manière ou d'une autre, sur cette intégration : certaines d'entre elles se contentent de mentionner l'adhésion à une organisation ou une institution internationale, d'autres sont plus explicites sur ce point, les raisons de ce choix n'étant pas toujours claires. Dans ce contexte, un rôle primordial est joué par les cours constitutionnelles des États membres, qui sont censées veiller à la protection des constitutions nationales, mais aussi garantir le respect des obligations découlant de l'adhésion à l'Union et la conformité des valeurs nationales à celles de l'Union. L'instance qui décide, en dernier ressort, de l'étendue des pouvoirs délégués, est la Cour de justice de l'Union européenne, dont la jurisprudence peut rendre floue et variable la portée des dispositions nationales mentionnées. L'article se consacre essentiellement à l'analyse des « clauses d'intégration » introduites dans les constitutions des États membres, qui met en lumière une grande variabilité de leurs teneurs, déterminées par des critères nationaux, la nature du système juridique de l'État concerné, le moment de l'amendement de la constitution, ainsi qu'un certain nombre de circonstances subjectives comme la situation politique du pays au moment de l'amendement et l'attitude des citoyens vis-à-vis de l'intégration.

CZE [*Evropské klauzule v ústavách - opravdu jsou nezbytné?*]
Existence Evropské unie a jejího právního řádu se zcela zásadně dotkla tradičního nazírání na formy státu a mezinárodního práva, tak jak na ně bylo pohlíženo do poloviny 20. století. Většina autorů se nepokouší o definici unie, nýbrž vyhledává rozdíly mezi ní a státem nebo mezinárodními organizacemi a obdobně lze označit i snahy o charakteristiku unijního práva. Právě tyto nejasnosti motivovaly jednotlivé země, aby se ve svém vnitrostátním právu vyrovnaly s fenoménem přenosu kompetencí na evropskou úroveň. Zatímco vztah vnitrostátního a mezinárodního práva a s ním související otázka suverenity byl vyřešen již poměrně dávno, evropská integrace přináší novou podobou tohoto problému. Ve všech ústavách členských států unie je v nějaké podobě vztah k této integraci řešen, a to buď tak, že se zde hovoří o mezinárodní organizaci či instituci, aniž je tato specifikována, nebo se tak naopak děje výslovně, přičemž důvod řešení nebývá povětšinou jasný. Významnou roli ve vztahu k unijnímu právu hrají ústavní soudy členských států,

Czech Yearbook of International Law®

které mají bdít nad ochranou národních ústav, ale i zajišťovat naplnění závazků států plynoucích z členství v unii a konformitu národních hodnot s hodnotami unie. Tím, kdo určuje konkrétní rozsah přenesení kompetencí je v konečné instanci Soudní dvůr Evropské unie, díky jehož judikatuře se někdy stává hranice určená zmíněnými ustanoveními ve vnitrostátních právních řádech značně nezřetelnou a pohyblivou. Jádro článku se věnuje rozboru tzv. integračních klauzulí v ústavách členských států, na jehož základě lze dospět k závěru, že jejich formulace jsou značně odlišné a jedná se o výsledek daný především hledisky uvnitř jednotlivých zemí, povahou jejich právního řádu, dobou, kdy byla změna ústavy provedena i řadou dalších subjektivních okolností, jakými byla stávající politická situace v dané zemi a postoje jejich obyvatel k integraci, které způsobily tak vysokou míru plurality úprav.

| | |

POL [*Klauzule europejskie w konstytucjach – czy naprawdę są konieczne?*]
Powstanie Unii Europejskiej i jej porządku prawnego przyniosło ze sobą zasadnicze zmiany w spojrzeniu na niektóre tradycyjne instytucje, w tym przede wszystkim na suwerenność państwową. Na integrację zareagowały wszystkie kraje członkowskie unii m.in przez wprowadzenie tzw. klauzul integracyjnych do swoich konstytucji. Artykuł analizuje ich treść, zwracając uwagę na to, że w poszczególnych sformułowaniach znajdują się znaczne różnice, przy czym autorzy poszukują odpowiedzi na pytanie o przyczyny tych rozbieżności, które często nie są do końca jasne.

DEU [*Europaklauseln in den Verfassungen - sind sie wirklich unumgänglich?*]
Die Entstehung der Europäischen Union und des Gemeinschaftsrechts veränderte die Betrachtungsweise bestimmter traditioneller Rechtsinstitute, insbesondere dann der Staatshoheit, auf grundlegende Weise. Auf die Existenz dieser Integration reagierten sämtliche Mitgliedsstaaten mit der Aufnahme sog. Integrationsklauseln in ihre Verfassungen. Der vorliegende Beitrag analysiert deren Inhalt und legt dar, dass zwischen den einzelnen Formulierungen erhebliche Unterschiede bestehen; dabei stellen sich die Autoren die Frage nach den Gründen für diese Abweichungen, die oft nicht ganz klar sind.

RUS [*Европейские положения в конституциях — действительно ли они необходимы?*]

Возникновение Европейского союза и его правопорядка привело к существенным изменениям во взглядах на некоторые традиционные институты, прежде всего на суверенитет государства. На существование этой интеграции отреагировали все государства — члены ЕС, включив так называемые интеграционные положения в свои конституции. В статье рассматривается их содержание и подчеркивается, что в некоторых формулировках имеются существенные различия. Авторы также задают себе вопрос о причинах этих различий, которые во многих случаях даже не вполне очевидны.

ESP [*¿Son las cláusulas europeas en las constituciones realmente imprescindibles?*]

La creación de la Unión Europea y de su ordenamiento jurídico provocó cambios fundamentales en la percepción de ciertos institutos tradicionales, ante todo, la soberanía del Estado. Todos los Estados miembros respondieron a esa integración mediante, entre otras cosas, la inserción de las llamadas cláusulas de integración en sus constituciones. El texto analiza su contenido y recalca que existen diferencias fundamentales en las distintas versiones. Los autores se preguntan sobre el porqué de estas diferencias que, a menudo, no resultan del todo evidentes.

| | |

Bibliography

THE EUROPEAN CONSTITUTION AND NATIONAL CONSTITUTIONS: RATIFICATION AND BEYOND, The Hague: Kluwer Law International (ANNELI ALBI, JACQUES ZILLER eds., 2007).

PRAWO UNII EUROPEJSKIEJ. ZAGADNIENIA SYSTEMOWE (European Union Law. System Issues), Warsaw: Publisher Economic Law and Practise (Jan Barcz ed., 2006).

VOJTĚCH BELLING, LUKÁŠ KOLLERT, SUVERENITA PANOVNÍKA, LIDU A STÁTU V MODERNÍ POLITICKÉ FILOSOFII (Sovereignty of the Ruler, People and State in Modern Political Philosophy), Ústí upon Elbe (2017).

VOJTĚCH BELLING, ZROZENÍ SUVERÉNA: POJEM SUVERENITY A JEHO KRITIKA V MODERNÍ POLITICKÉ A PRÁVNÍ FILOSOFII: SUVERENITA A NORMATIVNÍ KONSTRUKCE REALITY (Birth

Czech Yearbook of International Law®

of the Sovereign: the Term of Sovereignty and Its Critique in Modern Political and Legal Philosophy: Sovereign and Normative Construction of Reality), Brno (2014).

DAVID BLANCHARD, LA CONSTITUTIONNALISATION DE L'UNION EUROPÉENNE, Rennes: Editions Apogée (2001).

FRANÇOIS BORELLA, ÉLEMENTS DE DROIT CONSTITUTIONNEL, Paris: Presses de Sciences Po (2008).

Francisco Balaguer Callejón, *La fragmentation du pouvoir constituant*, *in* LE POUVIOIR CONSTITUANT AU XXIE SIECLE, not stated: Institut Univesitaire Varenne (Francisco Balaguer Callejón, Stéphane Pinon, Alexandre Viala, eds., 2017).

PODSTAWOWE PROBLEMY STOSOWANIA KONSTYTUCJI RZECZYPOSPOLITEJ POLSKIEJ. RAPORT WSTĘPNY (Basic Problems of Applying of the Constitution of the Republic of Poland. Preliminary Report), Warsaw: Sejm Publishing House (Kazimierz Działocha ed., 2004).

LOUIS FAVOREU AND TEAM, DROIT CONSTITUTIONNEL, Paris: Dalloz (2005).

MARIÁN GIBA, SÚDNA KONTROLA ÚSTAVNOSTI VE FRANCÚZKU (Judicial Supervision of the Constitutionality in France), Bratislava: Wolter Kluwer (2017).

Luke Glanville, *The Myth of Traditional Sovereignty*, 57(1) INTERNATIONAL STUDIES QUARTERLY (2013).

GEORG JELLINEK, VŠEOBECNÁ STÁTOVĚDA (General State Sciences), Prague (1906).

KAREL KLÍMA, KOMENTÁŘ K ÚSTAVĚ A LISTINĚ (A Commentary on the Constitution and the Charter), Pilsen: Publishing Aleš Čeněk (2009).

KAREL KLÍMA, TEORETICKÁ VÝCHODISKA EVROPSKÉ ÚSTAVNOSTI (The Theoretical Basis of the European Constitutionality, in Instytucje prawa konstytucyjnego w dobie integracji europejskiej (The Institutions of Constitutional Law in the Era of the European integration), Warsaw: Sejm Publishing (2009).

KAREL KLÍMA, ÚSTAVNÍ PRÁVO (Constitutional Law), Pilsen (3rd ed. 2006).

Artur Kozak, *Deficyt demokracicji a intergracja europejska* (The Democracy Deficit and European Integration), *in* AKSJOLOGICZNE I PRAKTYCZNE ASPEKTY INTEGRACJI EUROPEJSKIEJ (Axiological and Practical Aspects of European Integration) Wrocław, University of Wrocław Publisher (Ewa Kozerska, Tomasz Scheffler eds., 2007).

ALEKSANDRA KUSTRA, PREPISY I NORMY INTEGRACYJNE W

KONSTYTUCJACH WYBRANYCH PAŃSTW CZŁONKOWSKICH UE (Transposing and Integration Standards for the Consulates of the EU Member States), Toruń: Dom Organizatora (2009).

Zdeněk Kűhn, Jan Kysela, *Na základě čeho bude působit komunitární právo v českém právním řádu?* (On What Basis Community Law Will Work in Czech Legal Order?), 1 PRÁVNÍ ROZHLEDY (Legal Insights) (2004).

Zdeněk Kűhn, *Ještě jednou k ústavnímu základu působení komunitárního práva v českém právním řádu* (Once Again to the Constitutional Basis of the Influence of Community Law in Czech Legal Order), 10 PRÁVNÍ ROZHLEDY (Legal Insights) (2004).

JIŘÍ MALENOVSKÝ, MEZINÁRODNÍ PRÁVO VEŘEJNÉ: JEHO OBECNÁ ČÁST A POMĚR K VNITROSTÁTNÍMU PRÁVU, ZVLÁŠTĚ PRÁVU ČESKÉMU (Public International Law: Its General Part and Relation to National Law, Especially to Czech Law), Brno: Doplněk (2007).

Jiří Malenovský, *O 'chudokrevnosti' mezinárodních rozměrů české ústavy a možných terapiích* (About the 'Anemia' of the International Dimensions of the Czech Constitution and Possible Therapies), 7 PRÁVNÍK (Lawyer) (1997).

DAVID MILLER, BLACKWELLOVA ENCYKLOPEDIE POLITICKÉHO MYŠLENÍ (Blackwell´s Encyclopedia of Political Thought), Brno (1995).

MIROSLAV NOVÁK, ARONOVO POJETÍ SUVERENITY A SCHMITTOVA KRITIKA SVĚTOVÉHO STÁTU (Aron´s Concept of Sovereignty and Schmitt´s Critique of the World State).

THEO ÖHLINGER, HARALD EBERHARD, VERFASSUNGSRECHT, Wien: Facultas-WUV (2016).

Piirimäe Pärtel, Stephen Krasner, *in* SOVEREIGNTY IN FRAGMENTS THE PAST, PRESENT AND FUTURE OF A CONTESTED CONCEPT, Cambridge (Hent Kalmo, Quentin Skinner, ed., 2010).

VÁCLAV PAVLÍČEK, ÚSTAVNÍ PRÁVO A STÁTOVĚDA: I. DÍL OBECNÁ STÁTOVĚDA (Constitutional Law and State Sciences: 1st part General State Sciences), Prague (1998).

Eugeniusz Piontek, *Konstytucje państw członkowskich v porządku prawnym unii europejskiej (Constitutions of the Member States in the Legal Order of the European Union), in* INSTYTUCJE PRAWA KONSTYTUCYJNEGO W DOBIE INTEGRACJI EUROPEJSKIEJ (Institutions of Constitutional Law in the Era of the European Integration), Warsaw: Sejm Publishing (2009).

JIŘÍ PRAŽÁK, ZÁKLADNÍ RYSY VŠEOBECNÉHO PRÁVA STÁTNÍHO (The Basic Features of General State Law), Praha (Prague): Jednota právnická (Legal Unity) (1900).

Czech Yearbook of International Law®

SACHA PRECHAL, DIRECTIVES IN EC LAW, Oxford: Oxford University Press (2005).

JANA RESCHOVÁ, EVROPSKÝ KONSTITUCIONALISMUS: ZDROJE, FORMY A TENDENCE (The European Constitutionalism: Sources, Forms and Tendenciess, Prague: Publishing house Oeconomica (2003).

DENYS SIMON, KOMUNITÁRNÍ PRÁVNÍ ŘÁD (Community Legal Order), Prague: ASPI (2005).

QUENTIN SKINNER, O STÁTĚ (About the State), Praha (Prague): Oikomenh (2013).IVO ŠLOSARČÍK, POLITICKÝ A PRÁVNÍ RÁMEC EVROPSKÉ INTEGRACE (Political and Legal Scope of the European Integration), Prague: Wolters Kluwer (2010).

JIŘÍ ZEMAN, PŘISTOUPENÍ K EU A NUTNOST PROVÁDĚNÍ ÚSTAVNÍCH ZMĚN (Assession to the European Union and the Need of Making Constitutional Changes), Brno: Masarykova univerzita (Masaryk University) (2009).

VLADIMÍR ZOUBEK, PRÁVOVĚDA A STÁTOVĚDA: ÚVOD DO PRÁVNÍHO A STÁTOVĚDNÍHO MYŠLENÍ (Legal Sciences and State Sciences: the Introduction to Legal and State-Sciences Thinking), Pilsen (2010).

Maria Viktorovna Mazhorina

The Transformation of the State and the 'denationalization' of Law in the Context of Private International Law

Key words:
globalization | Private International law | Public International Law | state sovereignty | rule of law | applicable law | lex mercatoria | arbitration | commercial arbitration | interpretation of the term 'rules of law' | non-state law | UNCITRAL model law | transnational law | denationalization of law

Abstract | Law is developing in line with the society which has suffered structural changes as a result of globalization. The latter has changed the face of the world, spurred the transformation of the State and its sovereignty and furthered the denationalization of Law. As the Law develops it must be adequate for this new society. The biggest changes are taking place within Private International Law, where we see an increase in the number of norm-making actors and the changing character of norm-making itself, the growth and changes in the process of delocalization of law, the standardization of Law and search for a new legal identity, an unprecedented growth of non-state regulatory norms and searching for ways to legitimize them, a vibrant development of alternative non-state and supranational systems for trans-boundary dispute resolution, paradigm shifts in the sphere of legal consciousness, caused by interpretations of the notion of 'rules of law,' and an updating of the institution of autonomous legal qualification, to name a few. All this creates an effect of parallel social realities, with two colliding systems of regulating trans-boundary relationships and two dispute resolution systems developing based on State law and non-State law. The doctrines of Global / Transnational / Non-State law arising from it demand interpretation and conceptualization within the Private International Law paradigm.

Maria Viktorovna Mazhorina is a candidate of legal sciences, and an associate professor of the Private International Law Department at the Kutafin Moscow State Law University. She is the author and co-author of books on Private International Law and Law of International Commercial Contracts, as well as the author of over 40 publications on Public International and Private International Law, including cross-border transactions, transboundary disputes and international commercial arbitration. She serves as the Research Supervisor for post-graduate students, who have prepared dissertations seeking the degree of a candidate of legal sciences. She is also a practicing lawyer and the author of several legal opinions on the application of foreign law in Russian courts and arbitral tribunals. E-mail: mazhorinamaria@gmail.com

The reported study was funded by RFBR according to the research project № 18-011-00883.

'For as long as we have been aware of it, the whole history of mankind has been marked by its movement towards greater and greater unity. Such unity is achieved by the most varied means – not only by those who work actively for it, but also by those who try to resist it.'

L.N. Tolstoy[1]

'...for the craving for universal unity is the third and last anguish of men. Mankind as a whole has always striven to organize a universal state.'

F. Dostoyevsky[2]

I. Introduction: Globalization and Some Effects on the Law

7.01.   At the turn of the 21st century the world entered a new stage of its development, related to globalization,[3] which predetermines and explains significant changes in the whole system of normative regulation in the sphere of trans-boundary relationships as a concept of Private International Law. Globalization is considered a process that encompasses the causes and consequences of transnational and trans-cultural integration of human and non-human activities.[4] It is characterized by the trans-territoriality and trans-nationality of the resulting processes.

7.02.   Professor of Law Jürgen Basedow, a German legal scholar, director of the Max Planck Institute for Comparative and International Private Law, refers to globalization through the concept of 'Open Society' that is based on commerce leading

---

The article was prepared within the project of the Russian Foundation for fundamental research (РФФИ) № 18-011-00883 'Information sovereignty: from issues of determining the jurisdiction of the State to online dispute resolution'.

1   TOLSTOY LEV NIKOLAYEVICH, Толстой Л.Н. Круг чтения *(Reading circle)*, Eksmo, Moscow 13-14. (2015).

2   DOSTOYEVSKY FYODOR, Достоевский Ф.М. Братья Карамазовы. Часть вторая. Книга пятая *(The Brothers Karamazov. Part two. The fifth book)*.

3   See DAVID B. GOLDMAN, GLOBALIZATION AND THE WESTERN LEGAL TRADITION: RECURRING PATTERNS OF LAW AND AUTHORITY, Cambridge: Cambridge University Press The Edinburgh Building, (2007); GLOBALIZATION AND PRIVATE LAW: THE WAY FORWARD, Cheltenham, Northampton: Edward Elgar Publishing 488 (Michael Faure, André van der Walt ed., 2010), ROLAND ROBERTSON, GLOBALIZATION: SOCIAL THEORY AND GLOBAL CULTURE, London: Sage (1992); Paul Schiff Berman, *From International Law to Law and Globalization*, 43 COLUMBIA JOURNAL OF TRANSNATIONAL LAW, 485-556 (2005); Ulrich Sieber, A *Legal Order in a Global World – The Development of a Fragmented System of National, International, and Private Norms*, 14 MAX PLANCK YEARBOOK OF UNITED NATIONS LAW, 1-49 (2010); WILLIAM TWINING, GLOBALISATION & LEGAL THEORY, London/Edinburgh/Dublin: Butterworths 279 (2000); Maria V. Zacharova, Захарова М.В. Влияние глобализации на юридическую карту мира *(The impact of globalization on the legal map of the world)*, 3 LEX RUSSICA 417-444 (2011).

4   Nayef R.F. Al-Rodhan, Definitions of Globalization, A Comprehensive Overview and a Proposed Definition, available at: http://citeseerx.ist.psu.edu/viewdoc/download?doi=10.1.1.472.4772&rep=rep 1&type=pdf (accessed on 26 December 2017).

to more open national boundaries, the gradually increasing interdependence of societies and economies as well as the internationalization of separate individuals' lives. In this respect globalization as an irreversible process seems to be just an accelerated tendency towards a greater interpenetration across national boundaries that originated in 1980-1990s and has been the driving force of the Open Society.[5]

7.03.   The idea of the Open Society is seen a bit differently by the sociologist Manuel Castells. He writes, in the context of information in modern society, about the 'Network Society' which is a dynamic open system with production, power and experience networks at its core.[6] According to the author's definition, a network is a set of interconnected nodes, while a node varies depending on the kind of concrete networks in which it is connected.[7] For example, when speaking about a global financial flow network, nodes can be stock markets and supporting centers providing them with different services.

7.04.   For the American sociologist Immanuel Maurice *Wallerstein, globalization is a new highly efficient system of global economy management, based on* the global spreading of Western ideology. Such an ideology creates a new feeling of identity replacing the traditional framework and a former way of living.[8] In fact, *globalization* leads to a society lacking in the traditional features of sociality: its national, historical, cultural or even legal identity. This approach is consistent with concepts of the Europeanization of Law,[9] the Americanization of Law,[10] its Westernization or even 'McDonaldization'.[11]

7.05.   One way or another the process of *globalization* is seriously transforming the modern world order, with the primary cause of all current changes evidently being economic globalization. We are witnessing not just the cooperation of national economies, but their combining into a single, though not homogenous,

---

[5]   JÜRGEN BASEDOW, THE LAW OF OPEN SOCIETIES – PRIVATE ORDERING AND PUBLIC REGULATION OF INTERNATIONAL RELATIONS: GENERAL COURSE ON PRIVATE INTERNATIONAL LAW, Moscow: Norma 13 (2016).
[6]   Manuel Castells, The Rise of the Network Society Second edition with a new preface, available at: https://deterritorialinvestigations.files.wordpress.com/2015/03/manuel_castells_the_rise_of_the_network_societybookfi-org.pdf (accessed on 27 December 2017), p. 501.
[7]   Manuel Castells, *Supra* note 6, at 501. See also Manuel Castells, *Materials for an Exploratory Theory of Network Society,* 51 THE BRITISH JOURNAL OF SOCIOLOGY 5-14 (2000).
[8]   IMMANUEL *WALLERSTEIN, Валлерстайн И.* Конец знакомого мира: Социология XXI в. (*The end of the familiar world: Sociology of XXI century*), Moscow: Logos 6 (2003).
[9]   Sjef van Erp., *European Private Law and Legal Globalisation,* 6(1) ELECTRONIC JOURNAL OF COMPARATIVE LAW (2002).
[10]   Duncan Kennedy, *Three Globalizations of Law and Legal Thought: 1850-2000, in* THE NEW LAW AND ECONOMIC DEVELOPMENT: A CRITICAL APPRAISAL, Cambridge: Cambridge University Press 19-73 (David M. Trubek, Alvaro Santos ed., 2006).
[11]   Roland Robertson, *Supra* note 3, p. 467.

Czech Yearbook of International Law®

global economic system, based on the principle of global interdependence. A global economy, being a historically new reality, can operate in real-time as a single system on the whole planet.[12] The era of economic globalization is at the same time the era of political localization.[13]

7.06. Globalization of the economy leads to globalization of Law. Previously developed State regulatory mechanisms do not meet the standards of the new economic world order. With the 'face of the world' changed, Law must change as well. The contemporary legal map of the world is a multicolored patchwork quilt of national legal systems. Such a map is currently bulging at the seams with national boundaries becoming meaningless and turning into formal lines on political maps of the world due to the statuses of States being transformed. The legal framework cannot preserve the same character of autonomous sets of legal norms any longer. It requires rethinking and reinterpretation through the lens of the global economic and social foundations. Thus the former legal architecture has not yet collapsed completely but it is getting more and more undermined by the supranational, cross-national and transnational economically-oriented actors in the context of State sovereignty getting weaker and undergoing some changes. The new legal architecture, still being in its embryonic stage, is just getting conceptualized locally. The legal field is in a state of emergency, with an urgent and chaotic search for new legal models, forms and mechanisms for normative regulation of the arising social relationships. We might have a chance to witness Network Law emerging as a legal framework of the Network Society which is developing in the same way as the fibrous root system characteristic of some plants.

7.07. Private International Law is an economically-oriented branch of Law and is at the vanguard of the relevant and most obvious changes. At the same time some other branches of law (mainly Public ones) are characterized by a serious time lag effect.

7.08. William Twining, Quain Professor of Jurisprudence Emeritus from University College London, has described the following predictable changes in Law caused by globalization: the emergence of new subjects with a strong transnational orientation; historically national objects being shifted towards transnational dimensions; a growing awareness of pluralism and multiculturalism; the necessity of the systematic rethinking and

---

[12] Manuel Castells, Кастельс М. Информационная эпоха: экономика, общество и культура *(The information age: economy, society and culture)*, available at: http://www.gumer.info/bibliotek_Buks/Polit/kastel/02.php (accessed on 26 December 2017).
[13] *Ibid.*

re-evaluation of certain issues, namely the Western canons of law and referring to Non-Western legal traditions for some answers to contemporary problems.[14] As the German legal scholar and sociologist Gunther Teubner justly says, the emerging global markets undermine the verifiable potential capacity of national politics and the possibility of legal regulation. Globalization shows power is being transferred from State actors to economic actors.[15]

7.09. There are two key tendencies developing in Law which predetermine other changes:

> 1) State status being transformed in the political structure of society and State sovereignty getting weaker;
>
> 2) the privatization and denationalization of Law.

It is obvious that both processes are closely interrelated. It is very difficult to determine the order of priority in the cluster of 'State status transformation' – 'denationalization of Law' the same way as it is difficult to say which came first – the chicken or the egg. Moreover it does not sound oxymoronic any more for Legal Science to speak about Law without a State. The issue has even become the focus of studies within post-jurisprudence or jurisprudence without the State and Law.[16]

II.   The Transformation of the Status and Sovereignty of the State

7.10. One of the essential 'products' of globalization is the changing of the states' actual status in the political structure of society. This problem has become international and interdisciplinary in nature, challenging the scholarly community as well.[17] Thus at

---

[14]   See William Twining, Globalisation and Legal Scholarship. Montesquieu Lecture, 2009, available at: https://lapa.princeton.edu/uploads/2011-0210%20Twining%20Paper.pdf (accessed on 30 October 2017).

[15]   Gunther Teubner, Global private regimes: Neo-spontaneous law and dual constitution of autonomous sectors in world society? available at: https://www.jura.uni-frankfurt.de/42852650/global_private_regimes. pdf (accessed on 10 October 2017).

[16]   Yu. A., Vedeneev, Веденеев Ю.А. Юридическая наука в системе междисциплинарных связей (*Legal science in the system of interdisciplinary links*), 6 LEX RUSSICA 13 (2017).

[17]   See DAVID J. BEDERMAN, GLOBALIZATION AND INTERNATIONAL LAW, New York: Palgrave Macmillan X–XI, 176 (2008); Daniele de Carolis, *The Process of Harmonisation of the law of international commercial arbitration: Drafting and diffusion of uniform norms*. PhD thesis, University of Trento, 2010, available at: http://eprints-phd.biblio.unitn.it/214/1/dissertation.pdf (accessed on 22 October 2017); ABRAM CHAYES, ANTONIA H. CHAYES, THE NEW SOVEREIGNTY: COMPLIANCE WITH INTERNATIONAL REGULATORY AGREEMENTS, Harvard University Press (1995); JEAN L. COHEN, GLOBALIZATION AND SOVEREIGNTY: RETHINKING LEGALITY, LEGITIMACY, AND CONSTITUTIONALISM, Cambridge University Press 442 (2012); Gráinne de Burca, *Developing Democracy Beyond the State*, 46(2) COLUMBIA JOURNAL OF TRANSNATIONAL LAW (2008); Anne-Marie Slaughter, *Disaggregated Sovereignty: Towards the Public Accountability of Global Government Networks*, 39(2) GOVERNMENT AND OPPOSITION 162 (2004); Julie Mertus, *Considering Non-state Actors in the New Millennium: Toward Expanded Participation in Norm Generation and Norm Application*, 32 NYU JOURNAL OF INTERNATIONAL LAW AND POL. 553 (2000); Harold H. Koh, Review Essay: Why do Nations Obey Law?, *Faculty Scholarship Series*. Paper 2101, available at: http://digitalcommons.law. yale.edu/fss_papers/2101 (accessed on 30 November 2017).

the University of Bremen, Germany, the Collaborative Research Center on Transformations of the State has been created, studying different aspects of the evolution of State and Law over the current period of time as well as projecting the future prospects of the Sovereign State.[18]

7.11.   Jean-Bernard Auby, Professor and Director of the Center on Changes in Governance and Public Law at Sciences Po in Paris, remarked vividly that globalization cuts the institution of State sovereignty to the heart.[19] President of the Carnegie Endowment for International Peace, Jessica Tuchman Mathews discusses the decline of States and emergence of non-State actors.[20] German sociologist Ulrich Beck thinks that globalization intensifies the processes in which national States and their sovereignty get entwined in the maze of trans-national actors and get dominated by their power, orientation and identity.[21]

7.12.   When analyzing the process of a State status being transformed, one can enumerate a number of issues: the weakening of State sovereignty; State demonopolization in the political and, as a result, legal arenas; the decentralization of powers and authority as well as the rise of private actors performing the traditional functions of states.

7.13.   Karim Benyekhlef, Professor of Law at University of Montreal, Canada, and Fabien Gélinas, Professor of Law at McGill University, believe that digital technologies and those means of communication based on them, challenge the principle of national sovereignty with sovereignty itself becoming a fluctuating concept.[22]

7.14.   Castells writes about de-legitimatization of the State and the crisis of the nation State as a sovereign unit. The fact that the State's orders cannot be completely executed discredits both its power and legitimacy. The globalization of capital, the growth in the number of parties represented in the government institutions and the decentralization of powers and authority and their delegation to regional and local governments create new geometries of power, possibly giving rise to a new form of the State – the Network State. It is the nation States that will survive but not their sovereignty.[23]

---

[18]   http://www.sfb597.uni-bremen.de/pages/forProjekte.php?SPRACHE=en (accessed on 11November 2017).
[19]   JEAN-BERNARD AUBY, LA GLOBALIZATION, LE DROIT ET L'ETAT (*Globalization, Law and State*), Paris: LGDJ-Lextenco ed., 95 (2010).
[20]   Jessica T. Mathews, *Power Shift*, 76(1) FOREIGN AFFAIRS 50-67 (1997).
[21]   ULRICH BECK, RISIKOGESELLSCHAFT: AUF DEM WEG IN EINE ANDERE MODERNE (*Risk Society: towards a new Modernity*), Frankfurt am Main: Suhrkamp (1986).
[22]   Karim Benyekhlef, Fabien Gélinas, *The International Experience in Regard to Procedures for Settling Conflicts Relating to Copyright in the Digital Environment*, 35(4) COPYRIGHT BULLETIN 7 (2001).
[23]   Manuel Castells, *Supra* note 12.

7.15. Martha Minow, Professor of General Jurisprudence at Harvard Law School and Harvard University Distinguished Service Professor, describes three spheres whose developments influence the status of the modern State: the expansion of private actors performing functions or actions formerly performed by state actors; the increased insertion of arbitration clauses in consumer contracts and the increased use of the Internet and digital communication by consumers and businesses.[24]

7.16. In Russia there have also been studies devoted to the processes of State institutions and State sovereignty getting transformed in the context of globalization. Thus, Nadezhda Pastukhova, Professor of Law at Moscow State Law University, writes that 'the consistent development of globalization in the world has provided some scholars with grounds for developing the idea of the so-called 'post-sovereignty world order'.[25] Globalization is transforming the role of the State in the contemporary world: information, financial and other globalization-related processes reduce the powers of national governments to control and manage the internal political situation. Many functions formerly performed by governments are delegated to transnational corporations and civil society institutions.[26] Elena Voinikanis, the leading researcher in Law at Higher school of Economics, says that the processes of globalization cast doubt on the State's monopoly role in creating laws and administering justice.[27] The Russian comparativist Maria Zakharova believes that the actors driving globalization of law can be classified into two big groups: those having the powers and authority of the State, and public and private actors at the supranational and cross-national levels of functionality.[28] The contemporary international system is considered to be a system of multilevel governance,[29] in which the State is just *primus inter pares*.

7.17. The consequences of the transformation of a State status are manifested in Law, and a new legal reality is being formed in the 21st century creating a new future for Law. Private actors, like the

---

[24] Martha Minow, *Alternatives to the State Action Doctrine in the Era of Privatization, Mandatory Arbitration, and the Internet: Directing Law to Serve Human Needs*, 52 HARVARD CIVIL RIGHTS-CIVIL LIBERTIES LAW REVIEW 146-167 (2017).

[25] NADEZHDA B. PASTUKHOVA, Пастухова Н.Б. Проблемы государственного суверенитета (*Problems of state sovereignty*), Moscow: Norma 45-46 (2006).

[26] *Ibid*, at 220.

[27] Elena A. Voinikanis, Парадигмальный сдвиг в современном праве (*Paradigm shift in modern law*), 1 PHILOSOPHY POLITICS AND LAW: COLLECTION OF SCIENTIFIC WORKS 138-161 (Vorobyev ed., 2010).

[28] Maria V. Zakharova, *Supra* note 3, at 433-434.

[29] *Ulrika Mörth*, Soft Law and New Modes of EU Governance – A Democratic Problem? Paper presented in Darmstadt November 2005, available at: http://www.mzes.uni-mannheim.de/projekte/typo3/site/fileadmin/research%20groups/6/Papers_Soft%20Mode/Moerth.pdf (accessed on 7 November 2016).

global business community and business elites represented by transnational and multinational organizations and supranational agencies have largely contributed to this transformation, not only (sometimes, rather than) governmental bodies. Europeans are getting more and more accustomed to the idea that most of their laws are initiated not by their own nation state, but by EU institutions.[30]

7.18.   The legal community is plagued by the question of who will become the contemporary legislator and law maker: the State or some entity alongside it with which the State shares its sovereignty? The situation in Law is getting more complicated in the context of IT development. Now, when modern society is greatly dependent on digital resources to communicate, store, distribute and acquire information, there arises the issue of the State's information sovereignty. Who and what will manage and regulate the relevant relationships in this situation, and by which law, if any? What is the contemporary society governed by – the State or Facebook?

7.19.   In the sphere of regulating trans-boundary Private Law relationships the leaders in developing the relevant norms have, for many years now, been using UNCITRAL, UNIDROIT, the Hague Conference on Private International Law, as well as the International Chamber of Commerce (ICC) and other agencies. Internationally oriented law firms (particularly American and British firms) are strengthening their impact on the processes of standardization. They have created new types of contracts which become standard and cause other norms to be created. Bar associations and arbitral tribunals support these processes. A number of actors creating sources which consolidate world scale results from below in different spheres, has grown. The international business community plays an active role in norm-making. Its most active and highly-professional segment includes experts, the Business Elite, adjudicators, the Chamber of Commerce and Industry members, members of professional associations, and scientists.[31]

7.20.   The Law seems to be getting separated from the State, and losing its nature immanent to the State. The boundaries of legal regimes no longer coincide with State boundaries. Besides, the number of legal regimes need not be the same as the number of nation States.[32] The answer to the question of who makes Law

---

[30]   Roger Cotterrell, *What Is Transnational Law?* 37(2) LAW & SOCIAL INQUIRY 500 (2012).

[31]   Alec S. Sweet, *The New Lex Mercatoria and Transnational Governance*, JOURNAL OF EUROPEAN PUBLIC POLICY 627–646 (2006).

[32]   *Andreas Fischer-Lescano*, Gunther *Teubner, Regime-Collisions: The Vain Search for Legal Unity in the Fragmentation of Global Law*, 25 MICHIGAN JOURNAL OF INTERNATIONAL LAW 999-1046 (2004).

brings about the answer to another question: What is Law? Thus the changing pool of law-makers forms a new paradigm for the contemporary understanding of Law.

III. 'Denationalization' of Private International Law

7.21. Law has crossed the boundaries of the Nation State,[33] so today the concept of privatization or denationalization of Law is being actively developed.[34] The concepts of 'private global norm-production'[35] and 'private law and order'[36] have become a trend haunting foreign legal thought. The private global norm-production, based on non-state actors' norm-making, is associated in literature with the apolitical procedure of developing Law.[37]

7.22. The stunning multiplication of the norm-making actors and denationalization of legal regimes lead to the development of the concept referred to as globalization of Law.[38] However, in different branches of Law the globalization-driven changes are happening

---

[33] Roger Cotterrell, *Supra* note 30, at 500–524.

[34] Anne Peters, Isabella Pagotto, *Soft Law as a New Mode of Governance: A Legal Perspective*, 4 NEWGOV: NEW MODELS OF GOVERNANCE 5-6 (2006).

[35] See Gunther Teubner, *Breaking Frames: The Global Interplay of Legal and Social Systems*, 45(1) AMERICAN JOURNAL OF COMPARATIVE LAW 157 (1997); GLOBALIZATION AND PRIVATE LAW: THE WAY FORWARD, Cheltenham, Northampton: Edward Elgar Publishing 17 (Michael Faure, André van der Walt eds., 2010).

[36] See MATH NOORTMANN, CEDRIC RYNGAERT, NON-STATE ACTOR DYNAMICS IN INTERNATIONAL LAW: FROM LAW-TAKERS TO LAW-MAKERS, Ashgate (2010); Fabrizio Cafaggi, A comparative analysis of transnational private regulation: legitimacy, quality, effectiveness and enforcement, available at: http://www.eesc.europa.eu/resources/docs/a-comparative-analysis-of-transnational-private-regulation-fcafaggi_12062014.pdf (accessed on 1 September 2017); Matthias Goldmann, *A matter of perspective: Global governance and the distinction between public and private authority (and not law)*, 5(1) GLOBAL CONSTITUTIONALISM 48-84 (2016); Marc Amstutz, *Global (Non-)Law: The Perspective of Evolutionary Jurisprudence*, 9(4) GERMAN LAW JOURNAL 465-476 (2008); Gunther Teubner, *Supra* note 15; Jürgen Basedow, *Supra* note 5, at 90-220; Peer Zumbansen, *Transnational private regulatory governance: ambiguities of public authority and private power*, 76 LAW AND CONTEMPORARY PROBLEMS 117-138 (2013); Ralf Michaels, Nils Jansen, *Private Law Beyond the State? Europeanization, Globalization, Privatization'*, 54 THE AMERICAN JOURNAL OF COMPARATIVE LAW 843-890 (2006); Sofia B. Aguilar, Supranational Systems of Dispute Resolution and their Integration into Domestic Legal Systems: A View of the Latin American Experience, available at: http://digitool.library.mcgill.ca/webclient/StreamGate?folder_id=0&dvs=1510331151991~117&usePid1=true&usePid2=true (accessed on 11 September 2017); Joel Bakan, *The Invisible Hand of Law: Private Regulation and the Rule of Law*, 48 CORNELL INTERNATIONAL LAW JOURNAL 279-300 (2015); Colin Scott, Fabrizio Cafaggi, Linda Senden, *The Conceptual and Constitutional Challenge of Transnational Private Regulation*, 38(1) JOURNAL OF LAW AND SOCIETY 1-19 (2001).

[37] Francesco Galgano, *The New Lex Mercatoria*, 2(1) ANNUAL SURVEY OF INTERNATIONAL & COMPARATIVE LAW 109 (1995).

[38] Andrea di Robilant, *Genealogies of Soft Law*, 54(3) THE AMERICAN JOURNAL OF COMPARATIVE LAW 500 (2006). See also: JODY FREEMAN, MARTHA MINOW, INTRODUCTION TO GOVERNMENT BY CONTRACT: OUTSOURCING AND AMERICAN DEMOCRACY, MA: Harvard University Press 552 (2009); Paul Schiff Berman, *From International Law to Law and Globalization*, 43 COLUMBIA JOURNAL OF TRANSNATIONAL LAW 485-556 (2005); Klaus P. Berger, *Transnational Commercial Law in the Age of Globalization*, available at: http://www.imeryurdaneta.com/archivos/clases/art_432__BERGER%20-%20Transnational%20Commercial%20Law%20in%20the%20Age%20of%20Globalization.pdf (accessed on 10 November 2017).

Czech Yearbook of International Law®

at different rates. The visible impact that globalization has had is on International Law, Ecological Law, International Private Law, International Trade Law (*lex mercatoria*), International Banking Law, Information Law, International Taxation Law, International Civil Procedure, International Commercial Arbitration. Another sphere breaking the ardent influence of globalization is the Financial Market.[39] The institution of E-commerce is overlapping at several legal, economic, and value-based dimensions. The evolution of the Internet has brought about a previously unknown phenomenon of *lex electronica* or *lex networkia.*[40]

7.23. Another modern concept is the Doctrine of Transnational Law,[41] referred to as the proto concept[42] and its varieties, such as the concepts of Transnational Commercial Law,[43] Global Law[44] and others. The terms of 'Transnational Law' and 'Global Law'[45] are often used as synonyms. The quintessence of Transnational Law are those norms that do not fall under any category which returns us to the debate as to what Law is and what its future is. Craig Scott, Professor of Law and Director of the Nathanson Centre on Transnational Human Rights, Crime and Security, at Osgoode Hall Law School of York University, Toronto, Canada, considers that Transnational Law is an invitation to see the legal developments through the lens of legal pluralism.[46] Actually the concepts of the Global/Transnational Law, 'Denationalization' of Law, and the State's lost monopoly right in creating norms are closely related.[47]

7.24. An American lawyer, Professor of Law at The George Washington University, Paul Schiff Berman remarks ironically that to some, the very mention of globalization will seem old hat having been a nuisance for a rather long time. However 'legal scholars are so focused on the official organs of legal power –

---

[39] Maria V. Zacharova, *Supra* note 3, at 434-435.

[40] See E.J. Valauskas, Lex Networkia: Understanding the Internet community, First Monday, [S.l.], oct. 1996, available at: http://www.ojphi.org/ojs/index.php/fm/article/view/490/411>. (accessed on 24 December 2017).

[41] See PHILIP C. JESSUP, TRANSNATIONAL LAW, New Haven: Yale *University* Press 113 (1956); César Arjona, Transnational Law as an Excuse. How teaching law without the state makes legal education better, ESADE Working Paper, № 219, October 2011. p. 20.

[42] Colin Scott, *Transnational Law as a Proto-Concept*, 10(6,7) GERMAN LAW JOURNAL 864 (2009).

[43] See Ross Cranston, *Theorizing Transnational Commercial Law*, 42 TEXAS INTERNATIONAL LAW JOURNAL 597-617 (2007).

[44] See DAVID J. BEDERMAN, GLOBALIZATION AND INTERNATIONAL LAW, New York: Palgrave Macmillan 244 (2008).

[45] See RAFAEL DOMINGO, THE NEW GLOBAL LAW, Cambridge: Cambridge Univ. Press (2010); GIULIANA Z. CAPALDO, THE PILLARS OF GLOBAL LAW, Ashgate: Aldershot (2008).

[46] Colin Scott, *Supra* note 42, at 868-875.

[47] See Gunther Teubner, *The Two Faces of Janus: Rethinking Legal Pluralism*, 13 *CARDOZO L. REV.* 1443-1462 (1991); Paul Schiff Berman, *From International Law to Law and Globalization*, 43 COLUMBIA JOURNAL OF TRANSNATIONAL LAW 507-511, 538-540 (2005).

nation-state governments - that they have been less likely to embrace ideas about norm-development in non-state arenas.'[48] Many autonomous fragments of the world society such as the globalized economy, science, technology, mass media, etc. are developing an enormous demand for regulating norms which cannot be satisfied by national or international institutions. The most prominent contemporary private legal regimes are the *lex mercatoria* and *lex digitalis*.[49]

7.25.   Professor of Transnational Law at King's College London, Peer Zumbansen thinks that the dilemma of the nation states weakening as a result of globalization is accentuated by such processes as creating legally binding norms outside the State institutions.[50] Professor Ulrich Sieber, Director at the Max Planck Institute for Foreign and International Criminal Law in Freiburg, Germany, believes that globalization leads to the 'transnational applicability and enforceability of law'.[51] In Private Law the 'transnational applicability' appears where there is a collision of norms, in forum shopping. It is more and more often that private actors create non-governmental instruments which are not part of the national, international or supranational law. Private actors assume the responsibility for the stagnating process of Law harmonization, whose results are far from being satisfying. Examples of such private law-making include home-made law by professional associations, international commercial arbitration, codes of behavior developed by research institutions, results of business associations' self-regulation, principles, guidelines, and contract forms, to name a few.[52]

7.26.   Basedow relates the growing role of private norm-making to the States no longer having information regarding the assessment of the social and economic situation. The process of opening the States and their economies blurs the notion of typical trans-boundary cases resulting in national legislators losing the opportunity to create a mechanism for their legal regulation. As a result private norm-making steps forward to play the leading role, as it is much more aware of the relevant facts and changes happening in the society and world economy. Understanding that national laws cannot provide a system of legal certainty, private actors develop strategies to solve the problem, anticipating the States' actions.[53] Likewise, Professor

---

48   Paul Schiff Berman, *Supra* note, at 490.
49   Andreas Fischer-Lescano, Gunther Teubner, *Supra* note 32, *at* 1010.
50   Peer Zumbansen, *Supra* note 36, at 117-138.
51   Ulrich Sieber, *Supra* note 3, at 1-49.
52   *Ibid.*
53   Jürgen Basedow, *Supra* note 5, at 26, 65-69.

Czech Yearbook of International Law®

of Law Remy Cabrillac says that globalization has undermined the omnipotence of the national law which has become relative and subservient.[54]

7.27.   Twining rightly says that globalization poses three challenges for the traditional (Western) jurisprudence. First, it challenges the 'black box theories', treating nation States, societies, legal systems and legal regimes as closed and impervious entities that can be studied in isolation. Second, it challenges the idea that the study of law and legal theory can be restricted to two types of legal ordering, namely municipal state law and public international law. Finally, it challenges the adequacy of much of the present conceptual framework and vocabulary of legal discourse for discussing legal phenomena.[55] Twining is supported by other scholars agreeing that the concept of Law based on the dichotomy of the Municipal State Law and Public International Law is inadequate for considering the new actors emerging on the global stage.[56] Other scholars also support the necessity of a 'language change' and introducing new terminology. They claim that the old terminology was developed exclusively for State Law[57] and that the language of the scholastic and dogmatic jurisprudence can neither fix nor reflect the legal reality. An American lawyer and legal scholar, Harold Hongju Koh, Professor of International Law at Yale Law School, joining the discussion, says that two traditional dichotomies, 'National - International law', and 'Public - Private Law', are breaking apart,[58] Sieber compares the situation to the Middle Ages. He argues that there is no direct correlation between State power and law and order, no distinct separation between Private and Public Law, and a 'seamless' transition taking place between the norms of law and other regulators.[59]

7.28.   Other authors go even further, offering ideas which undermine the target dichotomies from the other side. They state that all norms of national law might be public in their nature, while globally all laws might be private in their nature.[60] Thus, Professor of Public Law Christoph Möllers, encouraging the discussion about the flexibility of the boundaries between Public and Private Law says that all domestic (national) law can become

---

[54]   See Rémy Cabrillac, Кодификации / Les codifications (*Codifications*), Moscow: Statut 480 (2007).
[55]   William Twining, *General Jurisprudence*, 15(1) UNIVERSITY OF MIAMI INTERNATIONAL AND COMPARATIVE LAW REVIEW 1-59 (2014); See also WILLIAM TWINING, GLOBALISATION & LEGAL THEORY, Cambridge *University* Press (2000).
[56]   See Daniele de Carolis, *Supra* note 17.
[57]   *Ibid.*
[58]   Harold H. Koh, Transnational Legal Process, available at: http://digitalcommons.law.yale.edu/cgi/viewcontent.cgi?article=2902&context=fss_papers (accessed on 2 December 2017), p. 184.
[59]   Ulrich Sieber, *Supra* note 3, at 1-49.

[60]   See Ralf Michaels, Nils Jansen, *Supra* note 36, at 843-890.

public, with International Law becoming Transnational Private Law at same time.[61] In the context of Private International Law the consequences of the denationalization of Law can clearly be seen. Firstly, there is a stronger and modified process of delocalization of law. The influence of International Law and non-traditional legal sources is *de facto* increasing.[62] However, international agreements are losing their former importance as traditional forms of delocalization of law and are being partly replaced by model laws, with unification giving way to harmonization. At international/interstate levels, one unique development has been the creation of homonymous documents which are practically identical in their contents, and differing only in their form. For example, the UNCITRAL project is devoted to enforcing international commercial settlement agreements achieved through conciliation. The Draft Convention and Draft Model Law are likewise in the process of development.[63] This UNCITRAL Model Law approach is still in active development, taking a form similar to the New York Convention.[64]

7.29. The Delocalization of Private Law is preconditioned by increasing standardization. Unification results in a set of uniform norms and a uniform law enforcement practice, while standardization is, to some extent, indifferent to the National Law but it is most efficient in the sphere of non-state regulation and practice typification. An American legal scholar, Professor *Harold J. Berman* says that Law is no longer perceived as a whole, as corpus juris, but rather as a body of norms adopted *ad hoc* and formally put together. Law is more often seen as a non-historical entity, lacking in continuity. Law is growing increasingly fragmented and subjective, aiming rather at convenience that morality, and with practitioners caring more about instant results rather than consistency and continuity.[65]

7.30. Secondly, there is an unprecedented avalanche-like growth in the amount of non-state regulatory norms. These are incorporated in specialized non-governmental codes, and are more or less autonomous from the sources of legal regulation. It is interesting how the contents of the relevant documents change. There

---

[61] Christoph Möllers, *Transnational Governance without a Public Law?, in* TRANSNATIONAL GOVERNANCE AND CONSTITUTIONALISM, Hart Publishing 329-330 (Christian Joerges, Inger-Johanne Sand, Gunther Teubner, eds., 2004).
[62] GLOBALIZATION AND PRIVATE LAW: THE WAY FORWARD, Cheltenham, Northampton: Edward Elgar Publishing 2 (Michael Faure, André van der Walt eds., 2010).
[63] The Working group materials are available at: https://documents-dds-ny.un.org/doc/UNDOC/LTD/V17/083/22/PDF/V1708322.pdf?OpenElement.
[64] This refers to Convention on the Recognition and Enforcement of Foreign Arbitral Awards 1958 (UNSITRAL).
[65] *HAROLD J. BERMAN, Западная традиция* права: эпоха формирования (*The Western tradition of law: the era of the formation*), Moscow: Infra-M (2nd ed., 1998).

are, of course, traditional bodies of norms and rules which are renewed from time to time and contain customary rules. These include INCOTERMS, UCP,[66] URC,[67] Institute Cargo Clauses,[68] and others.[69] But alongside these are acts of non-state regulation, making attempts to codify and interpret the *lex mercatoria*, such as the UNIDROIT Principles of International Commercial Contracts,[70] Principles of European Contract Law — PECL,[71] *and the CENTRAL* List of *lex mercatoria* Principles, Rules and Standards,[72]). Finally, documents have been developed that are aimed at creating new practices in the sphere of conflict of laws and substantive regulation of trans-boundary relationships. These include the Draft Common Frame of Reference (DCFR),[73] the Hague Principles on Choice of Law in International Contracts,[74] A-national rules as the applicable law in international commercial contracts with particular reference to the ICC Model Contracts.[75] Thus, 'gathering and fixing' have been replaced by 'codifying and interpreting', and finally getting transformed into 'creating and characterizing'. From the non-official codification of trade customs we have arrived at the applicable law, which is, in fact, a bloodless revolution in normative regulation of trans-boundary relationships and, even more importantly, in the sphere of promoting legal consciousness. The appearance of such codified sources of non-state regulation norms challenges not only the contents of Private Law, but also the way its nature must be shaped.

7.31.   Norms of non-state regulation are not legitimate from the traditional or legalistic point of view, as they are not created by a legislator. However, due to their being widely applied in practice, they cannot be ignored by scholarship any longer and require reinterpretation. Professor of European Private Law at Maastricht University and director of the Maastricht European Private Law Institute, Jan Smits says it is now time to find a new source of legitimacy for legal rules. It is clear that this new source of legitimacy cannot be found in the authority of the State and in

---

[66]   Uniform Customs and Practice for Documentary Credits, available at: http://store.iccwbo.org/icc-uniform-customs-and-practice-for-documentary-credits
[67]   Uniform Rules for Collections. Available at: http://store.iccwbo.org/icc-uniform-rules-for-collections
[68]   Available at: https://www.ctplc.com/media/72243/Institute-Cargo-Clauses-2009.pdf
[69]   For example ICC Uniform Rules for Bank Payment Obligations, Pub No.750, ICC 2013, ISBN 978-92-842-0189-1
[70]   Available at: https://www.unidroit.org/instruments/commercial-contracts/unidroit-principles-2016
[71]   Available at: http://www.jus.uio.no/lm/eu.contract.principles.parts.1.to.3.2002
[72]   Available at: http://www.trans-lex.org/principles
[73]   Available at: http://ec.europa.eu/justice/policies/civil/docs/dcfr_outline_edition_en.pdf
[74]   Available at: http://www.hcch.net/upload/wop/gap2014pd06rev_en.pdf
[75]   Available at: http://store.iccwbo.org/content/uploaded/pdf/Developing%20neutral%20legal%20 standa rds%20for%20Intl%20contracts.pdf.

Czech Yearbook of International Law®

the decisions of national parliaments.[76] Private law is understood more as an organism than product of an explicit design. What is really interesting in this respect is the author's attitude to the alternative sources of legitimacy for private law rules, which cannot be seen as only a result of lawmakers' activities but rather provided through jurisdictional competition. Market players are free to choose those norms which are best for regulating the emerging relationships, and select the most efficient normative models. The demand for such norms and their efficiency partly depend on the norm-making efforts of their authors or actors. In this respect, informed deliberation on Private Law norms among specialists may lead to greater legitimacy than a general debate among non-specialists.[77] Professional communities developing modern codified sets of non-state regulation norms appear to be more competent in doing this than the legislative bodies of States. Private law is probably the most scholarship-based area of law, saturated with doctrine and accomplishments of different schools of thought, so many of its norms result from doctrinal codification. For example, the DCFR, providing definitions of legal terms, fundamental principles and model rules, can be used as a 'toolbox' by a European legislator, as a source of inspiration for the ECJ and national courts, and as an optional code for contracting parties that want to make the CFR the law applicable to their contract. All these functions imply that the DCFR is only applicable if the relevant actors prefer it over national law. If the DCFR is not made applicable, the drafters are held accountable for the lack of success of this particular legal regime.[78] Thus the traditional approach to norm-making through the fusion of legal will and regulatory enforcement practices is being replaced by a new method – norm-making by non-state actors through doctrinal interpretation and professional generalization of the 'best practices' contained in codified documents, legitimized by the business community in the context of jurisdictional competition.

7.32.   Fabrizio Marrella, Professor of International Law and of International Business Law at the University of Venice, considers documents similar to the UNIDROIT Principles as a new instrument for international arbitrators. When a dispute requires application of the national law, arbitrators apply those of the national law norms which correlate with the UNIDROIT Principles. In other words the UNIDROIT Principles are used by

---

[76]   GLOBALIZATION AND PRIVATE LAW: THE WAY FORWARD, Cheltenham, Northampton: Edward Elgar Publishing 24-27 (Michael Faure, André van der Walt eds., 2010).

[77]   Ibid, pp. 24-27.

[78]   Ibid.

arbitrators to grant a transnational status to national law norms. The author refers to the method as the T-test or TNT-test for legal decisions made based on the domestic law.[79] Thus, the norms of non-state regulation act as sort of a standard for those of national law and a mechanism for their adapting to regulating trans-boundary relationships. They smooth over the negative aspects of conflict of laws regulation, so choice of foreign law does not feel for a counterparty to be a leap into the unknown or wandering in the dark. Instead, it ensures some certainty that in case of a conflict the court will be guided by those norms of national law which correlate with the international principles of trans-boundary trade, contained in unofficial codifications.

7.33. Thirdly, denationalization of law manifests itself through a vigorous development of alternative non-state and supranational systems of Dispute Resolution.[80] International commercial arbitration as a process of resolving disputes is going through another Renaissance. Access to national courts is *de jure* not limited, but has been *de facto* downplayed by the growing popularity of arbitration and the widespread market. The State is losing its monopoly in the sphere of resolving trans-boundary private law disputes. In fact, the circle has been closed. There is an abundance of non-state regulatory norms with quasi-legal grounds for their application available and with a growing development of successful practical uses. All this is backed by the State's coercive power – the mechanism for admission and enforcement of foreign arbitral awards based on the 1958 New York Convention. This is unbelievable, particularly from the perspective of the positivist legal paradigm.[81] An autonomous system of dispute resolution has been developed based on the principle of arbitrators' autonomy of will, constantly strengthening its positions.

7.34. It is in International Commercial Arbitration that another revolutionary tendency is forming, which is related to paradigm shifts in legal consciousness. Arbitration turns away from the model in which national law and order are seen as an exclusive legal framework for resolving a dispute. This is stipulated in most

---

[79] Fabrizio Marrella, Choice of Law in Third-Millennium Arbitrations: The Relevance of the UNIDROIT Principles of International Commercial Contracts, available at: http://www.cisg.law.pace.edu/cisg/biblio/marrella.html#v (accessed on 11 December 2013).
[80] Sofia B. Aguilar, Supranational Systems of Dispute Resolution and their Integration into Domestic Legal Systems: A View of the Latin American Experience, available at: http://digitool.library.mcgill.ca/webclient/StreamGate?folder_id=0&dvs=1510331151991~117&usePid1=true&usePid2=true (accessed on 10 November 2017).
[81] Maria V. Mazhorina, Мажорина М.В. Lex mercatoria: средневековый миф или феномен глобализации? (*Lex mercatoria: Medieval Myth or Phenomenon of Globalization?*), The Higher School of Economics, 1 PRAVO. ZHURNAL VYSSHEY SHKOLY EKONOMIKI, (LAW JOURNAL OF THE HIGHER SCHOOL OF ECONOMICS) 4-19 (2017).

modern arbitration rules through the use of the term 'rules of law' in relation to determining the applicable law. The term 'rules of law', clearly known by any national lawyer in the context of Legal Positivism, is acquiring a new sacral meaning in international arbitration. An increasing number of professionals in the sphere of international arbitration can consider themselves privy to a certain ciphered meaning of the phrase,[82] a sort of commercial secret knowledge, which can often predetermine the outcome of resolving a trans-boundary dispute on merits. The veil of mystery was removed from rules of law by the Hague Principles on Choice of Law in International Contracts[83] in 2015. Article 3 of the Principles contains an unprecedented rule, according to which a reference to law (made in a contract) includes rules of law that are generally accepted on an international, supranational or regional level as a neutral and balanced set of rules, unless the law of the forum provides otherwise. Following the Hague Conference on Private International Law practically any norms including, predominantly, non-state ones, contained in various codes can become the applicable law which can only be national law according to the national collisional rules. The Commentary to the Hague Principles clearly stipulates that the term 'rules of law' is used to refer to the norms having non-state sources.[84] That means that 'rules of law' have been independent from the State in their ontology. Moreover, according to most arbitration rules, if the parties to a dispute have not chosen the applicable law, the arbitration tribunal may apply the rules of law which 'they find appropriate'. Thus, through the norms of non-state regulation there has taken place interpretation of the term 'rules of law', with a graceful substitution of notions. Arbitration is not limited in its choice to the law of any particular state, with the autonomous principle of free will of the parties being, to some extent, replaced by the autonomy of the free will of the arbitrators. The arbitration award thus passed, even if based on the norms of non-state regulation, gets incorporated in the national enforcement system through the mechanism provided for in the 1958 New York Convention. In this regard Farshad Sadafi Chaghooshi, an Iranian lawyer and a member of Quebec Bar and Iranian Bar Association, asks whether international commercial arbitration is an autonomous legal system.[85]

---

[82] See Maria P. Bardina, *Determination of Substantive law by International Commercial Arbitration in Russian law, ICAC Rules and Arbitration Practice, in CZECH AND CENTRAL EUROPEAN YEARBOOK OF ARBITRATION, 2013: Borders of Procedural and Substantive Law in Arbitral Proceedings (2013).*

[83] Available at: http://www.hcch.net/upload/wop/gap2014pd06rev_en.pdf

[84] Available at: http://www.hcch.net/upload/wop/gap2014pd06rev_en.pdf

[85] Farshad S. Chaghooshi, Is International Commercial Arbitration an Autonomous Legal System?, A Thesis Submitted to McGill University in partial fulfillment of the requirements of the degree of Master of

Likewise, Catharine *Titi*, a Research Scientist at the French National Centre for Scientific Research (CNRS), w*rites of an arbitrator as a norm-maker.*[86] Can we say that the *arbitrator, being an enforcer, becomes a norm-maker*? It is doubtful. The *arbitrator*, broadly interpreting 'rules of law' and relying on the principles of delocalization and arbitral autonomy, is more likely to go beyond the scope of legal consciousness promoted by the States. International commercial arbitration, based on state law enshrined in international agreements, builds a new legal architecture in the process of norm enforcement.

7.35.   Fourthly, signs of Private International Law denationalization can also be seen in such a seemingly private issue as the problem of legal assessment. In accordance with the State legal paradigm, legal assessment of relationships must be carried out based on the *lex fori* which is stipulated in most modern codified norms of Private International Law. However, with the growing bulk of non-state regulation norms, there arises the question of using States' interpretative material and referring to the institution of autonomous assessment.[87] Professor of Law Alexander J. Belohlavek says that for the purposes of independent assessment national courts have to forget about any national legal acts within Contract Law and any national assessment of contractual and non-contractual obligations. Instead, they should refer to some fictitious legal Esperanto. It is independent assessment that, providing a unique opportunity to make Law less formal, offers a unique and revolutionary solution in reference to a foreign element.[88] The present-day institution of autonomous assessment easily fits into the practice of international commercial arbitration rather than that of national courts. Within the arbitration framework it is not only possible but actually necessary to apply the Principles of the European Law of Obligations, containing some interpreting rules which are to be taken into consideration when interpreting the EU member states' national norms.[89] Autonomization of

Law, Faculty of Law McGill University Montreal, June 2013, available at: http://digitool.library.mcgill.ca/webclient/StreamGate?folder_id=0&dvs=1515802385181~741 (accessed on 30 November 2017).

[86]   *Titi, C., Тити К.* Арбитр как нормотворец: правотворческий процесс в инвестиционном арбитраже *(The arbitrator as a lawmaker: the law-making process in investment arbitration)*, Institute for Law and Public Policy, 14(2) MEŽDUNARODNOE PRAVOSUDIE (INTERNATIONAL JUSTICE) 85-99 (2015).

[87]   See Maria V. Mazhorina, Трансграничные договорные обязательства: проблема правовой квалификации *(Cross-border contractual obligations: the problem of legal qualification)*, The Higher School of Economics, 2 PRAVO. ZHURNAL VYSSHEY SHKOLY EKONOMIKI, (LAW JOURNAL OF THE HIGHER SCHOOL OF ECONOMICS) 143-159 (2016).

[88]   See ALEXANDER J. BELOHLAVEK, Белоглавек, А.И, Европейское международное частное право – договорные связи и обязательства *(European private international law – contractual arrangements and commitments)*, In 2 volumes, Volume 1. Kiev: Takson 106-113. (2010).

150 | [89]   See ALEXANDER J. BELOHLAVEK, ARBITRATION LAW AND PRACTICE IN THE CZECH

The Transformation of the State and the 'denationalization' of Law in the Context ...

Czech Yearbook of International Law®

contemporary international commercial arbitration has taken various forms: from the autonomy of the arbitrators' free will to denationalization of judicial interpretation through shifting to 'rules of law'. Autonomous assessment comes as a logical development in this chain.

7.36. There is no doubt that all the above-mentioned processes are closely interrelated and create an effect of parallel social realities.[90] On the one hand, trans-boundary private law relationships are to be regulated within the traditional framework of Private International Law as a branch of National Law and by reference to International Civil Procedure and/or International Commercial Arbitration institutions. On the other hand, the same relationships can be regulated by non-state regulatory norms, primarily by reference to arbitration institutions and alternative means of dispute resolution (ADR). There is a growing risk of different levels of normative regulation colliding, which, in Private International Law parlance, can be described as the collision of law and non-law. At the same time the State dispute resolution system collides with the non-state one, with quite different practices of applying non-state regulation norms, developing in each of them.

7.37. Something very similar is happening at the interstate level. The fragmentation of International Law is accompanied by the springing up of specialized and relatively autonomous norms or sets of norms, legal institutions and spheres of legal practice.[91] Some lawyers see this as the erosion of Public International Law, the emergence of conflicting jurisprudence, the search for a convenient tribunal and loss of legal stability.[92] In the sphere of interstate regulation the concept of 'informal international lawmaking' has appeared, which became the focus

REPUBLIC (WITH REGARD TO THE ARBITRATION LAW IN SLOVAKIA), Prague: Linde Praha 2650 (1st ed., 2009).

[90] See Maria V. Mazhorina, Эволюция правопонимания: парадигмальные сдвиги в международном частном праве, или когда международный коммерческий арбитраж покончит с правом? (Evolution of legal understanding and law enforcement: Paradigm shifts in private international law (or when the international commercial arbitration will kill the law?), Kutafin Moscow State Law University (MSAL), 10 LEX RUSSICA 88-102 (2017).

[91] Report of the International Law Commission Fifty-seventh session (2 May - 3 June and 11 July - 5 August 2005), pp. 212-222, available at: http://www.refworld.org/cgi-bin/texis/vtx/rwmain/opendocpdf.pdf?reldoc=y&docid=4a716c0e2 (accessed on 27 November 2017). See: Martii Koskenniemi, Päivi Leino, Fragmentation of International Law? Postmodern Anxieties, 15 LEIDEN JOURNAL OF INTERNATIONAL LAW 553-579 (2002); Martti Koskenniemi, International Law: Between Fragmentation and Constitutionalism, available at: http://www.helsinki.fi/eci/Publications/Koskenniemi/MCanberra-06c.pdf (accessed on 28 November 2017).

[92] Report of the International Law Commission Fifty-seventh session (2 May - 3 June and 11 July - 5 August 2005), pp. 214, available at: http://www.refworld.org/cgi-bin/texis/vtx/rwmain/opendocpdf.pdf?reldoc=y&docid=4a716c0e2 (accessed on 27 November 2017).

of study for the Project, launched by the Hague Institute for the Internationalization of Law in 2009.[93]

IV.   Conclusion

7.38.   Contemporary trans-boundary Private Law relationships have the nature of a network while the weakening States are still trying to localize their regulation. As Castells says the world is developing in the dimension of flows, but people are trying to continue living in the dimension of places.[94] The network character of relationships implies decentralization, whereas Law in its formal doctrinal sense has a hierarchical structure.[95] In this regard, in relation to Private Law, a serious discrepancy or even a conflict has appeared, manifesting itself in the inadequacy of the fragmented and relatively static legal landscape and localized systems of dispute resolution for trans-boundary relationships integrated in the global network. As a response to the changing foundation the framework creates new Law and mechanisms for its application, which are non-state codified sets of norms and international non-judicial institutions.

7.39.   The type of State administration itself is changing. Bureaucracy is being replaced by 'adhocracy', a term coined by the futurologist Alvin Toffler, and defined as the power of intellectuals, summoned for a particular reason.[96] Such adhocracies involve coordinating the work of numerous temporary work groups, appearing and then finishing their activities following the rate of changes in the surrounding environment.[97] These social changes are echoed by the processes taking place in Law. 'Adhocracy' in Private International Law can be seen in norm-making where the State is being replaced by the cosmopolitan legal elite, gathered in international and non-state agencies, chambers of commerce, arbitral tribunals, leading law firms. Spontaneous 'case-by-case' norm-making by private actors diminishes the role of the State as the monopolist in the sphere of norm-making.

7.40.   The informational foundation of society raises its sensitivity to external effects, increasing the speed and pace of life, and expanding instability and impermanence of ties. A society which was formerly based on permanence and continuity is getting transformed into a society advocating brevity, modularism, substitutability and a rapid depreciation of knowledge,

---

[93]   Available at: http://www.informallaw.org (accessed on 10 October 2015).
[94]   See Manuel Castells, *Supra* note, at 6.
[95]   Elena A. Voinikanis, *Supra* note 27, at 143.
[96]   ALVIN TOFFLER, THE THIRD WAVE, New York: William *Morrow* 215 (1980).
[97]   A term coined by futurist Alvin Toffler in 1970. See ALVIN TOFFLER, FUTURE SHOCK, New York: Random House 505 (1970).

information, and things. Thus the sphere of normative regulation shows an unprecedented interest towards the norms of non-state regulation. The latter, being short-lived, flexible and renewable, are actually becoming standardized *ad hoc* law and serve as an antipode to firm, static and localized national law. In society, and especially in its business community, there is a growing demand for a more subjective, precedent based, pragmatic, momentary, mobile law having no national identity, whose application would require minimal effort. The 'New' Law is in search for its new identity.

7.41.   In accordance with the changing architecture of the world, a multi-layer pluralistic normative architecture is developing with numerous normative non-hierarchical subsystems, most of which are not recognized by or typical for modern jurisprudence. Thus the issue of conflict of laws, being the major problem in Private International Law, clearly shows the practical consequences of legal pluralism, which nowadays has turned into the theory referred to as 'Global Bukowina' that refers to a territory with numerous non-state normative orders, and coined in an article by Teubner.[98] The legitimacy of these orders is supported through their recognition by private companies, persons and other actors within trans-boundary relationships, i.e. by actual addressees, as well as through their application within the framework of quasi-judicial institutions. The normative landscape, which initially seemed to be patchy and fragmented,[99] together with the perceived chaos of normative regulation, on closer scrutiny turns out to be adequate for a Network Society – the world of astatic, intersecting and overlapping networks. The multilayer, multilevel and multi-component reality creates a congruent regulatory framework.

7.42.   Globalization has triggered a transformation of the State and its sovereignty, leading to the denationalization of Law. We have come so close to the phenomenon which cannot be ignored, for it has crashed down, like a giant tsunami, onto the former jurisprudence, threatening to wipe it off the face of the Earth. It is non-state law, bawling and squalling of its arrival and demanding to be interpreted and conceptualized. There is a growing probability that various levels of normative regulation and different dispute resolution systems, within the framework of which is developing quite a distinct regulatory enforcement practice, will come into conflict with each other.

---

[98]   Gunther Teubner, *Global Bukowina: Legal Pluralism in the World Society, in* GLOBAL LAW WITHOUT A STATE, Dartmouth: Brookfield 3-28 (Gunther Teubner ed., 1997).
[99]   Peer Zumbansen, *Transnational Comparisons: Theory and Practice of Comparative Law as a Critique of Global Governance,* 1 COMPARATIVE RESEARCH IN LAW & POLITICAL ECONOMY 1-20 (2012).

Czech Yearbook of International Law®

7.43. There is no doubt that all the above-mentioned processes are closely interrelated and create the so-called effect of the social reality, normative and institutional frameworks getting 'parallel'. Today trans-boundary relationships can be regulated, on the one hand, by the Private International Law norms, national law and international treaties and, on the other hand, by non-state regulatory norms through arbitration institutions and ADR. Non-state Law norms are getting, in fact, standardized by ad hoc Law and serve as the antipodes of the rigid, static, local National Law or extremely labor-intensive International Law. The current stage of social development is characterized by the fact that the future is not a continuation of the present. A new society, new civilization, new Law have been evolving. The key trends in the Law development in the context of States' transforming have been the changed legal consciousness, standardization and denationalization of Law.

| | |

Summaries

DEU [*Die Transformation des Staats und die „Entnationalisierung"*
des Rechts im Kontext des internationalen Privatrechts]
Das Recht entwickelt sich zusammen mit der Gesellschaft,
und diese hat infolge der Globalisierung gewisse strukturale
Änderungen durchgemacht. Die Globalisierung hat das Antlitz
der Erde verändert, die Transformierung von Staaten und
deren Souveränität beschleunigt und zur Entnationalisierung
des Rechts beigetragen. Die Rechtsentwicklung muss dieser
neuen Gesellschaft Rechnung tragen. Die größten Änderungen
finden auf dem Felde des internationalen Privatrechts statt;
unter den Beispielen wären zu nennen: der zahlenmäßige
Anstieg der Verfasser von Normen und die geänderte Natur
der Normenschaffung als solcher, die Entwicklung und
Änderung des Prozesses für die Delokalisierung des Rechts, die
Standardisierung des Rechts und die Suche nach einer neuen
rechtlichen Identität, der beispiellose Anstieg nichtstaatlicher
Regulierungsvorschriften und die Suche nach Wegen zu
deren Legitimierung, das energische Wachstum alternativer
(nichtstaatlicher und überstaatlicher) Systeme für die Beilegung
grenzüberschreitender Konflikte, die paradigmatischen
Verschiebungen im Bereich des Rechtsverständnisses, die durch
die verschiedenen Auslegungen des Begriffs „Rechtsnorm"

The Transformation of the State and the 'denationalization' of Law in the Context ...

Czech Yearbook of International Law®

ausgelöst wurden, sowie die Aktualisierung des Instituts der autonomen rechtlichen Qualifikation. All das zusammen genommen löst einen Effekt paralleler sozialer Realitäten aus, mit zwei unvereinbaren Systemen zur Regulierung grenzüberschreitender Beziehungen und zwei Systemen für die Beilegung von Streitigkeiten, die sich aus dem Nährboden bzw. Spannungsfeld des staatlichen Rechts und des nichtstaatlichen Rechts entwickeln. Die sich hieraus speisenden Doktrinen vom globalen/supernationalen/nichtstaatlichen Recht bedürfen der Interpretation und Konzeptualisierung innerhalb des Paradigmas des internationalen Privatrechts.

CZE [*Transformace státu a „odnárodnění" práva v kontextu mezinárodního práva soukromého*]

Právo se vyvíjí společně se společností, která v důsledku globalizace prodělala určité strukturální změny. Globalizace změnila tvář světa, urychlila transformaci státu a jeho svrchovanosti a přispěla k odnárodnění práva. Vývoj práva musí této nové společnosti odpovídat. Největší změny se odehrávají na poli mezinárodního práva soukromého, kde můžeme pro ilustraci uvést například nárůst počtu normotvůrců a měnící se povahu normotvorby jako takové, rozvoj a změny procesu delokalizace práva, standardizaci práva a hledání nové právní identity, bezprecedentní nárůst nestátních regulačních norem a hledání cest pro jejich legitimizaci, energický nárůst alternativních nestátních a nadnárodních systémů pro řešení přeshraničních sporů, posuny paradigmatu v oblasti právního vědomí způsobené výklady pojmu „právní normy", jakož i aktualizaci institutu autonomní právní kvalifikace. To vše vytváří efekt paralelních sociálních realit se dvěma kolidujícími systémy regulace přeshraničních vztahů a dvěma systémy řešení sporů, které se vyvíjejí na základě státního práva a nestátního práva. Z toho plynoucí doktríny globálního/nadnárodního/nestátního práva vyžadují interpretaci a konceptualizaci v rámci paradigmatu mezinárodního práva soukromého.

| | |

POL [*Transformacja państwa i „wynarodowienie" prawa w kontekście międzynarodowego prawa prywatnego*]

Globalizacja spowodowała zmiany strukturalne w społeczeństwie, transformując państwo i jego suwerenność. To z kolei doprowadziło do wynarodowienia prawa. Główną konsekwencją tych zmian w międzynarodowym prawie prywatnym jest np.: wzrost liczby prawodawców i zmiana charakteru prawodawstwa jako takiego, bezprecedensowy wzrost niepaństwowych norm regulacyjnych oraz autonomizacja niepaństwowych mechanizmów rozstrzygania sporów transgranicznych. Wynikające z tego doktryny prawa globalnego/ponadnarodowego/niekrajowego wymagają interpretacji i konceptualizacji w ramach paradygmatu prawa międzynarodowego prywatnego.

FRA [*La transformation de l'État et la « dénationalisation » du droit dans le contexte du droit international privé*]

La mondialisation a entraîné des changements structurels au sein de la société, tout en imposant des transformations au niveau de l'État et de sa souveraineté. Ceci a déclenché le processus de dénationalisation du droit. Dans le domaine du droit international privé, ces changements impliquent, entre autres, un nombre croissant d'instances législatives et une mutation des processus législatifs, une multiplication sans précédent de normes de régulation non étatiques, ainsi qu'une autonomisation des mécanismes non étatiques de règlement des litiges transfrontaliers. Les doctrines du droit mondial/ supranational/non étatique nécessitent ainsi une analyse et une reconceptualisation au sein du paradigme du droit international privé.

RUS [*Трансформация государства и 'разгосударствление' права в контексте международного частного права*]

Глобализация породила перестройку социума, трансформацию государства и его суверенитета, что привело к 'разгосударствлению' права. В международном частном праве ключевыми последствиями таких изменений стали: увеличение числа субъектов нормотворчества и изменение характера самого процесса создания норм, беспрецедентное разрастание массива норм негосударственного регулирования, автономизация механизмов негосударственного разрешения трансграничных споров и пр. Возникшие в связи с этим доктрины глобального/транснационального/ негосударственного права требуют своего осмысления и концептуализации в парадигме международного частного права.

Czech Yearbook of International Law®

ESP [*La transformación del Estado y la "desnacionalización" del derecho en el contexto del derecho privado internacional*]
La globalización ha provocado cambios estructurales de la sociedad trasformando el Estado y su soberanía, lo que produjo posteriormente la "desnacionalización" del derecho. A las principales consecuencias de estos cambios en el derecho privado internacional pertenecen, por ejemplo: mayor número de legisladores y el carácter cambiante de la adopción de leyes como tal; incremento sin precedentes de normas regulatorias no estatales; autonomización de mecanismos no estatales para la solución de litigios trasfronterizos. Las doctrinas del derecho global/supranacional/no Estatal que derivan de allí, precisan de interpretación y conceptualización dentro del paradigma del derecho privado internacional.

| | |

Bibliography

JÜRGEN BASEDOW, THE LAW OF OPEN SOCIETIES – PRIVATE ORDERING AND PUBLIC REGULATION OF INTERNATIONAL RELATIONS: GENERAL COURSE ON PRIVATE INTERNATIONAL LAW, Moscow: Norma (2016).

Maria P. Bardina, *Determination of Substantive law by International Commercial Arbitration in Russian law, ICAC Rules and Arbitration Practice, in CZECH AND CENTRAL EUROPEAN YEARBOOK OF ARBITRATION, 2013: Borders of Procedural and Substantive Law in Arbitral Proceedings (2013).*

ALEXANDER J. BELOHLAVEK, Белоглавек, А.И, Европейское международное частное право – договорные связи и обязательства *(European private international law – contractual arrangements and commitments)*, In 2 volumes, Volume 1. Kiev: Takson (2010).

ALEXANDER J. BELOHLAVEK, ARBITRATION LAW AND PRACTICE IN THE CZECH REPUBLIC (WITH REGARD TO THE ARBITRATION LAW IN SLOVAKIA), Prague: Linde Praha (1st ed., 2009).

DAVID J. BEDERMAN, GLOBALIZATION AND INTERNATIONAL LAW, New York: Palgrave Macmillan (2008).

Paul Schiff Berman, *From International Law to Law and Globalization*, 43 COLUMBIA JOURNAL OF TRANSNATIONAL LAW (2005).

CASTELLS, M., THE RISE OF THE NETWORK SOCIETY SECOND EDITION WITH A NEW PREFACE, Wiley-Blackwell (2010).

JEAN L. COHEN, GLOBALIZATION AND SOVEREIGNTY:

RETHINKING LEGALITY, LEGITIMACY, AND CONSTITUTIONALISM, Cambridge University Press (2012).

Roger Cotterrell, *What Is Transnational Law?* 37(2) LAW & SOCIAL INQUIRY (2012).

Ross Cranston, *Theorizing Transnational Commercial Law*, 42 TEXAS INTERNATIONAL LAW JOURNAL (2007).

Francesco Galgano, *The New Lex Mercatoria*, 2(1) ANNUAL SURVEY OF INTERNATIONAL & COMPARATIVE LAW 109 (1995).

GLOBALIZATION AND PRIVATE LAW: THE WAY FORWARD, Cheltenham, Northampton: Edward Elgar Publishing (Michael Faure, André van der Walt ed., 2010).

PHILIP C. JESSUP, TRANSNATIONAL LAW, New Haven: Yale *University* Press (1956).

Andreas Fischer-Lescano, Gunther *Teubner, Regime-Collisions: The Vain Search for Legal Unity in the Fragmentation of Global Law*, 25 MICHIGAN JOURNAL OF INTERNATIONAL LAW 999-1046 (2004).

Jessica T. Mathews, *Power Shift*, 76(1) FOREIGN AFFAIRS (1997).

Martha Minow, *Alternatives to the State Action Doctrine in the Era of Privatization, Mandatory Arbitration, and the Internet: Directing Law to Serve Human Needs*, 52 HARVARD CIVIL RIGHTS-CIVIL LIBERTIES LAW REVIEW (2017).

Ralf Michaels, Nils Jansen, *Private Law Beyond the State? Europeanization, Globalization, Privatization*, 54 THE AMERICAN JOURNAL OF COMPARATIVE LAW (2006).

ROLAND ROBERTSON, GLOBALIZATION: SOCIAL THEORY AND GLOBAL CULTURE, London: Sage (1992).

Colin Scott, *Transnational Law as a Proto-Concept*, 10(6,7) GERMAN LAW JOURNAL 864 (2009).

Alec S. Sweet, *The New Lex Mercatoria and Transnational Governance*, JOURNAL OF EUROPEAN PUBLIC POLICY (2006).

Gunther Teubner, *Breaking Frames: The Global Interplay of Legal and Social Systems*, 45(1) AMERICAN JOURNAL OF COMPARATIVE LAW 157 (1997).

Gunther Teubner, *Global Bukowina: Legal Pluralism in the World Society, in* GLOBAL LAW WITHOUT A STATE, Dartmouth: Brookfield (Gunther Teubner ed., 1997).

WILLIAM TWINING, GLOBALISATION & LEGAL THEORY, London/Edinburgh/Dublin: Butterworths 279 (2000).

Yu. A. Vedeneev, Юридическая наука в системе междисциплинарных связей (*Legal science in the system of interdisciplinary links*), 6 LEX

RUSSICA 13 (2017).

Elena A. Voinikanis, Парадигмальный сдвиг в современном праве *(Paradigm shift in modern law)*, 1 PHILOSOPHY POLITICS AND LAW: COLLECTION OF SCIENTIFIC WORKS 138-161 (Vorobyev ed., 2010).

Maria V. Zacharova, Влияние глобализации на юридическую карту мира (*The impact of globalization on the legal map of the world*), 3 LEX RUSSICA 417-444 (2011).

Peer Zumbansen, *Transnational private regulatory governance: ambiguities of public authority and private power*, 76 LAW AND CONTEMPORARY PROBLEMS 117-138 (2013).

Josef Mrázek

The Modern Concept of State Sovereignty in International Law

Key words:
Sovereignty | sovereign | equality | independence | globalization | human rights | international law | the UN Charter

JUDr. Josef Mrázek, DrSc., is based at the Institute of State and Law of the Academy of Sciences of the Czech Republic and is a member of the Faculty of Law, University of West Bohemia, Pilsen, Czech Republic. He is an Attorney at Law in Prague, as well as the author of about 300 writings in International Law, including several books. E-mail: mrazek.ak@gmail. com

Abstract | *State sovereignty is a legal and political concept that has been transformed by globalization and the development of international legal order. This article refers primarily to external sovereignty. The transfer of certain competencies to international organizations and development of human rights necessarily reduce the competencies of individual States. The concept of State sovereignty still reflects the fact that States are the main and decisive subjects of international law. The sovereignty of States is not a static notion, but it has a changing character along with the development of international community. Despite pre-existing objections the author of this article considers the principle of sovereignty as one of the basic principles of international law, probably still the Grundnorm (basic norm) of the international legal order. Sovereignty is also an obligatory property of any independent State. There is no end of sovereignty as some authors might suggest. But it is true that there is often an abuse of sovereignty in politics and States then invoke the principle of sovereignty or sovereign equality. Several authors have mentioned the myths or mythology of State sovereignty. This approach may indicate the idea that sovereignty is in demise. The idea that the sovereign State has been omnipotent is admittedly unrealistic and false.*

The erosion of state sovereignty does not mean that State sovereignty has already lost its meaning as the basic principle of international law. The sovereignty of State has been naturally justified and protected. The author of this article describes the modern concept of State sovereignty in the era of globalism. Developments in political, commercial and military spheres have in fact resulted to some loss of sovereign powers by individual States.

| | |

I.   Introduction

8.01.   The aim of this article is to clarify the meaning and value of State sovereignty, mainly in contemporary international law. Today, the sovereignty of a State is confronted by the challenge of globalization, and various spheres of international community life such as communications, technological advances, business, the environment, science, culture, international terrorism, war crimes and crimes against humanity. The world order is influenced not only by sovereign States, but also by *the interaction* of various international and regional organizations, governmental and non-governmental organizations, and political and business groups. The appropriate description of sovereignty in international law and in international relations is closely connected with the notion and character of a *State*. The notion of sovereignty is a legal construct reflecting the decision-making power of the State bodies. The sovereignty of a State is also influenced by international law in general. State sovereignty cannot be an excuse from the duties required by international law. The international interdependence of States in all spheres of international life has been increasing and this process necessarily affects the sovereign governance of all States.

8.02.   The international legal order has been based on the sovereignty of States. State sovereignty is one of the basic principles of modern international law. At the same time sovereignty is a necessary political feature as well as the *property* of any independent state.[1] Globalization and the altered conditions for the life and behavior of peoples and States in the international community begs the question of 'whether, in the early twenty-first century, the concept of sovereignty still has an object in the real world and fulfils a function that justifies its continued use,

---

[1]   The literature upon sovereignty is rather extensive. See e.g. HANS KELSEN, DAS PROBLEM DER SOUVERÄNITÄT UND DIE THEORIE DES VÖLKERRECHTS, Tübingen 1-85 (1920); IAN BROWNLIE, PRINCIPLES OF PUBLIC INTERNATIONAL LAW, Oxford 288-295 (1984); LUIS HENKIN, RICHARD C. PUGH, OSCAR SCHACHTER, HANS SMIT, INTERNATIONAL LAW, CASES AND MATERIALS, St. Paul 286-318 (1987); CHARLES ROUSSEAU, DROIT INTERNATIONAL PUBLIC, Paris: Tome II 56-93 (1974); PETER MALANCZUK, AKEHURSTS'S MODERN INTRODUCTION TO INTERNATIONAL LAW 1718 (1997); FRANCIS HARRY HINSLEY, SOVEREIGNTY, Cambridge University Press 1-236 (1986); HURST HANNUM, AUTONOMY, SOVEREIGNTY AND SELF-DETERMINATION, University of Pennsylvania Press 14-27 (2011).

or if the changes in recent decades have cut the 'ground out from under it'.[2] The process of globalization has certainly contributed to some *erosion* of sovereignty in international law. Former UN Secretary Kofi Annan maintained that 'globalization has limited the ability of states to control their economies, regulate their financial policies, and isolate themselves from environmental damage and human migration...'.[3] The process of globalization will continue with all its implications for national governments and individuals as well. The concept of State sovereignty will reflect new changes resulting from globalization and the role of State will probably continue to change toward more *limited sovereignty*. The evolution of the concept of State sovereignty will not be unequivocal in consequence of different interests of States, especially from the so-called *Great Powers* and their often-ambiguous positions.

8.03. In literature we may find also very skeptical views with regard to the meaning of State sovereignty. Scholars Yale H. Ferguson and Richard W. Mansbach refer to 'the myths of State Sovereignty'. The proponents of this approach stress the 'relocation of various components of sovereignty into supranational, governmental or private institutions'. They go on to argue that States are now 'less sovereign, less autonomous and less able to awe, protect or inspire citizens'.[4] Beyond stating the myth and ambiguities surrounding sovereignty these authors insist that a number of contemporary States have been enfeebled or have completely ceased to meet the demands of their citizens. They see a gap or abyss between sovereignty and authority. Various non-sovereign actors such as Hizbullach in Lebanon according to these authors enjoy even a greater legitimacy than the State. In sum, these authors claim that States *share* authority with other *polities* and are 'confronted by 'transnational' and subnational authority challenges'.[5] This nihilistic approach to the meaning of sovereignty is not quite new. Already in 1925 Harold J. Laski suggested that the term *sovereignty* should be abandoned. He wrote: 'It would be of lasting benefit to political science if the whole concept of sovereignty were surrendered. That the fact with which we are dealing is power...'.[6] Power surely is not reason to avoid the notion of sovereignty, because power itself is an integral part and condition of state sovereignty.

[2]   DIETER GRIMM, SOVEREIGNTY: THE ORIGIN AND FUTURE OF A POLITICAL AND LEGAL CONCEPT, New York: Columbia University Press xiii-xiv (2015).
[3]   Kofi Annan, Annual Report to the General Assembly, at 33 (1999).
[4]   Yale H. Ferguson & Richard W. Mansbach, The Myths of State Sovereignty, available at: http://www.saisjournal.org/posts/the-myths-of-state-sovereignty (accessed on 27 July 2018).
[5]   *Ibid.*, at 4-5, 9.
[6]   HAROLD J. LASKI. GRAMMAR OF POLITICS, Allen& Unvin 44-5 (1925).

8.04. I maintain that State sovereignty still plays a central role in both the internal and international life of every State under the new political and economic conditions of the present world. Globalization is a real feature of our life. International legal sovereignty reflects the real status of every State in the international legal system. Political, economic and military integration is confronting the individual States with delimitation and some reduction of their supreme State power. State sovereignty has been redefined in the process of globalization and integration, but any dreams about world State and government remain a mere unrealistic vision. It is true that within Europe the EU created supranational *governance* with a serious impact on national sovereignty of individual members.

II.   The Notion of State Sovereignty

8.05. At the beginning of the 20th century, the famous and distinguished international lawyer, professor Lassa Oppenheim wrote about sovereignty thusly:

> There exists perhaps no conception the meaning of which is more controversial than that of sovereignty. It is an indisputable fact that this conception from the moment when it was introduced into political science, until the present day, has never had a meaning which was universally agreed upon.[7]

8.06. The notion of sovereignty was introduced to International law by Jean Boden (1529-1596) in his work *Six Livres de la République* (1577). The word sovereign was derived from Latin *superanus*. In France the word *souverain* meant a political or religious authority which had no other authority above itself. In support of the policy of absolutism by Louis XI of France he defined sovereignty as 'the perpetual power within a state'. He maintained that sovereignty as a supreme power belongs to a monarch without any restriction except the command of God and the law of nature.[8] In Bodin's view, sovereignty was an attribute of the king (*majestas est summa in cives ac subditos legibus que soluta potestas*).[9] Bodin's position has often been interpreted such that a monarch as sovereign is not responsible to anybody and is not bound by any law. Bodin's ideas have been

---

[7]   LASSA FRANCISS LAWRENCE OPPENHEIM. INTERNATIONAL LAW, London, New York: Longmans § 66, 65 (1905, 1912, 1928).

[8]   JEAN BODIN, SIX LIVRES DE LA REPUBLIQUE, Frankfurt (1644).

[9]   HERSCH LAUTERPACHT, OPPENHEIM´S INTERNATIONAL LAW, Vol. I, London: Peace, Longman, 120 (1955); ANDRE GARDOT, JEAN BODEN: SA PLACE PARMI LES FONDATEURS DU DROIT INTERNATIONAL, Recueil des Cours de l´Academie de Droit International, Vol. IV (RCADI) 545 (1934).

used to justify absolutism in the internal political order. There is some controversy of the interpretation of Bodin's writing. It is generally acknowledged that pursuant to Bodin a sovereign was bound by certain basic rules derived from divine law, the law of nature or reason and by the law common to all nation (*ius cogens*). However, it remains questionable if sovereignty according to Bodin was also restricted by the constitutional law of state.[10]

8.07.   Samuel von Puffendorf (1637-1694) characterized sovereignty as the supreme, but not absolute power in a State which may be constitutionally restricted.[11] John Locke (1632-1704) on the other hand maintained that a State is an original sovereign and that all highest competences are derived from the people´s sovereignty.[12] The authors of the sixteenth and seventeenth century on the whole agreed that sovereignty is indivisible.

8.08.   The doctrine of 'popular sovereignty' was expressed in the US Declaration of Independence (1776) and in the French constitution of 1791. The English lawyer John Austin (1790-1859) stated that sovereignty was vested in a nation´s parliament. He characterized law as a general command of a sovereign. This characteristic was not valid in cases of international law and he did not even consider international law as law.[13] In the twentieth century in the USA the theory of 'pluralistic sovereignty' was established. It was exercised by various political, economic, social or religious groups' domination of the government of the individual State.[14]

8.09.   Sovereignty was characterized by Hersch Lauterpacht as a 'supreme authority, an authority which is independent of any other earthly authority.' In his view, sovereignty 'in the strict and narrowest sense' implies 'independence all round within and without the border of the country.'[15] Ian Brownlie stated that 'sovereignty and equality by states represent the basic constitutional doctrine of the law of nations, which governs a community consisting primarily of states having a uniform

10   THE NEW ENCYCLOPAEDIA BRITANICA, Vol. 11, Micropaedia 56 (2002).
11   SAMUEL PUFFENDORF, ON THE LAW OF NATURE AND NATIONS, Oxford (1934).
12   JOHN LOCKE, TWO TREATIES OF GOVERNMENT, Cambridge University 123 (1988). Available on http://www.efm.hris.ac.uk/het/locke/government.pdf (accessed on 23 May 2018).
13   John Austin, The Province of Jurisprudence of Determined, Stanford Encyclopedia of Philosophy, Stanford University, 8 February 2018, available at: https://plato.stanford.edu/entries/austin-john/ (accessed on 23 May 2018).
14   LEON DUGUIT, LAW IN THE MODERN STATE, New York (1919); HUGO KRABBE, L'IDEE MODERNE DE L'ETAT, Recueil des Cours de l´Academie de Droit International (RCADI), Vol. III (1926); also DIE LEHRE VON DER RECHTSSUVERÄNITÄT (1906); HAROLD LASKI, THE STATE IN THEORY AND PRACTICE, New York (1968); also THE FOUNDATION OF SOVEREIGNTY AND OTHER ESSAYS (1926).
15   HERSCH LAUTERPACHT, OPPENHEIM´S INTERNATIONAL LAW, A TREATIES, London 118-19 (1955).

legal personality'. With regard to international law he added: 'If international law exists, then the dynamics of state sovereignty can be expressed in terms of law, and as states are equal and have legal personality, sovereignty is in a major aspect a relation to other states (and to organization of states) defined by law'.[16] The last edition of Oppenheim´s International Law stated:

> 'The concept of sovereignty was introduced and developed in political theory in the content of the power of the rules of the state over everything. Sovereignty was in other words, primarily a matter of international constitutional power and authority conceived as the highest, underived power within the state with exclusive competence therein'.[17]

8.10. In the Russian textbook of International Law of 1986 sovereignty was defined as a 'state´s complete authority over its own territory and independence in international relations'.[18]

8.11. Max Huber, the sole arbitrator in the case Island of Palmas stated that 'sovereignty in relations between states means independence'. In his view 'independence in relation to area of the globe is the right to exercise his function within the state, excluding any other State'.[19] It is possible to say that this definition given by Max Huber has achieved broad acceptance among international law scholars. Today, sovereignty is mostly defined as the supremacy of the State in its territory and independence from other States. Sovereignty is still the cornerstone of modern international law and the relations among States. The principle of sovereignty also has a fundamental impact on the whole system of international governmental organizations, including their basic rights and duties. Sometimes State sovereignty is defined as the independence of State power inside the State territory and outside its frontiers as well. However, to equate the notion of *sovereignty* with the term *independence* is not quite correct, as these terms are not equivalent. The notion of sovereignty is wider than that of independence, which is only one attribute of a State's sovereignty. Sovereignty includes the positive power of a State for its various activities including territorial and personal jurisdiction. Sovereignty belongs to the State as political organization of the people. The State as a whole

---

[16] IAN BROWNLIE, PRINCIPLES OF PUBLIC INTERNATIONAL LAW, Oxford University Press 287 (4th ed. 1990).

[17] OPPENHEIM´S INTERNATIONAL LAW, Vol. I Peace, Longman 125 (Robert Jennings, Arthur Watts eds., 1992).

[18] THEORY OF INTERNATIONAL LAW, Moscow 137 (Grigorij I. Tunkin ed., 1970).

[19] Reports of International Arbitral Awards, Island of Palmas (*U.S.* v. *Netherlands*), Vol. 2, at 821, 838 (1928).

has been exercising its sovereign rights and duties through the activities of various State bodies, such as the government, parliament and the judiciary.

8.12. The State exercises supreme authority over all physical and legal persons in its own national territory and it is formally independent in its international relations. A manifestation of internal sovereignty can be found in the adoption of Constitution and other laws of the country, in the building of armed forces and facilities, and in penal and civil jurisdiction over all persons and organizations within its state borders. Territorial sovereignty is also reflected in lawmaking activities and in all State functions which are necessary for ordinary governance. Sovereignty also implies authority over the national resources of the country. Constitutional law answers the question of who is entitled to supreme authority within the State.

III. Sovereignty and the UN Charter

8.13. The UN Charter does not define the notion of sovereignty. Article 2(1) states that the Organization 'is based on the principle of the sovereign equality of all its Members'. This *two-pieces* principle embodies both principles of *sovereignty* and *equality* of States. The UN Charter contains specific restrictions on its membership. States must be *peace-loving* and must accept all Charter obligations and the obligations of international law developed under the Charter. States are subject to good-faith obligations (preamble, Article 1 and 2). The members of the UN are sovereign and equal with limitations according to the Charter (see for example the powers of the UNSC and especially the extra-sovereign powers of the five permanent members – the right to veto). There is often a tension and controversy between member States and UN bodies about the scope of international concern and matters reserved to the internal jurisdiction of States.

8.14. In connection with the principles of *sovereign equality* it is necessary to mention the Declaration of Principles of International Law Concerning Friendly Relations and Cooperation Between States in accordance with the UN Charter from 24 October 1970, adopted by consensus.[20] The Declaration at that time was lauded as the major legal achievement. The Declaration states that 'all States enjoy sovereign equality and have equal rights and duties'. They are equal members of the international community, notwithstanding differences

---

of an economic social, political or other nature. According to this Declaration, sovereign equality includes the following propositions:

- States are judicially equal;
- each State enjoys the rights inherent in full sovereignty;
- each State has the duty to respect the personality of other States;
- the territorial integrity and political independence of the State are inviolable;
- each State has the right to freely choose and develop its political, social, economic and cultural systems;
- each State has the duty to comply fully in good faith with its international obligations and to live in peace with other States.

IV.   Rethinking State Sovereignty

8.15.   The origin and history of State sovereignty is closely associated with the organization of political authority of States and within States. The origin of modern State sovereignty was organized on a Westphalian model which was based mainly on the principle of territoriality. Westphalian sovereignty was considered violated when external actors influenced State sovereignty and the independence of any State through various forcible actions, including interventions. The concept of sovereignty was originally developed as an internal concept. Later this internal concept of sovereignty was transferred to the international level. The relationship among States on the international level is characterized by their equality and independence.

8.16.   The concept of State sovereignty particularly changed at the end of the twentieth century. The international institutions and international protection of human rights have qualitatively changed the nature of international law. After the Second World War the traditional international system was expanded by numerous international governmental organizations, almost importantly by the United Nations and its specialized organizations. Human rights instruments together with developing international law have confronted many claims based on the traditional concept of State sovereignty. Changes in the notion of sovereignty will have a serious impact on many diverse topics in international as well as in internal domestic law and external sovereignty.

8.17.   State sovereignty is being eroded by globalization. States are not always able or willing to control and regulate the flow of goods and even persons across their borders. The technological base of globalization is provided by the rapid growth in communication and information technologies which are available worldwide. Globalization has contributed to increasing productivity and the expansion of market economies. Globalization also brings negative implications such as an extensive illegal migration, criminality, illegal drug trade, money laundering, financial instabilities and economic crises.

8.18.   The mutual interdependence of peoples has been increasing and the world population is rapidly growing. There are demographic pressures, especially in the Middle East and Africa; we may see increasing dependence of governments on foreign capital, including investments. It remains an open question if the process of *globalization* or *globalism* will bring future *prosperity* to people or more risks to their lives, including a struggle over natural resources. Globalization is also to some extent an outcome of economic and political integrations. Globalism is a real feature of our life. The international legal order was traditionally connected with sovereignty of States. We may see today that State sovereignty has tended to be reduced. This trend has been shaping a common political life of people. Sovereignty was based on a nationally organized community. The classical international law recognized 'full' and 'not-full' sovereign States. This division also implied that sovereignty was divisible.

8.19.   Sovereign States, as a rule, have imposed limitation on their national sovereign rights in support of international cooperation. Certain sovereign rights and powers of individual States have been limited by the membership of States in international organizations. This limitation is particularly obvious in connection with the transfer of these rights to transnational organizations of an integrationist character. By becoming a member of the European Union, member States conferred substantial rights to this organization, and even some constitutional rights. For some observers the membership in the EU may in the future bring the statehood of individual States into question. Others have decisively denied this possibility.[21] The Treaty establishing the European Union requires an ever closer union among European States. It seems, however, that the people of Europe are not in favor of a super-state. Therefore emphasis has been put on the principle of subsidiarity in EU decision- making. However, it is clear that member States have irrevocably transferred part of their sovereign powers to the EU. In this sense the member States have to some extent reduced their sovereignty or they are *sharing sovereignty* with the EU.

---

[21]   See Robert Jennings, Arthur Wats, Oppenheim´s International Law, *Supra* note 17, at 126.

Czech Yearbook of International Law®

Member States have agreed to act in some fields together rather than individually. This approach has been called a 'pooling' of sovereignty.[22]

8.20.   Challenges to the scope of sovereignty can also be found in the domains of international criminal jurisdiction, the norms of international humanitarian law and the international protection of human rights. On the other hand even international criminal jurisdiction may serve as the protection of the State sovereignty of other States (see e.g. the Rome Statute). Outlawing acts and crimes of aggression protect the territorial integrity and political independence of sovereign States. There are various forms of sovereignty abuse, violating both the rights and obligations of sovereign States. An abuse of sovereignty may also be carried out by States creating serious threats to international security and to the independence of States.

8.21.   Sovereignty is closely tied to the principle of State immunity and jurisdiction. The State cannot use the principle of sovereignty to avoid its legal responsibilities for violations of international law in all matters called *acta jure gestionis*. On the other hand, *acta jure imperii*, the performance of State functions are protected by the principle of *sovereign equality*, which States are entitled to invoke.

8.22.   The independence of the State in international relations is limited by the independence and legal equality of other sovereign States. The power of governments to decide the methods of governance must be in compliance with international law, including human rights norms and rule of law principles. The powers of the modern State are internationally distributed mainly among executive, legislative and judicial bodies. International organizations, the development of international trade, transnational corporations and the migration of people have a considerable impact on the notion of *sovereignty*.

8.23.   The US 'National Security Strategy' of 2017 has also stressed the meaning of sovereignty. The Nationality Security Strategy begins with a determination to protect American people, the American way of life and American interests. This Strategy puts America first. It recognized the benefits of an interconnected world, where 'information and commerce flow freely. But according to this document and to President Donald Trump, it does not mean that the United States should abandon its rights and duties as a sovereign state...' Already in his foreword to this Strategy President Trump pursued 'this beautiful vision – a world of strong, sovereign, and independent nations, each

22   Konrad Schiemann, *Europe and the loss of sovereignty*, (56) ICLQ 485 (2007).

Czech Yearbook of International Law®

with own cultures and dreams...'[23] The Introduction to the US Strategy proclaimed that 'peace, security, and prosperity depend on strong, sovereign nations' and that the US 'protect that American sovereignty' by defending its institutions, traditions, and principles. In conclusion this National Security Strategy 'acknowledges the central role of power in international politics' and 'affirms that sovereign states are the best hope for a peaceful world.'[24] This US approach to 'the principles of sovereignty clearly indicate its extraordinary relevance in international relations.

8.24. Some authors distinguish between *negative* and *positive* sovereignty. Negative sovereignty is characterized as 'formal-legal conditions' indicating immunity from external interference. Positive sovereignty indicates a substantive and empirical dimension, which negatively sovereign States may or may not enjoy.[25] Negative sovereignty was construed as a legal or quasi-legal act of recognition of empirical sovereignty. Positive sovereignty was marked as the core of statehood. According to this approach, States may be 'positively sovereign yet oppressive, undemocratic, and deeply unjust'. The Third Reich was used as an example of a 'positively sovereign state'. The difference between *negative* and *positive* sovereignty is based mainly on *philosophical* or *sociological* approach that has no substantial impact on international law. International law should mostly pay attention to the external sovereignty of the State but internal sovereignty can't be neglected.[26] David Held is mentioning 'liberal international sovereignty'. This approach means that, effective State power is challenged by the principles of self-determination democracy, and human rights as the proper basic of sovereignty.[27] Some authors maintain that only the establishment of supranational institutions with some limited sovereign powers can allow States to exercise sovereignty and people´s self-determination in a meaningful way.[28]

---

[23] National Security Strategy, December 2017, pp. I-II, 1-2, 7.
[24] *Ibid.*, at 55.
[25] See Zezen Mutaqin, *Negative Sovereignty and Positive Sovereignty, Why the Great Powers Invade Outlaw States*, 1(4) CANTERBURY AMICUS CURIE LAW JOURNAL 44 – 61 (2017); Robert H. Jackson, *Negative Sovereignty in Sub-Saharan Africa*, 12(4) REVIEW OF INTERNATIONAL STUDIES 247 – 264 (1968).
[26] Miriam Ronzoni, *Two Conception on State Sovereignty and Their Implications for Global Institutional Design*, 15(5) JOURNAL CRITICAL REVIEW OF INTERNATIONAL SOCIAL AND POLITICAL PHILOSOPHY, 579 (2012); available at: https://mnv.tandfonline.com/doi/pdf...13698230.2012.72730 (accessed on 27 July 2018).
See 'Telle qu'elle se présente dans la théorie classiquie du droit des gens, la notion de souveraineté, revêt, comme en droit interne, un aspect positif et un aspect négatif. Au point de vul positif, elle se caractérise par le pouvoir de donner des ordres inconditionnés; au point de vue négatif elle se défrinit par le droit de n'en recevoir d'acune autre autorité humaine. Charles Rousseau, Droit International Public, Paris t. I 1974, p. 62
[27] David Held, *The Changing Structure of International Law: Sovereignty Transformed? in* THE GLOBAL TRANSFORMATIONS READER: AN INTRODUCTION TO THE GLOBALIZATION DEBATE, Cambridge: Polity Press 164 (David Held, Anthony McGreen eds., 2003)
[28] Miriam Ronzoni see *Supra* note 26;

Czech Yearbook of International Law®

V. Sovereignty as Responsibility

8.25. The interdependence among individual States themselves and in relation to international organizations, including the supranational communities has been increasing. This process has been also affecting the concept of State sovereignty. The relationship between the State and its citizens can not be considered as a purely domestic affair any longer. States also have special human rights obligations towards foreigners in their territories, including refugees approaching their borders. States are rather reluctant to accept broad commitments to foreigners and to their interests. The 2001 Report of the International Commission on Intervention and State Sovereignty (the Report) considered the concept of sovereignty as *responsibility* of the State to protect its citizens.[29] According to the Report, State authorities are responsible for the protection of the lives and safety of their citizens and the promotion of their welfare. Besides, State authorities are responsible to the international community for their actions and omissions. There is a controversial opinion that the Report supports intervention for the protection of human rights, when major harm to civilization is occurring and the State in question is unable or unwilling to end the harm, or even if the State itself is the perpetrator. The concept of sovereignty as *responsibility* is not to be overestimated. It remains to some extent rather controversial. José E. Alvarez, the famous American author described the responsibility to protect (R2P) as *schizophrenia*, and warned against turning the idea of 'Responsibility to protect' from 'political rhetoric to legal norm'. He asks whether the R2P justifies the preemptive use of force.[30]

VI. Sovereignty and Humanity

8.26. A new concept of State sovereignty is connected with humanity. In this sense author Eyal Benvenisti has argued that 'in a densely populated and deeply integrated world, sovereignty should be understood as also involving a trusteeship toward humanity at

---

ROBERT H. JACKSON, QUASI-STATES: SOVEREIGNTY, INTERNATIONAL RELATIONS AND THE THIRD WORLD, Cambridge: Cambridge University Press 26-28 (1990).
[29] The Responsibility to protect, available at: http:responsibility-toprotect.org. According to the Report of the formal Secretary-General, the responsibility to protect ,lies, first and foremost, with individual state, whose primary *raison d´etre* and duty is to protect its population. But if national authorities are unable or unwilling to protect their citizens, then the responsibility shifts to the international community...' In Larger Freedom: Toward Development, Security and Human Rights for All. Report of the Secretary-General, par 135, UN Doc. A/592005 & annex.
[30] José E. Alvarez, *The Schizophrenia of R2P in: Human Rights intervention, and the Use of Force, in* COLLECTED COURSES OF THE ACADEMY OF EUROPEAN LAW, Oxford: Oxford University Press X12, 275-284 (Philip Alston, Ean MacDonald eds., 2008).

large...'[31] The sovereign as trustee must then 'yield to the interests of others when such a concession is costless to itself'. 'Sovereigns are entitled to award priority to the interests and values of their citizens.'[32]

8.27. Anne Peters argues that the principle of sovereignty 'is being ousted from its position as a *Letzbegründung* (first principle of international law)'. She is stressing that State sovereignty is not merely limited by human rights, but 'should be seen to exist only in function of humanity'. In her view sovereignty has thus been 'humanized'.[33] She insists that the 'responsibility to protect (R2P)' definitely 'ousted the principle of sovereignty from its position as *Letzbegründung* (first principle) of international law'.[34] Peters expressly derived the normative statues of sovereignty from *humanity*. She maintained that State sovereignty remains *foundational* only in a historical or ontological sense and 'systematically, non-intervention- not sovereignty-is constitutive for international legal order'.[35] The concept of *humanized* sovereignty is in the present international conditions rather controversial and probably premature. Various objections to her position may be raised. This is an idealistic doctrinal approach which does not so far respond to the reality of interstate relations and practice.

8.28. In the UN Charter the principle of sovereignty has been *transformed* into the principle of *sovereign equality* of States, which is still a basic principle of international law. The principle of *independence* and non-*intervention* results directly from State sovereignty. It is rather difficult to separate the principle of non-intervention from the principle of sovereignty. Sovereignty of a State was always based on *state power* and not on *humanity*. The theories of sovereignty were based on nationalism even in 19th century. There is hitherto no dismissal of State sovereignty. A sovereign State is obliged to respect basic human rights and international legal order. A concern for humanity is a legitimate claim for the sovereignty of any State.

8.29. There are also objections that humanization of sovereignty seems to open the way for humanitarian intervention. It is not possible with credibility to maintain that the prohibition on intervention is normatively derived from concerns for humanity

---

[31] Eyal Benvenisti, *Sovereigns as Trustees of Humanity: On the Accountability of States to Foreign Stateholders*, 107(2) AJIL 295, 313, 332 (2013).

[32] *Ibid.*, at 300, 314, 320.

[33] Anne Peters, *Humanity as the A and Ω of Sovereignty*, 20(3) EJIL 513 (2009).

[34] *Ibid.*, at 514. See Report of the International Comission on Intervention and State Sovereignty (ICISS), The Responsibility to Protect (2001), available at: http.://www.iciss.ca/pdf/Commission-Report.pdf (accessed on 27 July 2018).

[35] *Ibid.*, at 514-515.

only. This concept would be in discrepancy with history and the development of international law. It is difficult to deny that sovereignty is the basic feature of an independent State, its characteristic property and inalienable right. The claim that State sovereignty has its source and telos only in humanity[36] is unconvincing, despite the legal duty of every state to protect human rights. For Peters the principle of humanity serves as foundation of the international legal system. Peters contention that 'the humanization of sovereignty' has shifted the focus from rights of States to 'the needs of humans' and 'has thus promoted a significant evolution in international law in the direction of a legal obligation of the Security Council to take humanitarian action ',[37] has no relevant support in the UN Charter or in customary international law. Peters' idea that the UNSC is constrained by the *rule of law* is on the whole true, but there are no enforcement measures against this highest authority in the UN collective security system. It is unclear for example how it is possible to review the SC decisions as Peters suggests. The ICJ has no right to review the SC actions. Neither the UN Charter nor the Statue of the ICJ admit it. There is no task and possibility for the ICJ under the UN Charter to review the decisions of the UNSC.

8.30.   Peters' position has been in some respects criticized. Opponents have stated that 'it was premature to characterize the R2P principle as an emerging international legal norm', when there is 'no will to enforce commitment to it'. It was also observed that Peters 'relegated sovereignty to the statues of a second-order norm', even if it still operates as a threshold to limit intervention. Likewise it was objected that Peters´ claim that rule of law also governs decisions of the UNSC is made 'without analyzing the interrelationship between international law and politics...'[38] Another author mentioned that 'it is unclear that the Security Council is constrained by the Rule of Law', as proposed by A. Peters. In addition if R2P were considered as a relevant rule of international law 'a veto could be eventually considered illegal in the face of mass atrocity'.[39] Peters presented an *illegal* veto as a possible outcome of the adoption of R2P principles into international law. But it must be emphasized here that the notion of *limiting* the veto proposed originally in the Report of the International Commission on State Sovereignty was not included

---

[36]   See Anne Peters, *Supra* note 28, at 543.
[37]   *Ibid.*, at 540-547.
[38]   Amrita Kapur, *Humanity as the A and Ω of Sovereignty: Four Replies to Anne Peters*, 20(3) EJIL (2009).
[39]   Emily Kidd White, *Humanity as the A and Ω of Sovereignty: Four Replies to Anne Peters*, 20(3) EJIL 547-8 (2009).

in the Final document of the UN World Summit in 2005.[40] It is not the aim here to analyze in detail R2P and its relationship to sovereignty. Nevertheless this document obviously illustrates an impact of the development in international law including the influence of UN bodies on the notion of State sovereignty.

VII. Sovereignty and Rule of Law

8.31. The sovereignty of States has been closely connected with the rule of international law, which represents the basic value of legality. The rule of law in the international realm constrains the government and lawmakers. They are bound to show that they are devoted to the principle of legality in all of their dealings.[41] There are different ways of defining the rule of law. It is possible to say that the rule of law is a fundamental principle both in internal and international law as well.

8.32. For the UN, the rule of law 'refers to a principle of governance in which all persons, institutions and entities public and private, including the State itself, are accountable to laws that are publically promulgated, equally enforced and which are consistent with international human rights norms and standards. It requires, as well, measures to ensure adherence to the principles of supremacy of law, equality before the law, fairness in the application of the law, separations of powers, participation in decision making, legal certainty, avoidance of arbitrariness and procedural and legal transparency'.[42]

8.33. The concept *rule of law* has been already embodied in the UN Charter. The preamble proclaimed the aim:

> to establish conditions under which justice and respect for the obligations arising from treaties and other sources of international law can be maintained; to unite our strengths to maintain international peace and security; to reaffirm faith in fundamental human rights, in the dignity and worth of the human person, in the equal rights of men and woman and of nations large and small.

8.34. Article 1(1) is stressing the principles of justice and international law by solving international disputes or situations which might lead to a breach of the peace. Declaration on Principles of International Law Concerning Friendly Relations and Co-

---

[40] UN Doc. A/RES/60/1, 15 Sept 2005, paragraphs 138-139.

[41] Jeremy Waldron, *The Rule of International Law*, 30(1) HARWARD JOURNAL OF LAW & PUBLIC POLICY 25-26 (2006).

[42] Report of the Secretary-General on the Rule of Law and Transitional Justice in Conflict and Post-Conflict Societies, Doc. S/2004/616, Chapter III, paragraph 6, p. 4.

operation among States in Accordance with the Charter of the UN of 1970 stressed that the Declaration would contribute to the strengthening of world peace and constitute a landmark in the development of international law and of relations among states promoting the rule of law among nations and particularly the universal application of the principles embodied in the Charter.[43]

8.35. There are many articles addressing the issue of the rule of law in the international sphere, constraining governments within their national systems. Some authors start with the statement that the rule of law in international law is complicated by the fact that there is 'no overarching world government from whom we need protection'. It may be a suitable to think that if the rule of law operates in the international sphere, it must operate to 'protect the interests of the formal subjects of international law, nations states'. An opinion even appeared, that rule of law and 'sovereignty are antithetical terms'.[44]

8.36. The old ideas of world government or world police are idealistic and unrealistic conceptions. International law presumes the community of States. Author Jeremy Waldron's arguments that individuals, not States are 'the bearers of ultimate value' and that the State just 'exists for the sake of human individuals' are not sufficient to exclude States from the rights and obligations resulting for them from the rule of law.

8.37. There is also an opinion that 'sovereign states benefit only indirectly from the rule of law (for instance, in their relationships to one another), but not directly as agents of international law'. In this connection it was argued that non-democratic States are sovereign and benefit from all rights and duties of a sovereign State, but international sovereignty and democracy are sometimes held to be in *tension*.[45]

VIII. Conclusions

8.38. At the beginning of the twenty-first century sovereignty can no longer be understood in terms of 'Wesphalian sovereignty'. The contemporary notion of sovereignty attempts to restrain State sovereignty in favour of international cooperation, mutual values and prevention of human rights abuses. Non-state actors have a growing importance in international relations but it does not mean that State sovereignty is, as a matter of principle

---

[43] A/RES/25/2625, 24 October 1970.

[44] See Jeremy Waldron, *Are Sovereigns Entitled to the Benefit of the International Rule of Law?* 22(2) EJIL 315, 321, 325 (2011).

[45] Samantha Besson, *Sovereignty, International Law and Democracy*, 22(2) EJIL 373, 382 (2011).

declining in importance. The basic legal status of sovereignty politically, economically and legally is preserved in international law in a legally modified form. State sovereignty has remained the basic principle of contemporary international law. States are also main subjects or persons of international legal order. The position or status of a State in the international community depends on many factors as the recognition by other States, the possibility to become a member of international governmental organizations, and the ability to enter into agreements with other states. As a basic rule of international law all sovereign States are juridicially equal, but from the political, economic or military view they are in fact unequal.

8.39.   State sovereignty has been to some extent redeveloped in the process of globalization and international cooperation. Globalization and integration have affected even the notion of statehood and the essential functions of any State. But developing countries have remained extremely sensitive to any limitation of their sovereignty. They still highly value sovereignty as a *cornerstone* of international relations and a guaranty of their existence. It is naive to suppose that State sovereignty is likely to disappear and to expect progress towards an old idea of pan-European or even world government.

8.40.   Peter Malanczuk in his textbook with regard to sovereignty stated, that while in the West the doctrine of sovereignty has been losing much ground in view of increasing international interdependence, developing countries still value it highly as a 'cornerstone of international relations' to protect their recently gained political independence.[46] The former Soviet Union and socialist states have continuously emphasized the principle of sovereignty and territorial integrity, including the inviolability of frontiers.

8.41.   The idea of absolute sovereignty is undoubtedly an outdated concept, which was in the history of foreign relations never fully realized. In modern international law there are many factors contributing to its erosion, including international law itself, the growing number of international organizations, the internationalization of human rights protection, and the growing interdependence and co-operation among states. But there is no sign that sovereignty of the State is likely to disappear in future.

There are different theories among realists, liberal interdependence theorists or critical theorists who are arguing

---

[46]   PETER MALANCZUK, AKEHURST´S MODERN INTRODUCTION TO INTERNATIONAL LAW, London: Routledge 18 (1997).

Czech Yearbook of International Law®

about sovereignty and its practical role in world politics in the post-Cold war era. But the development in a realm of international relations, as we can see nowadays, is rather complicated. The term *state sovereignty* has been used in various meanings as 'Westphalian sovereignty', 'interdependence sovereignty' or 'international legal sovereignty', to name a few. There are sometimes different approaches to the notion of *sovereignty*. Since the second half of the twentieth century it is apparent that the classical approach to sovereignty has been changed from independence and supreme authority of a State in favor of sovereignty as interdependence and cooperation among States, where the freedom and independence of States are limited both by the freedom of other States and by international law.

8.42.   The author of this article does not support the idea of ending State sovereignty. It still remains the basic principle for policy making of a State. Sovereignty under international law, however has been modified with regard to development in the real political life of individual States and of the international community a whole.

| | |

Summaries

FRA   [*La conception moderne de la souveraineté dans le droit international contemporain*]

On entend par souveraineté d'un État, la conception juridique et politique de son pouvoir, modifiée à l'époque actuelle par les processus de mondialisation et par les avancées de l'ordre juridique international. Le présent article se focalise avant tout sur les aspects extérieurs de la souveraineté. La délégation par l'État de certains pouvoirs aux organisations internationales et le développement de la protection des droits de l'Homme imposent nécessairement des restrictions au pouvoir de l'État. Toutefois, il n'en reste pas moins que le concept même de la souveraineté de l'État implique que c'est bien l'État qui représente le sujet principal du droit international. La notion de souveraineté n'est pas rigide, mais peut varier en fonction des besoins de la communauté internationale. Malgré les objections et les doutes existants, l'auteur du présent article considère que le principe de souveraineté, pilier du droit international, représente la norme fondamentale de l'ordre juridique international. En outre, la souveraineté est une caractéristique définitoire de tout État indépendant. La « fin de la souveraineté », évoquée par certains auteurs, est un concept erroné. Il faut cependant admettre que les cas d'abus et de violation de la souveraineté dans la vie politique sont fréquents, ce qui pousse les États à invoquer les principes de souveraineté ou d'égalité souveraine. D'autres auteurs parlent du « mythe » ou de la « mythologie » de la souveraineté de l'État, laissant sous-entendre que la souveraineté est une notion vouée à la disparition. D'un autre côté, l'idée d'un État souverain, tout-puissant et doté de pouvoirs illimités, est également irréelle et mal fondée.

La souveraineté de l'État, malgré l'érosion qu'elle subit, n'a pas perdu son statut de principe fondamental du droit international. Il va sans dire que la souveraineté d'un État doit être protégée et respectée. L'auteur du présent article ne partage pas l'avis que la souveraineté a perdu sa position centrale dans le droit international, malgré sa métamorphose à l'heure de la mondialisation. Suite aux évolutions au niveau politique, économique et militaire, certains pouvoirs des États souverains ont disparu ou ont été limités.

CZE [***Moderní pojetí suverenity v soudobém mezinárodním právu***]

Suverenitou státu se rozumí právní a politická koncepce státní moci modifikovaná v současnosti procesem globalizace a rozvojem mezinárodního právního řádu. Tento článek se vztahuje především k vnější suverenitě. Přechod určitých pravomocí ze státu na mezinárodní organizace a rozvoj ochrany lidských práv nutně omezuje pravomoci jednotlivých států. Nicméně koncepce státní suverenity stále odráží skutečnost, že státy představují hlavní a rozhodující subjekty mezinárodního práva. Pojem státní suverenity není statickým pojmem, nýbrž má proměnlivý charakter v závislosti na vývoji mezinárodního společenství. Navzdory existujícím námitkám a pochybnostem považuje autor tohoto článku zásadu suverenity za jeden ze základních principů mezinárodního práva, za „základní normu" mezinárodně právního řádu. Suverenita je rovněž obligatorní vlastností každého nezávislého státu. Nelze v žádném případě hovořit o „konci" suverenity, jak se domnívají někteří autoři. Je ovšem pravdou, že často dochází ke zneužití a porušování suverenity v politice a státy se pak oprávněně dovolávají principu suverenity nebo svrchované rovnosti. Několik autorů hovoří o „mýtu" nebo „mythologii" státní suverenity. Tento přístup má naznačovat, že idea suverenity již odumírá. Rovněž myšlenka, že suverénní stát je všemocný a neomezený ve svém chování, je ovšem nerealistická a falešná.

Eroze stání suverenity neznamená, že státní suverenita ztratila svůj význam základního principu mezinárodního práva. Suverenita státu musí být přirozeně chráněna a respektována. Autor tohoto článku nesdílí názor, že suverenita ztratila své postavení základního principu v mezinárodním právu, a to i přes svou transformaci v éře globalismu. Rozvoj v politické, hospodářské i vojenské oblasti ovšem vedl k určité ztrátě nebo omezení některých pravomocí suverénních států.

| | |

POL   *[Nowoczesne postrzeganie suwerenności we współczesnym prawie międzynarodowym]*

Suwerenność państwa to podstawowa właściwość każdego niepodległego kraju oraz jedna z podstawowych zasad prawa międzynarodowego. Na treść zasady suwerenności wpływa obecnie proces globalizacji, rozwój międzynarodowej ochrony prawnej praw człowieka i cały porządek prawa międzynarodowego. Błędem byłoby jednak stwierdzenie, że suwerenność to kategoria przeszłości, co zdają się sugerować niektórzy autorzy. Szczególnie wrażliwe na własną suwerenność są nie tylko kraje „rozwojowe", ale również mocarstwa. Świadczy o tym np. polityka obecnej administracji amerykańskiego prezydenta D. Trumpa.

DEU   *[Die moderne Souveränitätsauffassung im Völkerrecht von heute]*

Die Souveränität ist grundlegende Eigenschaft eines jeden eigenständigen Staats und eines der grundlegenden Prinzipien des Völkerrechts. Mit welchem Inhalt der Grundsatz der Souveränität zu füllen ist, das wird gegenwärtig vom Globalisierungsprozess bestimmt, sowie von der Entwicklung des völkerrechtlichen Schutzes der Menschenrechte und der völkerrechtlichen Ordnung insgesamt. Freilich wäre es ein Fehler zu glauben, dass staatliche Souveränität eine bereits überwundene Kategorie darstellt, wie manche Autoren zu glauben scheinen. Wenn es um die eigene Souveränität geht, sind nicht nur „Entwicklungsländer", sondern auch Großmächte besonders empfindlich. Davon zeugt z.B. die Politik der gegenwärtigen US-Regierung unter Präsident Trump.

RUS [*Передовая концепция суверенитета в современном международном праве*]

Суверенитет государства является основным свойством каждого независимого государства и одним из основных принципов международного права. В настоящее время на содержание принципа суверенитета влияет процесс глобализации, развитие международно-правовой защиты прав человека и всего международного правопорядка. Однако было бы ошибкой полагать, что суверенитет государства представляет собой исчерпавшую себя категорию, как считают некоторые авторы. Особенно чувствительны к суверенитету не только «развивающиеся» страны, но и сверхдержавы. Об этом свидетельствует, например, политика нынешней администрации США президента Трампа.

ESP [*La interpretación moderna de la soberanía en el derecho internacional contemporáneo*]

La soberanía del Estado constituye una característica principal de cada Estado independiente y uno de los principios fundamentales del derecho internacional. El contenido del principio de soberanía está siendo influenciado por el proceso de la globalización, el desarrollo de la legislación internacional relativa a la protección de derechos humanos y de todo el ordenamiento jurídico internacional. Sin embargo, sería un error opinar, como parecen hacer varios autores, que la soberanía del Estado constituye una categoría superada. No solo países "en vías de desarrollo", sino también potencias mundiales se muestran especialmente sensibles en relación con su soberanía, lo que corrobora, por ejemplo, la política de la actual administración americana del presidente Trump.

Bibliography

José E. Alvarez, *The Schizophrenia of R2P in: Human Rights intervention, and the Use of Force, in* COLLECTED COURSES OF THE ACADEMY OF EUROPEAN LAW, Oxford: Oxford University Press X12, (Philip Alston, Ean MacDonald eds., 2008).

Eyal Benvenisti, *Sovereigns as Trustees of Humanity: On the Accountability of States to Foreign Stateholders*, 107(2) AJIL (2013).

Samantha Besson, *Sovereignty, International Law and Democracy*, 22(2) EJIL (2011).JEAN BODIN, SIX LIVRES DE LA REPUBLIQUE,

Frankfurt (1644).

IAN BROWNLIE, PRINCIPLES OF PUBLIC INTERNATIONAL LAW, Oxford University Press (4th ed. 1990).

LEON DUGUIT, LAW IN THE MODERN STATE, New York (1919).

ANDRE GARDOT, JEAN BODEN: SA PLACE PARMI LES FONDATEURS DU DROIT INTERNATIONAL, Recueil des Cours de l´Academie de Droit International, Vol. IV (RCADI) (1934).

DIETER GRIMM, SOVEREIGNTY: THE ORIGIN AND FUTURE OF A POLITICAL AND LEGAL CONCEPT, New York: Columbia University Press (2015).

FRANCIS HARRY HINSLEY, SOVEREIGNTY, Cambridge University Press 1-236 (1986); HURST HANNUM, AUTONOMY, SOVEREIGNTY AND SELF-DETERMINATION, University of Pennsylvania Press (2011).

David Held, *The Changing Structure of International Law: Sovereignty Transformed? in* THE GLOBAL TRANSFORMATIONS READER: AN INTRODUCTION TO THE GLOBALIZATION DEBATE, Cambridge: Polity Press (David Held, Anthony McGreen eds., 2003).

LUIS HENKIN, RICHARD C. PUGH, OSCAR SCHACHTER, HANS SMIT, INTERNATIONAL LAW, CASES AND MATERIALS, St. Paul (1987).

ROBERT H. JACKSON, QUASI-STATES: SOVEREIGNTY, INTERNATIONAL RELATIONS AND THE THIRD WORLD, Cambridge: Cambridge University Press (1990).

Robert H. Jackson, *Negative Sovereignty in Sub-Saharan Africa*, 12(4) REVIEW OF INTERNATIONAL STUDIES (1968).

OPPENHEIM´S INTERNATIONAL LAW, Vol. I Peace, Longman (Robert Jennings, Arthur Watts eds., 1992).

Amrita Kapur, *Humanity as the A and Ω of Sovereignty: Four Replies to Anne Peters*, 20(3) EJIL (2009).

HANS KELSEN, DAS PROBLEM DER SOUVERÄNITÄT UND DIE THEORIE DES VÖLKERRECHTS, Tübingen (1920).

HUGO KRABBE, L'IDEE MODERNE DE L'ETAT, Recueil des Cours de l´Academie de Droit International (RCADI), Vol. III (1926).

HAROLD LASKI, THE STATE IN THEORY AND PRACTICE, New York (1968).

HAROLD J. LASKI. GRAMMAR OF POLITICS, Allen& Unvin (1925).

HERSCH LAUTERPACHT, OPPENHEIM´S INTERNATIONAL LAW, Vol. I, London: Peace, Longman (1955).

JOHN LOCKE, TWO TREATIES OF GOVERNMENT, Cambridge

University 123 (1988).

PETER MALANCZUK, AKEHURST´S MODERN INTRODUCTION TO INTERNATIONAL LAW, London: Routledge (1997).

Zezen Mutaqin, *Negative Sovereignty and Positive Sovereignty, (Why the Great Powers Invade Outlaw States*, 1(4) CANTERBURY AMICUS CURIE LAW JOURNAL (2017).

LASSA FRANCISS LAWRENCE OPPENHEIM, INTERNATIONAL LAW, London, New York: Longmans (1905, 1912, 1928).

Anne Peters, *Humanity as the A and Ω of Sovereignty*, 20(3) EJIL (2009).

SAMUEL PUFFENDORF, ON THE LAW OF NATURE AND NATIONS, Oxford (1934).

Miriam Ronzoni, *Two Conception on State Sovereignty and Their Implications for Global Institutional Design*, 15(5) JOURNAL CRITICAL REVIEW OF INTERNATIONAL SOCIAL AND POLITICAL PHILOSOPHY (2012).

CHARLES ROUSSEAU, DROIT INTERNATIONAL PUBLIC, Paris: Tome II (1974).

Konrad Schiemann, *Europe and the loss of sovereignty*, (56) ICLQ (2007).

THEORY OF INTERNATIONAL LAW, Moscow 137 (Grigorij I. Tunkin ed., 1970).

Jeremy Waldron, *Are Sovereigns Entitled to the Benefit of the International Rule of Law?* 22(2) EJIL (2011).

Jeremy Waldron, *The Rule of International Law*, 30(1) HARWARD JOURNAL OF LAW & PUBLIC POLICY (2006).

Emily Kidd White, *Humanity as the A and Ω of Sovereignty: Four Replies to Anne Peters*, 20(3) EJIL (2009).

Daniela Nováčková | Andrea Holíková

The Application of Transparency Rules in Investment Arbitration as a Requirement of Sovereignty

Key words:
investment policy | foreign investment | transparency | globalization | rules

Abstract | The development of investment relations involves the protection of investors' rights, the protection of the interests of states and the correct application of the rules of international investment law. This article analyses in a broader context a case concerning the operation of foreign business entities in the territory of the Slovak Republic. The present case is interesting for international investment theory and practice, especially in terms of the jurisdiction of the International Centre for Settlement of Investment Disputes and the application of transparency rules in international investment arbitration. The authors sought to clarify the contradictions between the legal views of the plaintiffs (claimants) and the defendant (respondent), which were decisive for the issue of the arbitration award, and to identify the causes of the dispute between foreign business entities and the Slovak Republic.

| | |

Professor JUDr. Daniela Nováčková, PhD., has long been interested in issues regarding International Investment Relations. Throughout her time working at the Ministry of Finance of the Slovak Republic, she was engaged and entailed in process preparation, negotiations, and in the closing of bilateral investment treaties for the Slovak Republic. In addition to theoretical expertise, she has had also practical experience in the field of investment arbitrage procedures. At the present time, she works at the Faculty of Management, Comenius University in Bratislava, and lectures International Economic Law, as well as European Law. Subsequently, in her scholarly research activity she examines economic support issues for foreign investors and financial protection of foreign investment.
E-mail: daniela. novackova@fm.uniba.sk

Ing. JUDr. Andrea Holíková is the head of the in-house investment treaty arbitration team for the Slovak Government. Her title is Director of the Department of Specific Legal Affairs of the Ministry of Finance of the Slovak Republic.

I. Introduction

9.01. As part of its membership in several international organisations, the Slovak Republic removed the obstacles of free movement of capital and created the conditions for the inflow of foreign investments. As a consequence of the removal and the introduction of non-discrimination based on nationality within the framework of the Slovak Commercial Code, several foreign companies came to Slovakia. These included EuroGas Inc., an oil and gas company incorporated under the laws of the United States (EuroGas), and Belmont Resources Inc., a company incorporated under the laws of Canada (Belmont).

> As head of her legal team within the Slovak Republic, Andrea Holíková is charged with the defense of the country against claims brought by foreign investors against the State under bilateral and multilateral investment treaties. Andrea Holíková coordinates and leads an in-house team who work on these arbitrations, as well as an external legal team from many of the largest firms in the world. E-mail: andrea.holikova@mfsr.sk

9.02. In the course of their business activities, these companies searched for mineral deposits in Slovakia. These foreign companies (EuroGas and Belmont) filed a complaint with the International Centre for Settlement of Investment Disputes (ICSID) based on alleged infringement of *the Treaty between the United States of America and the Czech and Slovak Federal Republic.*[1] The treaties were known as the *Treaty Concerning the Reciprocal Encouragement and Protection of Investment,* entered into force on 19 December 1992, and the *Agreement between Canada and the Slovak Republic for the Promotion and Protection of Investments,* entered into force on 14 March 2012.[2] Additionally, they were concerned about alleged restrictions of mining rights. At the same time, EuroGas and Belmont claimed before the arbitration tribunal that the principles of fair and equitable treatment and denial of justice were violated. One of the consequences of globalization is that it enables the development of international investment relations and provides for the movement of capital. This study clarifies the essential facts and circumstances relating to the arbitration case. The goal of this scholarly study is to present the current the application of rules in the Slovak Republic, with broader implications to international investment law.

---

[1] Treaty between the United States of America and the Czech and Slovak Federal Republic Concerning the Reciprocal Encouragement and Protection of Investment. Act. No. 183/1993.

[2] Agreement between Canada and the Slovak Republic for the Promotion and Protection of Investments. Act No. 6/2012.

II. Methodology

9.03. The main method of the study is the analysis of the case filed by *the EuroGas, and Belmont* v. *the Slovak Republic* (Case No. ARB/14/14).[3] We applied two methods of analysis and synthesis in the drafting of this study. First, we have analyzed the opinions of experts on the principle of transparency. In turn, we have been monitoring the relationships and processes between the facts, as well as the nature of the interrelationships between them, in order to produce a broader synthesis. We have relied on scholarly literature, the case law of the courts and international treaties related to the investments and the movement of capital. Secondly, the authors not only have theoretical knowledge but also applied practical experience in this area in writing this scholarly study. The analysis of the study is structured as follows: First, we will discuss theoretical aspects, and the legal and theoretical aspects of transparency measures in ICSID. Subsequently, we will focus on the practical aspects, with an analysis of the substantive arguments and facts having influenced the decision of the ICSID in the case.

III. Theoretical and Legal Aspects of Transparency Rules

9.04. In the interest of introducing fair rules in the field of investment relations, international organizations adopt rules with different legal nature. The United Nations General Assembly adopted a resolution on 10 December 2014 entitled the 'Convention on Transparency in Treaty-based Investor-State Arbitration' (69/116).[4] The Convention is known as the 'Mauritius Convention on Transparency'. The major aim of the Convention was to provide an instrument for the application of the UNCITRAL Rules on transparency to disputes arising under existent investment treaties. The Mauritius Convention on Transparency established a new level of enhancing transparency in Investor - State treaty arbitration. It modernized the rules on transparency that would be included in modern investment treaties with the goal of higher quality Investor - State arbitration. The Mauritius Convention on Transparency created mechanisms that allow public access to necessary information about disputes, proceedings, arbitrators and final awards. It

---

[3] *EuroGas Inc. and Belmont Resources Inc.* v. *Slovak Republic*, ICSID Case No. ARB/14/14, 2014, available at: https://www.italaw.com/cases/3210 (accessed on 4 June 2018).
[4] United Nations: Convention on Transparency in Treaty-based Investor-State Arbitration, 2014, available at: http://www.unis.unvienna.org/unis/en/pressrels/2014/unisl210.html (accessed on 5 June 2018).

established a harmonized legal framework for a fair and efficient settlement of international investment disputes. Its goals were to increase transparency and accountability and promote good governance.[5]

9.05. 'Transparency can be introduced in two ways. It can be introduced as a requirement in the investment treaty on which the arbitration is based and it can also be introduced into arbitration rules.'[6]

9.06. The United States and Canadian model bilateral investment treaties were the first to introduce provisions granting the public access to investor-State dispute hearings and documents (Article 29 of the United States' Model). At present the Agreement between Canada and the Slovak Republic for the Promotion and Protection of Investments, which entered into force on 14 March 2012 contains a provision on transparency in the framework of arbitration proceedings (Annex B).

9.07. Transparency can be introduced in three ways: in the rules of international organisations, in investment treaties and in the decision of the investments tribunal. International investment arbitrations contribute to legal certainty and to the development of international investment law. Legal theory considers the decisions of the courts (case law) as the main source of the law in the common law system. Precedent is recognised as the formally binding source of law in Anglo-American legal culture and in international law. In this connection we can point out several cases. The tribunal in *Suez and others v. Argentina* (ICISD Decision, *Suez v. Argentina*, ICSID ARB/03/17 & 19)[7] held that 'public acceptance of the legitimacy of international arbitral processes, particularly when they involve states and matters of public interest, is strengthened by increased openness and increased knowledge as to how these processes function' (Case No ARB/03/19, paragraph 22).[8]

9.08. The transparency rules have already been applied in cases *Iberdrola, SA and Iberdrola Energia SAU v. Bolivia* (PCA Case

---

[5]   United Nations: Convention on Transparency in Treaty-based Investor-State Arbitration, 2014, available at: http://www.unis.unvienna.org/unis/en/pressrels/2014/unisl210.html (accessed on 5 June 2018).

[6]   Fola Adeleke, *The Role of Law in Assessing the Value of Transparency and the Disconnect with the Lived Realities under Investor-State Dispute Settlement*, Working Paper No. 06/2015 November 2015, University Bern. World Trade Institut 14 (2015).

[7]   *Suez, Sociedad General de Aguas de Barcelona S.A., and InterAguas Servicios Integrales del Agua S.A. v. The Argentine Republic*, (formerly Aguas Provinciales de Santa Fe S.A, Suez, Sociedad General de Aguas de Barcelona, S.A.) ICSID Case No. ARB/03/17, 2010, available at: https://www.italaw.com/cases/1048 (accessed on 5 June 2018).

[8]   *Suez, Sociedad General de Aguas de Barcelona, S.A.and Vivendi Universal, S.A. v. Argentine Republic*, ICSID Case No. ARB/03/19, 2018 (formerly *Aguas Argentinas, S.A., Suez, Sociedad General de Aguas de Barcelona, S.A.and Vivendi Universal, S.A. v. Argentine Republic*), available at: https://www.italaw.com/cases/1057 (accessed on 5 June 2018).

No 2015-05)[9] and *BSG Resources Limited* v. *Republic of Guinea* (ICSID Case No ARB/14/22).[10]

9.09. Transparency has been addressed by several authors at the international level. Abraham Chayes and Antonia Handler Chayes define transparency 'as the availability and accessibility of knowledge and information about the meaning of norms, rules, and procedures established by the treaty and practice of the regime, and the policies and activities of parties to the treaty and of any central organs of the regime as to matters relevant to treaty compliance and regime efficacy.'[11]

9.10. Rawlins defines transparency as 'the deliberate attempt to make available all legally releasable information, whether positive or negative in nature, in a manner that is accurate, timely, balanced and unequivocal, for the purpose of enhancing the reasoning ability of the public and holding organisations accountable for their actions, policies, and practices.'[12]

9.11. Transparency and equal treatment enables the public to understand better investment policy, by which the system of international investment arbitration becomes more credible and effective. Introducing transparency reduces suspicions of lobbying and protectionism. Effective transparency efforts by decision-makers require self-discipline, which guarantees the stability, legality and legitimacy of their arbitration awards and their justifications. The possibility of public control in the area of investment disputes increases the motivation of decision-making bodies to perform their tasks in the best possible way and in accordance with the applicable legislation. 'The transparency elements in most of these principles focus on the traditional objective of transparency provisions to eliminate information costs and institutional risks facing investors. Some of these principles have an additional focus on balancing State and investor rights and obligations to facilitate the sustainable development of the host State.'[13] In this connection we are of the opinion that transparency is an important principle in international investment law. In investment arbitration there

---

[9]   *Iberdrola, S.A. and Iberdrola Energía, S.A.U.* v. *Plurinational State of Bolivia*, PCA, ICSID Case No. 2015-05, 2016, available at: https://www.italaw.com/cases/3659 (accessed on 5 June 2018).
[10]   *BSG Resources Limited, BSG Resources (Guinea) Limited and BSG Resources (Guinea) SÀRL* v. *Republic of Guinea*, ICSID Case No. ARB/14/22, 2015, available at: https://www.italaw.com/cases/3688 (accessed on 5 June 2018).
[11]   ABRAHAM CHAYES, ANTONIA HANDLER CHAYES, THE NEW SOVEREIGNTY. Cambridge, Mass: Harvard University Press 135-153 (1995).
[12]   Brad Rawlins, *Give the emperor a mirror. Toward developing a stakeholder measurement of organizational transparency*, JOURNAL OF PUBLIC RELATIONS RESEARCH 75 (2009).
[13]   UNCTAD: Transparency UNCTAD Series on Issues in International Investment Agreements II New York and Geneva, 2012, et. 3, available at http://unctad.org/en/PublicationsLibrary/unctaddiaeia2011d6_en.pdf. (accessed on 5 June 2018).

is a tension between the consensual commercial character of a dispute and an increasing need to offer transparent proceedings where a public interest is involved.[14] In addition to the principle of transparency, we also incorporate the principle of responsibility and greater democratic legitimacy to the decision-making process in investment arbitration. The Slovak Republic to full extent supports transparency rules not only through investment rules, but also on a practical level.

IV.   The Coordination of the Development of International Investment Relations

9.12.   Due to the development of international economic and investment relations in Slovakia the number of foreign companies doing business in Slovakia has grown. The Slovak Republic entered into international obligations as the subject of international law beginning in 1993. The coordination over the Bilateral Investment Treaties has been entrusted to the Ministry of Finance of the Slovak Republic. The Ministry of Finance of the Slovak Republic has more than a decade of experience with the successful defence of the Slovak Republic in international investment arbitration. Looking over this period it can be stated that the balance of the Slovak Republic's results obtained in the field of international investment arbitration against a State is exceptionally positive in global comparison with the other defendant States. The Slovak Republic faced eleven international investment arbitrations with the claimed compensation in the overall amount almost 1,840 billion euro. It was not successful only in the first arbitration, specifically the commercial arbitration between the bank ČSOB, JSC (Czecho-Slovak Commercial Bank, the joint stock company) and the Slovak Republic. The reason for filing this case was the financial claim of the ČSOB, JSC that was related to the credits provided within the framework of the recovery of the company (No. ARB/97/4).[15]

9.13.   The Ministry of Finance of the Slovak Republic learned during international investment arbitration to effectively manage crisis situations as well as to successfully manage challenging and complicated legal disputes. It gained know-how in guiding the Ministry of Finance them tactically and it set up a mechanism

---

[14]   Maciej Zachariasiewicz, *Amicus Curiae in International Investment Arbitration: Can It Enhance the Transparency of Investment Dispute Resolution?* 29(2) JOURNAL OF INTERNATIONAL ARBITRATION 205–224 (2012).

[15]   Československá *obchodní banka, a.s.* v. *Slovak Republic*, ICSID Case No. ARB/97/4), 2004, available at: https://icsid.worldbank.org/en/Pages/cases/casedetail.aspx?CaseNo=ARB/97/4 (accessed on 5 June 2018).

for legal disputes held against the State. This has led to the Ministry of Finance of the Slovak Republic being the first public institution in the world to receive a world-renowned institutional award in 2016 (Financial Times - Most innovative law firms: In-house legal teams).

9.14. In on-going arbitration it is essential and primary for the Ministry of Finance to defend the interests of the Slovak Republic as[16] a whole. For the Slovak Republic, International investment arbitrations represent, in the end, the 'account exposure', or, respectively, the forum of last resort for assessing the rate of implementation of international commitments stemming from bilateral investment treaties. In the case of a State's loss in international investment arbitrage, public interest or specially protected public goods, such as water, mineral wealth or public funds, can be indirectly jeopardized. Similar aspects can be also observed in big domestic disputes held against the Slovak Republic.

9.15. Due to its membership in the European Union the Slovak Republic in concluding the international treaties in the field of investment relations fully complies with the EU Regulation No 1219/2012 of the European Parliament and of the Council of 12 December 2012 establishing transitional arrangements for bilateral investment agreements between Member States and third countries (OJ EU L 351.20.12.2012). Within the meaning of this regulation the negotiations on agreement on the protection and mutual support of investments can take place only on the basis of prior authorisation of the European Commission. The negotiated bilateral investment agreement is subsequently subjected to the authorisation of the European Commission. The Slovak Republic has concluded more than 50 international agreements of this type. Nonetheless, due to its membership in the European Union the international agreements in force had to be amended to comply with the legal acts of the European Union. They are international treaties and thus they prevail over the laws under Article 7 paragraph 5 of the Constitution of the Slovak Republic. The barriers of free movement of capital have been removed by the membership of the Slovak Republic in the EU. A significant part of international investment law is formed by the case law established during the disputes where the Slovak Republic was one of the parties to the proceedings. It helps to clarify the phenomena and processes related to investments and brings certain rules into investment relations. Within the

---

[16] Available at: http://rankings.ft.com/innovativelawyers/most-innovative-law-firms-2016-in-house-legal -team (accessed on 5 June 2018).

framework of international investment arbitration there are a number of cases that can be used as examples, however, we have opted for this case involving the Slovak Republic as the defendant.

V.   State Sovereignty over Natural Resources

9.16.   State sovereignty and the sovereign right of a State for the protection of its mineral and natural resources is also related to 'the problem to be discussed below'. The sovereignty of the State can be defined as the biggest independent power of the State, i.e. the independence of State power from any other power that cannot be limited in any way. 'Permanent sovereignty over natural resources is a firmly established standard of international law that authorizes states to exercise exclusive jurisdiction over natural resources and all components of the natural environment within their national boundaries.'[17] The Slovak Republic has the sovereignty principle anchored in the Constitution of the Slovak Republic in the following wording: 'The territory of the Slovak Republic is integral and indivisible'. 'Borders of the Slovak Republic may be changed only by a constitutional law.' (Act No.460/1992) The economic basis of the sovereignty of the Slovak Republic is enshrined in Article 4 of the Constitution of the Slovak Republic. This Article stipulates that 'Mineral resources, caves, underground waters, natural healing sources and streams are a property of the Slovak Republic.' It can be briefly stated that the sovereignty of the Slovak Republic includes State ownership of mineral resources, underground waters, natural healing sources and streams, territorial integrity, and the State budget. It follows from the above that mineral wealth is the property of the State. Subsequently we can also talk about the constitutional principle of the protection of mineral resources in Slovakia. In addition to the Constitution of the Slovak Republic, Law no. 44/1988 Coll. on the Protection of the Use of Mineral Resources in its Article Section 5 paragraph 5 also regulates that mineral resources are owned by the Slovak Republic, as mineral resources are not renewable and must be protected and used effectively. A sovereign State has natural resources in its territory and decides independently on their

---

[17]   Petra Gümplová, *Restraining permanent sovereignty over natural resources*, 53 ENRAHONAR. QUADERNS DE FILOSOFIA, 93-114 (2014), available at: https://ddd.uab.cat/pub/enrahonar/enrahonar_a2014v53/enrahonar_a2014v53p93.pdf (accessed on 5 June 2018)

use. In this context the Slovak Republic has an exclusive right to issue mining permits for mineral resources located in its territory as well as to determine the rights and obligations for all involved subjects and entities. The State acts as a sovereign, which includes the condition that it will act responsibly, will protect its national interests, and protect the security and lives of its citizens, as well as mineral wealth and its efficient use.

VI.   Case Study

9.17.   By the end of December 2013 the Slovak Republic received a notification about the dispute of the claim from EuroGas, and Belmont. They were claimants in the case, and were alleged shareholders of the mining company Rozmin Ltd., that owned the mining authorisation to extract talc in Gemerská Poloma, Slovakia. After the expiration of a 6 month deadline for friendly settlement of the dispute on 25 June 2014, the two foreign companies filed a notification to commence arbitration in the International Centre for Settlement of Investment Disputes (ICSID). This formally started the arbitration proceedings against the Slovak Republic. This was conducted under the Convention on the Settlement of Investment Disputes between States and Nationals of Other States, which entered into force on 14 October 1966 (ICSID Convention). Investment disputes are resolved under various international bodies which apply different rules.

9.18.   The international investment arbitration proceedings were initiated due to a violation of The Treaty between the United States of America and the Czech and Slovak Federal Republic Concerning the Reciprocal Encouragement and Protection of Investment, and an Agreement between Canada and the Slovak Republic for the promotion and protection of investments (entering into force in the year 2012).

9.19.   Despite the media coverage of damages to the Slovak Republic in the amount up to $ 1.65 billion, the foreign investors claimed compensation of damages in the amount of a minimum of 240 billion Euro for the alleged removal of mining authorisation as a consequence of the decisions taken by the Slovak administrative authorities and courts.

9.20.   In order to clarify the factual situation we consider it useful to point out the fact that in the year 1997 the District Mining Office in Spišská Nová Ves approved the transfer of mining rights from the Geological Survey (a State-owned entity) to the company Rozmin, Ltd. In the same year the Mining Office in Spišská Nová Ves issued mining authorisation to company Rozmin, Ltd. that

Czech Yearbook of International Law®

enabled it to perform mining activities in the mining site until 31 December 2002 subject to complying with the conditions of the originally determined mining site and mining rights to the Gemerská Poloma.

9.21. The Claimants stated that EuroGas first became an indirect shareholder of Rozmin in 1998, when EuroGas GmbH, a wholly-owned subsidiary of EuroGas incorporated in Austria, purchased an interest in one of Rozmin's three initial shareholders. Then, in 2002, as a result of subsequent stock purchase agreements, EuroGas GmbH became the direct owner of a 33% interest in Rozmin (*infra* paragraph 40 No. ARB/14/14). On 24 February 2000, Belmont allegedly acquired a 57% share in Rozmin. *(infra* paragraph 42 No. ARB/14/14).

9.22. In the meantime the National Council of the Slovak Republic approved an amendment to the Law on the Protection and Use of Mineral Resources (Mining Law) that entered into force as of 1 January 2002. It was decisive for the claimants that Article 27 paragraph 12 of the amendment of the Mining Law of 2002 introduced a new rule relating to subjects with the determined mining area. According to the valid legal regulation if such an entity does not start mining within three years from the designation or if mining is interrupted for a period of more than three years, the mining authority either cancels its decision on the designation of a mining area or it designates it to another entity. With regard to the fact that in the period between 1 January 2002 and 1 January 2005 the company Rozmin, Ltd. was not mining in the determined area nor did it perform other related activities necessary to mining. Consistent with Article 27 paragraph 12 of the Mining Law the mining rights were revoked from the company and were to be awarded to a new company at the beginning of the year 2005. The Slovak authorities did this on the basis of the fact that Rozmin did not use the mining authorisation for talc in Gemerská Poloma within the three years and thus did not act in accordance with its original investment intention.

9.23. Claimants argued that revocation and assignment of mining rights to another entity was unjustified and unlawful, on the basis of decisions of the Slovak courts rendered in proceedings subsequently instituted by company Rozmin Ltd. The claimants indicated that the decisions of the Slovak court required the local authorities to renew the expired mining authorisation in Gemerská Poloma to Rozmin, Ltd. On the contrary, the Slovak Republic, in the arbitration proceedings claimed that it was stated in the decisions of the Slovak courts that the process of assignment of mining rights was not appropriate from the point of view of international law due to procedural, and not substantive deficiencies and that the mining area had to be assigned to a third person according to the applicable legal regulation. The Slovak mining authorities repeatedly proceeded in accordance with decisions of Slovak courts, remedied all the procedural deficiencies and re-assigned the mining rights to another company.

9.24.   The dispute was divided procedurally by the arbitration tribunal in such a way that the jurisdiction and substance of the dispute were dealt by the tribunal in the first phase of arbitration proceedings. If the tribunal would reach the conclusion that it was competent to hear the case and that one or two international treaties were infringed, only then would it decide in the second phase of arbitration proceedings about the amount of compensation required by both claimants.

9.25.   The tribunal rendered its decision in August 2017 on the basis of arguments raised by the Slovak Republic that challenged the jurisdiction of ICSID in the case. The tribunal accepted these challenges to jurisdiction raised by the Slovak Republic and held that it was not competent to hear the case and to decide in the dispute. The ICSID ruling enabled the parties to file a request for the annulment of the decision of the tribunal. The company EuroGas appealed the decision of the tribunal which was in favour of Slovakia.

9.26.   The tribunal unanimously accepted the objections to jurisdiction raised by the Slovak Republic in the dispute in relation to the claimant EuroGas. As regards the claimant Belmont, the tribunal in the ratio of 2:1 recognised the time limitation of the possibility to settle the dispute that was introduced by the new bilateral investment agreement between the Slovak Republic and Canada in 2012. The tribunal recognised that the dispute arose in 2005, when the amendment of the Mining Law had to be applied for the first time when the mining area in Gemerská Poloma was assigned to another company.

9.27.   In regards to the claimant EuroGas it was found in the course of arbitration that the original company EuroGas incorporated under US laws went bankrupt in 2004 and in 2005 another company with the same name EuroGas was established. This information was not disclosed to the Slovak Republic until the arbitration proceedings. The company incorporated in 1985 in Utah as 'EuroGas, Inc' was dissolved abolished in 2001 and went bankrupt in 2004. In the course of bankruptcy proceedings the company representatives established the new company in

Utah with the same name 'EuroGas Inc', with its seat in the same address and with the same directors and managers. After the finalisation of the bankruptcy proceedings both companies seemingly merged.

The objection to jurisdiction raised from the side of the Slovak Republic consisted in claiming that it is not possible to validly qualify the company 'EuroGas II' as an investor under the provisions of Agreement between the United States and the Czech and Slovak Federative Republic for the Promotion and Protection of Investments on the basis of the ownership of shares in company EuroGas GmbH, who was the direct shareholder in the company Rozmin, Ltd. at the time of re-assignment of mining rights to the company Rozmin, Ltd. With the aim to prove this jurisdictional objection and with a legal analysis of the legal order of state of Utah, the Slovak Republic reached the conclusion that such a transaction would not be possible without infringement of the respective laws. With regard to the fact that the company 'EuroGas I' did not come out from the bankruptcy proceedings with its share owned in the company Rozmin, Ltd., the company EuroGas II could never own the investment and therefore the tribunal did not have the jurisdiction to hear this case related to EuroGas II.

9.28. In order to establish its jurisdiction in relation to the company EuroGas II the tribunal held that company EuroGas II had to prove two conditions. First, it had to prove that at the time when the bankruptcy proceedings in state of Utah on 19 March 2007 were closed, the company EuroGas I Ltd. owned shares in the company EuroGas GmbH and thus the company owned the claim relating to the re-assignment of the mining rights in 2005. Secondly, it had to prove that the company EuroGas I validly transferred its claim relating to the re-assignment to the company EuroGas II.

9.29. The tribunal held that the claimant company 'EuroGas II' did not provide any grounds on the basis of the laws of the State of Utah which could confirm the validity of the merger of two companies. Since this merger was unlawful, no rights that were claimed in the arbitration proceedings could be transferred to the claimant 'EuroGas II'. For this reason the tribunal held that the companies 'EuroGas I' and 'EuroGas II' merged unlawfully, and that the claims for talc related to the re-assignment of the mining area that were subject-matter of the arbitration proceedings could not be transferred from the company 'EuroGas I' to the company 'EuroGas II'.

9.30. In the case of company Belmont Resources the tribunal acknowledged the limitations of time for resolving the alleged dispute that was introduced by the new Agreement between Canada and the Slovak Republic for the Promotion and Protection of Investments of 2012. The Slovak Republic claimed that the tribunal was not competent *ratione temporis* (in terms of time jurisdiction). In its Article 15 paragraph 6 of the Agreement between Canada and the Slovak Republic for the Promotion and Protection of Investments it is established that 'this Agreement shall apply to any dispute which has arisen not more than three years prior to its entry into force'. This agreement entered into force as of 14 March 2012. The Slovak Republic therefore argued stating that the tribunal has competence to decide only in disputes that arose from 14 March 2009 or later and that alleged claim of company Belmont arose only in 2005, when the mining area was assigned to third person. However, the claimants argued that some of the court proceedings held in the Slovak courts started in relation to the re-assignment of the mining area to a third person were finished only after 2009.

9.31. After having considered all facts and submitted evidence, the tribunal did not accept the arguments of the claimants, according to which the investor could revoke the infringement of the law from the side of the Slovak authorities.

9.32. Furthermore, it was in this case for the first time that the identification of third party financing costs related to the dispute on the side of claimants was successful. The decision confirms that security for costs orders are the exception, even where the claimants have third party funding (see Saint Lucia (ICSID Case No ARB/12/10)).[18]

9.33. At the same time the Slovak Republic has unprecedentedly applied the so-called 'denial of benefits'. The tribunal's judgment also contributed to the widening of jurisprudence in international investment law by its way of identifying the origin of dispute.

VII.   Research Results

9.34. International investment arbitrations have their origin mainly in alleged infringement of the rules stipulated in bilateral investment treaties concluded between sovereign States with the aim to promote and protect investments. However, a real legal ground should exist so that the arbitration proceedings can commence and the causal link can be established between

---

[18]   *RSM Production Corporation* v. *Saint Lucia*, ICSID Case No. ARB/12/10, 2010, available at: https://www.italaw.com/cases/2706 (accessed on 5 June 2018).

infringed rights of the entitled subjects and the damage. The given dispute represents the fundamental contribution not only to theory, but also to practice, because it brought some unprecedential elements from the point of view of the development of international investment law. It is in international investment arbitration where transparency of these proceedings has been considerably increased due to the application of the Agreement between Canada and the Slovak Republic for the Promotion and Protection of Investments, which entered into force on 14 March 2012, and specifically regarding its *'transparency'* provisions of Annex B. This Agreement regulates the transparency rules as well. Besides the judgement and procedural decisions of the tribunal all submissions of procedural parties were published, as well as the transcript and video record from the five day proceedings. Such publicity of arbitration proceedings contributes to the strengthening of the institute of justice, impartiality, fairness and credibility of the ICSID. Such an attitude has a fundamental significance for business entities, since it has not only a legal, but also an ethical dimension. Transparency in this context could also be understood as making information public in an understandable manner, including the substantive information on the arbitration proceedings and decisions of international arbitration tribunals. As a result, investment arbitration has a chance to earn a better reputation and through public participation contribute to an increase of democratic principles of accountability, and the legitimacy of States involved in investment disputes in the public eye.

VIII. Conclusion

9.35. An open investment environment contributes to the growth of GDP, the growth of employment, and regional development around the world. Nonetheless it is essential for everyone to apply the same rules. New investment trends in the current round of globalization are focused on international cross-border mergers and acquisitions. Foreign investment is increasingly focusing on the search for new markets and strategic assets. The Slovak Republic became attractive for foreign companies that were interested in realizing their business intentions there. On the basis of the synthesis of knowledge we reached the conclusion that not every business entity is doing business in compliance with good morals *(bonos mores)*. Just and fair decisions of the arbitration tribunal helped us to understand the truth and the background relations concerning the business activities of foreign companies in Slovakia. The evidence and suitable legal argumentation from the side of the Slovak Republic have contributed to a fair and just decision of arbitration tribunals. At the same time the foreign companies made use of their right for a fair trial.

| | |

Summaries

DEU [*Die Anwendung der Transparenzregeln im Investitionsschiedsverfahren als sich aus der Souveränität ergebende Anforderung*]
Die Autorinnen analysieren in ihrem wissenschaftlichen Beitrag den vom Internationalen Zentrum zur Beilegung von Investitionsstreitigkeiten entschiedenen Fall des Abbaus nicht erneuerbarer Rohstoffe auf dem Gebiet der Slowakei. Verfahrensbeteiligte waren kommerzielle ausländische Unternehmen einerseits und die Slowakische Republik andererseits. Die ausländischen Rechtsträger beriefen sich im Schiedsverfahren auf die Verletzung der Bestimmungen des bilateralen Investitionsschutzabkommens als Auslöser für die Streitigkeit. Im Artikel klären die Autorinnen den Begriff der Staatshoheit in den breiteren Zusammenhängen und verweisen auf das Recht von Staaten, über die Bodenschätze im Eigentum des Staats zu verfügen und diese zu schützen. Geklärt wird außerdem das ausschließliche Recht nationaler Autoritäten, Abbaugenehmigungen für Bodenschätze innerhalb ihres Gebiets zu erteilen und die Rechte und Pflichten derjenigen zu bestimmen, die Abbaurechte erworben haben. Das Ergebnis des o.g. Schiedsverfahrens ist nicht nur für die Theorie des internationalen Investitionsrechts von Bedeutung, sondern auch für die schiedsrichterliche Praxis, insofern als in der vorliegenden Streitigkeit die Transparenzregeln zur Anwendung kamen.

CZE [*Aplikace pravidel transparentnosti v investiční arbitráži jako požadavek vyplývající ze suverenity*]
Autorky ve svém vědeckém článku rozebírají případ rozhodovaný Mezinárodním střediskem pro rozhodování investičních sporů týkající se těžby nerostných surovin na území Slovenské republiky. Účastníky řízení byly zahraniční podnikatelské subjekty a Slovenská republika. Zahraniční podnikatelské subjekty uváděly jako důvod sporu projednávaného v rozhodčím řízení porušení ustanovení dvoustranné smlouvy o ochraně investic. V článku autorky v širších souvislostech objasňují institut státní suverenity

a poukazují na právo státu disponovat a chránit nerostné bohatství, jehož vlastníkem je stát. Objasňují rovněž výlučné právo národních autorit vydávat povolení k těžbě nerostných surovin na svém území a určovat práva a povinnosti pro všechny subjekty, které získaly těžební práva. Výsledek rozhodčího řízení má význam nejen pro teorii mezinárodního investičního práva, ale i pro praxi rozhodčího řízení, neboť v daném sporu byla aplikována pravidla transparentnosti.

| | |

POL   [*Stosowanie zasad transparentności w arbitrażu inwestycyjnym jako wymóg wynikający z suwerenności*]
Niniejszy artykuł naukowy stara się zwrócić uwagę na problemy prawne dotyczące działalności na terenie Słowacji zagranicznych przedsiębiorstw, które zainicjowały międzynarodowe postępowanie arbitrażowe przeciwko Słowacji. Zagraniczna spółka handlowa korzysta wówczas ze swojego prawa do sprawiedliwego procesu. Przedmiotem sporu między stronami było wydobycie surowców kopalnych na Słowacji. Zagraniczne spółki handlowe domagały się wydania orzeczenia potwierdzającego naruszenie umowy dwustronnej w sprawie ochrony inwestycji. W niniejszym artykule naukowym zwrócono uwagę na fakt, że środki dowodowe oraz właściwa argumentacja prawna ze strony Republiki Słowackiej przyczyniły się do wydania sprawiedliwego orzeczenia przez trybunał arbitrażowy.

FRA   [*L'application des règles de transparence dans l'arbitrage d'investissement à la lumière de la souveraineté*]
Le présent article se propose d'aborder les problèmes juridiques relatifs à certaines entreprises étrangères actives sur le territoire de la République slovaque et qui ont intenté une procédure d'arbitrage internationale à l'encontre de cet État. Ces entreprises étrangères ont fait valoir leur droit à un procès équitable, l'objet du litige étant l'extraction minière en Slovaquie. Leur demande tendait à ce que le juge constate qu'il y a eu violation d'un contrat bilatéral relatif à la protection des investissements. Les moyens de preuve, ainsi qu'une argumentation adéquate de la part de la République slovaque, ont contribué à ce que la chambre arbitrale rende une décision équitable.

RUS [*Применение правил прозрачности в инвестиционном арбитраже как требование, вытекающее из суверенитета*]

Целью данной научной статьи является определение правовых проблем, связанных с действием иностранных предпринимательских субъектов на территории Словацкой Республики, которые были инициаторами международного арбитража против Словакии. Иностранные торговые компании воспользовались своим правом на справедливый процесс. Предметом спора между субъектами была добыча полезных ископаемых в Словакии. Иностранные торговые компании требовали вынести решения о нарушении двустороннего договора о защите инвестиций. Кроме того, данная научная статья указывает на тот факт, что средства доказывания, а также соответствующие юридические аргументы Словацкой Республики способствовали справедливому вынесению решения составом арбитражного суда.

ESP [*La aplicación de las normas de transparencia en el arbitraje de inversiones como un requisito derivado de la soberanía*]

El objetivo del presente texto científico es llamar la atención sobre cuestiones jurídicas relacionadas con la actividad de empresas extranjeras en el territorio de la República Eslovaca que iniciaron un procedimiento de arbitraje internacional contra Eslovaquia. Las compañías mercantiles extranjeras hicieron uso de su derecho a un proceso justo. El litigio entre las partes radicaba en la extracción de materias primas minerales en Eslovaquia. Las compañías mercantiles extranjeras reivindicaban una decisión según la que el contrato bilateral sobre la protección de la inversión había sido violado. Entre otros, el presente artículo científico señala que los medios probatorios, así como la adecuada argumentación jurídica empleada por parte de la República Eslovaca contribuyeron a una resolución justa por parte de la sala de arbitraje.

||||

Bibliography

Fola Adeleke, *The Role of Law in Assessing the Value of Transparency and the Disconnect with the Lived Realities under Investor-State Dispute Settlement*, Working Paper No. 06/2015 November 2015, University Bern. World Trade Institut (2015).

ABRAHAM CHAYES, ANTONIA HANDLER CHAYES, THE NEW SOVEREIGNTY. Cambridge, Mass: Harvard University Press (1995).

Petra Gümplová, *Restraining permanent sovereignty over natural resources*, 53 ENRAHONAR. QUADERNS DE FILOSOFIA, 93-114 (2014).

Brad Rawlins, *Give the emperor a mirror. Toward developing a stakeholder measurement of organizational transparency*, JOURNAL OF PUBLIC RELATIONS RESEARCH 75 (2009).

Maciej Zachariasiewicz, *Amicus Curiae in International Investment Arbitration: Can It Enhance the Transparency of Investment Dispute Resolution?* 29(2) JOURNAL OF INTERNATIONAL ARBITRATION (2012).

Czech Yearbook of International Law®

Peter Papáček

The Impact of the Deteriorating Environment on the Status and Roles of States

Key words:
deteriorating environment | State sovereignty | restriction | common good | protection | control

Abstract | This paper deals with the status and role of a sovereign State in connection to the deteriorating environment, requiring some global protection and control. The environmental arena is globally accepted as one of the most important for global welfare and sustainable development. For that reason it is not surprising that this area can influence the role and status of a State. The first section introduces the very meaning of State sovereignty and its connection to the environment. The second section deals with the issue of the restriction of State sovereignty. It asks how States got to the point that under pressure of the common good they had to restrict their authoritative power on their own territories. The importance of international law and international agreements are highlighted. As a case, the article focuses on the Gabčíkovo-Nagymaros Project case which is based in the Slovak Republic. Analysis of this case gives us a good sense of how the international law is connected to environmental control and protection can limit the sovereign role of the States even if the object is on its own territory. The third section explains the problems of implementation of international environmental obligations and the complicated political situation connected to it. The problems could be based on the costs of the fight against the environment´s deterioration and the costs of industrial development. The complicated political situation reflects the need of the public for a good quality environment. The last section deals with environmental non-government organisations which are a reflection of the civil

JUDr. Peter Papáček
is a PhD student at the Institute of Public Law, Faculty of Law, Pan-European University, Bratislava, Slovak Republic. His Dissertation is focused on the theme of 'Legal responsibility for environmental losses'. He finished his Mgr. studies at Pan-European University in 2016 and stood for his Viva exam in 2017, also at the Pan-European University. He actively participates in different projects in the field of criminal law and attends various international conferences.
E-mail: peter.papacek@gmail.com

sector´s will and with its role to put pressure on a State to reach changes in this area.

| | |

I.　Introduction

10.01. Every State is sovereign in the autonomy of decisions relating to its territory, citizens, constitution, mechanism of power and relations with other subjects. State sovereignty has gone through a lot of changes because of various social and cultural events and processes. That is the reason why we can not talk about absolute sovereignty, because regulated international relations have led to a situation in which States can not unilaterally set the application of some rules. It means that the State can not unilaterally change its borders with other States, unilaterally pollute emissions into its neighbour States or unilaterally disrespect the human rights of another State's citizens in their territory. States are bound by the rules of international law, but they do not have to submit to the will of other States. We have to distinguish between internal and external State sovereignty. Internal sovereignty is considered as an abstract principle which declares the legitimate power authority. According to authors professor Ján Svák, et al., the sovereign power of the State as a principle of its internal power can be understood in two ways. First it can be understood as supreme power, whose decisions are not derived from anyone else. Secondly, it can be understood as unlimited power, to whom everybody on its territory is subjected.[1]

10.02. Besides these authors, noted author Hassan deals with the meaning of sovereignty and he identifies three meanings of it. First, State sovereignty can be a distinctive characteristic of States as constituent units of the international legal system. Secondly, Sovereignty can be a freedom of action with respect to all matters and which a State is not under any other legal obligation. Finally, Sovereignty describes the minimum amount of autonomy required to be accorded the status of a sovereign State.[2]

---

[1]　JÁN SVÁK, ĽUBOR CIBULKA, KAREL KLÍMA, ÚSTAVNÉ PRÁVO SLOVENSKEJ REPUBLIKY, VŠEOBECNÁ ČASŤ, Bratislava: EUROKÓDEX, 779 – 782 (2009).

[2]　Daud Hassan, *Territorial Sovereignty and State Responsibility – An Environmental Perspective*, 45(3-4)

10.03. Further, regarding external State sovereignty it is important to mention that it means the conservation of the State´s safety and the non-interference in its territory. First of all, territory is a substantial attribute of Statehood which declares and defines the area where the State can exercise and enjoy its sovereignty. States are independent of any other State authorities. Thanks to this concept of territorial sovereignty, States are able to act freely including in the environmental arena, because they have the right to pollute within their borders at a self-determined level – in accordance with international treaties. The rise of many environmental problems have led to the widespread acceptance of the idea of environmental responsibility, but still not in every State. According to this idea some concessions are necessary to limit territorial sovereignty for the common good of our planet. This is clearly seen in the statement of a former Australian Ambassador for the Environment to the United Nations: 'The concept of absolute sovereignty of States will have to make concessions as never before in face of today's emerging crisis. There will have to be a high degree of willing subordination of national sovereignty in favour of the common good of all nations'. One of the basic principles of international law is that a State has to act so as not to harm the interests of another State. What this means in this case is an international obligation for States to control and reduce environmental pollution. This contribution focuses on the aforementioned concessions in the field of territorial sovereignty in favour of environmental development and control. These concessions are made because of international treaties and international law which are a very important basis for environmental development and control. International law and international treaties play an important role because in many of cases environmental damage does not affect only the jurisdiction of one State, but also foreign jurisdictions of the global commons. Non-respecting international environmental obligations cannot be excused by territorial sovereignty. Many international principles support the above-mentioned environmental obligations and a breach of them will incur the responsibility of the breaching State.

II.   The Restriction of State Sovereignty

10.04. According to international law every State has an obligation to act so as not to harm the interests of the neighbour States. Historically, the first treaty dealing with this issue from an environmental perspective was the Frontier Treaty (1960) between the Netherlands and the Federal Republic of Germany. It laid down a principle for the prevention of excessive pollution in the boundary waters of States in its Article 58 as follows:

> 1. The Contracting Parties undertake to give due regard, in the performance of their tasks in the field of water management, to the neighbouring State´s interests in the boundary waters. To that end, they agree to take or to support all measures required to establish and to maintain within the section of the boundary waters situated in their respective territories such orderly conditions as will mutually safeguard their interests, and they shall neither take nor tolerate any measures causing substantial prejudice to the neighbouring State.
>
> 2. In performing the obligations undertaken in paragraph 1, the Contracting Parties shall in particular take or support, within an appropriate period of time, all measures required:
>
> …
>
> (e) To prevent such excessive pollution of the boundary waters as many substantially impair the customary use of the waters by the Neighbouring State.[3]

10.05. Today there are a lot of international treaties which set up obligations for States where it is relevant for environmental damage. This means that in case of the same harmful activities affecting other States there will be an obligation for the polluting State to make reparations. The above discussed issue is connected to the principle of good neighbourliness which expert Kari Hakappää defined as follows: 'No State may conduct, promote or sustain in its territory activities which cause other than inconsiderable and usual damage in the territory of a neighbouring State'.[4] According to this principle it is unambiguous that for a favourable environment with the neighbour States, a sovereign State must practice its State power in a restricted, rather than absolute way. There are a lot of cases that are connected to the aforementioned principle, where the possibility of the deterioration of the environment caused

---

[3] JOHAN G. LAMMERS, POLLUTION OF INTERNATIONAL WATERCOURSES, Martinus Nijhoff Publishers: Hague 117 (1984).
[4] Kari Hakapää, *Marine Pollution in International Law: Material Obligations and Jurisdiction*, Helsinki: Suomalainen Tiedeakatemia, 141 (1981).

some international issues because of States acting to freely. One example is the Trail Smelter Arbitration (*United States* v. *Canada*)[5] where the emission of sulphur dioxides in the course of normal operation of a Canadian copper smelter damaged crops and vegetation in the United States of America, or the Lake Lanoux Arbitration (*France* v. *Spain*)[6] where Spain sought influence with France regarding the diversion of lake waters as part of a hydro-electric project. The most interesting case in this area in Slovak republic is the Gabčíkovo-Nagymaros Project (*Hungary* v. *Slovakia*).[7]

II.1.   The Gabčíkovo-Nagymaros Case

10.06.   The International Court of Justice (ICJ) in the Hague, Netherlands, decided the case of the Gabčíkovo-Nagymaros Project between Hungary and the Slovak Republic on the 25th of September 1997. Hungary and the former Czechoslovakia (ČSR) signed a contract in 1977 concerning the construction of water works with the purposes of electricity production, combating floods and increasing the navigation on the river Danube. Unfortunately, in May 1989, Hungary unilaterally finished the construction works without a statement or consideration on their part of the project. Due to that, from November 1991 the ČSR had to realize their part of the project in an alternative form. Hungary unilaterally cancelled the realization of the project and later resigned from the contract with the reasoning that it would pose a serious risk for the environment in Hungary and particularly for Budapest´s water supply. The ČSR decided to proceed with the project but in an altered form on their territory. On 24 October 1992 the Gabčíkovo step was started by reserving the Danube river basin in a manner consistent with the altered form. The mentioned judicial decision of the ICJ in 1997 confirmed the validity of the contract from 1977, the succession of the Slovak Republic after the ČSR's dissolution, and declared the construction of an alternate solution known as the Čuňovo step. The ICJ decided that both sides, Hungary and Slovakia, should review the issue again in the context of the water work´s effect on the environment in the favour of the harmonization of economic development with environmental protection. In particular, they should find a satisfactory solution

---

[5]   For the full text of the Arbitration see: http://legal.un.org/riaa/cases/vol_III/1905-1982.pdf
[6]   For the full text of the Arbitration see: http://www2.ecolex.org/server2.php/libcat/docs/COU/Full/En/COU-143747E.pdf
[7]   For the full text of the judgment see: https://www.icj-cij.org/files/case-related/92/092-19970925-JUD-01-00-EN.pdf

for the amount of water entering the old Danube bed and the shoulders situated on both banks of the river. The ICJ decided that the two States breached their legal obligations and called them to make a binding treaty, taking into account the changes that have taken place since 1989. The following provides a short summary of the ICJ´s decision in this case.[8]

10.07. First, Hungary was not entitled to interrupt and later withdraw from part of the works in 1989. It was required to undertake this project, being the subject of the contract signed in 1977 between Hungary and ČSR and the means connected with it. Secondly, the ČSR was authorized to take part in the preparatory works in November 1991 with the aim to realize a temporary solution known as variant C, but was not authorized to unilaterally put it into operation on October 1992. Thirdly, the notification made by Hungary in May 1992 on the termination of the treaty from year 1977 and the means associated with it did not have a legal effect. In other words, this notification was not in force and did not regulate the relations between the two parties. Finally, Slovakia, as a successor State of the ČSR, became one of the contracting parties from the 1977 agreement. As regards the behaviour of both parties in the future, the ICJ ruled as follows:

a) Hungary and Slovak republic shall, in good faith and taking into account the existing situation, negotiate and take all necessary measures to ensure the achievement of the objectives of the treaty from 1977.

b) Unless otherwise agreed between the parties, a common operating regime for the water works in Slovak territory shall be established in accordance with the 1977 treaty.

c) Each party must compensate the other for damages caused by its behaviour.

d) The settlement concerning the construction and operation of the water works shall be carried out in accordance with the provisions of the treaty from 1977 and its related provisions. The ICJ has ruled that the environmental law standards that have emerged relate to the performance of the contract and that both parties may by common agreement take them into account when applying several articles of the contract. The ICJ decided that both sides, in order to reconcile economic development with environmental protection, should re-examine the effects of the use of the Gabčíkovo power plant on the environment. In particular, they have to find a satisfactory

---

[8] Rozsudok v súdnom spore medzi Maďarskom a SR o Gabčíkovo – Nagymaros. available at: http://www.teraz.sk/slovensko/rozsudok-v-sudnom-spore-medzi-madarsko/280752-clanok.html (accessed on 14 August 2017)

Czech Yearbook of International Law®

solution in terms of the volume of water entering the old Danube bed and the water arms situated on both banks of the river.

10.08. Many years after this decision of the ICJ the two States signed a memorandum for the ICJ in Hague. The joint statement shortly summarized the process and the results of negotiations between the States. It even contains common conclusions where the parties opine that it would be premature to move the case of the waterworks before the ICJ. This means that the current status quo will be maintained at the international court.

10.09. From table 1, the principal differences in the positions of government delegations will be clearly seen regarding this issue:[9]

Table 1

Opinion of the Slovak government delegation	Opinion of the Hungarian government delegation
Nagymaros section of river Danube	
Build the Nagymaros level or other level fulfilling the aims of the 1977 treaty.	Do not build a Nagymaros level or other similar project.
In the Nagymaros area increase the water level in the Danube river by upheaval, a stage, without any further fortification of the bottom and banks, except for flood barriers.	Prevent further excessive water level drops in the Danube by fortification of the bottom and banks by gabions and rocky outcrops, narrowing of the sailing track, dredging and building shoots.
Ensure flood protection by completing the construction of the Nagymaros or other level on this section of the Danube.	Ensure flood protection without building other waterworks by other additional works.
Produce electricity at Nagymaros or at another lower level-built suitable place, averaging around 1000 GWh per year.	Do not generate electricity at Nagymaros.
Creating conditions for high quality production of electricity at Gabčíkovo.	Do not create conditions for high quality electricity production at Gabčíkovo.

---

[9]   II. Rozsudok Medzinárodného súdneho Dvora., available at: http://www.gabcikovo.gov.sk/old. gabcikovo.gov.sk/doc/zbornik_04/kapitola%202/kap2_text.htm#_ftn11 (accessed on 14 August 2017)

Improve the sailing conditions in the section between Gabčíkovo and Budapest as recommended by the Danube commission for class Vic. for boat cruises with a dive of up to 3,5m and navigational width of 180m. The Slovak republic has already built a dyke along the entire length of the Danube.	Deteriorate the navigation conditions (reclassify) to class VIb for boat cruises with a dive of up to 2.5m and cruising width of 80-150m.
Ensure the interconnection of the Danube waterway with an internal waterway of international significance to the Váh river.	Do not ensure the cruising connection of the Danube river with the Váh by swelling, but rather in some other way such as building a barrage at the river Váh´s aperture in the Danube.
The permanent drop of the bottom and water level of the Danube river between Gabčíkovo and Budapest is considered as an unfavourable ecological process.	The fall of the Danube river´s bottom and water level between Gabčíkovo and Budapest is considered to be a natural ecological process.
The Danube bed and the Danube tributaries in the Nagymaros section are considered to be ecologically important and the solution of ecological issues should be realized by swelling the Danube´s water level.	The Danube tributaries in the Nagymaros section are considered to be ecologically more important and the solution to ecological issues has to be done by dredging and deepening.

Costs	
The total cost corresponds to the build-up of the barrage for water level rising on which the hydroelectric power plant can be placed. Other investments for the upgrading and maintenance of the cruising way are minimal. In the opinion of the Slovak government, the cost of the barrage and the hydroenergetic part should be not higher than the costs specified by the Hungarian side for the provision of a cruise according to their proposal.	The total costs (according to prices in 1999) of the construction of the fortification on the Danube river for a period of 50 years is 136 689 million HUF. Additional costs should be added to this. This will include the elimination of shipping obstacles, the limitation of drops, the provision of international cruises, and the permanent maintenance of cruising ways.
For the Slovak side the Hungarian proposal results in additional costs, such as the construction of a barrage for the cruises between Danube and Váh, and additional flood protection to provide irrigation water in the lower part of river Ipeľ.	For the Hungarian side their proposal results in additional costs for flood protection, for the construction of infrastructure or the bridge in the Visegrád region and others.
Gabčíkovo section of river Danube	
Linking the Dunakiliti barrage to regulate the Danube level and flowing into the Hungarian tributary systems. Flood protection mainly in the Szigetköz area.	Not using the Dunakiliti barrage.
The involvement of Čuňovo water works as an integration component of the Gabčíkovo level into the contractual regime.	The Hungarian side had not submitted proposals for it in this plan.

Securing the swallow of the water in the Danube river with weirs under Čuňovo. For one weir approximately 100 000 – 200 000 m3 of material are assumed to be constructed.	Securing the swallow of the water in the Danube river by building a new meandering channel from more weirs on it, 70 000 m3 of rock blocks or by tilting the old bed and graveling (11 million m3 over a 30 km stretch).
Production of top quality electricity at Gabčíkovo level according to the Joint Contracting Project.	The exclusion of top quality service. Lower quality of produced energy.
Connection of the tributary system with the old Danube riverbed in several places.	Connection of the tributary system with the old Danube riverbed in several places.
All types of cruises in the old Danube riverbed under certain negotiated conditions.	Ensuring a small sport cruising on the Danube and its tributaries.
Flows to the old Danube riverbed and the tributary system under the 1977 treaty are: minimal flow in the old Danube bed 50 m3/s, in the vegetation period 200 m3/s. The agreement from 1955 talks about 400 m3/s in annual average, in winter at least 250 m3/s an in summer, excluding floods, up to 600 m3/s.	According to the ecological justification of the Hungarian party in the winter period, at least 20 - 40 m3/s must be allowed into the old Danube bed and in the vegetation period 400 m3/s. In the winter season 20 m3/s must be allowed to flow into the tributary system and 90 m3/s in the vegetation period.

Costs	
The total cost of adaptation in the old Danube riverbed corresponds to the construction of 6 – 9 weirs with a height of 2 to 4 m. By connecting the old Danube riverbed with tributaries in the floodplains, the process of the Danube´s meandering can begin. The old riverbed of the Danube and the entire flood must remain ready to pass flood discharges.	Costs, according to the materials of the Hungarian party, to reduce and increase the bottom of the river represents 34 – 36 billion HUF and maintenances costs in the first year 2 – 6 billion HUF. The Hungarian side estimates the cost of creating a meandering new Danube riverbed of 17 – 20 billion HUF and maintenance of 0,5 – 0,8 billion HUF per year.

10.10. This case is a very nice example of a situation where one physical object is in the point of interest of two States. Nevertheless some part of this object, in our case a river, is on the territory of one sovereign State. This State is not entitled to act authoritatively with the river´s organization, because its organization could change its environment which in turn can have an effect in a neighbour State. It means that the serious issues connected to the environment´s welfare change the sovereign role and status of a State to a more co-operational role even if the present object is on its territory.

III.   Implementation Problems of Environmental Obligations and 'Greening' Policy

10.11. A significant problem for the deteriorating environment is industrial production. Companies try to avoid environmental costs and pass them to the users of the products. What does it mean for a sovereign State? For categorization purposes we can divide States into developed countries and developing countries in economic transitions based on their environmental responsibility.

10.12. For the developing countries it is typical that they do not have the will to undertake the high cost connected to environmental problems. It is because of the fear that it could markedly restrict their industrial development which they sense as the guarantee of the State´s future welfare.[10] According to Men Quing-nan,

---

[10]   Daud Hassan, *Territorial Sovereignty and State Responsibility – An Environmental Perspective*, 45(3-4)

the costs of environmental control are of two kinds. First there are transitional costs, which involve the adaptation of existing plants and equipment, management practices, technology, and labour and consumption patterns in ways that reduce damage to the environment and the cost of environment-induced shifts in the location of production. Secondly, there are recurring costs, which require more resource inputs per unit of output or consumption, or, less use of resources in order to avoid environmental spill-overs.[11]

10.13. This situation can seriously polarize society, because these costs can slow down the economic growth of the country. On the other hand there is a need to find a balance between economic development and the environmental welfare. Because of the different interests of political groups and non-governmental organizations (NGOs), issues like this can lead to internal political conflicts which can result in the instability of the government and thus in the sovereign role of the State. So, regarding developing countries it is possible to observe that they are not really interested in the protection of the world community´s common interest, but they pursue their own needs and interests. Their priorities are much more poverty and debt servicing and not the common interest of environmental welfare and responsible environmental management. The high costs of environmental development are the reason for undermining the effort to find a solution for this issue, so logically it means that if the capacity of one State is not enough for the solution of this issue than there is a need to co-operate with other States. It is absolutely important for developing States to understand that if their capacity is not enough for all activities then some concessions are needed to be taken, even if it means some restrictions of their sovereignty in the favour of the common welfare.[12] To keep the environment in a good quality and to protect it requires an effective legal concept, which is quite complicated to apply because of the different levels of political will, economic priorities or social situations. If there is an absence of specific standards of environmental protection at a global level setting various obligations for States, then the States frequently violate environmental obligations. This happens because they are in a role of a sovereign State and everything connected to the environment is a matter of national

---

ENVIRONMENTAL POLICY AND LAW 140 (2015).

[11] MEN QUING-NAN, LAND BASED MARINE POLLUTION, INTERNATIONAL LAW AND DEVELOPMENT, London: Graham and Trotman, 40 (1987).

[12] Daud Hassan, *Territorial Sovereignty and State Responsibility – An Environmental Perspective*, 45(3-4) Environmental Policy and Law 141–143 (2015).

concern. They are not bound by international law in this area, which can limit the supreme power of the State even on its own territory if the deteriorating environment is in danger. The Harmon doctrine directly argued that environmental pollution is a right of the territorial sovereign. This variant of national control seems to be problematic and non-effective, because it could lead to some issues connected to global environmental development and inhibits protection against its deterioration.[13] Today this territorial point of view seems to be an archaism because the transboundary and common environmental objects need international legislative protection and global will to fight against deterioration. Cooperation is necessary even if it restricts the State´s sovereign role on its territory in the environmental arena. That kind of regulation by international law is a kind of warranty for the States against not harming each other and it has met with a very positive response all over the world, enjoying great acceptance.

IV.   The Impact of Environmental NGO´s on the State´s Role

10.14.   Today, environmental NGOs play an irreplaceable role in the international community. They focus on serious cross-border environmental problems which States cannot solve as individual sovereigns and where they cannot act alone. Such environmental problems which can cause deterioration include global warming, ozone-depletion, overpopulation, etc.. The growing intensity of serious environmental problems spurred the creation of groups like environmental NGOs and their power is increasing so rapidly it may become necessary to ask whether the State´s role is a necessary factor in progressive environmental change. The power and strength of environmental NGOs and the reason of their existence is based in the lack of political will in individual States in this area. This passivity in this area was typical even for the international level. There could be various reasons for this political passivity. One of them is the lack of accountability because environmental problems do not belong to one nation. There is also the problem of collective inactivity. This expression refers to the fear by a State of not profiting from help given by another State, or if that other State will enjoy the greater benefits of the solved problem. The most important reason is the restriction of its supreme power according to some

---

[13]   Terry L. Anderson, J. Bishop Grewell, *It Isn´t Easy Being Green: Environmental Policy Implications for Foreign Policy, International Law, and Sovereignty*, 2(2) CHICAGO JOURNAL OF INTERNATIONAL LAW 435 (2001).

international agreements or treaties where a State can be forced to take some actions even if it does not have a direct interest in that issue.[14]

10.15. Environmental NGOs are actually representatives of the civil sector via groups of people with the same interests who want to solve cross-border environmental issues by various forms of co-operation. They undertake serious research and they lobby local and even national governments, and put international organizations and corporations under pressure.

10.16. They achieve their purposes by the co-operation with the public because they alert them and point to some serious problems and with the helping hand of the public they can seriously pressure the State to act in the favour of the public will. Two examples of great environmental NGOs are Greenpeace or the Friends of the Earth. Compared to States, environmental NGOs are not bounded by territorial sovereignty, but they can act wherever it is needed. In today´s political situation governments have started to co-operate with some environmental NGOs in cases of new legislation in the area of environmental protection. They do this because they are afraid of situations where the environmental NGOs weaken the State´s control over its own affairs and strengthen their own position. For example in the Narmada Bachao Andolan and the Brazilian Rubber Tapper Movement case we could see that the State was unable to control the environmental NGO´s activity and the NGO´s international effort resulted in an effective change within the State.[15]

V.   Conclusion

10.17. Maybe at first sight environment does not seem to be an important factor connected to the State´s role or status. However, after some analysis of the deteriorating environment´s impact at a global level it can clearly be seen that the environmental question is one of the areas which restricts the State´s sovereign position and the freedom of its power even on its own territory in favour of the common good. The most effective tool to fight against this deterioration is in international law and international agreements in the area of environmental protection and control. It is an effective tool of protection and control, but it does place some limits to the sovereign role of the State. Nevertheless this is a tool of control and protection that is globally accepted

---

[14]   Marissa A. Pagnani, *Environmental NGOs and the Fate of the Traditional Nation-State*, 15(4) GEORGETOWN INTERNATIONAL ENVIRONMENTAL LAW REVIEW 793 (2003).
[15]   Marissa A. Pagnani, *Environmental NGOs and the Fate of the Traditional Nation-State*, 15(4) GEORGETOWN INTERNATIONAL ENVIRONMENTAL LAW REVIEW 804–805 (2003).

and it gives some kind of safety for citizens. Unfortunately, the acceptation of this tool is not in every State, but the number of them is increasing. Among the final recipients of a good quality environment is our whole human population. That is the reason why it is important to engage civil society in the matters of environmental protection and control. Those citizens created environmental NGO´s for the purpose of common welfare which they can reach by putting States under the pressure of civil society. Finally it can only be concluded that the State sovereign role and it's authoritative status are the only way for dealing with the deteriorating environment. A deteriorated environment leaves us no territory to live in and no territory to practice the status of sovereignty.

| | |

Summaries

DEU   [*Der Einfluss der Umweltverschlechterung auf Stellung und Rolle des Staats*]

Der Beitrag befasst sich mit der Stellung und Rolle souveräner Staaten im Zusammenhang mit den sich verschlechternden Kenngrößen der Umwelt, die in einem gewissen Sinn des globalen Schutzes und der globalen Kontrolle bedürfen. Es sei festgehalten, dass hinsichtlich der besonderen Wichtigkeit des Bereichs Umwelt für das globale Wohl und die nachhaltige Entwicklung ein globaler Konsensus besteht. Von daher überrascht es nicht, dass dieser Bereich Einfluss auf die Rolle und Stellung des Staats haben kann. Im ersten Teil des Beitrags wird die Bedeutung der staatlichen Souveränität und deren Beziehung zur Umwelt vorgestellt, unter Darstellung der Ansichten verschiedener bekannter Autoren. Der zweite Teil befasst sich mit der Frage der Beschränkung der Staatshoheit. Zur Erklärung werden historische Situationen herangezogen, in denen Staaten unter dem Druck des Gemeinwohls ihre autoritative Macht auf dem eigenen Staatsgebiet beschränken mussten. Betont wird außerdem die Bedeutung des Völkerrechts und diverser internationaler Abkommen und Verträge. Am besten eröffnet sich das Verständnis für die theoretischen Aspekte über praktische Fallstudien. Deshalb widmet sich der Beitrag u.a. dem Fall Gabčíkovo-Nagymaros, der in diesem Bereich zumeist mit der Slowakei in Zusammenhang gebracht wird. Die Analyse dieses Falls vermittelt eine gute Vorstellung davon, wie das internationale Recht in Verbindung mit dem Schutz der Umwelt und der Kontrolle der Einhaltung von Umweltschutzauflagen die souveräne Position eines Staats auch dann beschränken kann, wenn sich das betreffende Objekt des umweltschützerischen Interesses auf dessen Staatsgebiet befindet. Ein dritter Teil klärt die Probleme im Zusammenhang mit der Umsetzung internationaler Verpflichtungen im Bereich des Umweltschutzes und die komplizierten politischen Konstellationen, die sich dabei ergeben können: Probleme im Sinne der Kostenabwägung zwischen den Aufwendungen im Kampf gegen die Umweltverschlechterung und den Aufwendungen für die industrielle Entwicklung, und politische Komplikationen im Sinne des Bedürfnisses und des Rufs der Allgemeinheit nach unversehrter, „guter" Umwelt. Der letzte Teil des Beitrags befasst sich mit den Nichtregierungsorganisationen im Bereich Umwelt, die die Interessen des zivilen Sektors vertreten, und deren Aufgabe, Druck auf den Staat auszuüben, um auf Änderungen in diesem Bereich hinzuwirken.

CZE **[*Vliv zhoršujícího se životního prostředí na postavení a úlohu státu*]**

Článek se zabývá postavením a úlohou suverénního státu v souvislosti se zhoršujícím se životním prostředím, které vyžaduje určitou globální ochranu a kontrolu. Je nutno poznamenat, že oblast životního prostředí je celosvětově přijímána jako jedna z nejdůležitějších pro globální blaho a udržitelný rozvoj. Proto není překvapivé, že tato oblast může ovlivnit úlohu a postavení státu. První část představuje samotný význam státní svrchovanosti a také její vztah k životnímu prostředí. Prezentovány jsou zde i názory různých známých autorů. Druhá část se zabývá otázkou omezení státní moci. Vysvětluje historický aspekt, jak se státy dostaly do situace, že pod tlakem společného dobra musely omezit svou autoritativní moc i na svém území. Kromě toho se zdůrazňuje význam mezinárodního práva a mezinárodních smluv. Nejlepším způsobem, jak porozumět teoretickým aspektům, jsou případové studie. Proto se tento článek dále zabývá i případem Gabčíkovo-Nagymaros, který je v této oblasti nejčastěji spojován se Slovenskou republikou. Rozbor tohoto případu poskytuje dobrou představu o tom, jak mezinárodní právo spojené s ochranou a kontrolou životního prostředí může omezit suverénní postavení státu i v případě, že předmětný objekt životního prostředí se nachází na jeho území. Dále jsou ve třetí části objasněny problémy implementace mezinárodních závazků v oblasti životního prostředí a komplikovaná politická situace, která je s ní spojena. Problémy mohou spočívat v nákladech

*v boji proti zhoršování životního prostředí a nákladech na
průmyslový rozvoj a komplikovaná politická situace odráží
potřebu veřejnosti pro kvalitní životní prostředí. Poslední část
se zabývá nevládními organizacemi činnými v oblasti životního
prostředí, které odrážejí zájmy civilního sektoru, jakož i jejich
úlohou vyvíjet tlak na stát, aby se dosáhlo změn v této oblasti.*

| | |

POL [*Wpływ pogarszającego się stanu środowiska na status i rolę
państwa*]
*Artykuł poświęcony statusowi i roli państwa w związku
z pogarszającym się stanem środowiska. Konkretnie omawia
czynniki wpływające na suwerenność państwa na jego własnym
obszarze. Wpływ ten może prowadzić do ograniczania
autorytarnej władzy państwa na korzyść dobra wspólnego.
Instrumenty prawne, pomagające w osiągnięciu tego stanu
w sferze środowiska to różne traktaty międzynarodowe
i prawo międzynarodowe, które nakładają na państwa pewne
zobowiązania. Wreszcie artykuł zajmuje się problemami
implementacji wynikającymi z powyższej potrzeby regulacji
międzynarodowych kosztem suwerennej władzy państwa.*

FRA [*La dégradation de l'environnement et son influence sur le
statut et le rôle de l'État*]
*Le présent article se consacre au statut et au rôle de l'État
dans le contexte de la dégradation de l'environnement. Plus
particulièrement, il examine les facteurs susceptibles d'influencer
la souveraineté de l'État sur son propre territoire, et pouvant
résulter en une limitation du pouvoir de l'État au bénéfice du
bien commun. Les instruments juridiques applicables dans le
domaine de l'environnement sont les traités internationaux et
le droit international, imposant aux États diverses obligations.
L'article se penche également sur les problèmes liés à l'application
des normes internationales au détriment du pouvoir souverain
de l'État.*

RUS [*Влияние ухудшающегося состояния окружающей среды
на статус и роль государства*]
*В статье рассматривается статус и роль государства
в связи с ухудшающимся состоянием окружающей среды.
В частности, факторы, влияющие на суверенитет
государства на его собственной территории. Это
влияние может привести к ограничению авторитетной*

государственной власти в пользу общего блага. Правовые инструменты, способствующие достижению такого состояния в области окружающей среды, состоят из различных международных договоров и норм международного права, которые приносят государствам определенные обязательства. И последнее, но не менее важное: в статье рассматриваются проблемы имплементации, вытекающие из вышеупомянутой необходимости международного регулирования в ущерб суверенной власти государства.

ESP [*La influencia del deterioro medioambiental en la posición y la función del Estado*]

El escrito versa de la posición y la función del Estado en relación con el deterioro medioambiental, concretamente, con los factores que influencian la soberanía del Estado en su propio territorio. Tal influencia puede provocar la restricción del poder autoritario del Estado a favor del bien común. Los instrumentos jurídicos que contribuyen a la consecución de tal estado medioambiental se plasman en diferentes tratados internacionales y en el derecho internacional que conllevan varias obligaciones para los Estados. El artículo se enfoca asimismo en cuestiones relacionadas con la implementación que deriva de la necesidad descrita más arriba de la legislación internacional en detrimento del poder soberano del Estado.

| | |

Bibliography

Terry L. Anderson, J. Bishop Grewell, *It Isn´t Easy Being Green: Environmental Policy Implications for Foreign Policy, International Law, and Sovereignty*, 2(2) CHICAGO JOURNAL OF INTERNATIONAL LAW (2001).

Kari Hakapää, *Marine Pollution in International Law: Material Obligations and Jurisdiction*, Helsinki, SUOMALAINEN TIEDEAKATEMIA (1981).

Daud Hassan, *Territorial Sovereignty and State Responsibility – An Environmental Perspective*, 45(3-4) ENVIRONMENTAL POLICY AND LAW (2015).

JOHAN G. LAMMERS, POLLUTION OF INTERNATIONAL WATERCOURSES, Hague: Martinus Nijhoff Publishers (1984).

Marissa A. Pagnani, *Environmental NGOs and the Fate of the Traditional Nation-State*, 15(4) GEORGETOWN INTERNATIONAL

ENVIRONMENTAL LAW REVIEW (2003).

MEN QUING-NAN, LAND BASED MARINE POLLUTION, INTERNATIONAL LAW AND DEVELOPMENT, London: Graham and Trotman (1987).

JÁN SVÁK, ĽUBOR CIBULKA, KAREL KLÍMA, ÚSTAVNÉ PRÁVO SLOVENSKEJ REPUBLIKY, VŠEOBECNÁ ČASŤ, Bratislava: EUROKÓDEX (2009).

Marieta Safta

European Criminal Law as a Form of Transnational Law

Developments through the Constitutional Review

Key words:
*European criminal law
| constitutional control |
constitutional courts*

Abstract | The emergence of European criminal law is a product of debate and crisis. Its creation is a reaction to perceived security risks, rather than anything else – provision of security having been the driver in the creation of European criminal law".[1] Even if the European Union's involvement in criminal law has generated significant challenges and tensions, developments in this area continue at a sustained pace. For a comprehensive approach to the evolution of European criminal law, the issue must be addressed both from the perspective of the EU and the Member States as well as from the perspective of the Court of Justice of the EU and the Constitutional Courts of the Member States. Constitutional control can be considered as a catalyst in building a European law, its importance being significant. This is all the more so since, as the studies in the field reveal, criminal law has undergone a contemporary revolution in constitutional significance. The extent to which the constitutional courts explore the constitutional foundations of criminal norms is very different, being influenced by national tradition. An increasingly profound constitutional approach to criminal law issues is, however, undeniable. At the same time, by using the jurisprudence of international and supranational courts, as

Ph.D Marieta Safta is an Associate Professor at „Titu Maiorescu" University of Bucharest, Faculty of Law, First Assistant-Magistrate of the Constitutional Court of Romania.
Email: marietasafta@ yahoo.com

---

[1]   MASSIMO FICHERA & JENS KREMER, LAW AND SECURITY IN EUROPE: RECONSIDERING THE SECURITY CONSTITUTION (Jens Kremer eds., 2013)., apud Kimmo Nuotio, European Criminal Law, in The Oxford Handbook of Criminal Law, Oxford University Press 1121 (Markus D. Dubber, Tatjana Hornle, eds., 2016).

Czech Yearbook of International Law®

well as comparative law, the constitutional courts contribute to the approximation of legal systems – including on the dimension of criminal law – at a European level. This approach serves to strengthen mutual trust, a basic principle of the EU. Starting from these premises, the present study analyzes the evolution of European criminal law through the point of view of constitutional control.

| | |

I.   Introduction

11.01. With the main milestones of the Maastricht Treaty (1992/1993), where the criminal field was circumscribed to Justice and Home Affairs, and the adoption of the Convention on the Protection of the Financial Interests of the European Communities in 1995,[2] the development, alongside the Amsterdam Treaty (1997/1999), of an extensive regulatory framework for the control of crime and the building of an area of freedom and justice, the establishment of Eurojust by Council Decision 2002/187 / JHA,[3] the Framework resolution system,[4] the developments towards a European criminal law are remarkable. At present, the provisions relating to the area of freedom, security and justice are integrated into the main body of the Treaties of the European Union (EU), the area being part of the shared competence of the EU with the Member States. Article 82 (1) of the Treaty on the Functioning of the European Union[5] establishes in this sense that *"Judicial cooperation in criminal matters in the Union shall be based on the principle of mutual recognition of judgments and judicial decisions and shall include the approximation of the laws and regulations of the Member States in the areas referred to in paragraph 2 and in Article 83. The European Parliament and the Council, acting in accordance with the ordinary legislative procedure, shall adopt measures to: (a) lay down rules and procedures for ensuring recognition throughout the Union of all forms of judgments and judicial decisions; (b) prevent and settle conflicts of jurisdiction between Member States; (c) support the training of the judiciary and judicial staff; (d) facilitate*

---

[2]   Council Act of 26 July 1995 drawing up the Convention on the protection of the European Communities' financial interests (95/C 316/03).

[3]   Council Decision 2002/187/JAI of 28 February 2002 setting up Eurojust with a view to reinforcing the fight against serious crime.

[4]   For more, Kimmo NUOTIO, EUROPEAN CRIMINAL LAW, THE OXFORD HANDBOOK OF CRIMINAL LAW, Oxford University Press 1115-1138 (Markus. D. Dubber, Tatjana Hörnle eds., 2016).

[5]   Official Journal of the European Union C 326/81.

cooperation between judicial or equivalent authorities of the Member States in relation to proceedings in criminal matters and the enforcement of decisions." The competence of the European Union to adopt measures on criminal law is provided for in Article 83 TFEU, which establishes the following in the first two paragraphs: *„(1) The European Parliament and the Council may, by means of directives adopted in accordance with the ordinary legislative procedure, establish minimum rules concerning the definition of criminal offences and sanctions in the areas of particularly serious crime with a cross-border dimension resulting from the nature or impact of such offences or from a special need to combat them on a common basis. These areas of crime are the following: terrorism, trafficking in human beings and sexual exploitation of women and children, illicit drug trafficking, illicit arms trafficking, money laundering, corruption, counterfeiting of means of payment, computer crime and organized crime. On the basis of developments in crime, the Council may adopt a decision identifying other areas of crime that meet the criteria specified in this paragraph. It shall act unanimously after obtaining the consent of the European Parliament. (2) If the approximation of criminal laws and regulations of the Member States proves essential to ensure the effective implementation of a Union policy in an area which has been subject to harmonization measures, directives may establish minimum rules with regard to the definition of criminal offences and sanctions in the area concerned. Such directives shall be adopted by the same ordinary or special legislative procedure as was followed for the adoption of the harmonization measures in question, without prejudice to Article 76."*

11.02. As the doctrine emphasizes, "the emergence of European criminal law is a product of debate and crisis. Its creation is a reaction to perceived security risks, rather than anything else – provision of security having been the driver in the creation of European criminal law".[6] Even if, as has been shown, the European Union's involvement in criminal law has generated significant challenges and tensions,[7] developments in this area continue and the recent adoption of Council Regulation (EU) 2017/1939 of 12 October 2017 implementing enhanced cooperation with regard to the establishment of the European Public Prosecutor's Office (Henceforth known as the EPPO Regulation) is further evidence for this development. For a comprehensive approach,

---

[6]   MASSIMO FICHERA & JENS KREMER, LAW AND SECURITY IN EUROPE: RECONSIDERING THE SECURITY CONSTITUTION (Jens Kremer eds., 2013)., apud Kimmo Nuotio, *Ibid.*, at 1121.
[7]   For more, PAUL CRAIG & GRAINNE DE BURCA, DREPTUL UNIUNII EUROPENE – COMENTARII, JURISPRUDENȚĂ ȘI DOCTRINĂ, Hamagiu Publishing House 1113 (2017).

the issue of the development of European criminal law must be addressed both from the perspective of the EU and the Member States, and also from the perspective of the Court of Justice of the European Union(CJEU) and constitutional courts. For example, in its Lisbon judgment, the German Federal Court likewise emphasized the particular nature of criminal law and held that EU criminal law competence must be interpreted narrowly and consistent with the constitutionally protected specificities of criminal law.[8] Constitutional control thus reveals itself as a catalyst in the work of building a European law, its importance being significant. This is all the more so since, as the studies in the field reveal, criminal law has undergone a contemporary revolution in constitutional significance.[9] The extent to which the constitutional courts explore the constitutional foundations of criminal norms is very different, being influenced by national traditions, but without denying an increasingly profound constitutional approach to criminal law issues. Substantive criminal law, the principle of criminal liability, become a "laboratory" for the constitutional, focusing and advancing classic questions of constitutional interest.[10] At the same time, by using the jurisprudence of international and supranational courts – and here we are referring to the European Court of Human Rights (ECHR) and the CJEU as well as the comparative law, the constitutional courts contribute to the approximation of the legal systems – including the criminal law dimension at European level.

11.03. Starting from these premises, the present study analyzes the evolution of European criminal law in terms of constitutional review, highlighting the developments in this respect at the level of the Constitutional Court of Romania (CCR). In view of the large number of decisions it has made in criminal matters, we will limit the scope of analysis only to the constitutional review of the rules contained in the Criminal Code, so only to the *a posteriori*, concrete constitutionality review, exercised under Article 146(d) of the Constitution (exceptions of unconstitutionality)[11] and only in regards to substantive criminal law. Of course, the most relevant, in terms of the effect they produce, are the decisions by which the CCR accepted the exceptions of unconstitutionality

---

[8]   K.Nuotio, *Ibid.*, at 1123.

[9]   BENJAMIN L. BERGER, CONSTITUTIONAL PRINCIPLES, THE OXFORD HANDBOOK OF CRIMINAL LAW, Oxford University Press 422 (Markus D. Dubber, Tatjana Hörnle, eds., 2016).

[10]   In this regard, broadly,Benjamin L.Berger, *Ibid.*, at 422.

[11]   According to Article 146 letter d) of the Constitution of Romania, the Constitutional Court" *decides on objections as to the unconstitutionality of laws and ordinances, brought up before courts of law or commercial arbitration; the objection as to the unconstitutionality may also be brought up directly by the Advocate of the People;"*

invoked, and found the unconstitutionality of the criticized norms, with the consequence of obliging the legislator to adopt norms in line with the Constitution and European standards of reference.

II. Evolution of CCR jurisprudence in the area of substantive criminal law[12]

II.1. Introductory remarks

11.04. The current Constitution, which marked the passage of Romania from a totalitarian regime to a democratic one, was published in the Official Gazette of Romania, Part I, no. 233 of November 21 1991 and entered into force following its approval by the national referendum of December 8 1991. This was amended and supplemented by the Law for the revision of the Romanian Constitution no. 429/2003,[13] approved by the national referendum of October, 18-19 2003. The Constitution of 1991 enshrined in Romania the European model for the control of the constitutionality of laws, and the Constitutional Court was established[14] as an independent authority, with the role of guaranteeing the supremacy of the Constitution. We have pointed out[15] that even if the constitutional regulation, developed by organic law, gave it considerable powers and a special status among the public authorities, the main consolidation of the Constitutional Court, as well as the constitutional control, are the result of its own activity. The challenges that the Court has encountered and overcome during this period should be emphasized - those concerning the effects/the authority of the Constitutional Court's acts and those concerning the reception of international law in the framework of constitutional control (especially the interpretation and application of Article 20 of the Constitution – *International Treaties on Human Rights*). Jurisprudence on the provisions outlined in the Criminal Code is illustrative in this regard, marking a development of constitutional control and a growing connection of the CCR to the common European values.

11.05. Also relevant to this study (together with the dates mentioned 1991 – adoption of the Constitution, 2003 – the revision of the

---

[12] Just exception of unconstitutionality regarding Criminal Code

[13] Published in the Official Gazette of Romania no. 758 of 29 October 2003; republished, with the updating of the names and giving the texts a new numbering, in the Official Gazette of Romania no. 767 on 31 October 2003.

[14] On 6 June 1992.

[15] Tudorel Toader, Marieta Safta, *Evoluția constituționalismului în România*, 1 REVIEW OF CONSTITUTIONAL LAW 156, 156-204 (2015).

Czech Yearbook of International Law®

Constitution, 1992 – the establishment of the Constitutional Court), are the dates of adoption, respectively modification, of the Romanian Criminal Code. Upon the entry into force of the Constitution, the Criminal Code of 1969[16] was and remained in force.[17] The new Criminal Code of Romania was adopted in 2009[18] and entered into force on 1 February 2014. As far as the 1969 Criminal Code is concerned, the challenges with regard to the exercise of constitutional control were the reception of criminal law institutions in the new constitutional, democratic order, with the consequence that institutions incompatible with the latter were eliminated. After the accession of Romania to the European Union, in the context of substantive reforms in the field, namely the adoption of a new Criminal Code, constitutional control also meant a process of building and connecting to European values, starting from the premise that *"the adoption of the new Criminal Code was imposed from a teleological point of view for reasons whose public source is given both by the regulations adopted at the level of the European Union for the realization of the common space of freedom, security and justice, as well as by the new criminal philosophy of the Romanian state."* (Decision no. 265/2014,[19] paragraph 35).

II.2. Jurisprudential developments during 1992-2013 (the Criminal Code of 1969)

11.06. From the analysis of the jurisprudence it is noted that during the period 1992-2013, the constitutionality examination was carried out (with few exceptions) by strictly comparing the norms criticized to those of the Constitution in force in 1991, without comparative law elements or references to international rights and fundamental freedoms documents. In essence, the Court sanctioned institutions incompatible with the new democratic regime, namely that of *"public wealth"*, respectively the differential protection of private property in relation to the holder, and applied the principle of non-retroactivity of the law with its exceptions. We could say that it is almost an exercise of assimilation of the new constitutional principles/ values, expressly enshrined in the fundamental law. Especially since the very principle of the non-retroactivity of the law was

---

[16] Law no. 15/1968 on the Criminal Code of Romania, The Official Bulletin of Romania 79-79 bis/21 June 1968
[17] According to Article 150 (1) of the 1991 Constitution *"Laws and all other legal acts remain in force, insofar as they do not contradict the present Constitution."*
[18] Law no.286 / 2009, published in the Official Gazette of Romania no.510 of 24 June 2009, and entered into force on 1 February 2014.
[19] Published in the Official Gazette of Romania, Part. I, no.372 din 20 May 2014.

innovatively brought by the Romanian constituent legislator to the rank of constitutional principle.[20]

11.07. Thus, in 1993, the CCR issued five decisions by which were admitted the exceptions of unconstitutionality concerning the provisions of the Criminal Code, respectively no.31/1993,[21] no.32/1993,[22] no.33/1993,[23] no.38/1993,[24] no.49/1993.[25] In all cases, the Court found that the term *"public wealth"*, a term which itself had become inappropriate in the new constitutional order, can only include goods which form the exclusive object of public property (defined by the rules constitutional provisions in force). As a consequence, the texts of the Criminal Code that used the term "public wealth" were found to be partially abrogated, remaining to be applied only to goods forming the exclusive object of public property, and only from the date of implementation of the Constitution.

11.08. In 1994, The Court issued nine admission decisions,[26] 8 of which targeted the rules of the Criminal Code referring to the public wealth (no.11/1994,[27] no.12/1994,[28] no.13/1994,[29] no.18/1994,[30] no.24/1994,[31] no.52/1994,[32] no.56/1994,[33] no.128/1994)[34] and one case related to Article 200 of the Criminal Code, which criminalized "same-sex relationships" (Decision no.81/1994).[35]

11.09. In 1995, no admission decision was given regarding the rules of the Criminal Code, and in 1996, a single admission decision was issued regarding the provisions of Article 238 of the Criminal Code, criminalizing, under the name of *"offense brought to the authority"* damages of reputation, threats, hitting or any acts of violence committed against one of the persons referred to in Article 160 in connection with its activities and of such nature as to prejudice the authority. The provisions of Article

---

[20] On another occasion, I appreciated that this is an element of originality of the Romanian Constitution in 1991, as a reflex of the Commission's request to include in the body of the fundamental law guarantees that would prevent the repetition of profound injustices of the past; Tudorel Toader, Marieta Safta, Evoluția constituționalismului in România, *Ibid.*

[21] Published in the Official Gazette of Romania, Part. I, no.13 on 19 January 1993.

[22] Published in the Official Gazette of Romania, Part. I, no.126 on 23 May 1994.

[23] Published in the Official Gazette of Romania, Part. I, no.278 on 30 November 1993.

[24] Published in the Official Gazette of Romania, Part. I, no.176 on 26 July 1993.

[25] Published in the Official Gazette of Romania, Part. I, no.126 on 23 May 1994.

[26] Some of them pronounced in the appel; at present, the organic law of the CCR no. 47/1992 provides that all the cases of the jurisdiction of the Court are settled by the Plenum of the Court, and the decisions pronounced are final and generally binding.

[27] Published in the Official Gazette of Romania, Part. I, no.126 on 23 May 1994.

[28] Published in the Official Gazette of Romania, Part. I, no.126 on 23 May 1994.

[29] Published in the Official Gazette of Romania, Part. I, no.152 on 17 June 1994.

[30] Published in the Official Gazette of Romania, Part. I, no.343 on 12 December 1994.

[31] Published in the Official Gazette of Romania, Part. I, no.29 on 08 February 1995.

[32] Published in the Official Gazette of Romania, Part. I, no.29 on 08 February 1995.

[33] Published in the Official Gazette of Romania, Part. I, no.156 on 22 June 1994.

[34] Published in the Official Gazette of Romania, Part. I, no.86 on 08 May 1995.

[35] Published in the Official Gazette of Romania, Part. I, no.14 on 25 January 1995.

160 of the Criminal Code criminalized under the name of *"an attack that threatens the security of the state"* the attempt against the life, physical integrity or health of a person carrying out an important state or public activity of circumstances that make the deed a threat to the security of the state. In the same line of jurisprudence of 1993-1994, the Court held that the determination of the crimes in Article 238 and Article 160 of the Criminal Code was made with reference to *the power structures and the system of values existing at the time of the drafting of the Criminal Code.* As this system of values no longer exists at the moment, being replaced by that established by the Constitution of 1991, the Court found that the provisions of Article 238 of the Criminal Code are partially abolished, according to Article 150(1) of the Constitution, remaining in force only insofar as the incriminatory deeds concern a person carrying out an important state activity (Decision no.25/1996).[36]

11.10. In 1997, the Court issued two admission decisions concerning the provisions of the Criminal Code. These are the provisions of Article 81(4) of the Criminal Code concerning *conditional suspension of the service of a sentence* on the grounds that it leads to discrimination on the basis of wealth, in the sense that the defendant who does not have the possibility of covering the damages before the conviction decision cannot have access to the suspended sentence. (Decision no. 463/1997).[37] The second admitted exception was the text of Article II paragraph 1 of Law no.140/1996 for amending and supplementing the Criminal Code, according to which: *"The provisions of the present law on conditional release do not apply to those with final sentences before the law came into force except for those who have circumvented the execution".* The Court held that the conditions for granting probation to convicts for intentional offenses became harsher, because the fractions of punishment to be executed for probation had increased. On the other hand, according to the provisions of paragraph 1 of Article II of the law, these provisions do not apply to those with final sentences before the law entered into force, except for those who have escaped its execution. *Per a contrario*, the provisions of the new law regarding probation are to apply to convicts who receive final sentences after the entry into force of the new law, but for crimes committed before aforementioned date, as well as to those previously convicted who have circumvented the execution of their sentence. These provisions on the incidence

---

[36] Published in the Official Gazette of Romania, Part. I, no.324 on 04 December 1996.
[37] Published in the Official Gazette of Romania, Part. I, no.53 on 06 February 1998.

of criminal law in relation to the acts committed prior to its entry into force are in clear contradiction with the provisions of Article 15(2) of the Constitution which enshrined the principle of non-retroactivity of the law, except for the more favorable criminal law,[38] therefore being unconstitutional (Decision no.214/1997).[39]

11.11. In 1998, two admission decisions concerning the rules of the Criminal Code were issued. The first of these, applying the regulations of the Decision No. 463/1997 *mutatis mutandis*, found the unconstitutionality of Article 86(4)[1] of the Criminal Code that regulates the problems related to the *"suspension of service of a sentence under supervision"* under conditions identical to the *"conditional Suspension of service of a sentence"* of Article 81, paragraph 4 of the same Code (Decision no.25/1998).[40] By the second decision, the Court found the unconstitutionality of Article (2) of the Criminal Code, which established for the private property of the state a preferential legal regime, based on the institution of the prior complaint. The Constitution ensures, however, in Article 41(2)[41], an equal protection of private property, regardless of whether it belongs to the state or to another legal or natural person and, implicitly, prohibits criminal law from containing separate regulations regarding the protection of private property (Decision no.177/1998).[42]

11.12. The three admission decisions passed in 1999 by the Constitutional Court also sanctioned differentiated regulations regarding the protection of private property enshrined in the criminal law, and the provision was therefore unconstitutional *"unless it is wholly or partly of the state"* in Article 214 paragraph 3 of the Criminal Code (Decision no.5/1999),[43] the provision *"except if it is wholly or partly of the state"* provided for in Article 217(6) of the Criminal Code (Decision no.150/1999)[44] and the provision *"unless it is wholly or partly of the state"* in Article 220(4) of the Criminal Code (Decision no.165/1999).[45]

11.13. In the period 2000-2010, the Court issued a single admission decision of an exception of unconstitutionality regarding the rules of the Criminal Code (Decision no.303/2001).[46] The subject of the exception of unconstitutionality was the provisions

---

[38] When revising the Constitution in 2003, an exception to this principle was introduced, namely the more favorable contraventional law.
[39] Published in the Official Gazette of Romania, Part. I, no.234 din 08 September 1997.
[40] Published in the Official Gazette of Romania, Part. I, no.143 din 08 April 1998.
[41] At present Article 44 paragraph (2).
[42] Published in the Official Gazette of Romania, Part. I, no.77 din 24 February 1999.
[43] Published in the Official Gazette of Romania, Part. I, no.95 din 05 May 1999.
[44] Published in the Official Gazette of Romania, Part. I, no.605 din 10 December 1999.
[45] Published in the Official Gazette of Romania, Part. I, no.624 din 21 December 1999.
[46] Published in the Official Gazette of Romania, Part. I, no.809 din 17 December 2001.

of Article II(2) of the Government Emergency Ordinance no.89/2001 amending and completing certain provisions of the Criminal Code on offenses regarding sex life.[47] CCR found that the provisions of the new criminal law, being obviously more severe, cannot be applied to the acts committed before their entry into force and the provisions of Article II(2) of the Government Emergency Ordinance no.89/2001, which refer to their application in relation to the previously committed act, are obviously unconstitutional, as they are contrary to the provisions of Article 15(2) of the Constitution, according to which only the "more favorable criminal law" constitutes the exception to the principle of non-retroactivity of the law.

11.14. In 2011, the admission decision for the exception of the unconstitutionality of the provisions of the Criminal Code of article 74[1] was pronounced, on the grounds that, by conditioning the reduction of the penalty limits of a certain procedural moment, respectively until the solution in the first instance of the case, the principle of equality of citizens in the face of the law, enshrined in Article 16(1) of the Constitution is affected. The Court also held that both paragraph 1 and paragraph 2 of Article 74[1] of the Criminal Code use such ambiguous and imprecise terminology that they deprive the rule of predictability, thus violating the constitutional and conventional provisions relating to the right to a fair trial (Decision no. 573/2011).[48]

11.15. In 2012, a single unconstitutionality exception in the matter was admitted, regarding the provisions of Article 124 of the Criminal Code, with the marginal title the *special prescription*, as amended by Article I, pt. 3 of Law no.63/2012 for amending and supplementing the Criminal Code of Romania and Law no.286/2009 on the Criminal Code, published in the Official Gazette of Romania, Part I, no.258 of 19 April 2012, according to which:" *The prescription removes the criminal liability for any interruption if the limitation provided for in Article 122 is exceeded once again.*" The Court found that the criticized rules are constitutional insofar as they do not prevent the application of the criminal law more favorably to the deeds committed under the old law. (Decision no.1092/2012)[49]

11.16. In 2013, no admission decision in this matter was made.

11.17. Concerning the cases in which the considerations of the decisions have also used the ECHR case-law, the most significant is Decision no.81/1994, cited above, in which the CCR noted that

---

[47]   Published in the Official Gazette of Romania, Part. I, no.338 din 26 June 2001.
[48]   Published in the Official Gazette of Romania, Part. I, no.363 din 25 May 2011.
[49]   Published in the Official Gazette of Romania, Part. I, no.67 din 31 January 2013.

Article 200(1) of the Criminal Code (which criminalizes same-sex sexual relationships) is unconstitutional insofar as it applies to sexual relationships between people of the same sex having reached the age of majority, freely consented, not committed in public or having produced public scandal. The special significance of the decision also appears in historical context, 1994 being a reference for the protection of human rights in Romania, while marking the accession to the Convention for the Protection of Human Rights and Fundamental Freedoms.[50] As the Court held in the aforementioned decision, « *if, as long as Romania has not been a member of the Council of Europe and has not adhered to the European Convention on Human Rights, the interpretation of Article 8 of the Convention, through the case law of the European Court of Human Rights in Strasbourg, had no relevance to Romanian legislation and jurisprudence after Romania's accession to the Council of Europe and accession to the European Convention on Human Rights (Law no. 30/1994, published in the Official Gazette of Romania, Part I, no.135 of May 31, 1994) the problem's data has fundamentally changed. It is the Constitution of Romania makes this change mandatory by stating in Article 20 paragraph (1), that its provisions on the rights and freedoms of citizens will be interpreted and applied in accordance with the Universal Declaration of Human Rights, with the pacts and other treaties to which Romania is a party, the European Convention on Human Rights, since May 31, 1994, has become such a treaty. Moreover, paragraph (2) of Article 20 of the Constitution enshrines the principle of the priority of the rule of international law: "If there are inconsistencies between the covenants and treaties on fundamental human rights, to which Romania is a party, and the internal laws, priority international regulations"*».

11.18. In order to rule on the unconstitutionality of the incrimination of same-sex consensual relations, the Court applied the ECHR jurisprudence on the right to intimate life, holding that «*in many countries, it is now accepted that homosexual relationships between adults who have consented to them represent a dimension of the intimate life of the individual and therefore can not be penalized. This idea came after a period of searches. Thus, even the European Court of Human Rights in Strasbourg in 1976 rejected the idea that there was a general European moral, the concept of good morals having to be understood by the provisions of national laws. Later, however, the Court reverted to this point of view (Dudgeon Business 1981, Norris 1987, Modinas*

---

[50] Denumită în continuare CEDH.

Business 1993), considering that homosexual relations between adults in private, with their consent, do not contradict good morals and therefore are not of a nature to violate Article 8 of the European Convention on Human Rights, [...]". The European Court has suggested through these decisions the amendment of the legislation of the member countries of the Council of Europe in the sense of the new interpretation of Article 8 of the Convention. The same idea is also found in Amendment No.8 of the Parliamentary Assembly of the Council of Europe to the Report on Romania's application for membership of the Council of Europe, which expresses the hope that Romania will not delay to amend its legislation in the sense that art. The Criminal Code no longer regards homosexual acts committed in private between adults who have consented to them as an offense. It must be admitted that the expression of good morals can acquire different meanings in relation to religions and ideologies. The right, as a social phenomenon, cannot ignore the evolutionary tendencies of contemporary society, including inter-human relations, even if, at some point, the legislative and jurisprudential solutions appear to contradict the traditional moral precepts». The CCR noted that there is such an inconsistency between Article 8 of the CEDH as interpreted by the ECHR and Article 200(1) of the Romanian Criminal Code, which obliges the Constitutional Court of Romania to make an appropriate decision, concluding that the removal the conflict between the domestic criminal law and the text of the CEDH, as this text is interpreted by the ECHR, leads to the partial admission of the exception of unconstitutionality regarding Article 200(1) of the Criminal Code. This decision was a cornerstone of further jurisprudence, in which the valorization of the CEDH and also the ECHR jurisprudence has become more and more substantial.

11.19. As for the other decisions, it concerns Decision no. 573/2011, cited above, referring to the principle of equality, where the Court referred to the application of Article 14 of Protocol 12 to the CEDH. In the same decision, the CCR invoked the conventional provisions on the right to a fair trial, as a result of the lack of clarity and predictability of the rule, with reference to the ECHR jurisprudence. It is also about Decision no. 1092/2012, cited above, whereby the CCR invoked ECHR jurisprudence in the application of Article 7 of the Convention.

II.3. Jurisprudential developments during 2014-2018 (New Criminal Code)

11.20. The New Criminal Code, adopted through the simplified legislative procedure of the Government assuming responsibility upon a bill,[51] has led to both substantive discussions (including criticism regarding the way of adoption, which did not allow an analysis in the specialized committees and debates in the Parliament), postponement of entry in force to prepare the reception of new institutions, changes, and also more complex approaches from the perspective of constitutional review.

11.21. In 2014, six unconstitutionality exceptions concerning the provisions of the Criminal Code were admitted. Thus, by Decision no. 78/2014,[52] for the same reasons set out in Decision no. 1092/2012, cited above, the Court found that the provisions of Article 118(2)(a),² of the Criminal Code of 1969, according to which *„Extended confiscation shall be ordered if the following conditions are met cumulatively: (a) the value of the property acquired by the convicted person within a period of 5 years before and, where appropriate, after the offense has been committed, up to the date of the referral, clearly outweighs the revenue it has obtained licitly"* is constitutional insofar as it allows the application of more favorable criminal law.

11.22. A reference decision was pronounced in the same year on the provisions of Article 5 of the Criminal Code, with the marginal name *Applying the more favorable criminal law until the final judgment of the case.* Thus, by the precited Decision no. 265/2014, the CCR accepted the unconstitutionality exception and found that the provisions of Article 5 of the Criminal Code are constitutional insofar as they do not allow the combination of successive laws in the establishment and application of the more favorable criminal law. CCR based its arguments, inter alia, referencing the provisions of Article 7(1) of the ECHR and the judgment of 18 July 2013, pronounced in the case of *Maktouf and Damjanović against Bosnia and Herzegovina.* From the perspective of the present study, it is a reference decision because it places the new criminal policy and the new regulation in the field, subject to the new Romanian Criminal Code in the context of serving the common space of freedom, security and justice in the European Union. As the subsequent jurisprudence will reveal, the Romanian Constitutional Judge continued to carry out his analysis in this context, including when he addressed the

---

[51] http://www.cdep.ro/pls/proiecte/upl_pck2015.proiect?cam=2&idp=10255 (accessed on 31 December 2018).

[52] Published in the Official Gazette of Romania no. 273 of 14 April 2014.

legislator by means of an appeal decision, to regulate with the observance of the European framework in the matter.[53]

11.23. Indeed, even in the next admission decision of the matter in the same year, respectively Decision no.356/2014,[54] the Court characterize the nature and purpose of the confiscation institution by referring to the Communication from the Commission to the European Parliament and the Council, COM (2008) 766 final, showing that « *it was essential to discourage organized crime activities by dispossessing the offenders of the proceeds from the offense. Organized crime groups build large-scale international networks and obtain substantial profits from various criminal activities. The confiscation and recovery of assets held by criminals is a very effective way of combating organized crime, primarily aimed at profit. Confiscation prevents the use of criminal assets as a source of funding for other criminal activities, removes the risk of compromising confidence in financial systems and corrupting legitimate society. Confiscation has a dissuasive character because it strengthens the principle that "crime does not bring income". This could help eliminate the negative patterns offered by offenders to local communities. In some cases, measures to confiscate the proceeds of crime allow the pursuit of decision-makers within criminal organizations, which are rarely investigated and prosecuted»*. It goes on to say that «*in the case of offenses with serious consequences and consequences both at national and transnational level, the Court notes the emergence of a concept / principle that offenses must not generate profit/ income — „crimes does not pay". Also, in the doctrine, it was noted that the measure of confiscation of property is nothing more than an option of criminal policy and a means of repression and re-education of those committing such crimes. Everything that is a specific manifestation of organized crime should be included in this category.*». Placing it in this context of criminal policy and invoking the *living law theory* has allowed the identification of constitutional bases for the extended confiscation measure. We could say that this is a re-interpretation of the constitutional presumption of the licit nature of wealth correlated with European instruments – both the EU and the Council of Europe – in order to combat organized crime. Thus, the exception of unconstitutionality was upheld, the Court found that the provisions of Article 118(2)(a)[2], of the 1969 Criminal Code are constitutional insofar as the extended confiscation does not apply to goods acquired prior to the entry into force of Law No.

---

[53] Decision no.405/2016, published in the Official Gazette of Romania, Part. I, no.517 on 8 July 2016.
[54] Published in the Official Gazette of Romania, Part. I, no.691 din 22 September 2014.

63/2012 for the amendment and completion of the Romanian Criminal Code and Law No. 286/2009 on the Criminal Code. It is not necessarily the admission solution that draws attention here. It is the broad argument of the Court, which for the above reasons, in fact supports the constitutionality of the extended confiscation (problematic through the interpretation of the Constitutional Court has given so far to the presumption of acquiring of the property, enshrined in Article 44, paragraph 8 of the Constitution.)[55]

11.24. The following decision, no.508/2014[56] by which the Constitutional Court upheld the exception of unconstitutionality of the provisions of Article 159(3) of the Criminal Code and found that they are constitutional insofar as they apply to all defendants brought before the date of entry into force of Law no.286/2009 on the Criminal Code and for which, at that time, the moment of the reading of the document instituting the proceedings had been exceeded does not impose special considerations. There was, *mutatis mutandis*, the same reasoning as in the Decision no.1.470/2011. However, the next one, Decision no.732/2014,[57] is illustrative of the new approach of the CCR, which uses the case law of the CJEU for the first time in this field, in substantiating the considerations of an admission decision. Thus, the CCR accepted the exception of unconstitutionality and found that the phrase „*at the time of gathering biological samples*" of the provisions of Article 336(1) of the Criminal Code is unconstitutional because it violates the constitutional provisions of Article 1(5) on the principle of respect for the law and Article 20 on the preeminence of international human rights treaties over domestic laws, compared to the provisions of Article 7(1) on the lawfulness of incrimination in the ECHR. The Court ruled that" *this phrase lacks the predictability of the rule of criminality, provided that the principle of lawfulness and the lawfulness of criminality require the legislator to legislate by texts sufficiently clear and precise to be enforceable, including by ensuring that those concerned are able to comply with the statutory limitation".* In addition to ECHR jurisprudence on the interpretation and application of Article 7 of the Convention, the CCR has also invoked the case-law of the CJEU which "*implicitly acknowledged the need to respect the legitimate*

---

[55] For a punctual and analytical treatment of this issue, see Marieta Safta, *Prezumția dobândirii licite a averii și confiscarea averilor ilicit dobândite în jurisprudența curții constituționale a României. Cadrul constituțional de referință pentru reglementarea confiscării extins,* 2(1) TRIBUNA JURIDICĂ, ASE PUBLISHING HOUSE, BUCHAREST 107-127 (Romanian language version) 128-147 (English language version) (2011).

[56] Published in the Official Gazette of Romania, Part. I, no.843 din 19 November 2014.

[57] Published in the Official Gazette of Romania, Part. I, no.69 din 27 January 2015.

expectations of citizens to whom legal regulation is addressed, for example in its judgment of 29 June 2010 in Case C-550/09 – Criminal proceedings against E. and F., paragraph 59".

11.25. In 2015, two admission decisions concerning the provisions of the Criminal Code were issued. Through Decision no.11/2015,[58] following the established jurisprudence line, the CCR established that the provisions in Article 112(2)(a) of the Criminal Code are constitutional insofar as the extended confiscation does not apply to assets acquired prior to the entry into force of Law no.63/2012 for amending and supplementing the Romanian Criminal Code and the Law No. 286/2009 on the Criminal Code. Through Decision no.603/2015,[59] The Court accepted the objection of unconstitutionality and found that the phrase *"commercial relations"* in the provisions of Article 301(1) of the Criminal Code to be unconstitutional; moreover, it admitted the objection of unconstitutionality and found the phrase *"or within any legal person"* in the provisions of Article 308, paragraph (1) of the Criminal Code, with reference to Article 301 of the Criminal Code to be unconstitutional. In the first case The Court sanctioned the ambiguity of the law, and in the second case, the Court found that the criminalization of conflict of interest in the private environment is an unjustified violation of the economic freedom and the right to work of persons exercising, with or without remuneration, either permanently or temporarily, a task of any kind within any legal persons.

11.26. In 2016, the CCR issued a single admission decision regarding the Criminal Code, also illustrative of the present study. Thus, through Decision no.405/2016[60] The Court found that the provisions of Article 246 of the 1969 Criminal Code and Article 297(1) of the Criminal Code criminalizing abuse of office are constitutional inasmuch as through the phrase *" fulfills in a defective manner" " within the meaning of this is understood to be "fulfills by breaking the law".* The above-mentioned texts read as follows: *„The act of a civil servant who, in the exercise of his or her duties, knowingly does not perform an act or does so defectively and thereby causes harm to the legal interests of a person shall be punished by imprisonment from 6 months to 3 years."* (Article 246 of the 1969 Criminal Code); *"The act of a civil servant who, in the exercise of his professional duties, does not perform an act or does so defectively and thereby causes damage or injury to the legitimate rights or interests of a natural person or a legal person*

[58] Published in the Official Gazette of Romania, Part. I, no.102 din 09 February 2015.
[59] Published in the Official Gazette of Romania, Part. I, no.845 din 13 November 2015.
[60] Published in the Official Gazette of Romania, Part. I, no.517 din 08 July 2016.

is punishable by imprisonment to 2 to 7 years and the ban on the exercise of the right to take up a public office." (Article 297(1) of the Criminal Code). A year later, the Court ruled on the same solution to Article 248 of the 1969 Criminal Code, according to which *„The act of a civil servant who in the exercise of his professional duties does not perform an act or performs it in a defective manner and thereby causes a significant disturbance to the goodwill of an organ or state institution or other entity those referred to in Art. 145 or damage to her property shall be punished by imprisonment from 6 months to 5 years."* Practically, the court pronounced two sentences on these texts at an interval of approximatively one year (2016 and, respectively, 2017), in which it found that the provisions of Articles 246 and 248 of the Criminal Code of 1969 and Article 297(1) of the Criminal Code are constitutional insofar as the phrase *"fulfills in a defective manner"* in their content is understood to be *"fulfills by breaking the law".* At the same time, it dismissed the objection of unconstitutionality as inadmissible regarding the lack of a threshold of damage and the circumstances of the injury caused by committing the act of abuse of office.

11.27. The pronouncement of these exceptions of unconstitutionality[61] has led the CCR to establish a case-law centered on the principle of proportionality, materialized and applied on several stages. By addressing, on a note of proportionality, the margin of appreciation of the legislator for the implementation of criminal policy, the Court has established two broad criteria that the legislator has to observe in the drafting of criminal rules: *the degree of intensity necessary for the application of a criminal penalty, the legislator having to dose the use of criminal means depending on the protected social value; the 'ultima ratio' principle,* which requires that the legislature, when exercising its power to legislate in criminal matters, *should take account of the principle that criminalization of an act must intervene as a last resort in the protection of a social value.* The Court made the reasoning and circumstantiations not only in the context of its own evolutionary jurisprudence under this aspect,[62] but

---

[61] Decision no.392 of 6 June 2017 published in the Official Gazette of Romania no.504 of 30 June 2017, Decision no. 405 of 15 June 2016, published in the Official Gazette of Romania, Part I, no. 517 of 8 July 2016.
[62] Also see Decision no.683 of 19 November 2014, published in the Official Gazette of Romania, Part. I, no.47 on 20 January 2015, on the legislative solution that set the threshold for over 90 days of hospitalization of the victim of of a traffic accident involving personal injuries that attracts the incidence of criminal law, with the consequence of decriminalizing the deeds that caused injuries that required medical care below this threshold, the Court held that *„the legislator has the right to place the constitutional protection of non-criminal value in the area of civil delictual liability",* thus, implicitly, it accepted the thesis that the incidence of criminal liability is conditioned by a certain degree of seriousness or a certain level of impairment of the value protected by the criminal regulation; in this sene, Decision no.824 of 3 December 2015, published in the Official Gazette of Romania, Part. I, no.122 of 17 February 2016.

also in a framework of European and comparative law. In the recitals of the pronounced resolutions, the Communication from the Commission to the European Parliament, the Council, the Economic and Social Committee and the Committee of the Regions towards a European Union criminal policy on criminal matters were explicitly invoked: Ensure the effective implementation of EU policies through criminal law, COM/2011/0573, pt.2.2.1 — Necessity and proportionality — criminal law as a last resort (ultima ratio) — where it is stated that *"criminal investigations and sanctions can have a significant impact on citizens' rights and have a stigmatizing effect. Therefore, criminal law must always remain a last resort. Therefore, the legislator should consider whether measures other than criminal law, such as administrative or civil penalty schemes, could not sufficiently ensure policy enforcement and whether criminal law could address more effective issues."* Also, the CCR invoked the jurisprudence of the constitutional courts (The Constitutional Court of Lithuania, The Constitutional Tribunal of Portugal, The Constitutional Court of Hungary) as well as documents of the European Commission for Democracy through Law (Venice Commission) or other entities – Report on the Relationship Between Political and Criminal Ministerial Responsibility (Venice, 8 - 9 March 2013). The Court invoked, *mutatis mutandis*, the statutes of the Venice Commission to the effect that national criminal provisions on 'abuse of office', 'abuse of power' and similar expressions must be interpreted narrowly and applied at a high level so that they can be invoked only in cases which are serious, such as serious crimes against national democratic processes, violation of fundamental rights, undermining the impartiality of the public administration, and so forth [...]. Moreover, additional criteria should be imposed such as, for example, the requirement of serious intention or negligence. For cases of "abuse of office" or "abuse of power" involving economic interests, the requirement of a personal gain may be considered appropriate either for the person concerned or for example, a political party. [...] insofar as the criminal provisions of "abuse of office" and "abuse of power" are invoked against ministers for actions that are mainly of a political nature, then this must be done as the last solution (ultima ratio). Moreover, the level of sanctions must be proportionate to the offense committed and not be influenced by political considerations and disagreements. The CCR also noticed upon analyzing the quality and predictability of some regulations that incriminated abuse of office, that the European

Court of Human Rights held that the concerned dispositions of criminal law, as well as their interpretation were inherited from the old Soviet legal system. Thus, the national authorities have faced the difficult task of applying these legal rules in the context of the new market economy (the Decisions of 25 June 2009 pronounced in the case of *Liivik* v. *Estonia*, paragraph 97). According to the jurisprudence of the European Court of Human Rights, Article 7(1) of the Convention for the Protection of Human Rights and Fundamental Freedoms, which enshrines the principle of the lawfulness of incrimination and punishment (*nullum crimen, nulla poena sine lege*), in addition to the prohibiting, in particular, the extension of the content of existing offenses to acts which previously did not constitute an offense, also provides for the principle that criminal law should not be interpreted and applied extensively to the detriment of the accused, for example by analogy. It follows that the law must clearly define the applicable offenses and penalties. This requirement is fulfilled when a person has the opportunity to know the acts and omissions that can incur its criminal liability and the punishment that they risk under their authority from the actual legal normative text itself if necessary by interpreting it through the courts and obtaining appropriate legal assistance.

11.28. In 2017, for reasons similar to those that substantiated the decision on the crime of abuse of service, the CCR found that the provisions of Article 249(1) of the 1969 Criminal Code and of Article 298 of the Criminal Code concerning negligence in service are constitutional in so far as by the phrase *"fulfills in a defective manner"* in their content is meant *" fulfilled by breaking the law "*.(Decision no.518/2017)[63]

11.29. Apart from the two mentioned decisions, the CCR also pronounced two decisions in the same year for admitting exceptions of unconstitutionality regarding the Criminal Code. Namely, through Decision no.224/2017,[64] The Court found that the legislative solution contained in Article 355 paragraph (1) of the Criminal Code, which does not criminalize the driving on the public roads of an agricultural or forestry tractor without a driving license, is unconstitutional. Then, through Decision no.369/2017,[65] The Court found that the phrase *"and against the same passive subject"* in the provisions of Article 35 paragraph (1) of the Criminal Code, according to which *"The offense is continued when a person repeats, at different intervals, but*

[63] Published in the Official Gazette of Romania, Part. I, no.765 din 26 November 2017.
[64] Published in the Official Gazette of Romania, Part. I, no.427 din 09 June 2017.
[65] Published in the Official Gazette of Romania, Part. I, no.566 din 17 July 2017.

in the same resolution and against the same passive subject, actions or inactions that each have the content of the same offense." is unconstitutional. In this case too, the recitals of the CCR decision are consistently based on ECHR jurisprudence; pronouncing a broad comparative analysis on the notion of "continued offense" by the ECHR in the case of *Rohlena against the Czech Republic.* (The Ruling of 27 January 2015). From this perspective, the CCR has considered it necessary to change its jurisprudence on the provisions of Article 35(1) of the Criminal Code, taking into account the evolution of the legislation, the doctrine and the judicial practice in the matter of the continued offense and reevaluating the impact of the criticized provisions in terms of the exclusion of their application in many situations where it cannot reasonably justify the incidence of the criminal treatment of the offense contest.

11.30. Lastly, 2018 debuted in the matter with a decision whereby the CCR found the legislative solution which provides for the interruption of the term of the limitation of criminal liability to be unconstitutional through the fulfillment of *"any act of the procedure in question"*, from the provisions of Article 155(1) of the Criminal Code (Decision no.297/2018).[66] In essence, the court held that it is necessary to guarantee the foreseeable nature of the effects of the provisions of Article 155(1) of the Criminal Code against the person who committed an act provided for by the criminal law, including by ensuring that it is possible to know the appearance of the interruption of the course of the limitation of the criminal liability and the commencement of the new prescription period. With the occasion of the establishing procedural acts that are not communicated to the suspect or the accused and which have the effect of interrupting the limitation of the criminal liability, accepting the contrary solution means creating a state of perpetual uncertainty for the person concerned. This happens due to the impossibility of reasonable appreciation of the timeframe in which it can be criminally liable for the acts committed, an uncertainty that may last until the special prescription period provided for in Article 155(4) of the Criminal Code. The CCR also noted that the legal issue invoked by the authors of the objection of unconstitutionality was the subject of legislative activity and the control of constitutionality and legality in other European states. Thus, in countries such as Estonia, Finland, France, Germany, Italy, Malta, the Netherlands, Portugal, Slovakia and Spain, interruption of the limitation of criminal liability is done

---

[66] Published in the Official Gazette of Romania, Part. I, no.518 on 25 June 2018.

through procedural documents communicated to the suspect or accused, or involving their presence before the judicial bodies, or by acts that directly address the settlement of the criminal legal relationship of conflict. At the same time, according to the case law of the Federal Constitutional Court of Germany, the general constitutional guarantees remain applicable and must be respected in terms of limitation periods on criminal liability. This includes, in particular, the principle of the protection of legitimate expectations and the general requirement of legal clarity and specificity deriving from the principle of the rule of law (BVerfGE 50, 42 <47>; BVerfG, Order of the Third Chamber of the Second Senate on 26 November 2003 — 2 BvR 1247/01, 2 BvR 1248/01 —), as well as the principle of proportionality (BVerfG, Order of the Third Chamber of the Second Senate on 26 November 2003 — 2, BvR 1247, 1248/01 —). In view of the above considerations, the Court found that the previous legislative solution provided for in Article 123(1) of the 1969 Criminal Code fulfilled the conditions of predictability imposed by the constitutional provisions analyzed in the present case because it provided for the interruption of the limitation of the limitation of criminal liability only by fulfilling an act, which according to the law, had to be communicated, in the case in which the person concerned was in the position of the accused or the defendant.

III.   Conclusions

11.31. As has been shown,[67] in a Europe that strives to establish a common market, the differences between the legal systems of the Member States can potentially be detrimental; economic integration must be followed by legal integration, "at least to a certain point". Since the nature of the criminal law is itself at the core of national sovereignty, the choice for any part of criminal law to fall within the exclusive competence of the European Union has been disputed, the Member States and the Union having shared competence of judicial cooperation, with the application of the principle of subsidiarity. Recent developments, such as the regulation of the European Prosecutor's Office, show, however, that at least in the field of criminal law, it is becoming increasingly difficult to identify issues that would not fall within the competence of the European Union.

11.32. Of course, the constitutional courts do not create norms and do not elaborate public policies. However, constitutionality control

---

[67]   Kimmo Nuotio, *Ibid.*, at 1115-1138.

is one of the most powerful modeling factors for legislators' action and even public policies, as they have to be in line with the Constitution. Thus, the interpretation of Articles 20 and 148 of the Romanian Constitution, texts that connect the internal law with that of the European Union and human rights is essential for the reporting of the entire Romanian legal system to the European and international reference standards. The examination of the jurisprudence reveals the gradual opening of the CCR to an interpretation and approach of the criminal law in connection with the European Union regulations, respectively with standards of protection of the fundamental rights regulated or recommended by the EU institutions and also by de CEDO. It was not our intention to analyze the way in which European criminal law institutions are reflected in constitutional control but rather to illustrate a tendency in the approach and comparison which, in our view, can also be interpreted as a principle statement of necessity of regulation of some criminal law institutions, even the criminalization of acts, by reference to democratic models in the Member States of the European Union, and the Recommendations of the Venice Commission (see, for example, the regulation of abuse of service).

11.33. The approximation of national laws in criminal matters is not an objective in itself, but obviously serves to strengthen mutual trust, which is a basic principle of the EU. Ultimately, the creation of a European criminal justice must not only emerge as a reaction to crisis situations, such as the escalation of terrorism or organized crime, but, above all, as a common regulatory will to achieve a common criminal policy.

Summaries

DEU   [*Das europäische Strafrecht als Form des supranationalen Rechts. Die Entwicklung vermittels Revision des Verfassungsrechts*]
Die Entstehung des europäischen Strafrechts ist auf Diskussion und Krise zurückzuführen. Mehr als irgend etwas anderes ist seine Schaffung eine Reaktion auf wahrgenommene Sicherheitsrisiken – das Bedürfnis und der Wunsch, Sicherheit zu gewährleisten, sind die treibende Kraft hinter der Entstehung des europäischen Strafrechts. Obwohl das Engagement der Europäischen Union

im Bereich Strafrecht für enorme Herausforderungen und Spannungen sorgt, geht die Entwicklung in diesem Bereich mit stetem Tempo weiter. Eine Gesamtschau der Entwicklung des europäischen Strafrechts erfordert, dass wir uns mit der Frage sowohl aus Sicht der Europäischen Union und ihrer einzelnen Mitgliedsstaaten befassen, als auch aus Sicht des Europäischen Gerichtshofs und der Verfassungsgerichte der Mitgliedsstaaten. Die verfassungsrechtliche Kontrolle darf als Katalysator bei der Erbauung des europäischen Rechts gelten; ihr kommt enorme Bedeutung zu. Dies gilt umso mehr als das Strafrecht – wie diverse Studien bezeugen – derzeit im verfassungsrechtlichen Sinne eine Revolution durchmacht. Der Umfang, in dem die Verfassungsgerichte die verfassungsrechtlichen Grundlagen strafrechtlicher Normen prüfen, ist vielfältig und wird durch nationale Traditionen beeinflusst. Dass aber strafrechtliche Fragen immer intensiver aus dem Blickwinkel des Verfassungsrechts angegangen werden, ist nicht zu verleugnen. Zugleich tragen die Verfassungsgerichte dadurch, dass sie auf die Rechtsprechung internationaler und supranationaler Gerichte sowie das vergleichende Recht zurückgreifen, zur gegenseitigen Annäherung der Rechtsordnungen auf europäischer Ebene bei – auch und gerade im Strafrecht. Dies stärkt das wechselseitige Vertrauen, als ein Grundprinzip der EU. Von diesen Voraussetzungen ausgehend analysiert die vorliegende Studie unter dem Aspekt der verfassungsrechtlichen Kontrolle die Entwicklung des europäischen Strafrechts.

CZE [*Evropské trestní právo jako forma nadnárodního práva. Vývoj prostřednictvím revize ústavního práva*]
Vznik evropského trestního práva je výsledkem diskuse a krize. Jeho vytvoření je, spíše než cokoli jiného, reakcí na pociťovaná bezpečnostní rizika – zajišťování bezpečnosti je motorem vzniku evropského trestního práva. Přestože angažovanost Evropské unie v trestním právu je zdrojem velkých výzev a pnutí, vývoj v této oblasti pokračuje setrvalým tempem. Požadujeme-li komplexní přístup k vývoji evropského trestního práva, je potřeba se touto otázkou zabývat jak z hlediska Evropské unie a členských států, tak z hlediska Soudního dvora EU a ústavních soudů členských států. Ústavní kontrolu lze považovat za katalyzátor při budování evropského práva, její důležitost je značná. To platí o to více, jak potvrzují studie v dané oblasti, že trestní právo prodělalo v současné době revoluci v ústavněprávním významu. Rozsah, v jakém ústavní soudy zkoumají ústavní základy trestněprávních norem, je velmi rozmanitý, ovlivňovaný národními tradicemi. Nepopiratelný je však prohlubující se

ústavněprávní přístup k trestněprávním otázkám. Současně platí, že využíváním judikatury mezinárodních a nadnárodních soudů, jakož i srovnávacího práva, ústavní soudy přispívají ke sbližování právních řádů – včetně dimenze trestního práva – na evropské úrovni. Tento přístup posiluje vzájemnou důvěru, základní princip EU. Na základě těchto výchozích předpokladů tato studie analyzuje vývoj evropského trestního práva pohledem ústavněprávní kontroly.

| | |

POL [*Europejskie prawo karne jako forma prawa ponadnarodowego. Zmiany przez rewizję prawa konstytucyjnego*]
Zmiany europejskiego prawa karnego zasługują na uwagę zarówno z perspektywy Unii Europejskiej i państw członkowskich, jak i z perspektywy Trybunału Sprawiedliwości UE oraz sądów konstytucyjnych państw członkowskich. Kontrolę konstytucyjną należy uznać za katalizator w tworzeniu europejskiego prawa. W oparciu o te założenia w artykule przeanalizowano zmiany w europejskim prawie karnym z perspektywy kontroli na gruncie prawa konstytucyjnego.

FRA [*Le droit pénal européen en tant qu'une catégorie du droit supranational. Ses transformations au fil des révisions du droit constitutionnel*]
L'évolution du droit pénal européen doit être abordée sous plusieurs perspectives : celle de l'Union européenne et de ses États membres, mais aussi celle de la Cour de justice européenne et celles des cours constitutionnelles des États membres. Le contrôle constitutionnel joue un rôle de catalyseur dans la construction du droit européen. Partant de ces prémisses, la présente étude se propose d'analyser l'évolution du droit pénal européen à la lumière de son contrôle constitutionnel.

RUS [*Европейское уголовное право как форма наднационального права. Развитие путем пересмотра конституционного права*]
Развитие европейского уголовного права следует рассматривать как с точки зрения Европейского союза и государств-членов, так и с точки зрения Суда ЕС и конституционных судов государств-членов. Конституционный контроль можно считать своеобразным катализатором в процессе создания европейского права. Основываясь на этих исходных предпосылках, данная

статья анализирует развитие европейского уголовного права с точки зрения конституционно-правового контроля.

ESP **[*El derecho penal europeo como una forma del derecho supranacional. El desarrollo mediante la revisión del derecho constitucional*]**
El desarrollo del derecho penal europeo debe ser abordado tanto desde la perspectiva de la Unión Europea y los Estados miembros, como desde el punto de vista del Tribunal de Justicia de la UE y de los tribunales constitucionales de los países miembros. El control constitucional puede ser considerado un catalizador de la creación de la legislación europea. Partiendo de estas premisas, el presente estudio analiza el desarrollo del derecho penal europeo desde el punto de vista del control constitucional.

||||

Bibliography

BENJAMIN L. BERGER, CONSTITUTIONAL PRINCIPLES, THE OXFORD HANDBOOK OF CRIMINAL LAW, Oxford University Press (Markus. D. Dubber, Tatjana Hörnle eds. 2016).

PAUL CRAIG & GRAINNE DE BURCA, DREPTUL UNIUNII EUROPENE – COMENTARII, JURISPRUDENȚĂ ȘI DOCTRINĂ, Hamagiu Publishing House (2017).

MASSIMO FICHERA & JENS KREMER, LAW AND SECURITY IN EUROPE: RECONSIDERING THE SECURITY CONSTITUTION (Jens Kremer eds., 2013).

Tudorel Toader, Marieta Safta, *Evoluția constituționalismului în România*, 1 REVIEW OF CONSTITUTIONAL LAW 156 (2015).

Marieta Safta, *Prezumția dobândirii licite a averii și confiscarea averilor ilicit dobândite în jurisprudența curții constituționale a României. Cadrul constituțional de referință pentru reglementarea confiscării extins*, 2(1) TRIBUNA JURIDICĂ, ASE PUBLISHING HOUSE, BUCHAREST 107 (Romanian language version) 128 (English language version) (2011).

KIMMO NUOTIO, EUROPEAN CRIMINAL LAW, THE OXFORD HANDBOOK OF CRIMINAL LAW, Oxford University Press (Markus D. Dubber, Tatjana Hörnle eds., 2016).

Olha Starytska | Olena Tantsiura

Methodological Pluralism in the Interpretations of 'Protection' and 'Safeguard' as Implemented in Private International Law Regulations

Key words:
protection | safeguard | private law sphere | offense | encroachment | restoration | rights and freedoms | state bodies

Abstract | *The authors of this article studied the approaches to define and correlate the concepts 'protection' and 'safeguard' taking into consideration the peculiarities of their implementation in the field of private law regulation. The basis of the analysis is taken from the main widely held legal positions where these concepts are identified, contrasted, complimented or are considered as the guarantee of human and civil rights and freedoms. Each approach utilizes scholarly arguments which the authors discuss. Analyzing the current sources on a chosen issue, the authors come to the conclusion that there is terminological confusion when the content of one notion is opened using other content. Such mutual absorption of concepts or their substitution is criticized, a result of which is the authors' opinion that methodological pluralism exists in modern jurisprudence.*

| | |

Olena Tantsiura graduated from the National Academy of Internal Affairs (2007), Ukraine. She received a Ph.D. in jurisprudence from the same academy (2010). She is currently an associate professor in the Department of Civil Law and the Process of the Educational and Research Institute of Law of the National Aviation University, Ukraine, Kyiv. She specializes in the theory of state and law, theory of justice, intellectual property, private law, family law and commercial law. E-mail: olenagusareva@gmail.com

Olha Starytska has a Ph.D. in jurisprudence, graduating from the Institute of Air and Space Law of the National Aviation University, Ukraine, Kyiv (2008). She undertook post-graduate studies at the National Academy of Internal Affairs, Ukraine, Kyiv (2014). She currently works as an associate professor at the Department of Theory of the State and Law of the National Academy of Internal Affairs, Ukraine,

Czech Yearbook of International Law®

I. Introduction

Kyiv. She specializes in the theory of state, theory of law, theory of state power, consumer protection, intellectual property, private law and international private law. E-mail: ostar0811@gmail.com

12.01. For a long time, the problem of correlation of the legal concepts of 'protection' and 'safeguard' have been the subject of scholarly research by representatives of both theoretical and practical spheres of law. Against the background of modern social transformations and increasing attention to the provision of basic human rights and freedoms, the issue of substantive updating of commonly used terms will become more vital to make their implementation more efficient, effective and precise. This happens increasingly often when legislation is issued in a way that promotes legal conflicts, and the legislative body that initiated it proceeds from its own interests and relevant industry standards. That is why, in our opinion, the issue of the substantive part of any definition requires a broad systemic analysis, considering not only individual points of view, but also the established methodological approaches, verified by both the practice of their normative use and the practice of doctrinal interpretations.

12.02. The aim of this article is to systematize and analyze modern approaches to the understanding of the concepts of 'protection' and 'safeguard', as well as providing a justification of their correlation and identification given the peculiarities of their use in the private law sphere. The achievement of this goal will require the differentiation of modern approaches to the understanding of the concepts of 'protection' and 'safeguard', as well as their comparison according to the criterion of volume. Finally, we shall outline our vision concerning the use of these categories in the field of private law.

12.03. The aforementioned issues have been repeatedly studied by the representatives of theoretical scholarship[1] and specialists in civil law.[2] However, the problem of differentiating and comparing the scope and content of these concepts in two legal areas

---

[1] See for example: Serhii Alekseyev, *General theory of law*, 1 JURID. LIT. 361 (1981);SERHII BRATUS, RESPONSIBILITY IN LAW AND LEGALITY. ESSAY THEORY, Legal Literature 215 (1976); PETRO RABINOVYCH, FUNDAMENTALS OF THE GENERAL THEORY OF LAW AND STATE, Atika 176 (2001), etc.

[2] See for example: I Dzera, *Civil-legal remedies for the protection of property rights in Ukraine: author's abstract*, DPhD in jurisprudence, T. Shevchenko National University 18 (2001); OLIMPIAD IOFFE, SOVIET CIVIL LAW, Yurid. Lit. 472–473 (1967); LARYSA KRASAVCHIKOVA, PERSONAL LIFE OF CITIZENS UNDER THE PROTECTION OF THE LAW, Legal Literature 12 (1983); YAROSLAVNA SHEVCHENKO, OWNER AND OWNERSHIP, Naukovadumka 205 (1994); ZORISLAVA ROMOVSKA, PROTECTION IN THE SOVIET FAMILY LAW (1985); RUSLAN STEFANCHUK, CIVIL LAW OF UKRAINE, Precedent 361 (2005); GANNA OSETYNS'KA, CIVIL AND LEGAL PROTECTION OF CONSUMER RIGHTS ACCORDING TO THE UKRAINIAN LEGISLATION, DPhD in jurisprudence, Kyev's National University named after T.G.Shevchenko (2006).

(theoretical and practical) remains poorly studied and therefore relevant to further developments.

II.   Grouping by Peculiarities

12.04. With the aim of systematizing modern scholarly views on the understanding of the concepts of 'protection' and 'safeguard', it is appropriate to group them according to the criteria of the peculiarities of the sphere of private law regulation.

II.1.   'Protection' and 'Safety' as a Synonyms

12.05. Supporters of one of the main scholarly approaches are authors who consider the concepts of 'protection' and 'safeguard' of rights identical and use them synonymously. For example, Serhii Ozhegov defines the notion of 'to safeguard' as 'protecting, defending from attacks, from hostile actions, from danger.' At the same time, 'to protect' is interpreted as 'to keep, to defend, to keep in integrity, to save,' as well as 'to ensure that they are not harmful to anyone or anything.'[3] Thus, protection is safeguard, and safeguard is protection.

12.06. Using the criterion of the intended purpose, Zorislava Romovska believes that the purpose of protection is the regulation of social relations at the first stage and the definition of measures to protect a specific subjective right at the second stage. At the same time, the very opportunity to safeguard this right and its specific implementation is one of the factors of protection, and protection is only the result of the person's realization of the right to safeguard.[4]

12.07. The position of Romovska is somewhat controversial. Romovska's criterion for differentiation of these categories is unclear, and the scope of contents and application are obscured. Both safeguard and protection can be the outcome of the implementation of a particular subject's powers, and therefore the outcome of the implementation cannot be chosen as a criterion for distinguishing these two categories and corresponding legal phenomena.

12.08. The position of Oleksandr Sergeyev is of interest for scholarly studies. He points out that at the level within the broad concept of protection in scholarship and the practice of legislative

---

[3]   SERHII OZHEGOV, DICTIONARY OF THE RUSSIAN LANGUAGE, Rus. Yaz. 196 (1984).
[4]   ZORISLAVA ROMOVSKA, PROTECTION IN THE SOVIET FAMILY LAW (1985).; RUSLAN STEFANCHUK, CIVIL LAW OF UKRAINE, Precedent 361 (2005).; GANNA OSETYNS'KA, CIVIL AND LEGAL PROTECTION OF CONSUMER RIGHTS ACCORDING TO THE UKRAINIAN LEGISLATION, DPhD in jurisprudence, Kyev's National University named after T.G.Shevchenko (2006).

activity, the concept of protection is used in a narrow sense. Its use only covers those measures envisaged by the legislation that are aimed at the restoration or recognition of civil rights and the protection of interests in their violation or contestation. Thus, for example, Part 2 of Article 16 of the Civil Code of Ukraine establishes that there may be the following ways of protecting civil rights and interests: recognition of a right, recognition of a deed to be voided, restoration of the situation that existed before the violation, compensation for losses and other methods of compensation for material damage, and compensation for moral (non-material) damage.[5]

12.09. The Commercial Code of Ukraine contains a similar norm that stipulates that the rights and legitimate interests of economic entities are respectively protected by recognition of the presence or absence of rights; the recognition to void in whole or in part of acts of State authorities and local self-government bodies, acts of other entities that are in conflict with the law, infringement of the rights and legitimate interests of the subject of economic activity or consumers; invalidation of economic contracts; and indemnification.[6]

12.10. In this case, according to Sergeyev, protection is the safeguard of private rights.[7] Thus, Sergeyev equates the protection of rights with the safeguard of rights.

12.11. In the scholarly literature there is an approach, the essence of which is to fold one concept into another one.

12.12. This position is supported by Serhii Taranenko, who considers 'protection' and 'safeguard' as general and partial. Their differentiation is based on the presence or absence of a violated right and its restoration.[8] This opinion is shared by Oleksii Ulyanov, who notes that such an approach allows the determination of the peculiarities of the State bodies' activities in the mechanism of safeguarding the rights and freedoms of citizens.[9]

12.13. The problem with this approach is that even among the supporters of this position there are differences as to what kind of concept is generic, and which is specific, especially in the field of private law. As Serhii Vavzenchuk notes, some scholars believe

5 The Civil Code of Ukraine of 16 January 2003. Kyiv: Verkhovna Rada of Ukraine (Article 16).
6 Commercial Code of Ukraine of 16 January 2003. Kyiv: Verkhovna Rada of Ukraine (Article 20).
7 Aleksandr Sergeyev, *Civil law*, Prospect 334 (Yu Tolstoy ed. 1998).
8 SERHII TARANENKO, PROTECTION OF THE RIGHTS AND FREEDOMS OF CITIZENS IN PROCEEDINGS ON ADMINISTRATIVE VIOLATIONS AND THEIR PROVISION IN THE ACTIVITIES OF THE LAW ENFORCEMENT BODIES, DPhD in jurisprudence, National Academy of Sciences of Ukraine named after V.M. Koretsky Institute of State and Law 4 (2000).
9 OLEKSII ULYANOV, ADMINISTRATIVE-LEGAL PROTECTION OF THE RIGHTS OF CITIZENS BY THE MILITIA IN THE SPHERE OF PUBLIC ORDER, DPhD in jurisprudence, Odesa's Law institute of The National University of Internal Affaires 6 (2002).

that protection is a broader concept and covers safeguarding as a constituent element, while others argue that protection is an integral part of safeguarding.[10]

12.14. Supporting the above thesis, Maksym Legenchenko states that the issue of safeguarding of a right is a component of the broader concept of protection, which, along with the safeguarding of such a right, also contains mechanisms for its implementation and ways to prevent possible violations. The very concept of the 'safeguard of rights' is also an integral part of the protection of rights, which is exercised not only in the case of the violation of rights, but also primarily during its very realization. It is a system of legal norms aimed at the restoration of the violated or challenged rights and the provision of the interests of a person concerning the right belonging to them in the corresponding legal title. Legenchenko emphasizes that the actual restoration of the violated right is a characteristic feature of civil and economic/private legal safeguards, since the purpose of criminal or administrative/public safeguards of rights is primarily punishment of the offender for the committed wrongful act. Hence, a private legal safeguard is marked by its focus on the restoration of the violated right and securing the interests of an authorized person.[11] An example of securing a legal interest can be found in Part 2 of Article 386 of the Civil Code of Ukraine, which stipulates that the owner, who has grounds to foresee the possibility of violating their property right by another person, may apply to the court for the prohibition of actions which may violate their right or with the requirement to take certain actions to prevent such a violation.[12]

12.15. In our opinion, the aforementioned approach is the most reasonable and adapted to the sphere of private law regulation, since the concepts of protection and safeguard are interdependent and complementary elements of a single mechanism of legal regulation. They correlate with each other and have different spectra of manifestation, which depend on the particular circumstances of the case and the succession of legal consequences. At the same time, the presence of the fact of the offense may not be a reference point in the implementation of protection or safeguard in the field of private law.

---

[10] 'The second approach lie down to include one explored concept into another. The problem of this approach is that even among supporters of this position there is a discrepancy as to what kind of concept is generic, and which is a species. So, some scientists believe that protection is a broader concept and covers protection as a constituent element, while others argue that protection is the part of the protection.'

[11] Maksym Leghenchenko, *The concept of protection and security of right and their relationship*, 6(1) SCIENTIFIC BULLETIN OF THE KHERSON STATE UNIVERSITY LAW SCIENCES 171 (2014).

[12] The Civil Code of Ukraine of 16 January (2003). Kyiv: Verkhovna Rada of Ukraine (Article 386).

12.16. To summarize, some authors prefer scholarly approaches, according to which the definitions of 'protection' and 'safeguard' are identical or complementary.

II.2. 'Protection' and 'Safety' as Notions with Different Content

12.17. In modern scholarship there is another opinion,[13] according to which the concept of safeguard and protection cannot be identical and interchangeable. Such an approach clearly distinguishes and separates the concepts of 'protection' and 'safeguard' of rights, emphasizing that these are different in their content, concepts and phenomena.

12.18. For example, professor Olha Skakun is convinced that the protection of every right exists constantly and is aimed at ensuring the rule of law.[14] In addition, the protection envisages prevention, that is, not letting unlawful actions be taken. But the protection of rights and freedoms is the state of their lawful implementation and is under the control of social institutions, but without their intervention. The need to apply for the safeguard of rights appears only in the event of an impediment to their implementation, or violation, or threat of violation.

12.19. Safeguard, in Skakun's opinion, can be carried out through the interference of State bodies in the process of implementing rights and freedoms as a protective response to the objective factor of deviation from the rule of law and can be expressed in sanctions or liability.[15]

12.20. Analyzing this position, we arrive at the conclusion about partial displacement of concepts, where the protective reaction is in essence called a safeguard, and which occurs only in case of nuisance. At the same time, the protection, according to the author, coincides with the process of lawful implementation of a right. Unfortunately, it is impossible to distinguish between the content of the concepts under investigation and indicate their differences, without isolating the subjects and their role in the law-enforcement process. These include legal entities and subjects of law enforcement activity, including human rights' protection.

---

[13] Tamara Illaryonova, *The system of civil-law protection measures: the dissertation*, Dis. Doctors of Sciences in jurisprudence, Sverdlovsk 417 (1985); OLENA KOKHANOVSKA, THEORETICAL ISSUES OF INFORMATIONAL RELATIONS IN CIVIL LAW, Kyiv's University 463 (2006); YURII NOSIK, PROTECTION AND PROTECTION OF INFORMATION BY THE OWNER, Collection of Abstracts of the Participants of the 2nd National Scientific and Practical Conference of Students, Postgraduates and Young Scientists "System Analysis and Information Technologies" 178-182 (2000).
[14] OLHA SKAKUN, THEORY OF STATE AND LAW, Espada 230 etc. (2006).
[15] *Ibid.*, at 230.

12.21. Veniamin Gribanov draws attention to the fact that it is hardly right to reduce the content of the right to protection in the material sense only to the possibility to apply for the protection of the right to the relevant State or public bodies. The right to protection in its material and legal sense, that is, as one of the powers of subjective private law, is an opportunity to apply measures of coercive influence to the offender.[16]

12.22. Professor Olimpiad Ioffe defines protection in a broad and narrow sense, meaning nothing more than safeguarding property relations in the event of their violation.[17] In turn, Serhii Korneyev under the category of protection understands the system of measures that are intended to prevent violation of rights and interests of participants in civil legal relations, and security. In his opinion, it comes into force only in the case of violation of rights and interests.[18] Sergeyev, under the notion 'safeguard', in the narrow sense of this term, understands protection of civil rights, which 'is aimed at the restoration or recognition of civil rights and the protection of interests in their violation or contestation.'[19]

12.23. While considering the issue of the correlation between concepts of protection and safeguard on the example of personal life protection, Larisa Krasavchykova believes that protection has a three-tier structure, consisting of regulatory, providing and protecting. This is a category of legal regulation in general. Safeguard in this case is considered as a separate type of protection and is used in case of an existing offense.[20]

12.24. The nature of the content of the term is again vital. The question is whether it is only about the structure of the term, or about the structural levels of protection as a type of legal activity. It is supposed that behind each level there is a specific subject. Taking this into consideration, it is inappropriate to combine the regulatory function as rule-setting with judicial protection into a single category. In this case, we should talk not about the level of protection, but about the structural levels of the safeguarding mechanism.

12.25. Thus, some contemporary authors[21] adhere to a scholarly approach to the understanding and correlation of concepts of

---

[16] VENIAMIN GRIBANOV, IMPLEMENTATION AND PROTECTION OF CIVIL RIGHTS, Statute 106 (2001).

[17] OLIMPIAD IOFFE, SOVIET CIVIL LAW, Yurid. Lit.472–473 (1967).

[18] Serhii Korneev, *Obligations for causing harm. Civil law*, 2 WALTERS CLOUVER 615 (2006).

[19] Aleksandr Sergeyev, *Civil law*, Prospect 334 (Yu Tolstoy ed. 1998).

[20] LARYSA KRASAVCHIKOVA, PERSONAL LIFE OF CITIZENS UNDER THE PROTECTION OF THE LAW, Legal Literature 12 (1983).

[21] For example see: Dmytro Andreiev, *Administrative and legal remedies of security holders rights*, DPhD in jurisprudence, Institute of Legislation of the Verkhovna Rada of Ukraine 4 (2008).; N MALEYN, CIVIL LAW AND PERSONALITY RIGHTS IN THE USSR, Yurid. Lit. 192 (1981); S. Kozhevnykov, *Protection measures*

protection and safeguard. According to such an approach these legal categories are different in their content, and the same-named legal phenomena exist in parallel. At the same time, the necessity to safeguard private rights arises when they are violated or challenged by authorized persons in private legal relations, while protection always exists. Thus, the example of the aforementioned approach may be found in the provisions of Part 10 of Article 28 and 52 of the Law of Ukraine 'On Copyright and Related Rights'. According to this Law, personal non-material rights, provided for in Article 14, are protected indefinitely,[22] while for safeguarding copyright and/or related rights, subjects of copyright and related rights are entitled to apply in the prescribed manner to the court and other bodies in accordance with their jurisdiction.[23]

II.3.   'Protection' and 'Safety' as Elements of 'Legal Safeguard' and 'Legal Protection'

12.26. The supporters of the scholarly approach consider safeguard and protection of rights as constituent elements of broader concepts: 'legal safeguard' and 'legal protection.'

12.27. Nykolai Maleyin defines legal safeguard as a system of legal norms aimed at preventing an offense and eliminating its consequences,[24] including both protection and safeguard into the content of this concept. At the same time, according to professor Serhii Alekseyev, legal safeguard is a State-compulsory activity aimed at the restoration of the violated right and the enforcement of legal obligations.[25] In its turn, this only puts a security element into the specified term. Romovska draws attention to the essence of legal safeguard as the implementation of the measure of State coercion chosen by a law enforcement body, as well as the need to consider legal safeguard in dynamics as a process. This process consists of an origin expressed in the submitting of a claim and in completion on the execution of a court decision.[26] This is partially identical to the scholarly position of Alekseyev.

---

in Soviet law, Abstract PhD in jurisprudence, SVERDLOVSK 21 (1968).

[22]   About copyright and related rights. Law of Ukraine of 23 December 1993. Kyiv: Verkhovna Rada of Ukraine (Article 28).

[23]   About copyright and related rights. Law of Ukraine of 23 December 1993. Kyiv: Verkhovna Rada of Ukraine (Article 52).

[24]   NYKOLAI MALEYN, CIVIL LAW AND PERSONALITY RIGHTS IN THE USSR, Yurid.Lit. 192 (1981).

[25]   Serhii Alekseyev, *General theory of law*, 1 JURID. LIT. 361 (1981).

[26]   ZORISLAVA ROMOVSKA, PROTECTION IN THE SOVIET FAMILY LAW (1985); RUSLAN STEFANCHUK, CIVIL LAW OF UKRAINE, Precedent 361 (2005); GANNA OSETYNS'KA, CIVIL AND LEGAL PROTECTION OF CONSUMER RIGHTS ACCORDING TO THE UKRAINIAN LEGISLATION, DPhD in jurisprudence, Kyev's National University named after T. G. Shevchenko (2006).

12.28. However, in this case, the penitentiary system should be relocated from law enforcement to human rights protecting, which is not consistent with the current point of view of modern jurisprudence and the corresponding position of the representatives of legal practice.

12.29. A similar situation appears in the position of Iryna Dzera. Dzera introduced the definition of the safeguard of title to property as a system of active measures that are used by the owner and by competent State or other authorities. Such an approach is aimed at eliminating violations of property rights and imposing a duty to restore the violated right on the violator.[27] Thus, most scholars believe that the obligatory elements of legal safeguard are the bodies of State power.

12.30. On the other hand, in contemporary legal scholarship, there is an opinion that legal protection is a set of measures, methods and means defined by legal norms, to protect the subject from encroachment. At the same time, legal protection and protection of rights are not considered identical concepts, since legal protection is a law-making and law-enforcement activity carried out alongside norms of law and within the limits of legal norms. Conversely, protection of rights is an activity of observing rights and freedoms, protecting them from encroachment.[28]

12.31. Alongside this, Legenchenko points out that legal safeguard in most cases takes place after the violation of a right and is a part of a wider concept of 'protection of rights'. The definition of the concept of protection of rights is disclosed during the theoretical study of the relationship between this concept with the abovementioned concept of legal safeguard. From one point of view, we can assume that the protection of private rights and interests takes place at the stage before their violation, and legal safeguard takes place after. On the other hand, the question of the safeguard of right is an integral part of the general notion of protection, which also contains mechanisms for implementing such a right, and ways to prevent it from being violated.[29]

II.4. 'Protection' and 'Safety' as the Guarantee of Human and Civil Rights and Freedoms

12.32. Among other things, we should pay attention to such a scholarly approach, the use of which involves the consolidation

---

[27] Iryna Dzera, *Civil-legal remedies for the protection of property rights in Ukraine: author's abstract*, DPhD in jurisprudence, T. Shevchenko National University 18 (2001).

[28] Serhii Vavzenchuk, *Parity of Concepts "Protection" and "Safeguard" of the Labor Rights in the Current Legislation*, 1 FORUM PRAVA 46 (2010).

[29] Maksym Leghenchenko, *The concept of protection and security of right and their relationship*, 6(1) SCIENTIFIC BULLETIN OF THE KHERSON STATE UNIVERSITY LAW SCIENCES 170-171 (2014).

of concepts of protection and safeguard of rights in a single collective concept – the guarantee of human and civil rights and freedoms.

12.33. So, for example, Juliya Zhelihovska can be considered a supporter of this approach. Based on an analysis of the main provisions of domestic legislation, she substantiates that the use of the word 'protection' in many cases reduces it to the notion of 'safeguard.' In a number of normative acts in most cases it is indicated only in the title, by which it is reduced to the concept of 'guarantees of fundamental rights and the freedoms of man and citizen.' They constitute a system of norms, principles, conditions and requirements, which together ensure the protection of the rights and freedoms and legitimate interests of individuals.[30]

12.34. Most likely, it will be correct to talk about legal guarantees of the realization of human and civil rights and freedoms, and 'protection' and 'safeguard' are proposed to be included into the contents of these.

III.   Conclusion

12.35. Thus, on the basis of all mentioned above, it seems possible to conclude that in modern scholarly literature there is pluralism of views on the concepts of 'protection' and 'safeguard.' The absence of a single position regarding their interpretation is due to the difference in methodological approaches to the cognitive process, which results in the studied concepts being considered synonyms, constituting one whole or concepts that are completely different in their content.

12.36. Therefore, in generalizing the author's positions regarding the understanding of the terms 'protection' and 'safeguard' in order to comprehend them further, it is expedient to identify several approaches. These include integrative, structural, activity, and instrumental, and discriminating them allows us to reveal the general and specific characteristics in the nature of the investigated legal phenomena.

12.37. A characteristic feature of the understanding and use of these categories in the field of private law regulation is that, in its content, safeguard is included in the structure of the legal phenomenon of 'protection', which always exists, and provides for the restoration of the violated right.

---

[30]   J. Zhelihovska 'Value and delineation of concepts 'protection' and 'security'', 3 Scientific Bulletin of the International Humanitarian University Jurisprudence 18 (2015).

Summaries

DEU [*Methodologischer Pluralismus bei der Auslegung der Rechtsinstitute des „Schutzes" und der „Sicherstellung" gemäß deren Implementierung im internationalen Privatrecht*]

Die Autorinnen sind den verschiedenen Ansätzen nachgegangen, mit denen die Begriffe „Schutz" und „Sicherstellung" definiert und harmonisiert werden, unter Berücksichtigung der Besonderheiten, was deren Implementierung im Bereich des Privatrechts anbelangt. Die Grundlage für die Analyse entstammt den wichtigsten, auf breiter Ebene vertretenen rechtlichen Positionen, wo diese Begriffe identifiziert, verglichen, gepriesen oder als Garant für Menschen- und Bürgerrechte und -freiheiten betrachtet werden. Jeder Ansatz verwendet eine andere rechtstheoretische Argumentation, die von den Autorinnen hinterfragt wird. Im Zuge ihrer Analyse der aktuellen Quellen zu dem von ihnen gewählten Thema gelangen die Autorinnen zu dem Schluss, dass dort, wo sich der eine Begriff unter Verwendung des Inhalts des jeweils anderen Begriffs inhaltlich öffnet bzw. erweitert, eine terminologische Vermengung und Verwirrung eintritt. Diese wechselseitige begriffliche Absorption bzw. Ersetzung wird kritisch beleuchtet; die Autorinnen gelangen abschließend zum Fazit, dass in der modernen Rechtstheorie ein gewisser methodologischer Pluralismus besteht.

CZE [*Metodologický pluralismus při výkladech „ochrany" a „zabezpečení", jak jsou tyto instituty implementovány v mezinárodním právu soukromém*]

Autorky studovaly jednotlivé přístupy k definování a sladění pojmů „ochrana" a „zabezpečení" s přihlédnutím ke zvláštnostem jejich implementace v oblasti soukromoprávní regulace. Základ této analýzy je převzat z hlavních široce zastávaných právních pozic, kde jsou tyto pojmy identifikovány, porovnávány, chváleny nebo považovány za záruku lidských a občanských práv a svobod. Každý přístup využívá právně teoretické argumentace, o nichž autorky diskutují. Analýzou současných zdrojů týkajících se zvoleného tématu dospívají autorky k závěru, že při otevření obsahu jednoho pojmu s využitím obsahu druhého pojmu dochází k určitému terminologickému zmatení. Tato vzájemná absorpce pojmů nebo jejich substituování je předmětem kritiky,

přičemž výsledkem je názor autorek v tom směru, že v moderní
právní teorii existuje určitý metodologický pluralismus.

| | |

POL [*Pluralizm metodologiczny w interpretacji „ochrony"*
i „zabezpieczenia", jak wdraża się te instytucje
w międzynarodowym prawie prywatnym]
Autorzy artykułu analizują podejście do określania instytucji
ochrony „ochrony" i „obrony", a także porównują te instytucje
prawa w świetle specyfiki ich realizacji na gruncie prawa
prywatnego.

FRA [*Le pluralisme méthodologique dans l'interprétation des*
notions de « protection » et de « sécurité » à la lumière de
leur application dans le droit international privé]
Les auteurs du présent article se proposent d'analyser les
différentes approches des notions de « protection » et de
« sécurité » et de comparer ces deux institutions juridiques, tout
en réfléchissant sur leurs spécificités dans le domaine du droit
international privé.

RUS [*Методологический плюрализм в толковании терминов*
«охрана» и «защита» в соответствии с нормами
международного частного права]
Авторы статьи изучили подходы к определению и
сопоставлению понятий «охрана» и «защита» с учетом
особенностей их реализации в области регулирования
частного права.

ESP [*El pluralismo metodológico en la interpretación de los*
institutos de "protección" y "salvaguarda" de acuerdo con su
implementación en el derecho privado internacional]
Los autores del artículo analizan diferentes posturas a la
hora de determinar los institutos de "protección" y "defensa",
incluida la comparación de dichos institutos, en relación con las
particularidades de su ejecución en el marco de la regulación del
derecho privado.

Bibliography

Serhii Alekseyev, *General theory of law*, 1 JURID. LIT. (1981).

Dmytro Andreiev, *Administrative and legal remedies of security holders rights*, DPhD in jurisprudence, Institute of Legislation of the Verkhovna Rada of Ukraine (2008).

SERHII BRATUS, RESPONSIBILITY IN LAW AND LEGALITY. ESSAY THEORY, Legal Literature (1976).

Iryna Dzera, *Civil-legal remedies for the protection of property rights in Ukraine: author's abstract*, DPhD in jurisprudence, T. Shevchenko National University (2001).

VENIAMIN GRIBANOV, IMPLEMENTATION AND PROTECTION OF CIVIL RIGHTS, Statute (2001).

Tamara Illaryonova, *The system of civil-law protection measures: the dissertation*, Dis. Doctors of Sciences in jurisprudence, Sverdlovsk (1985).

OLIMPIAD IOFFE, SOVIET CIVIL LAW, Yurid. Lit. (1967).

OLENA KOKHANOVSKA, THEORETICAL ISSUES OF INFORMATIONAL RELATIONS IN CIVIL LAW, Kyiv's University (2006).

Serhii Korneev, *Obligations for causing harm. Civil law*, 2 WALTERS CLOUVER (2006).

S. Kozhevnykov, *Protection measures in Soviet law*, Abstract PhD in jurisprudence, SVERDLOVSK (1968).

LARYSA KRASAVCHIKOVA, PERSONAL LIFE OF CITIZENS UNDER THE PROTECTION OF THE LAW, Legal Literature (1983).

Maksym Leghenchenko, *The concept of protection and security of right and their relationship*, 6(1) SCIENTIFIC BULLETIN OF THE KHERSON STATE UNIVERSITY LAW SCIENCES (2014).

NYKOLAI MALEYN, CIVIL LAW AND PERSONALITY RIGHTS IN THE USSR, Yurid.Lit. (1981).

YURII NOSIK, PROTECTION AND PROTECTION OF INFORMATION BY THE OWNER, Collection of Abstracts of the Participants of the 2nd National Scientific and Practical Conference of Students, Postgraduates and Young Scientists "System Analysis and Information Technologies" (2000).

GANNA OSETYNS'KA, CIVIL AND LEGAL PROTECTION OF CONSUMER RIGHTS ACCORDING TO THE UKRAINIAN LEGISLATION, DPhD in jurisprudence, Kyev's National University named after T. G. Shevchenko(2006).

SERHII OZHEGOV, DICTIONARY OF THE RUSSIAN LANGUAGE,

Rus. Yaz. (1984).

PETRO RABINOVYCH, FUNDAMENTALS OF THE GENERAL THEORY OF LAW AND STATE, Atika (2001).

ZORISLAVA ROMOVSKA, PROTECTION IN THE SOVIET FAMILY LAW (1985).

RUSLAN STEFANCHUK, CIVIL LAW OF UKRAINE, Precedent (2005).

Aleksandr Sergeyev, *Civil law*, Prospect (Yu Tolstoy ed. 1998).

YAROSLAVNA SHEVCHENKO, OWNER AND OWNERSHIP, Naukovadumka (1994).

OLHA SKAKUN, THEORY OF STATE AND LAW, Espada (2006).

RUSLAN STEFANCHUK, CIVIL LAW OF UKRAINE, Precedent (2005).

SERHII TARANENKO, PROTECTION OF THE RIGHTS AND FREEDOMS OF CITIZENS IN PROCEEDINGS ON ADMINISTRATIVE VIOLATIONS AND THEIR PROVISION IN THE ACTIVITIES OF THE LAW ENFORCEMENT BODIES, DPhD in jurisprudence, National Academy of Sciences of Ukraine named after V. M. Koretsky Institute of State and Law (2000).

OLEKSII ULYANOV, ADMINISTRATIVE-LEGAL PROTECTION OF THE RIGHTS OF CITIZENS BY THE MILITIA IN THE SPHERE OF PUBLIC ORDER, DPhD in jurisprudence, Odesa's Law institute of The National University of Internal Affairs (2002).

Serhii Vavzenchuk, *Parity of Concepts "Protection" and "Safeguard" of the Labor Rights in the Current Legislation*, 1 FORUM PRAVA (2010).

Julyia Zhelihovska, *Value and delineation of concepts 'protection' and 'security'*, 3 SCIENTIFIC BULLETIN OF THE INTERNATIONAL HUMANITARIAN UNIVERSITY JURISPRUDENCE (2015).

Czech Yearbook of International Law®

Maidan Kuntuarovich Suleimenov

State Immunity: The Formation of the Immunity Doctrine

Keywords:
*arbitration | judicial
immunity | state responsibility
| civil law | absolute judicial
immunity*

Abstract | *This article analyzes the issues of immunity of a state from Court proceedings and arbitration proceedings. In recent years the Republic of Kazakhstan has faced the problem of immunity from Court proceedings as a result of the active participation of the State in private law matters. Lawsuits are increasingly filed against the Government or the National Bank as State bodies of the Republic of Kazakhstan in foreign State courts. Often accounts in foreign banks are blocked to secure the claim, and the property of Kazakhstan is seized abroad. The doctrine of limited immunity for foreign States is established in the Civil Procedure Code of the Republic of Kazakhstan. The doctrine of the absolute immunity of the Republic of Kazakhstan in civil law relations with a foreign element with the participation of the State is established in the Civil Code of the of the Republic of Kazakhstan. The author asserts that the incorporation of such a rule into the Civil Code cannot be recognized as justified. As for the relative weight of immunity from Court proceedings and arbitration proceedings, the author believes that consent to dispute consideration in arbitration does not mean a waiver of immunity from Court proceedings. Rather, consent to dispute consideration in the arbitration means consent to the enforcement of an arbitration award.*

**Maidan Kuntuarovich
Suleimenov** is the
Director of the Research
Institute of Private Law at
Caspian University and the
Chairman of Kazakhstani
International Arbitrage.
He is an academician
of National Academy of
Sciences of the Republic of
Kazakhstan, LL.D., and a
Professor.
E-mail:
maidansuleimenov@gmail.
com

| | |

I.   Introduction

13.01. In recent years the Republic of Kazakhstan faced the problem of judicial immunity as a result of the active participation of the State in private law activities. Lawsuits are increasingly filed in foreign State courts against the Government or the National Bank as State bodies of the Republic of Kazakhstan, and accounts in foreign banks are often blocked to secure the claim, such that the property of Kazakhstan is seized abroad.[1] There arises the question of the legality of presenting and satisfying such claims from the point of view of the judicial immunity of the State exempting the Republic of Kazakhstan from prosecution without its consent. Kazakhstan courts need to be prepared to deal with the above issue of legality.

13.02. We are used to viewing the State as a vehicle of public administration, and as a standalone and independent sovereign which limits its power only on a voluntary basis by signing international treaties with other States. However, the State also acts as a subject of civil law, albeit much less often. For example, the State enters into contracts through the bodies authorized by it, acquires property rights (particularly, property under abeyance), or inherits by will or law.

13.03. Because Kazakhstan's economy heavily depends on the country's vast oil and gas resources, the State's foreign loan agreements and subsoil use contracts are important to Kazakhstan. These loan agreements and subsoil use contracts are executed on behalf of Kazakhstan by competent authorities, such as the Government, the National Bank, and the Ministry of Finance, while the State is responsible for their breach through its treasury under Article 115.1 of the Civil Code of the Republic of Kazakhstan (the "Civil Code").[2]

13.04. According to Article 111 of the Civil Code "...in civil relations Kazakhstan acts on equal terms with other participants." Furthermore, Kazakhstan law provides that the rules applicable to legal entities equally apply to the State unless a relevant exemption applies.[3]

---

[1]   Applying this notion to Kazakh legal entities and individuals, they can bring claims against foreign countries, in particular, countries of the Commonwealth of Independent States (CIS), Vietnam or Mongolia in the courts of the Republic of Kazakhstan.

[2]   Civil Code of the Republic of Kazakhstan (General Part) adopted on 27 December 1994 and Civil Code (Special part), adopted on 1 June 1999. Article 115.1 of the Civil Code reads as follows: "The Republic of Kazakhstan is liable for its obligations with state treasury's property..."

[3]   "The rules determining the participation of legal entities in relations governed by the civil laws apply to the state unless otherwise specified in the legislative acts" (Article 114 of the Civil Code). Such exemption is provided, inter alia, by Article 422 of the Civil Procedure Code of the Republic of Kazakhstan (the "CCP") for the immunity of a foreign State.

13.05. According to Article 477 of the Code of Civil Procedure of the Republic of Kazakhstan (the "2015 CCP" or "CCP")[4] immunity of the State derives from its sovereignty, there are the following types of immunity:

> 1) Judicial immunity, i.e. immunity from the jurisdiction of one State in the courts of another State.
> 2) Provisional remedy, i.e. immunity, where no provisional remedy is allowed against the property of the State without the consent of such State.
> 3) Finally, there is immunity from enforcement of the judgment.

13.06. The State can voluntarily waive immunity. Such consent to a waiver of immunity should be clearly expressed and should concern one or all types of immunity.[5] Such a refusal can be expressed in three ways. First, it can be expressed in international treaties.[6] Second, it can be expressed in enactments, for example, such as the CCP. Finally, it can be expressed in specific civil law contracts. Thus, the specific feature of the legal regime of the State as a participant in international activities is the availability of State immunity from foreign jurisdiction.

13.07. Immunity has two aspects, one concerning a State implementing private law activities in the territory of another State, and two when it concerns the receiving State.[7] In the first case, immunity is the right of the State to be exempted from the jurisdiction of another State. Enforcement measures shall not be applied to the State on the part of judicial, administrative and other authorities of another State. In the second case, immunity is the refusal of the State to exercise its full territorial jurisdiction and to apply enforcement measures by its judicial, administrative and other State bodies.[8]

13.08. There are different approaches to the definition of immunity. Some scholars discuss limited sovereignty only.[9] Other scholars use the notion of 'functional' and 'limited' immunity as synonyms, while certain scholars believe that these are different concepts, and separate functional immunity and limited immunity.[10]

---

4   Code of Civil Procedure of the Republic of Kazakhstan adopted on 31 October 2015.
5   Article 477 of the CCP.
6   For example, the Bilateral Investment Treaty between the Republic of Kazakhstan and the United States, signed 19 May 1992; entered into force 12 January 1994.
7   M. DMITRIYEVA, INTERNATIONAL PRIVATE LAW, Prospect 248-250 (2000).
8   *Supra* note 7.
9   IGOR I. LUKASHUK, INTERNATIONAL LAW: TEXTBOOK. GENERAL PART, BEK publishing house, INTERNATIONAL PRIVATE LAW 301 (1996). / edited by N. I. Marysheva, Contract law company, Infra. M. 158-159 (2000).; L. P. Anufrieva, *International private law*, V.2. Special part, BEK PUBLISHING HOUSE 104 (2000).
10 VIKTOR P. ZVEKOV, INTERNATIONAL PRIVATE LAW, Norma-infra group 232 (1999).; I. O. Khlestova, *Issues of immunity of state in the laws and contractual practice of Russian Federation*, PROBLEMS

13.09. Functional immunity should be based on the essential delimitation of the functions of the State into two types: public and private law. When exercising public functions, the State should use unconditional immunity. However, upon exercising private legal activities the State should lose its immunity, and the very entry of the State into private law relations should be regarded as a waiver of immunity. Limited immunity, unlike functional immunity, should neither formulate a general principle of public activities-private activities, nor formulate general criteria, but should list specific cases when the limitation of State immunity is allowed.

13.10. A classic example of the implementation of limited immunity is the European Convention on State Immunity and the Additional Protocol to that Convention adopted by the Council of Europe on 16 May 1972 stipulating withdrawals from immunities in a number of cases where activities of the State are of a private law nature.[11]

13.11. The US Foreign Sovereign Immunities Act of 1976 states that immunity will not be recognized 'when the grounds for a suit are business conducted by a foreign state in the United States or an action made outside the United States in connection with business of a foreign country outside the United States if such action had direct consequences for the United States.[12] 'The property of a foreign country located in the United States and used for making business in that country shall not be subject to immunity from arrest measures to secure a suit and from measures for execution against property based on a court judgment. Paragraph 1603 (d) of this same US Act states that 'business means either regular commercial behavior or a specific commercial action or act'. The commercial nature of any operations is determined by the nature of behavior or specific action or act but not by its purpose.

13.12. The English State Immunity Law of 1978 which defines the commercial action by describing its nature and listing the types of the relevant contracts is based on similar positions.[13]

OF INTERNATIONAL PRIVATE LAW, CONTRACT LAW COMPANY 68.

[11] European Convention on State Immunity. Basle, 16.V.1972.
[12] US Foreign Sovereign Immunities Act, Title 28, paragraph 1605 (1976).
[13] UK State Immunity Act, Chapter 33, paragraph 3 (1978).

II.   The Formation of the Relative Immunity Doctrine in Kazakhstan

13.13. Initially, the concept of absolute immunity was included in the Civil Procedure Code of the Kazakh SSR.[14] The Code of Civil Procedure Code adopted in 1999 (the "1999 CCP") offered a different formula. As such, paragraph 1, Article 422 of the 1999 CCP stated:

> "The filing of a lawsuit against a foreign state, involving such state in participation in a case as a third person, seizing its property and impounding of its property to secure a claim and execution against such property shall be permitted provided only the competent authorities of the respective state give their consent, unless otherwise is provided by the law or by international treaty of the Republic of Kazakhstan."

13.14. 'Unless otherwise is provided by the law or international treaty,' meant that for the first time a theory of limited sovereignty was introduced in Kazakhstan. However, the interpretation of the above provision remained elusive since no such law was adopted until recently. Therefore, an absurd situation had arisen, when the Kazakh courts, based on Article 422 of the 1999 CCP, had to request a consent of the competent authorities of a foreign State to note a claim even when the State entered into a standard commercial transaction.[15]

13.15. A new chapter on jurisdictional immunity of foreign State and its property first introduced into the 1999 CCP[16] was later included in the 2015 CCP.[17] The 2015 CCP cemented the doctrine of limited immunity for foreign States. As such, Article 478 of the 2015 CCP states that a foreign State does not enjoy judicial immunity in the Republic of Kazakhstan if it carried out activities other than the sovereign power of the State including cases specified in Articles 484 to 491 of the Code. These articles mention that immunity does not apply in a number of areas, including disputes related to business, disputes with ownership

---

[14]   Article 435 of the Civil Procedure Code of Kazakh SSR read as follows: 'Bringing of a suit against a foreign state, security of suit and execution against the property of a foreign state located in the USSR may be permitted provided only the competent authorities of the state concerned give their consent.'

[15]   A new Chapter 46 on Jurisdictional Immunity of Foreign State and Its Property was introduced into the 1999 CCP, when it was amended on 5 February 2010. The provisions of the above chapter were later included in Chapter 57 of the CPC titled 'Proceedings on Cases Involving Foreign Persons' (Articles 477-500 of the CPC), with minor changes.

[16]   Chapter 46 of the 1999 CCP was introduced by the amendment on February 2010.

[17]   Chapter 57 of the Current CCP is titled 'Proceedings on cases involving foreign persons' (Article 477-500 of the CCP).

interest in legal entities, disputes concerning the rights to property, disputes on indemnification, disputes concerning intellectual property, disputes related to the operation of marine vessels and inland navigation vessels, and labor disputes.

13.16. This rule covers other types of jurisdictional immunity. The foreign State does not enjoy immunity from securing the claim and immunity from enforcement if the property of a foreign State located in the territory of the Republic of Kazakhstan is used and/or intended for use by a foreign State for purposes other than the exercise of the sovereign power of the State.[18]

III.   Immunity from Enforcement of a Judgment

13.17. Until the adoption of the 2015 CCP, there was no clarity on immunity from the enforcement of judgments in Kazakhstan. Article 480.2 of the CCP provides the following rule:

> "The consent of a foreign State to waive judicial immunity is not deemed its consent to waive immunity from securing a claim and immunity from a compulsory court order."

13.18. This means that the execution of a judgment against a foreign State requires obtaining a waiver of sovereignty from such a State in relation to the enforcement of a judgment.

13.19. Almost all conventions on mutual encouragement and protection of investment provide for consideration of disputes between an investor and the receiving State in arbitration. In Russian scholarly literature, such conventions are regarded as a waiver of judicial immunity.[19] Furthermore, some Russian scholars, consider submission of disputes to foreign arbitration or arbitral tribunal as a waiver of judicial immunity in accordance with the Article 23 of the Law On Production Sharing Agreements of Russian Federation.[20] I also expressed such an opinion pointing out that the State's waiver of immunity may be clearly expressed in international treaties, in legislative acts or in specific civil law contracts such as a production sharing contract.[21] Meanwhile, the above waiver covered only the consent of the State to submit disputes to international commercial arbitration[22].

---

[18] Article 492.3 of the CCP.
[19] SVETLANA. I. KRUPKO, INVESTMENT DISPUTES BETWEEN STATE AND FOREIGN INVESTOR, BEK 79 (2002).; Viktor P. Zvekov, *International Private Law*, NORMA-INFRA GROUP 234 (1999).
[20] JOHANNES RAT. PRODUCTION SHARING AGREEMENTS, ANALYSIS OF LEGAL REGULATION OF RELATIONS IN THE FIELD OF REALIZATION IN RUSSIAN FEDERATION. Walters Kluwer 109-110 (2008).
[21] Maidan K. Suleimenov and Y. G. Bassin, *Civil Law. Volume 3: Textbook*, ALMATY 446 (2004).
[22] What is meant by the submission of a dispute to an arbitration court? According to Professor Mark

Czech Yearbook of International Law®

13.20. The consent of the State to dispute consideration in foreign arbitration should not mean the State waived its judicial immunity. Judicial immunity should be limited to the jurisdiction of the courts of another State but not to the arbitration court, which is a non-governmental private institution. In general, any jurisdictional immunity, and not only judicial, is fundamentally connected with the public courts, whether it is the consideration of a dispute, security of a claim or enforcement.

IV.   Absolute Immunity for the Republic of Kazakhstan

13.21. By establishing the principle of the limited immunity for foreign States, the current 2015 CCP had finally eliminated a long gap in the laws of the Republic of Kazakhstan. However, along with these changes, the Civil Code included a rule which was completely illogical and contrary to these laws and common sense (the "Validity Rule"). The Validity Rule states as follows:

> "In civil relations with a foreign element, the Republic of Kazakhstan enjoys jurisdictional immunity in relation to itself and its property from the jurisdiction of the courts of another state including judicial immunity, immunity from the adoption of provisional measures and immunity from the execution of a judicial decision, unless otherwise is established:
>
> - in the international treaty of the Republic of Kazakhstan;
> - in a written agreement that is not an international treaty of the Republic of Kazakhstan;
> - by a statement in court or written notice within a particular case."[23]

13.22. Thus, the Validity Rule relates to the doctrine of the absolute immunity in civil law relations with a foreign element with

---

Moiseevich Boguslavsky, Doctor-at-Law, and an arbitrator of the International Commercial Court of Arbitration under the CCI of Russia: "[A]n arbitration award of the State means that the State waived jurisdictional/judicial immunity. As such, the consent of a foreign State to a dispute consideration in an arbitral tribunal does not automatically mean an acceptance of provisional measures and consent to the enforcement of an arbitral award. An international treaty on the protection of investment which provides that the State agrees to consider an occurring investment dispute through arbitration does not mean that it thereby agreed to take provisional measures to enforce the decisions." MARK M. BOGUSLAVSKIY, INTERNATIONAL PRIVATE LAW: TEXTBOOK, 5TH EDITION, Yurist 583 (2004).

Kazakhstan Article 482 of the CCP has the following rule in this regard: "If a foreign state expressed in writing its consent to arbitration of disputes with its participation that arouse or may arise in the future, it shall be recognized that, in relation to these disputes, it voluntarily agreed to waive judicial immunity in the matters relating to the exercise by the court of the Republic of Kazakhstan of its functions in relation to arbitration."

[23] The Law of 5 May 2010 included paragraph 2 in the Article 1102 of the Civil Code of the Republic of Kazakhstan.

the participation of the State. An attempt to establish absolute immunity for State property was undertaken in Russia when drafting a federal law entitled 'On Immunity of Property of the Russian Federation Abroad.' The above concept was criticized in scholarly literature as contradicting the universally recognized principles and rules of international law violating the sovereignty of the foreign States and has not yet been implemented.[24] However, Kazakhstan managed to realize a similar and problematic legal concept.

13.23. Inclusion of the Validity Rule in the Civil Code of the Republic of Kazakhstan cannot be justified. The Civil Code governs civil law relations, i.e. property and personal non-property relations. These are norms of substantive and private law. The State's immunity derives from the sovereignty of the State and is connected with the exemption from judicial jurisdiction. These are rules of public and procedural law. Therefore, in any case the Validity Rule does not fit in the Civil Code. If included in the Kazakhstan national laws, then it should be included only in the CCP.

13.24. It is obvious that the legislators who drafted the law decided deliberately not to include the Validity Rule in the CCP since it is quite obvious that the CCP governs the civil procedure in the territory of Kazakhstan only. The immunity of the State of Kazakhstan is not questioned in the CCP since the immunity of the State may refer only to the civil process in the territory of another State and cannot be governed by the Nation's Code of Civil Procedure. As noted earlier, the CCP governs procedural relations only in the territory of the Republic of Kazakhstan and cannot govern procedural relations in the territory of other States. The legislators who included a chapter on immunity in the 1999 CCP. However, again we are talking only about the immunity of foreign countries.

13.25. However, the same can be said about civil laws as well as about any other national laws. The Civil Code governs civil law relations in the territory of the Republic of Kazakhstan and cannot regulate civil law relations in the territory of other States. This also applies to civil law relations with a foreign element. The Civil Code can govern these relations in the territory of Kazakhstan only including relations with the participation of a foreign State, and cannot govern such relations in the territory of other States including relations with the participation of the

---

[24] SVETLANA. I. KRUPKO, INVESTMENT DISPUTES BETWEEN STATE AND FOREIGN INVESTOR, BEK 79 (2002).

Republic of Kazakhstan. In addition the proposed rule does point to civil law relations in the territory of foreign States.

13.26. It is clear that the legislators intend to protect the Republic's property abroad and to strengthen the judicial immunity of Kazakhstan. However, this may not be a feasible proposition. The theory of the absolute immunity prevailed throughout the world for a long time. According to such a theory, under no circumstances is a State subject to the courts of another State without its consent. However, at present the majority of States started following the theory of limited (or functional) immunity, according to which the State enjoys unconditional immunity in performing public functions. However, in the exercise of private law activities, it loses immunity, and entry of the State into private law relations is regarded as a waiver of immunity.

13.27. Under such terms, if a suit is brought against the Republic of Kazakhstan in any country, what laws shall be valid, the laws of such countries or Article 1102 of the Civil Code of the Republic of Kazakhstan? The answer results from the above that the adoption of rules of the new law contradicts the basic principles of delimitation of national, foreign and international law and shall not be valid abroad.

13.28. However, the negative consequences of adopting this rule are very significant. As this rule is stated in the Civil Code, then the courts of the Republic of Kazakhstan shall apply it and shall refuse on its basis to enforce judgments of foreign courts on claims to the Republic of Kazakhstan. Foreign courts acting on the basis of their law on the immunity of foreign States, having received such an obviously unlawful decision of the Kazakhstan court to refuse to enforce its award, will make a decision to seize the property of the Republic of Kazakhstan located abroad including accounts in foreign banks. The foreign court will be right because the rule of the Civil Code of the Republic of Kazakhstan does not and cannot have any legal significance for it.

13.29. While being aware of the fact that the Republic of Kazakhstan is helpless to undertake anything in its defense abroad, the drafters of amendments to the 1999 CCP tried to find some way to ensure the compliance of foreign States with the principle of the absolute immunity of the Republic of Kazakhstan. As such, the 1999 CCP included the following provisions that are reproduced in the 2015 CCP:

"1) Claims for damages caused by a violation by a foreign State of the jurisdictional immunity of the Republic of Kazakhstan and its property shall be made at the location of the claimant, unless otherwise provided by an international treaty ratified by the Republic of Kazakhstan (Clause 5, Article 31 of 2015 Civil Procedure Code of the Republic of Kazakhstan).

2) Seizure of money held in the territory of the Republic of Kazakhstan on the correspondent account of a foreign State shall be permitted on claims for recovery of losses caused by a violation by a foreign State of jurisdictional immunity of the Republic of Kazakhstan and its property (subparagraph 1, et.1, Article 156 of the Civil Procedure Code of the Republic of Kazakhstan of 2015).

3) A foreign State does not enjoy judicial immunity in the Republic of Kazakhstan as well as immunity from securing a claim and from enforcing a court order in disputes related to the violation by such foreign State of the jurisdictional immunity of the Republic of Kazakhstan and its property (Article 484 of 2015 Civil Procedure Code of the Republic of Kazakhstan)."

13.30. It is not likely that these measures would help Kazakhstan to deal with the laws of rest of the world but, on the contrary, would create unnecessary complications, both legal and diplomatic, and would not provide Kazakhstan with any significant benefits. Moreover, it would result in significant deterioration of Kazakhstan's image as a legal State. It is obvious even to the lay-person that the principle of double standards should be laid down in one and the same law, the CCP. A doctrine of limited immunity applies to a foreign State; however, the doctrine of the absolute immunity applies in the Republic of Kazakhstan.

13.31. The lawmaker's position on this issue contradicts not only the laws of foreign States but also international treaties. In this regard it is difficult to understand the logic of a lawmaker when, on one hand, the Civil Code and the CCP fix the doctrine of absolute immunity for Kazakhstan, while on the other hand, by the Law of 27 October 2009 of the Republic of Kazakhstan the parliament ratified the UN Convention of 2 December 1994 'On jurisdictional immunities of states and their property'.[25] The UN Convention is based on the establishment of a limited immunity doctrine. The CCP established almost the same conditions of non-application of the State immunity for the foreign countries as in the UN Convention. It means, therefore, that due to the priority of the international treaty over the national laws, the same restrictions will apply for Kazakhstan as for other States.

---

[25] Kazakhstanskaya Pravda, Issue 29 October 2009.

It turns out that the rules fixed in the Civil Code and the CCP of the Republic of Kazakhstan regarding the absolute immunity of Kazakhstan are simply empty talk and a manifestation of the legal incompetence of the Kazakhstan legislators.

| | |

Summaries

DEU   [*Immunität des Staats: Genese der Immunitätsdoktrin*]
Dieser Beitrag analysiert Fragen der gerichtlichen und schiedsgerichtlichen Immunität des Staates. In jüngeren Jahren hat sich die Republik Kasachstan angesichts der aktiven Beteiligung des Staats an privatrechtlichen Angelegenheiten mit dem Problem der gerichtlichen Immunität auseinandersetzen müssen. Immer häufiger wird bei ausländischen ordentlichen Gerichten Klage gegen die Regierung oder die Zentralbank als staatliche Stellen der Republik Kasachstan eingereicht. Oft werden Konten in ausländischen Banken eingefroren, um Ansprüche zu sichern, und wird Vermögen der Republik Kasachstan im Ausland konfisziert. Die Doktrin der beschränkten Immunität fremder Staaten ist in der Zivilprozessordnung der Republik Kasachstan verankert. Eine Doktrin der absoluten Immunität der Republik Kasachstan in privatrechtlichen Verhältnissen mit ausländischem Element und mit einer Beteiligung des Staates findet sich hingegen im Bürgerlichen Gesetzbuch der Republik Kasachstan. Der Autor behauptet, dass die Verankerung dieser Regel im Bürgerlichen Gesetzbuch nicht zu rechtfertigen ist. Was die relative Gewichtung der gerichtlichen und schiedsgerichtlichen Immunität anbelangt, so ist der Autor davon überzeugt, dass die Zustimmung zur Beurteilung einer Streitigkeit im Schiedsverfahren nicht automatisch den Verzicht auf gerichtliche Immunität bedeutet. Eine Zustimmung zur Beurteilung der Streitigkeit im Schiedsverfahren kommt vielmehr eher einer Zustimmung zur Vollstreckung des Schiedsspruchs gleich.

CZE   [*Imunita státu: vznik doktríny imunity*]
Tento článek analyzuje otázky soudní a rozhodčí imunity státu. V posledních letech se musí Republika Kazachstán, vzhledem k aktivní účasti státu v soukromoprávních věcech, vyrovnávat s problémem soudcovské imunity. U zahraničních obecných soudů jsou proti vládě nebo centrální bance jako státním orgánům Republiky Kazachstán stále častěji podávány žaloby. Často

Czech Yearbook of International Law®

dochází k blokování účtů v cizích bankách za účelem zajištění nároků, jakož i zabavování majetku Republiky Kazachstán v zahraničí. Doktrína omezené imunity cizích států je zakotvena v občanském soudním řádu Republiky Kazachstán. Doktrína absolutní imunity Republiky Kazachstán v občanskoprávních vztazích s cizím prvkem, je-li jejich účastníkem stát, je zakotvena v občanském zákoníku Republiky Kazachstán. Autor tvrdí, že zakotvení tohoto pravidla v občanském zákoníku nelze považovat za důvodné. Pokud jde o relativní váhu soudcovské a rozhodcovské imunity, je autor přesvědčen, že souhlas s posouzením sporu v rozhodčím řízení neznamená vzdání se soudní imunity. Souhlas s posouzením sporu v rozhodčím řízení spíše znamená souhlas s výkonem rozhodčího nálezu.

| | |

POL   [*Immunitet państwa: powstanie doktryny nietykalności*]
Artykuł poświęcony kwestiom immunitetu sądowego i arbitrażowego państwa. W prawie cywilnym procesowym Kazachstanu uregulowano doktrynę ograniczonego immunitetu państw trzecich, przy czym w kodeksie cywilnym uregulowano doktrynę absolutnej nietykalności Kazachstanu. Zdaniem autora artykułu, umowa stron odnośnie rozstrzygania w sporze w postępowaniu arbitrażowym (klauzula arbitrażowa) nie oznacza rezygnacji z immunitetu sądowego (zrzeczenie się immunitetu sądowego), a jedynie stanowi zgodę na przymusowe wykonanie orzeczenia arbitrażowego.

FRA   [*L'immunité de l'État : naissance de la doctrine de l'immunité*]
Le présent article aborde les questions de l'immunité juridictionnelle et arbitrale de l'État. Les règles de procédure civile de la République du Kazakhstan prévoient une immunité restreinte des États étrangers, alors que le Code civil édicte une immunité absolue de la République du Kazakhstan. L'auteur du présent article est d'avis qu'un accord stipulant le règlement des litiges moyennant une procédure d'arbitrage (clause compromissoire) n'emporte pas l'abandon de l'immunité juridictionnelle, mais uniquement un consentement à une exécution forcée de la sentence arbitrale.

RUS   [*Иммунитет государства: развитие доктрины иммунитета*]
В статье анализируются вопросы судебного и арбитражного иммунитета государства. В Гражданском

Czech Yearbook of International Law®

Czech Yearbook of International Law®

процессуальном кодексе Республики Казахстан закреплена доктрина ограниченного иммунитета для иностранных государств, при этом в Гражданском кодексе – доктрина абсолютного иммунитета Республики Казахстан. По мнению автора статьи, согласие на рассмотрение спора в арбитраже не означает отказа от судебного иммунитета, но означает согласие на принудительное исполнение арбитражного решения.

ESP   [*La inmunidad del Estado: creación de la doctrina de la inmunidad*]

El artículo analiza la inmunidad del Estado en el ámbito de la jurisdicción y del arbitraje. El Código procesal civil de la República de Kazajstán estipula la doctrina de la inmunidad restringida de los Estados extranjeros, mientras que el Código civil establece la doctrina de la inmunidad absoluta de la República de Kazajstán. El autor del texto opina que el acuerdo sobre la resolución de la controversia por medio del procedimiento arbitral (cláusula arbitral) no expresa una resignación a la inmunidad jurisdiccional (renuncia a la inmunidad jurisdiccional), sino que manifiesta un acuerdo con la ejecución forzosa del laudo arbitral.

| | |

Bibliography

Ludmila P. Anufrieva, *International private law*, V.2. Special part, BEK PUBLISHING HOUSE (2000).

MARK M. BOGUSLAVSKIY, INTERNATIONAL PRIVATE LAW: TEXTBOOK, 5TH EDITION, Yurist 583 (2004).

GALINA K. DMITRIYEVA, INTERNATIONAL PRIVATE LAW, Prospect 248-250 (2000).

JOHANNES RAT. PRODUCTION SHARING AGREEMENTS, ANALYSIS OF LEGAL REGULATION OF RELATIONS IN THE FIELD OF REALIZATION IN RUSSIAN FEDERATION. Walters Kluwer (2008).

Kazakhstanskaya Pravda, Issue (29 October 2009).

Irina O. Khlestova, *Issues of immunity of state in the laws and contractual practice of Russian Federation*, PROBLEMS OF INTERNATIONAL PRIVATE LAW, CONTRACT LAW COMPANY

SVETLANA I. KRUPKO, INVESTMENT DISPUTES BETWEEN STATE AND FOREIGN INVESTOR, BEK 79 (2002).

IGOR I. LUKASHUK, INTERNATIONAL LAW: TEXTBOOK. GENERAL PART, BEK publishing house, INTERNATIONAL PRIVATE LAW 301 (1996). / edited by N. I. Marysheva, CONTRACT LAW COMPANY, INFRA. M. 158-159 (2000).

Maidan K. Suleimenov and Y. G. Bassin, *Civil Law. Volume 3: Textbook*, ALMATY (2004).

VIKTOR P. ZVEKOV, INTERNATIONAL PRIVATE LAW, Norma-infra group 232 (1999).

Czech Yearbook of International Law®

Lyudmila V. Terenteva

Jurisdiction Issues in Cyberspace

Key words:
jurisdiction | *cyberspace* | *territory of the state* | *information* | *infrastructure*

Abstract | *One of the chief aims of this article is to examine some changes to the assertion of jurisdiction by States in cyberspace. This examination reveals a certain contradiction with the limited territorial jurisdiction of States due to the transnational nature of cyberspace. The article is centered on the new Russian and United States approaches to the jurisdiction of the State over national segments of cyberspace and infrastructural objects including server locations. The study of the jurisdiction question is also spurred by the need to address the problem of international jurisdiction of courts regarding civil cases in cyberspace. The present article aims to reveal some difficulties of the traditional criteria of the international jurisdiction based on physical geographical factors.*

Lyudmila V. Terenteva
is a candidate of legal sciences, and a senior lecturer at the Chair of Private International Law at Kutafin Moscow State Law University.
E-mail: terentevamila@ mail.ru

The reported study was funded by RFBR according to the research project № 18-011-00883.

| | |

I.   Introduction

14.01. The increasing use of cyberspace has vigorously changed the traditional approaches to jurisdiction. Cyberspace has no material physical borders, but the notion of jurisdiction of a State is based on some territorial features. Ignoring the problem of jurisdiction in cyberspace can threaten the sovereignty of a State. Thus jurisdiction over activities in cyberspace has become one of the main issues in establishing the rule of law in cyberspace.

14.02. Meanwhile some representatives of the cyberspace community have tried to divide the applicability of sovereign law and their online activities. For example, cyberlibertarian political activist John Barlow was one of the first thinkers who, even at the end of the 20th century, declared the independence of cyberspace from the applicable law of any State. The argument was that cyberspace was outside any country's borders.[1]

14.03. Though this kind of cyberspace separatism has waned, many of its followers continue to advocate in favor of legal immunity for online activities. The victory of the advocates of the opinion that cyberspace was subject to state regulation was demonstrated in the *Yahoo* case.[2] The U.S. company made images of Nazi memorabilia objects available in France. Such images were constitutionally protected in the United States where Yahoo was based, but illegal to display in France where the users were located and where Yahoo targeted advertising. Yahoo unsuccessfully claimed that the French court had no personal jurisdiction seeing that the alleged acts occurred on the U.S. soil and French law did not apply to the images because they were stored on a server in the United States. Search engine Yahoo also argued that compliance with French law would effectively require complete shutdown of its website worldwide. Yahoo has banned Nazi memorabilia from its U.S. auction sites but at the same time sued the French plaintiffs in the United States District for the Northern District of California claiming that the French decision could not be recognized in the United States as it would be incompatible with First Amendment to the Constitution of the United States, related to freedom of expression and would consequently violate U.S. public policy.

14.04. The Yahoo's case illustrates the situation where the laws of one country against some actions in cyberspace may conflict with

---

[1]   John P. Barlow, A Declaration of the Independence of Cyberspace, available at: https://www.eff.org/cyberspace-independence (accessed on 16 August 2018).

[2]   United States Court of Appeals, Ninth Circuit. - 433 F.3d 1199, *Yahoo! Inc. v. LICRA and UEJF*, 12 January 2006.

the laws of another country and may cause the extension of jurisdiction of one State over cyber activities in another State.

14.05. Today there is no doubt that relationships in the cyberspace can not be free from law in spite of any technology-based arguments. If we recognize that the cyberspace can not be outlawed, then on an analogy with this assumption it may be suggested that the cyberspace can not be outside the jurisdiction. This is in accord with the fact that jurisdiction is the practical authority granted to a legal body in order to apply its law. In fact despite the territorial aspect of jurisdiction states exercise jurisdiction over both cyber infrastructure located in the territory of the State and objects or activities in the virtual part of cyberspace. Yahoo's case also proved that any trans-boundary cyber activities would be subject to the regulation of territorial sovereigns.

II. The Concepts of 'Jurisdiction' and 'Territory of the State'

14.06. The legal term 'jurisdiction' is rather controversial as it is used by various branches of law and every branch attaches its own meaning. According to international public law jurisdiction is an important element of sovereignty, and refers to general power to exercise authority, granted to a State over a certain geographic area, territory or certain persons. It can be designated as jurisdiction of a State.[3]

14.07. Statehood is impossible in the absence of territory. International lawyer Michael Akehurst emphasized the territorial aspect of jurisdiction by identifying jurisdiction as territory.[4] It seems that the author did not perceive these concepts of 'jurisdiction' and the 'territory of the State' as equivalent, since it is known that the jurisdiction of the State can be carried out outside its territory. For example, the State has the right to execute prescriptive jurisdiction over its citizens in the territory of other States.

14.08. The territory of the State is understood as an attributive feature of the full prescriptive and enforceable jurisdiction of the State.[5] Full jurisdiction of the State is exercised over all persons and entities within the territory of the State but not within territory as an abstract category. Thus it should be noted here that the

---

[3] James Crawford, *Jurisdiction is an aspect or an ingredient or consequence of sovereignty*, in BROWNLIE'S PRINCIPLE OF PUBLIC INTERNATIONAL LAW, OUP 7 (8th ed. 2012).; Michael Akehurst, *A Jurisdiction in International law*, 46 (145) BYIL 15 (1972).; IGOR I. LUKASHUK, МЕЖДУНАРОДНОЕ ПРАВО. ОБЩАЯ ЧАСТЬ. (INTERNATIONAL LAW. A COMMON PART), Moscow 165-176 (2001).

[4] MICHAEL AKEHURST, A MODERN INTRODUCTION TO INTERNATIONAL LAW, London 102 (5th ed. 1985).

[5] IGOR I. LUKASHUK, МЕЖДУНАРОДНОЕ ПРАВО. ОБЩАЯ ЧАСТЬ. (INTERNATIONAL LAW. A COMMON PART), Moscow 165-176 (2001).

concepts of 'territory' and the 'territory of the State' are not equivalent.

14.09. The concept of the 'territory of the State' was not static throughout history. At the beginning of the twentieth century, the conception of territory was limited solely to the Earth's surface. In the 19th century Russian professor Andrey N. Ushakov under the notion of the State territory understood it as 'the space of land and water.'[6] Later the concept of the 'territory of the State' evolved due to the influence of political, geographic, and technological factors by means of including such spaces as the airspace, the continental shelf space and so on.

III. The Issue of Territoriality in Cyberspace

14.10. Airspace and continental shelf space have physical parameters, spatial extent and, consequently, can be considered as a territory of a State. New spaces demonstrate a phenomenon of virtual reality where social relations arise where there is neither territoriality nor physical tangibility. The logical question arises as to whether there are territorial limits to jurisdiction of the State actually existing in cyberspace?

14.11. The rapid development of telecommunications led to a scientific discussions whether the concept of 'territory' become an anachronism and whether the State lost control over cyberspace. Many authors confirmed 'the breaking of the geographical boundaries and distance'[7], 'the end to geography,'[8] 'the reducing of the effectiveness of the political, economic, legal authority rooted in geographical sovereignty.'[9]

14.12. Indeed some difficulties of determination of jurisdiction in cyberspace can be explained by the collision between the limited territorial competence of a particular State and the transnational, trans-boundary character of cyberspace. Taking into account that cyberspace must be subject to sovereignty and jurisdiction of state, UK Professors Nicholas Tsagourias and Russel Buchan considered that there is no inherent nexus between territory on the one hand and sovereignty and jurisdiction on the other hands. According to the authors the essence of sovereignty is

---

[6] ANDREY N. USHAKOV, МЕЖДУНАРОДНОЕ ПРАВО: ОСНОВНЫЕ ТЕРМИНЫ И ПОНЯТИЯ (INTERNATIONAL LAW: THE BASIC TERMS AND NOTIONS) Moscow 37 (1996).

[7] Jackson Adams, Mohamad Ubakajai, *Cyberspace: A New Threat to the Sovereignty of the State*, 4(6) 256-265 (2016).

[8] Jonathan Matusitz *Intercultural perspectives on cyberspace: An updated examination*, 24(7) JOURNAL OF HUMAN BEHAVIOUR IN THE SOCIAL ENVIRONMENT 713-724 (2014).

[9] Stephen Kobrin, *Electronic cash and the end of national markets*, 2(4) GLOBAL ISSUES 38 (1997).

a power and not a territory as the latter is only a container of power and not just as a place where powers are located.[10]

14.13. The abovementioned thesis is rather controversial as the concept of territory has a legal meaning. Equally important are both sovereignty and jurisdiction of State and also the frameworks of their implementation. Sovereignty and jurisdiction can not be defined if their boundaries are unknown. Both concepts of sovereignty and jurisdiction rely on the territory of a State and accordingly territory can not lose its legal meaning. At the same time the concept of territory can change its filling. The notion of territory can be expanded to new spaces as has been done in the past when the notion of territory was expanded to such spaces as continental shelves, sea space, ships and aircraft, space ships and space stations. Cyberspace as the area of social, economical and political relations also can be included in the concept of a territory of a State, provided that the notion of spaces ceases to be understood exclusively as a territorial and tangible aspect. In any case the interpretation of this kind of space as 'territory' must follow a certain degree of conventionality.

IV.   Approaches to the Problem of the Jurisdiction Issue in Cyberspace

14.14. In the characteristics that scholars assign to cyberspace, they mentioned as a rule, its 'unified character, indivisibility, irreducibility to the boundaries of physical space'[11], its 'mobility and variability, the absence of unambiguous geographical certainty, trans-boundary, multidimensionality and the absence of linearity and physical parameters'.[12]

14.15. What are the limits of the State's jurisdiction over cyberspace? There have been many approaches developed on a virtual framework to the solution of the jurisdiction issue in cyberspace. In the scholarly doctrine, there was an approach to cyberspace as a zone of common interests. Some commentators offered to determine zones of national jurisdiction on cyberspace by analogy, for example, with Arctic regions, outer space, the Moon and other heavenly bodies.[13] This approach to interpret cyberspace as *res communis* has certain difficulties. In

---

[10]   NICHOLAS TSAGOURIAS, RESERCH HANDBOOK ON INTERNATIONAL LAW AND CYBERSPACE, Elgar publishing, Cheltenham UK Northampton MA USA 18 (Edward R. Buchan ed., 2015).
[11]   Daria E. Dobrinskaya, *Cyberspace: the territory of modern life*, 24(1) BULLETIN OF MOSCOW UNIVERSITY 52-70 (2018).
[12]   E. L. Anselmo, *Cyberspace in International Legislation: Does the Development of the Internet Refute the Principle of Territoriality in International Law?*, (2) ECONOMIC STRATEGIES 25 (2006).
[13]   Darrel C. Menthe, Jurisdiction in Cyberspace: A theory of international spaces, available at: https:// repository.law.umich.edu/cgi/viewcontent.cgi?article=1163&context=mttlr. (accessed on 16 August 2018).

comparison with the Moon and other heavenly bodies that are the objects of public interest of different States, cyberspace is also the area of different private interests: business, communication, commercial contracts and other activity that cannot be the object of simultaneous regulation by several countries.

14.16.   Another approach to the question of jurisdiction in cyberspace that uses the principle of server location and the principle that presumes the jurisdiction of a State whose national domain was used for particular information was the subject of criticism at the end of the 20th century. David R. Johnson and David G. Post emphasized 'that although a domain name, when initially assigned to a given machine and may be associated with a particular Internet Protocol address corresponding to the territory within which the machine is physically located, the machine may move in physical space without any movement in the logical domain name space of the Net. Or, alternatively, the owner of the domain name might request that the name become associated with an entirely different machine, in a different physical location'.[14]

14.17.   Moreover the difficulties of the determination of the jurisdiction basing on domain zones can be explained by functional domains like «.com» «.org», «.int» that turn out to be out of the jurisdiction of a particular State.[15] For example, the Russian sector of cyberspace in the national domains zones .ru .su and .рф should accordingly fall under Russian legislation.[16]

14.18.   At the same time we may argue that in spite of the lack of an International treaty stipulating jurisdiction in cyberspace, the jurisdiction of a State in cyberspace has become the issue de jure in Russian law in recent times.

V.   Jurisdiction Issues in Cyberspace According to Russian Law

14.19.   The place of cyberspace in the structure of the information sphere appeared in the recent adopted Doctrine of Information Security of the Russian Federation approved by Decree of the President of the Russian Federation in 2016. It must be noted that the Doctrine operates on the notion of Internet and not cyberspace. The Doctrine defines the information sphere as a combination of information, information infrastructure objects,

---

[14]   David R. Johnson, Law And Borders: The Rise of Law in Cyberspace, Stanford Law Review 1367 1996 available at: https://cyber.harvard.edu/is02/readings/johnson-post.html. (accessed on 16 August 2018).
[15]   David R. Johnson. Law And Borders: The Rise of Law in Cyberspace, Stanford Law Review 1367 1996, available at: https://cyber.harvard.edu/is02/readings/johnson-post.html (accessed on 16 August 2018).
[16]   The non-profit organization 'Coordination Center for TLD .RU' is the administrator of the national top level domains .RU and .РФ (the national registry).

information systems and websites within the information and telecommunications network of the Internet, communications networks, information technologies, entities involved in generating and processing information, developing and using the above technologies, and ensuring information security, as well as a set of mechanisms regulating public relations in the sphere.[17]

14.20. It is especially noteworthy that the definition of the information infrastructure solves the issue of jurisdiction in cyberspace to a certain degree in the Executive Order on the '2017-2030 Strategy for the Development of an Information Society in the Russian Federation' signed by V. Putin on 9 May 2017.[18] The information infrastructure of the Russian Federation is defined as a combination of information infrastructure objects, information systems, cyberspace websites and communication networks located in the territory of the Russian Federation, as well as in the territories under the jurisdiction of the Russian Federation or used under international treaties signed by the Russian Federation.

14.21. Taking into account the fact that information systems and cyberspace sites do not have physical parameters and a physical location in the territory of the Russian Federation, the doctrine in fact extends the State's jurisdiction over the Russian segment of cyberspace, which is conditionally recognized as a territory.

14.22. Also the State's jurisdiction extends to the informational system. According to Federal Law "On Information, Information Technology and Protection of Information" 2006[19], this law refers to the totality of information contained in the databases and informational technologies and the technical facilities providing for its processing.

14.23. In this case a question arises about the sphere of jurisdiction. Relying on the definition of information infrastructure of the Russian Federation allows us to state that not only do information infrastructure objects, including servers located in Russia, fall under jurisdiction of Russia but that totality of information contained in the databases, servers and other equipment located in Russia are also under the jurisdiction of Russia. The analysis of Russian legislation, suggests that the sphere and limits of the sovereign power of the State concerning network space is determined only in the Decrees of the President but not

---

[17] Doctrine of Information Security of the Russian Federation, approved by Decree of the President of the Russian Federation No. 646 of 5 December 2016, available at: http://www.mid.ru/en/foreign_policy/official_documents/-/asset_publis her/CptICkB6BZ29/content/id/2563163 (accessed on 16 August 2018).

[18] Available at: http://en.kremlin.ru/acts/news/54477 (accessed on 16 August 2018).

[19] Available at: http://en.kremlin.ru/acts/news/55276 (accessed on 16 August 2018).

Czech Yearbook of International Law®

in the Constitution of Russia. This can be demonstrated by the reference to the fundamental law of Russia. According to Article 3, 4, 5, 67 and 79 of the Constitution of Russian Federation, the Russian Federation shall possess sovereign rights and exercise jurisdiction on the territory of Russia. According to Article 67 the territory of the Russian Federation shall include the territories of its subjects, inland waters and territorial sea, and the air space over them. The notion of 'territory of Russia' doesn't include the notion of 'cyberspace'. Meanwhile it is obviously important that the sphere and limits of the sovereign power of the State concerning network space also have to be reflected in the organic law of the State. All this allows us to conclude that the Decrees of the President actually extend Russian jurisdiction only over the national segment of cyberspace and information infrastructure objects including server locations in Russia.

VI. Jurisdiction Issues in Cyberspace According to US law: The case of *Microsoft Corp.* v. *United States*

14.24. The new American approach treats server location as irrelevant in determining jurisdiction. It was formulated in the Act entitled 'Clarifying Lawful Overseas Use of Data Act' or the 'CLOUD Act', and was signed by the U.S. President on the 23 of March 2018. The Cloud Act amended Title 18, United States Code and improved law enforcement access to data stored across borders.[20] The Cloud Act removed the obstacle in the form of the inability to access data stored outside the United States that are in custody, control or possession of telecommunications service providers that fall within the jurisdiction of the United States.

14.25. The history of the adoption of this act began with the Supreme Court case *Microsoft Corp.* v. *United States Department of Justice* regarding US access to emails stored in Ireland.[21] Microsoft contested its obligation to disclose Content Information stored exclusively in its Dublin, Ireland datacenter, in response to a government issued search warrant under the Stored Communication Act, arguing that US authority only extended to data located within the territorial boundaries of the United States.

---

[20] H.R.4943 — 115th Congress (2017-2018), available at: https://www.congress.gov/bill/115th-congress/house-bill/4943/text. (accessed on 16 August 2018).
[21] *Microsoft Corp.* v. *United States* (In re: Warrant to Search a Certain E-Mail Account Controlled & Maintained by Microsoft Corp.), 829 F.3d 197, 204– 205 (CA2 2016).

14.26. The Magistrate Judge denied Microsoft's motion.[22] On appeal, a panel of the Court of Appeals for the Second Circuit reversed the denial of the motion to quash and vacated the civil contempt finding, holding that requiring Microsoft to disclose the electronic communications in question would be an unauthorized extraterritorial application of s.2703 of the Stored Communications Act that did not apply to data outside the US.[23] On 6 February 2018, the Cloud Act of 2018 (H.R. 4943 and S. 2383) was introduced to the Congress and on 23 March 2018 it was signed by Donald Trump. According to the Section 2713 of the Cloud Act, "a provider of electronic communication service or remote computing service shall preserve, backup, or disclose the contents of a wire or electronic communication and any record or other information pertaining to a customer or subscriber within such provider's possession, custody, or control, regardless of whether such communication, record, or other information is located within or outside of the United States".[24] The Supreme Court granted the Department of Justice's petition to review the case and remanded the case to the United States Court of Appeals for the Second Circuit.[25]

14.27. Thus the Cloud Act solves the issue of the accessing data stored outside the United States even if foreign law prohibits communications-service providers from disclosing such data. Taking into account the transnational character of the biggest American IT companies, the adoption of the Act will facilitate expansion of US jurisdiction over the data of users of these companies. The prohibition of the transfer of data by the law of the location of these companies cannot be the only reason for the failure to provide data to the US authorities.

14.28. Therewith the Act also gives the opportunity to a provider of electronic communication service to the public or remote computing service to file a motion to modify or quash the legal process, if pursuant to legal process, that provider is being required to disclose the contents of a wire or electronic communication of a subscriber or customer. According to the Cloud Act the motion of provider may be satisfied if the following conditions are met. First, the customer or subscriber must not be a United States citizen and must not reside in the

---

[22] In re Warrant To Search a Certain E-Mail Account Controlled and Maintained by Microsoft Corp., 15 F.Supp.3d 466 (SDNY 2014).

[23] In re Warrant To Search a Certain E-Mail Account Controlled and Maintained by Microsoft Corp., 829 F. 3d 197, 222 (CA2 2016).

[24] 115th Congress 2nd Session S.2383. A Bill, available at: https://www.congress.gov/115/bills/s2383/BILLS-115s2383is.pdf. (accessed on 16 August 2018).

[25] *United States v. Microsoft Corp.* 584 U.S. (2018), available at: https://www.supremecourt.gov/opinions/17pdf/17-2_1824.pdf. (accessed on 16 August 2018)

United States. Second, the required disclosure would create a material risk that the provider would violate the laws of a qualifying foreign government. The Court may modify or quash the legal process only if the above provisions are met and if the court finds that, the interests of justice dictate that the legal process should be modified or quashed based on the totality of the circumstances (s.2713 (B)(2) Cloud Act).[26]

14.29. According to the s.2713 (3) of the Cloud Act the court for the purposes of making a determination of the interests of justice takes into the account the following the following circumstances: "the interests of the United States, including the investigative interests of the governmental entity seeking to require the disclosure; the interests of the qualifying foreign government in preventing any prohibited disclosure; the likelihood, extent, and nature of penalties to the provider or any employees of the provider as a result of inconsistent legal requirements imposed on the provider; the location and nationality of the subscriber or customer whose communications are being sought, if known, and the nature and extent of the subscriber or customer's connection to the United States; the nature and extent of the provider's ties to and presence in the United States; the importance to the investigation of the information required to be disclosed; the likelihood of timely and effective access to the information required to be disclosed through means that would cause less serious negative consequences; if the legal process has been sought on behalf of a foreign authority pursuant to section 3512, the investigative interests of the foreign authority making the request for assistance".[27]

14.30. The list of circumstances is rather extensive. The interests of the United States, including the investigative interests of governmental entities come first in the list, and the court will be more likely be concerned with them. The assessment of the interests of the qualifying foreign government in preventing any prohibited disclosure is likely to be secondary.

14.31. Therefore it is necessary to point out that assessment of circumstances by a court will be relevant only to a foreign government with which the United States has an executive agreement. This agreement has entered into force and provides to electronic communication service providers and remote computing service providers substantive and procedural opportunities similar to those provided in US law. There is no

---

[26] 115th Congress 2nd Session S.2383. A Bill, available at: https://www.congress.gov/115/bills/s2383/BILLS-115s2383is.pdf (accessed on 16 August 2018).

[27] 115th Congress 2nd Session S.2383. A Bill, available at: https://www.congress.gov/115/bills/s2383/BILLS-115s2383is.pdf (accessed on 16 August 2018).

opportunity for the provider to file a motion to modify or quash the legal process. If the US required disclosure would create a material risk for violation the laws of the foreign government that has no executive agreement with the US. Thus, it can be concluded that the equipment providing access to the data will fall under the jurisdiction of the State of its location, but it is unlikely that the jurisdiction of the State of the server's location can be extended to the data to which the server provides access. As has been mentioned earlier the State, in particular the US with the adoption of the Cloud Act, will also extend its jurisdiction to the data stored outside the United States even if foreign law prohibits communications service providers from disclosing.

14.32. This approach is rather problematic in the Russian Federation. The Russian Federation has not signed the Council of Europe Convention on cybercrime, adopted on 23 November 2001 in Budapest.[28] The reasons for this is the wording of paragraph 'b' of Article 32 of the Convention that allows trans-border access to stored computer data with consent or where publicly available. According to the paragraph a Party may, without the authorization of another Party access publicly available stored computer data, regardless of where the data is located geographically. Additionally, it may access or receive, through a computer system in its territory, stored computer data located in another Party, if the Party obtains the lawful and voluntary consent of the person who has the lawful authority to disclose the data to the Party through that computer system.

14.33. Russia's refusal to sign on to the Convention was explained by arguing that the wording of the paragraph 'b' of Article 32 contradicts the Russian legislation and is a violation of State sovereignty.[29]

14.34. Although the Convention covers issues of the protection of society against cybercrime, and the Cloud Act regulates the interaction between providers and US authorities regarding the data of US citizens located abroad, the common idea of both acts is similar. They allow the penetration into information networks of another State without the consent of the country in which these actions are performed.

14.35. From these two opposite conceptions followed opposing legal effects in the US and Russia regarding the jurisdiction in cyberspace.

---

[28] Council of Europe Convention on cybercrime, adopted on 23 November 2001 in Budapest, available at: https://www.coe.int/en/web/conventions/full-list/-/conventions/treaty/185 (accessed on 16 August 2018).
[29] 'Putin Defies Convention on Cybercrime', CNews (online), 28 March 2008, available at: http://www..crime-research.org/news/28.03.2008/3277/ (accessed on 16 August 2018).

VII. International Jurisdiction of Courts Regarding Civil Cases of Cyberspace in Australia and the US: the case of Dow Jones & Company Inc v Gutnick[30]

14.36. The actual range of jurisdiction problems is much wider. International private law defines the term of international jurisdiction as a proper court of a particular State handling civil disputes with a foreign factor between two or more private parties.[31]

14.37. The questions of jurisdiction should not be discussed separately in International private law and International public law bearing in mind that the jurisdiction of a State imposes limitations on the jurisdiction of courts. Dr. Dan Jerker B. Svantesson pointed out in his discussion of *Dow Jones & Company Inc* v. *Gutnick* that in a cyberspace context courts claiming criminal and civil jurisdiction face the same problems.[32]

14.38. It is very important to point out that stipulating a State's borders in cyberspace by domain registration simply is not enough. A State will assert its power over the effect of harmful acts in cyberspace that appear in its jurisdictions. That is why jurisdiction in Private International law should have additional bases to follow-up State authority.

14.39. Briefly it can be illustrated by the case of *Dow Jones & Company Inc* v. *Gutnick*. Gutnick alleged that part of an article created in New York defamed him and brought an action in the Supreme Court of Victoria in Australia against Dow Jones claiming damages. Gutnick lived in Victoria and was a well-known businessperson there, although he conducted business outside Australia including in the United States. The facts were that the allegedly defamatory content created in New York was uploaded to a server in New Jersey where it was available for access in Australia. The issue was whether the respondent could litigate his defamation action in the courts of Australia where the defamation law was stricter than in the US. The respondent's argument, accepted by the High Court, was that accessibility of the website in the case of defamation was sufficient to found jurisdiction. Here we can see that Cyberspace publishers bear some responsibility for understanding the laws of countries where possible plaintiffs reside and possess reputations. Dow

---

[30] *Dow Jones and Company Inc* v. *Gutnick* (2002) HCA 56 (2002) 210 CLR 433; 194ALR 433; 77 255.

[31] LASAR A. LUNTZ, КУРС МЕЖДУНАРОДНОГО ЧАСТНОГО ПРАВА (INTERNATIONAL PRIVATE LAW), Moscow 810 (2002).

[32] Dr Dan Jerker B. Svantesson. 'Place Of Wrong' in the Tort of Defamation - Behind the Scenes of a Legal Fiction. Bond Law Review. Volume 17, Issue 2 2005, available at: https://epublications.bond.edu.au/cgi/viewcontent.cgi?article=1308&context=blr. (accessed on 16 August 2018)

Jones was served under what is called the ‚extra-territorial‘ or ‚long-arm‘ jurisdiction of the Supreme Court of Victoria. These criteria of jurisdiction of the court were taken from US court practice.

14.40. Some criteria for asserting jurisdiction are based on physical geographical factors and cannot be transplanted into the cyberspace environment. Thus the question of jurisdiction in litigation focused on cyberspace should have special rules applicable to its specific character. It may be suggested that the more adequate criteria are stipulated in the US - certain minimum contacts with jurisdiction in which a legal action is brought.

14.41. The conception of long-arm jurisdiction is based on minimum contacts. This was developed by the US Supreme court for the first time in the case *International Shoe* v. *Washington* in 1945. Since then, the court has held that a person must have minimum contacts with a State, in order for a court in one State to assert personal jurisdiction over a defendant from another State.[33]

14.42. At the same time the opposite side of this can lead to some kind of multi-jurisdiction effect as the damage of harmful acts in cyberspace can appear in almost all jurisdictions. In order to avoid this effect courts could use the so-called sliding scale known in US.[34]

14.43. In *Zippo Manufacturing* v. *Zippo Dot Com, Inc.*, the court developed a passive versus active test-also known as the 'sliding scale' test. This test is where the court examined the level of interaction between a website and its viewers. If the website is a passive website that merely makes information available to residents of another State should they seek it, then jurisdiction in that foreign State would not be appropriate. If, however, the website is used to develop business contacts in another State or actively seeks out residents of that State, jurisdiction there would be appropriate. In the middle, where an interactive website allows a user to exchange information with the host computer, 'jurisdiction is determined by examining the level of interactivity and commercial nature of the exchange of information that occurs on the Web site.'[35]

---

[33]   *International Shoe* v. *State of Washington*, 326 U.S. 310 (1945).

[34]   *Zippo Manufacturing Co.* v. *Zippo Dot Com, Inc.*, 952 F.Supp. 1119, 1121 (W.D. Pa. 1997).

[35]   Ronald A. Brand, *Tort Jurisdiction In A Multilateral Convention: The Lessons Of The Due Process Clause And The Brussels Convention*, 26 Brook (1998).; Robert L. Hoegle, Christopher P. Boam, *The Internet and Jurisdiction International Principles Emerge but Confrontation Looms*, 3(1) THE JOURNAL OF WORLD INTELLECTUAL PROPERTY 43 (2000).

VIII. International Jurisdiction of Court in Cyberspace in Russia

14.44. There are some special jurisdictional rules for Cyberspace in Russian law. Article 247 of the 2002 Commercial Procedure Code provides ten bases for the competence of arbitral courts[36] in commercial disputes with a foreign factor. Such traditional criteria include the domicile of the defendant or place of business, the place of the contract's performance, and the place of harm-doing or effect of harmful acts. However, additionally Article 247 of the Commercial Procedure Code asserts the jurisdiction of the arbitral court if the case arises from a dispute connected with the State registration of names and other objects and rendering of services in the international association of networks 'Cyberspace' in the territory of the Russian Federation (Item 9 of Part 1 of Article 247). Actually there is no State registration of names in Russia as the administrator of the national top level domains .RU and .РФ (the national registry) is the non-profit organization 'Coordination Center for TLD .RU'. Moreover there is no legal definition of 'the international association of networks in cyberspace' in a legal act. Taking into account that the wording of the article is not clear, the Plenum of the Supreme court clarified that when Item 9 of Part 1 of Article 247 of the Commercial "Procedure Code is applied, disputes arising from relations pertaining to State registration of names and other objects and rendering of Cyberspace services on the territory of the Russian Federation should be regarded to include disputes pertaining to the protection of rights to results of intellectual activity and means of individualization of legal persons engaged in entrepreneurial and other economic activity, of goods, works, services and enterprises, used in registration of domain names in the Russian domain zone (national first-level domains and second-level domain zones, oriented at Russian users or including websites in Cyrillic alphabet), and if registration was performed on the territory of the Russian Federation (the registrar is a Russian person) – in other domain zones as well".[37]

14.45. Together with the before mentioned bases the Article 247 of the Commercial Procedure Code that permits arbitral courts to

---

[36] It's necessary to distinguish the competence of the State arbitral court of Russia which adjudicates commercial disputes and the International Commercial Arbitration Court at the chamber of commerce and industry of the Russian Federation. The latter would have jurisdiction if a dispute arose from contractual or other civil law relationships connected with foreign trade and where the place of business of at least one of the parties is located abroad and there is an agreement in writing between the parties to refer a dispute that has arisen, or may arise, between them to the International Commercial Arbitration Court.

[37] Ruling of the Plenary Session of the Supreme Court of the Russian Federation № 23, 27 June 2017, available at: http://test.vsrf.ru/Ruling/2017-23.pdf (accessed on 16 August 2018).

assert their jurisdiction if the dispute is most closely connected with territory of Russian Federation. This way of asserting jurisdiction seems very reasonable due to extending jurisdiction not only for companies and individuals incorporated or having their centers of operations domiciled within territory. It is also reasonable for the defendant's contacts with the forum. The principle of the closest connection is stipulated only in the arbitral procedure court of Russia and all civil disputes that have no commercial character must be adjudicated by civil courts whose competence is based on traditional criteria: the domicile of the defendant, the place of wrong-doing or effect of harmful acts and other.[38]

14.46. Given this, it would be reasonable to fix the competence of the Court on the principle of the closest connection in the Civil Procedure Code of the Russian Federation as well. The opposite side of this extension can lead to some kind of multi-jurisdiction effect as the backlash of harmful acts in cyberspace can appear in almost all jurisdictions. Moreover courts asserting their jurisdiction do not evaluate jurisdiction of foreign courts for a particular case. In order to avoid a multi-jurisdiction effect Russian courts could use the so-called sliding scale known in the US, and customized for an online world that is based on a determination of the level of interactivity associated with the website and its commercial nature.[39] The Court can assert jurisdiction over websites that conduct business over cyberspace and are therefore less likely to have a basis for personal jurisdiction over passive website which simply makes the information available to the user. It is worth pointing out that some amendments to the rules of the Civil Procedure Code relating to the jurisdiction of individual's disputes involving foreign persons entered into force on 1 January 2016. Item 2 of Part 3 of Article 402 Civil Procedure code provides that the competence of a Russian court is if the defendant has property located in the territory of the Russian Federation and/or distributes advertising in cyberspace, aimed at attracting the attention of consumers located on the territory of the Russian Federation. According to Item 11 of Part 3 of Article 402 Civil Procedure code, the Court is competent in cases of the deleting of search results by the search engine operator of links that allow access to information in cyberspace if the claimant has

---

[38] Ruling of the Plenary Session of the Supreme Court of the Russian Federation № 23, 27 June 2017, available at: http://test.vsrf.ru/Ruling/2017-23.pdf (accessed on 16 August 2018).
[39] CHRISTOPHER MCWINNEY, SEAN WOODEN, JEREMY MCKNOWN, JOHN RYAN, JOSEPH GREEN, THE 'SLIDING SCALE' OF PERSONAL JURISDICTION VIA THE CYBERSPACE, Dorsey & Whitney, LLP. 101 (2003).

a residence in the Russian Federation. Thus this item touches on some of the procedural aspects of the so-called 'right to be forgotten.' The 'right to be forgotten' was stipulated in the new Article 10.3 of the Federal Law No. 149-FZ 'On information, information technologies and protection of information' dated 27 July 2006 (as amended).

14.47. The Law stipulates a procedure when the operator's engines that distribute advertisements on the Internet aimed to attract the attention of consumers located on the territory of the Russian Federation is obliged at the request of a citizen to stop displaying the links of false and irrelevant information about the claimant or distributed with violation of the legislation of the Russian Federation. The exception is information containing events about some characteristics of criminal actions for which the terms of criminal prosecution have not expired and information about the commission by a citizen of a crime, for which the conviction has neither been expunged nor expired.[40]

IX.   Conclusion

14.48. The solution of the jurisdictional issue in cyberspace exclusively on the domestic level creates a conflict of interests of different States due to the intersection of their zones of influence with respect to a certain information infrastructure. As was demonstrated in the article the approach adopted in the US Cloud Act of 2018, which provides jurisdiction over data located on servers in foreign countries, contradicts the approach adopted in Russian legislation. From these two opposite conceptions we can see the opposite legal effects in the US and Russia.

14.49. The study of the jurisdiction question determines some problems of the international jurisdiction of courts regarding civil cases in cyberspace. From the analyses of the traditional criteria of asserting international jurisdiction it follows that some of them are based on physical geographical factors and cannot be applied to cyberspace. Thus the most reliable criteria of the competence of a court should be based on the principle of the closest connection. At the same time the grounds for jurisdiction must be stated in such way in order to exclude the

---

[40]   Amendments 'Federal Law No. 127-FZ entered into force 30.06.2018. The version of Federal Law on Information, Information Technologies and Protection of Information that incorporates all the amendments up to 'Federal Law No. 482-FZ of December 31, 2017 has not been translated into English yet. Russian version available at:
http://www.consultant.ru/document/cons_doc_LAW_61798/ (accessed on 16 August 2018).

multi-jurisdiction effect, being based only on the accessibility of information in cyberspace.

| | |

Summaries

FRA   [*La question de la compétence juridictionnelle au sein du cyberespace*]
Le principal objectif du présent article est d'analyser les changements qu'on observe dans la compétence des États au sein du cyberespace. L'analyse met en lumière la contradiction qui existe entre le pouvoir territorialement limité des États et la nature transfrontalière du cyberespace. L'article se focalise avant tout sur les nouvelles approches de la Russie et des États-Unis vis-à-vis du pouvoir de l'État sur les segments nationaux du cyberespace et sur les infrastructures, y compris la localisation des serveurs. L'étude des questions relatives à la compétence des juridictions s'avère de plus en plus nécessaire au vu des litiges civils ayant pour objet des relations juridiques au sein du cyberespace. Le présent article met en évidence certains aspects problématiques de l'approche traditionnelle de la compétence internationale, basée sur des critères géographiques.

CZE   [*Jurisdikční otázky kyberprostoru*]
Jedním z hlavních cílů tohoto článku je analyzovat některé změny uplatňování pravomoci států v kyberprostoru. Tato analýza odkrývá určitou kontradikci, zohledníme-li omezenou teritoriální pravomoc států, způsobenou přeshraniční povahou kyberprostoru. Článek se zaměřuje především na nové přístupy Ruska a Spojených států k pravomoci států nad národními segmenty kyberprostoru a infrastrukturními objekty, včetně umístění serverů. Studium otázky pravomoci (příslušnosti) je stále více žádoucí i z důvodu potřeby věnovat se problému mezinárodní pravomoci a příslušnosti soudů ve vztahu k civilněprávním případům realizovaným v kyberprostoru. Cílem tohoto článku je odhalit některé problémy tradičního kritéria mezinárodní pravomoci (příslušnosti) vycházející z fyzických geografických faktorů.

| | |

POL [*Kwestie jurysdykcji w cyberprzestrzeni*]

Artykuł zajmuje się kwestiami ograniczenia kompetencji (właściwość międzynarodowa) w odniesieniu do cybeprzestrzeni, co ze względu na charakter transgraniczny jest w pewnej opozycji do ograniczonych terytorialnie kompetencji sądowniczych państw. W artykule omówiono nowe rosyjskie i amerykańskie procedury określania kompetencji państwa w odniesieniu do segmentu krajowego cyberprzestrzeni oraz obiekty informatyki, w tym lokalizację serwerów. W związku z badaniem kwestii właściwości konieczne było również podjęcie problematyki określenia właściwości międzynarodowej sądów w odniesieniu do sporów na gruncie prawa prywatnego ze stosunków prawnych realizowanych w cyberprzestrzeni. Artykuł omawia szereg problemów związanych ze stosowaniem tradycyjnych kryteriów określania właściwości międzynarodowej za pomocą powiązania z konkretnym terytorium.

DEU [*Fragen der Zuständigkeit im Cyberspace*]

Der Beitrag widmet sich Fragen der Beschränkung der Rechtsgewalt (internationalen Zuständigkeit) betreffend den Cyberspace, welcher infolge seines grenzüberschreitenden Charakters in einem gewissen Gegensatz zur beschränkten territorialen Gerichtsbarkeit von Nationalstaaten steht. Im Artikel werden neue russische und amerikanische Ansätze zur Bestimmung der Hoheitsgewalt des Staats über das nationale Segment des Cyberspace und informationstechnische Objekte (einschließlich der physischen Unterbringung von Servern) abgehandelt. Die eingehendere Betrachtung dieser Fragen der Rechtshoheit hat außerdem Anstoß gegeben, sich mit dem Problem zu befassen, wie die internationale Zuständigkeit von Gerichten in privatrechtlichen Streitigkeiten zu bestimmen ist, wenn die zugrundeliegenden Rechtsbeziehungen sich im Cyberspace abspielen. Der Beitrag stellt dabei eine Reihe harter Nüsse vor, die es zu knacken gilt, wenn traditionelle Kriterien zur Bestimmung der internationalen Zuständigkeit (die eine konkrete territoriale Bindung voraussetzen) angewandt werden sollen.

RUS [*Вопросы юрисдикции в киберпространстве*]

Статья посвящена вопросам определения международной юрисдикции в отношении киберпространства, которое в силу своего трансграничного характера вступает в определенное противоречие с ограниченной территориальной юрисдикцией государств. В статье рассмотрены новые российские и американские подходы к

Czech Yearbook of International Law®

установлению юрисдикции государства над национальным сегментом Киберпространства и объектами информатизации, включая расположение серверов. Изучение вопроса юрисдикции также обусловило обращение к проблемам установления международной юрисдикции судов в отношении гражданских споров, вытекающих из отношений которые реализуются в киберпространстве. Статья обнаруживает ряд трудностей при применении традиционных критериев установления международной юрисдикции на основе привязки к определенной территории.

ESP　[*El ciberespacio – cuestiones jurisdiccionales*]
El artículo se dedica a las cuestiones relativas a la jurisdicción restringida (jurisdicción internacional) en relación con el ciberespacio que debido a su carácter trasfronterizo contradice, en cierto modo, la jurisdicción territorial limitada de los Estados. El texto examina las nuevas posturas adoptadas por Rusia y América a la hora de determinar la jurisdicción del Estado en el segmento nacional del ciberespacio y los objetos informáticos, incluida la ubicación de los servidores. El análisis de la cuestión de jurisprudencias ha revelado la necesidad de abordar el tema de definir la jurisprudencia internacional en el ámbito de controversias jurídico-privadas que surgen de relaciones jurídicas realizadas en el ciberespacio. El artículo plantea una serie de dificultades provenientes de la aplicación de criterios tradicionales para la definición de la jurisprudencia internacional mediante el vínculo con un determinado territorio.

| | |

Bibliography

Jackson Adams, Mohamad Albakajai, *Cyberspace: A New Threat to the Sovereignty of the State*, 4(6) 256-265 (2016).

Michael Akehurst, *A Jurisdiction in International law*, 46 (145) BYIL 15 (1972).

MICHAEL AKEHURST, A MODERN INTRODUCTION TO INTERNATIONAL LAW, London 102 (5th ed. 1985).

Erin L. Anselmo, *Cyberspace in International Legislation: Does the Development of the Internet Refute the Principle of Territoriality in International Law?*, (2) ECONOMIC STRATEGIES 25 (2006).

Ronald A. Brand, *Tort Jurisdiction In A Multilateral Convention: The Lessons Of The Due Process Clause And The Brussels Convention*, 26 Brook (1998).

James Crawford, *Jurisdiction is an aspect or an ingredient or consequence of sovereignty, in* BROWNLIE'S PRINCIPLE OF PUBLIC INTERNATIONAL LAW, OUP 7 (8th ed. 2012).

Daria E. Dobrinskaya, *Cyberspace: the territory of modern life*, 24(1) BULLETIN OF MOSCOW UNIVERSITY 52-70 (2018).

Robert L. Hoegle, Christopher P. Boam, *The Internet and Jurisdiction International Principles Emerge but Confrontation Looms*, 3(1) THE JOURNAL OF WORLD INTELLECTUAL PROPERTY 43 (2000).

David R. Johnson, *Law and Borders – The Rise of Law in Cyberspace*, STANFORD LAW REVIEW 34 (1996).

Stephen Kobrin, *Electronic cash and the end of national markets*, 2(4) GLOBAL ISSUES 38 (1997).

IGOR I. LUKASHUK, МЕЖДУНАРОДНОЕ ПРАВО. ОБЩАЯ ЧАСТЬ. (INTERNATIONAL LAW. A COMMON PART), Moscow 165-176 (2001).

LASAR A. LUNTZ, КУРС МЕЖДУНАРОДНОГО ЧАСТНОГО ПРАВА (INTERNATIONAL PRIVATE LAW), Moscow 810 (2002).

Jonathan Matusitz, *Intercultural perspectives on cyberspace: An updated examination*, 24(7) JOURNAL OF HUMAN BEHAVIOUR IN THE SOCIAL ENVIRONMENT 713-724 (2014).

CHRISTOPHER MCWINNEY, SEAN WOODEN, JEREMY MCKNOWN, JOHN RYAN, JOSEPH GREEN, THE 'SLIDING SCALE' OF PERSONAL JURISDICTION VIA THE CYBERSPACE, Dorsey & Whitney, LLP. 101 (2003).

Eli M. Noam, *The public telecommunications network: A concept in transition*, 37(1) JOURNAL OF COMMUNICATION NEW YORK 30–48 (1987).

NICHOLAS TSAGOURIAS, RESERCH HANDBOOK ON INTERNATIONAL LAW AND CYBERSPACE, Elgar publishing, Cheltenham UK Northampton MA USA 18 (Edward R. Buchan ed., 2015).

ANDREY N. USHAKOV, МЕЖДУНАРОДНОЕ ПРАВО: ОСНОВНЫЕ ТЕРМИНЫ И ПОНЯТИЯ (INTERNATIONAL LAW: THE BASIC TERMS AND NOTIONS) Moscow 37 (1996).

Czech Yearbook of International Law®

Natalia N. Viktorova

State Sovereignty and Protection
of International Investments

Key words:
state sovereignty | economic sovereignty | international investment | globalization | strategic sectors of economy | multilateral corporations

Abstract | The article is devoted to the problem of the alignment of State sovereignty with the protection of foreign investments. The problem of sovereignty is still one of the main issues studied in the theory of the State and law. Over time, the concept of sovereignty has changed. This problem is especially salient now - in the era of globalization - in connection with the attraction of foreign investment by States. In addition to positive factors, foreign investment may pose a threat to the security of States, so the legislation of many States provides mechanisms for restrictions on foreign investment in key, or strategic, spheres of the economy. States interested in attracting foreign investment enter into bilateral, multilateral investment agreements that provide some guarantees for foreign investors. According to some scholars, such international agreements limit the sovereignty of the State. This article discusses the fears of some experts that such international treaties may be dangerous for States, since they allow investors to utilize arbitration with claims against host States, and some investors abuse the investment treaty system.

Natalia N. Viktorova is a candidate of legal sciences, senior lecturer at the Chair of Private International Law at Kutafin Moscow State Law University.
E-mail: vozgik@mail.mipt.ru

The reported study was funded by RFBR according to the research project № 18-011-00883.

| | |

I.   Introduction[1]

15.01. The development of the law on foreign investment raises the question of its alignment with the national legislation of States and state sovereignty. In the scholarly doctrine there are different points of view on the problem under consideration.

15.02. The subject of State sovereignty is still given much attention in scholarship. There are different points of view regarding the concept of sovereignty, and its content. Modern concepts have emerged. Some experts consider sovereignty from the standpoint of the information revolution, others refer to globalization.[2]

15.03. State sovereignty is an attribute of a State to carry out its functions on its territory and abroad, in international relations, independently from other States. State sovereignty means 'the supremacy of state power, its unity and independence. In the literal sense, the word „sovereignty", derived from the Latin word *"supraneitas"* (from "supra" - above), means its supremacy or that characteristic of power by virtue of which it is the highest.'[3]

15.04. Prominent Russian scholar Iosif Levin considers that 'sovereignty is the supremacy of the state on its territory and independency from other states.'[4] The relationship between sovereignty and international law has found its legal embodiment in the principal of the sovereign equality of States. Under this principle, every State has the duty to fulfill its international obligations entirely and in good faith.[5]

15.05. The Declaration on Principles of International Law concerning Friendly Relations and Co-operation among States in accordance with the Charter of the United Nations adopted by the General Assembly on 24 October 1970 states that 'all States enjoy sovereign equality. They have equal rights and duties and are equal members of the international community, notwithstanding differences of an economic, social, political or other nature.'[6]

15.06. The concept of sovereignty arose as a result of long and bloody conflicts in Western Europe. The Thirty Years' War ended with the Peace of Westphalia in 1648. It proclaimed among

[1]   The reported study was funded by the Russian Foundation for Basic Research (RFBR) by RFBR according to the research project № 18-011-00883.
[2]   IGOR IVANOVICH LUKASHUK, МЕЖДУНАРОДНОЕ ПРАВО. ОБЩАЯ ЧАСТЬ (International Law. General Part), Moscow 52 (2005).
[3]   EKATERINA IVANOVNA KOZLOVA, OLEG EMELIANOVICH KUTAFIN, КОНСТИТУЦИОННОЕ ПРАВО РОССИИ (Constitutional Law of Russia), Moscow 165 (2003).
[4]   IOSIF DAVYDOVICH LEVIN. СУВЕРЕНИТЕТ (Sovereignty), Moscow 44 (2003).
[5]   IGOR IVANOVICH LUKASHUK, *supra* note 2, at 52.
[6]   The Declaration on Principles of International Law concerning Friendly Relations and Co-operation among States in accordance with the Charter of the United Nations adopted by the General Assembly on 24 October 1970, available at: http://www.un-documents.net/a25r2625.htm (accessed on 2 July 2018).

its participants the right to State territory and supremacy, the principles of equality, independence and sovereignty. The principles of the Westphalian system developed and changed in the course of time under the influence of the evolution of international relations, as well as new bilateral and multilateral treaties.[7]

15.07. The sovereignty of the State has not remained unchanged. It varies depending on specific historical conditions and is limited by the development of international law and the specific obligations that the States have assumed under international treaties.

II. Review Mechanisms for Foreign Investments

15.08. It is true that State sovereignty is changing. It depends on specific historical conditions.[8] For example, States have no right to adopt national laws contrary to generally recognized rights of peoples.[9] The problem of State sovereignty has become of particular importance because of the international investment process. Foreign investors are concerned with the protection of their investment, while the host States are concerned with the protection of national security. It is obvious that a balance must been achieved.

15.09. According to United Nations General Assembly resolution 1803 (XVII) of 14 December 1962 entitled 'Permanent sovereignty over natural resources' all States have the inalienable right 'to dispose of their natural wealth and resources in accordance with their national interest, and in respect for the economic independence of States.'[10]

15.10. As the UN Charter of Economic Rights and Duties of States of 12 December 1974 states: 'Every State has and shall freely exercise full permanent sovereignty, including possession, use and disposal, over all its wealth, natural resources and economic activities' (Article 2(1)).[11]

---

[7]   Vladimir Alekseevich Kartashkin, *Supremacy of International Law and State Sovereignty*, RUSSIAN YEARBOOK OF INTERNATIONAL LAW 16 (2013).

[8]   Vladimir Alekseevich Kartashkin, *supra* note 7, at 18.

[9]   IGOR IVANOVICH LUKASHUK, ГЛОБАЛИЗАЦИЯ, ГОСУДАРСТВО, ПРАВО, XXI ВЕК (Globalization, State, Law, XXI Century), Moscow 143 (2000).

[10] General Assembly resolution 1803 (XVII) of 14 December 1962 'Permanent sovereignty over natural resources', at 1, available at: https://www.ohchr.org/Documents/ProfessionalInterest/resources.pdf (accessed on 27 June 2018).

[11] The UN Charter of Economic Rights and Duties of States of 1 December 1974 was adopted by the General Assembly at its twenty-ninth session, at 4, available at: https://www.aaas.org/sites/default/files/SRHRL/PDF/IHRDArticle15/Charter_of_Economic_Rights_and_Duties_of_States_Eng.pdf (accessed on 27 June 2018).

15.11. Various States enter into investment treaties in the form of bilateral or multilateral investment treaties. The main task of the treaties is to promote and protect the investments of the individuals or legal entities of one contracting State on the territory of another contracting State.

15.12. The treaties provide for payment of prompt, adequate and effective compensation in cases of nationalization or expropriation. Many treaties set up a mechanism 'which is largely unique in international law'[12] to sue a host State in international arbitration.

15.13. The States may nationalize or expropriate foreign investments, but

> nationalization, expropriation or requisitioning shall be based on grounds or reasons of public utility, security or the national interest which are recognized as overriding purely individual or private interests, both domestic and foreign. In such cases the owner shall be paid appropriate compensation, in accordance with the rules in force in the State taking such measures in the exercise of its sovereignty and in accordance with international law.[13]

15.14. According to some scholars, 'State sovereignty is limited when the State recognizes certain norms of international law; when it ratifies a certain treaty...'[14] Another similar opinion notes that:

> As with every international agreement, an investment treaty reduces the scope of sovereignty for all parties to the treaty. In particular, an investment treaty will limit the sovereign right of a state to subject foreign investors to its domestic administrative legal system.[15]

15.15. The opposite position was expressed by a prominent Russian scholar Igor Lukashuk: 'By the conclusion of international treaties, a State does not limit its sovereignty. On the contrary, it realizes its sovereignty: the State creates not only responsibilities for itself but also acquires additional abilities to enjoy sovereign rights.'[16] This position was earlier supported in the Judgment of the Permanent Court of International Justice of 17 August

---

[12] Jesse Kennedy, *Protecting Regulatory Measures in Investment Treaty Law*, CZECH YEARBOOK OF INTERNATIONAL LAW, Volume IV 5 (2013).

[13] IGOR IVANOVICH LUKASHUK, *supra* note 9, at 2.

[14] Vladimir Alekseevich Kartashkin, *supra* note 7, at 14.

[15] Rudolf Dolzer, *The Impact of International Investment Treaties on Domestic Administrative Law*, 37 INTERNATIONAL LAW AND POLITICS 953, 972 (2005).

[16] IGOR IVANOVICH LUKASHUK, *supra* note 9, at 140.

1923 'S.S. Wimbledon' 'the right of entering into international engagements is an attribute of State sovereignty.'[17]

15.16. Each State has sovereignty 'and for this reason independently determines its economic policy and its economic space.'[18] States, being sovereign, may decide whether to allow foreign investors into their territory or not. States may regulate foreign investments on their territory, establish preferences and restrictions for foreign investors, and establish rules for the creation or liquidation of legal entities with foreign investments. 'And, if the state decides not to allow foreign investments either by adopting a general decision or by making special decisions, this will not entail the international responsibility of the state, and especially regarding the state of the investor.'[19] The investment treaties do not prohibit the host State from establishing control measures for foreign investment.

15.17. The inflow of foreign investments into the economy of a State is an ambiguous phenomenon. It is true that foreign capital is a prerequisite for successful development in the production sector of the economy of every state. But the establishment of foreign control over domestic enterprises may pose threats to the national security of a state. Foreign investments may threaten the economic sovereignty of a State that weakens its regulatory functions.

15.18. This problem has become especially acute in the era of globalization. It should be noted that today, due to globalization, the economy of every State cannot be isolated from the economy of other governments. Globalization is

> a worldwide process that links national socio-economic entities into a single global economic and social system. Social, economic and political activities acquire a world scale to such an extent that events in one part of the world can have immediate significance for individuals and their associations in the remotest parts of the global system.[20]

15.19. Today multinational corporations are the main players in the field of foreign investment. The negative aspects of multinational corporations are stressed by the scholar Muthucumaraswamy Sornarajah: 'The threat that the multinational corporation poses to the sovereign State was a preoccupation when multinational

---

[17] Judgment of the Permanent Court of International Justice of 17 August 1923 'S.S. Wimbledon', at 3, available at: http://legal.un.org/PCIJsummaries/documents/english/5_e.pdf (accessed on 3 July 2018).
[18] DOMINIQUE CARREAU, PATRICK JUILLARD, МЕЖДУНАРОДНОЕ ЭКОНОМИЧЕСКОЕ ПРАВО (International Economic Law), Moscow 350 (2002).
[19] DOMINIQUE CARREAU, PATRICK JUILLARD, *supra* note 18, at 353.
[20] IGOR IVANOVICH LUKASHUK, *supra* note 2, at 2.

corporations first started to invest abroad.'[21]. A multinational corporation is backed 'by its own immense financial resources as well as the power of its home State which stands behind it.'[22] The corporations 'may influence the political course of the States in which it seeks to invest. It could scuttle the economies of weak States simply by relocating its operations elsewhere.'[23]

15.20. The 'so-called measures of reasonable State intervention'[24] are of great importance for the protection of national interests.

15.21. Each State has the right to impose limitations on foreign investments on its territory. According to the UN Charter of Economic Rights and Duties of States, each State has the right to 'regulate and exercise authority over foreign investment within its national jurisdiction in accordance with its laws and regulations and in conformity with its national objectives and priorities. No State shall be compelled to grant preferential treatment to foreign investment.'[25] (Article 2(2)(a)).

15.22. Many States seriously limit foreign investments in 'the key branches of the economy on which the State sovereignty is based.'[26] These include the defense industry, the gas and oil industries, the communication sectors, the transport, health care, etc. They even exclude certain industries from being available for acquisition by foreign investors.

15.23. Such a mechanism is adopted, for example, by U.S. legislation. The Committee on Foreign Investment in the United States (CFIUS) is an inter-agency committee authorized to review transactions that could result in control of a U.S. business by a foreign person, in order to determine the impact of such transactions on the national security of the United States.[27] There are 16 critical infrastructure sectors 'whose assets, systems, and networks, whether physical or virtual, are considered so vital to the United States that their incapacitation or destruction would have a debilitating effect on security, national economic security, national public health or safety, or any combination thereof.'[28] They are the chemical sector, the communications

---

[21] MUTHUCUMARASWAMY SORNARAJAH, THE INTERNATIONAL LAW ON FOREIGN Investment, Cambridge 67 (2nd ed. 2007).

[22] *Ibid.*

[23] *Ibid.*

[24] Insur Zabirovich Farkhutdinov, *Foreign Investment: A Challenge for the State Sovereignty*, 3(28) MOSCOW JOURNAL OF INTERNATIONAL LAW 18 (2008).

[25] *Supra* note 10, at 4.

[26] VLADIMIR MIKHAILOVICH SHUMILOV, МЕЖДУНАРОДНОЕ ЭКОНОМИЧЕСКОЕ ПРАВО (International Economic Law), Rostov-on-Don 468 (2003).

[27] U.S. Department of the Treasury. The Committee on Foreign Investment in the United States (CFIUS), available at: https://home.treasury.gov/policy-issues/international/the-committee-on-foreign-investment-in-the-united-states-cfius (accessed on 29 June 2018).

[28] Homeland Security. Critical Infrastructure Sectors, available at: https://www.dhs.gov/critical-infrastructure-sectors (accessed on 29 June 2018).

sector, the defense industrial base sector, the energy sector, the food and agricultural sectors, and nuclear reactors.[29] During the review period, CFIUS members examine transactions in 'critical infrastructure sectors' in order to identify 'any national security concerns that arise as a result of the transaction.'[30]

15.24. The Russian Foreign Investment Strategic Law[31] introduced a review of foreign investments similar to the CFIUS mechanism. Foreign investors including Russian companies being under control of foreign investors need the authorization of the Governmental Commission on Control over Foreign Investments in the Russian Federation to acquire a controlling stake in a Russian company in any of 46 strategic sectors. These include but are not limited to the nuclear industry and nuclear security, arms production, aircraft and space, geological exploration of subsoil, production of minerals, natural monopolies, communication, mass media.

15.25. A similar mechanism is set up in Germany. According to the German Foreign Trade Act (*Außenwirtschaftsgesetz*) of 6 June 2013 there are two different procedures for foreign investment review: A sector-specific investment review and a general investment review. The sector-specific investment review applies where the target is an existing German company, 25% or more of the corporate investor voting rights are acquired, the investor is not a German resident, and the target's business activities are related to war weapons or IT security for classified information. The general investment review applies where the target is an existing German company, 25% or more of the voting rights are acquired, and the investor is not a resident of a European Union or European Free Trade Association member state. The acquisition may only be prohibited if it endangers German public order or security.[32]

15.26. In 2008, the United States Government Accountability Office made a review of the foreign investment policies of ten nations (Canada, China, France, Germany, India, Japan, the Netherlands, Russia, the United Arab Emirates, and the UK). The office compared the laws of the countries in the field of foreign investment in strategic spheres. The authors of the report note that 'in many ways the systems are similar to each other, where

---

[29] *Ibid.*
[30] *Supra* note 26.
[31] Russian Federal Law of 29 April 2008 No. 57-FZ 'On the Procedure for Foreign Investments in Business Entities Having Strategic Significance for State Defense and National Security', Collection of Legislation of the Russian Federation of 5 May 2008, N 18 Article 1940.
[32] Philipp Cotta and Christoph Heinrich. Aixtron and Ledvance: Climate Change for Chinese Investments in Germany? available at: http://blog.bblaw.com/aixtron-and-ledvance-climate-change-for-chinese-investments-in-germany (accessed on 27 June 2018).

most have a formal review process with an established time frame to assess security concerns.'

III.   Risks for Host States

15.27.   It should be noted that some investors abuse the system of investment arbitration. They attempt to create 'artificial jurisdiction over a pre-existing domestic dispute' abusing the system of investment treaty arbitration[33] in order to bring arbitration claims against host states under investment treaties. A good example is the case between the American company Transglobal Green Energy and the Republic of Panama.

15.28.   In 2003, a Panamanian company La Mina Hydro-Power Corp. owned by Panamanian national Julio Cesar Lisac had been awarded a concession to design, build and operate a hydroelectric power plant in Panama for 50 years. The State had the right to terminate the Concession Contract if the concessionaire failed to meet the deadlines stated in the contract. After the first year, the Panamanian authorities found that Mr. Lisac's company did not meet the requirements of the concession, terminated the agreement and later awarded the concession to another company. Mr. Lisac transferred part of his company's interests in the power plant project to Transglobal, a company incorporated in Texas.

15.29.   He submitted a dispute to the International Centre for Settlement of Investment Disputes against Panama on the basis of the bilateral investment treaty between the USA and Panama concerning the treatment and protection of investments. He alleged that Panama violated the Treaty having terminated the concession contract. In the award of 2 June 2016, the arbitral tribunal rejected the case 'on the ground of abuse by Claimants of the investment treaty system by attempting to create artificial international jurisdiction over a pre-existing domestic dispute.'[34]

15.30.   Thus, despite arbitrators being charged with policing 'the gates to investment treaty claims against states'[35] sometimes they fail to do so.

---

[33]   Stockholm Chamber of Commerce. ISDS Blog. *Transglobal Green Energy* v. *Panama*. 6 July 2016, available at: http://isdsblog.com/2016/07/06/transglobal-green-energy-v-panama/ (accessed on 3 July 2018).

[34]   *Transglobal Green Energy, LLC and Transglobal Green Panama, S.A.* v. *Republic of Panama*. ICSID Case No. ARB/13/28. Award, at 30, available at: https://www.italaw.com/sites/default/files/case-documents/italaw7336.pdf (accessed on 3 July 2018).

[35]   Diane Desierto, Arbitral Controls and Policing the Gates to Investment Treaty Claims against States in *Transglobal Green Energy* v. *Panama and Philip Morris* v. *Australia*, 22 June 2016, available at: https://www.ejiltalk.org/arbitral-controls-and-policing-the-gates-to-investment-treaty-claims-against-states-in-transglobal-green-energy-v-panama-and-philip-morris-v-australia/ (accessed on 3 July 2018).

15.31. Investment treaties may be dangerous for States because the mechanism provided by the treaties can be used by structures that are in conflicts with a State.[36] Such companies may invest their assets in a State through their subsidiaries on quasi-offshore jurisdictions such as the Netherlands, Luxemburg, or Switzerland. 'Residents' of these countries may submit a dispute with a State to an ad hoc arbitration tribunal or institutional arbitration tribunal despite the absence of an arbitration agreement between the 'investor' and the State.

15.32. A good example is the dispute between Russia and three shareholders of the Yukos Oil Corporation: Yukos Universal Ltd., Hulley Enterprises Ltd. and Veteran Petroleum Ltd. The companies were organized in Cyprus and the Isle of Man, but they were owned and controlled by Russian nationals. The companies 'never conducted any business there, and none of the shell companies or any of their Russian owners ever made any foreign investment in Yukos.'[37]

15.33. The companies initiated arbitration proceedings against Russia under the Energy Treaty (ECT) and accused Russia of violating obligations with respect to the claimants' investments under the ECT. So, the Treaty which Russia signed in 1994 but never ratified, turned out to be a 'delayed-action mine' for the Russian authorities.

15.34. It is obvious that the ECT protects foreign investments in the energy sector of the host State. In the case *the Yukos shareholders'* v. *Russia* the claimants were all nationals of the Russian Federation, and none of them ever made a foreign investment in Yukos. As the Ministry of the Russian Federation stated: it was 'a purely domestic dispute between the Russian Federation and the Russian nationals who previously owned Yukos and currently control the three offshore shell companies that commenced the international arbitral proceedings under the Energy Charter Treaty.'[38]

15.35. The awards of the *Yukos* case illustrate that international mechanisms of settlement of investment disputes may be a potential danger to host States. It is obvious that the States must be careful while entering into investment treaties, particularly with respect to the states' consent to the settlement by

---

[36] VLADIMIR ALEXANDROVICH KANASHEVSKY, МЕЖДУНАРОДНОЕ ЧАСТНОЕ ПРАВО (Private International Law), Moscow 298 (2016).
[37] Ministry of Finance of the Russian Federation, Press Release 'On writs filed by the Russian Federation seeking to annul the awards issued by an international arbitral tribunal in arbitrations commenced against the Russian Federation by the former shareholders of Yukos Oil Company' 6 February 2015, available at: http://old.minfin.ru/en/news/index.php?id_4=24358 (accessed on 3 July 2018).
[38] *Ibid.*

international arbitration of any disputes with foreign investors that may arise in the future.[39]

IV.   Conclusion

15.36.   The problem of sovereignty is still one of the main discussed issues in the law theory. It is especially salient now - in connection with the attraction of foreign investment by States. It is obvious that foreign investments play an important role in the development of economies of States. In addition to positive factors, foreign investment may pose a threat to the security of States. Due to their sovereignty, States may use the measures of reasonable State intervention and limit foreign investments in the strategic sectors of their economy. So the legislation of many States provides mechanisms for restrictions on foreign investment in key, or strategic, spheres of the economy.

15.37.   States interested in attracting foreign investment enter into bilateral, multilateral investment agreements that provide some guarantees for foreign investors. Such international agreements may limit the sovereignty of the State and may be dangerous for host States, since they allow investors to utilize arbitration with claims against host States. As was demonstrated in the article some investors abuse the investment treaty system. It is obvious that States must enter carefully into investment treaties.

| | |

Summaries

FRA   [*La souveraineté de l'État et la protection des investissements internationaux*]

Le présent article se consacre au problème de l'harmonisation de la souveraineté de l'État avec la protection des investissements étrangers. La souveraineté reste un des thèmes principaux de la théorie de l'État et du droit. La conception de la souveraineté a connu une évolution au cours du temps, ce qui devient particulièrement manifeste dans le contexte de la mondialisation, où les différents États cherchent à attirer des investissements étrangers. Ces investissements, mis à part les nombreux bénéfices qu'ils apportent, peuvent également représenter une menace pour la sécurité de l'État d'accueil. Pour cette raison, de nombreux États adoptent des normes législatives introduisant

[39]   VLADIMIR ALEXANDROVICH KANASHEVSKY, *supra* note 36, at 304.

Czech Yearbook of International Law®

des mécanismes destinés à limiter les investissements étrangers dans les secteurs économiques stratégiques. Les États désireux d'attirer les investissements étrangers concluent des accords bilatéraux ou multilatéraux relatifs au soutien et à la protection des investissements, qui offrent des garanties aux investisseurs étrangers. Selon certains théoriciens, ces accords internationaux limitent la souveraineté de l'État. L'auteur du présent article analyse les craintes exprimées par certains spécialistes par rapport au fait que ces accords internationaux représentent un danger pour l'État d'accueil parce qu'elles permettent aux investisseurs d'avoir recours aux procédures d'arbitrage pour faire valoir leurs droits à l'encontre des États d'accueil et que certains investisseurs abusent de ce système.

CZE   [*Státní svrchovanost a ochrana mezinárodních investic*]
Článek se věnuje problému sladění státní svrchovanosti s ochranou zahraničních investic. Svrchovanost je stále jedním z hlavních témat teorie státu a práva. Postupem času se koncepce svrchovanosti změnila. Tento problém vystupuje do popředí obzvláště nyní – v éře globalizace – v souvislosti se snahou jednotlivých států přilákat zahraniční investice. Kromě řady pozitivních faktorů mohou zahraniční investice představovat i hrozbu pro bezpečnost států. Proto právní předpisy řady z nich upravují mechanismy omezující zahraniční investice v klíčových či strategických hospodářských oblastech. Státy, které mají zájem na přilákání zahraničních investic, uzavírají dvoustranné či mnohostranné dohody o podpoře a ochraně investic, které zahraničním investorům skýtají určité záruky. Podle některých teoretiků tyto mezinárodní dohody omezují svrchovanost státu. V tomto článku autorka analyzuje obavy některých odborníků stran toho, že tyto mezinárodní dohody mohou být pro státy nebezpečné, jelikož investorům dovolují využívat rozhodčí řízení (arbitráž) k uplatňování jejich nároků proti hostitelským státům, přičemž někteří investoři systém dohod o podpoře a ochraně investic zneužívají.

| | |

POL   [*Suwerenność państwowa a ochrona inwestycji międzynarodowych*]
Artykuł poświęcony problematyce relacji między suwerennością państwową a ochroną inwestycji zagranicznych. Oprócz oczywistych problemów zagraniczne inwestycje mogą stanowić

zagrożenie m.in. dla bezpieczeństwa państwowego. Dlatego regulacje prawne w wielu państwach zakładają pewne ograniczenia dla inwestycji zagranicznych w obszarach kluczowych lub strategicznych z punktu widzenia gospodarki. Państwa, które są zainteresowane przyjmowaniem inwestycji zagranicznych, zawierają umowy bilateralne i multilateralne, które przewidują gwarancje dla praw zagranicznych inwestorów. Zdaniem niektórych specjalistów tego typu umowy międzynarodowe ograniczają suwerenność państwa. Z artykułu wynika, że specjaliści obawiają się, iż tego typu umowy międzynarodowe mogą być zagrożeniem dla państwa, ponieważ dopuszczają możliwość dochodzenia roszczeń przez nieuczciwych inwestorów w postępowaniu arbitrażowym przeciwko państwom przyjmującym daną inwestycję.

DEU [***Staatshoheit und der Schutz internationaler Investitionen***]
Der Beitrag befasst sich mit dem Problemkreis der Wechselbeziehungen zwischen staatlicher Souveränität und dem Schutz von Auslandsinvestitionen. Von weiteren grundlegenden Faktoren einmal abgesehen, können Auslandsinvestitionen eine Bedrohung für die Sicherheit des Staats darstellen. Deshalb sehen die Rechtsordnungen einer Reihe von Staaten vor, in Schlüsselindustrien und strategischen Wirtschaftszweigen bestimmte Beschränkungen für Auslandsinvestitionen einzuführen. Staaten, die daran interessiert sind, Auslandsinvestitionen ins Land zu bringen, gehen bilaterale und multilaterale internationale Verträge ein, in denen Garantien für die Rechte ausländischer Investoren vorgesehen sind. Nach Ansicht verschiedener Experten schränken diese internationalen Abkommen die Souveränität des Staates ein. Der Beitrag bringt die Sorge von Fachleuten zum Ausdruck, dass derartige internationale Verträge für den Staat deshalb gefährlich sein könnten, weil sie unredlichen Investoren die Möglichkeit einräumen, in Schiedsverfahren Ansprüche gegen das Gastgeberland (also den Staat, der die Investition empfängt) geltend zu machen.

RUS [*Государственный суверенитет и защита иностранных инвестиций*]
Статья посвящена проблеме соотношения государственного суверенитета и защите иностранных инвестиций. Помимо положительных факторов, иностранные инвестиции могут представлять угрозу для безопасности государства, поэтому законодательство многих государств предусматривает введение ограничений для иностранных инвестиций в ключевые,

или стратегические, сферы экономики. Государства, заинтересованные в привлечении иностранных инвестиций, заключают двусторонние, многосторонние инвестиционные соглашения, в которых предусматривают гарантии прав иностранных инвесторов. По мнению некоторых ученых, такие международные соглашения ограничивают суверенитет государства. В статье приводятся опасения специалистов по поводу того, что такие международные договоры могут быть опасны для государств, так как допускают возможность обращения недобросовестных инвесторов в арбитраж с исками к государствам, принимающим инвестиции.

ESP **[*La soberanía del Estado y la protección de la inversión internacional*]**

El texto versa de la relación entre la soberanía del Estado y la protección de la inversión extranjera. Dejando de lado otros factores fundamentales, la inversión extranjera puede constituir un peligro para la seguridad del Estado, por lo que la legislación de diferentes Estados presupone la implementación de restricciones para la inversión extranjera en los ámbitos clave o estratégicos de la economía. Los Estados interesados en recibir la inversión extranjera cierran convenios bilaterales o multilaterales que prevén garantías de derechos de los inversores extranjeros. Según la opinión de algunos expertos, tales convenios internacionales restringen la soberanía del Estado. Los autores expresan el temor de los expertos de que tales convenios pueden resultar peligrosos para los Estados, ya que posibilitan que los inversores deshonestos reclamen sus derechos en el procedimiento arbitral en contra de los Estados anfitriones (aquellos que reciben la inversión).

||||

Bibliography

DOMINIQUE CARREAU, PATRICK JUILLARD, МЕЖДУНАРОДНОЕ ЭКОНОМИЧЕСКОЕ ПРАВО (International Economic Law), Moscow (2002).

Rudolf Dolzer, *The Impact of International Investment Treaties on Domestic Administrative Law*, 37 INTERNATIONAL LAW AND POLITICS (2005).

Insur Zabirovich Farkhutdinov, *Foreign Investment: A Challenge for the State Sovereignty*, 3(28) MOSCOW JOURNAL OF INTERNATIONAL LAW (2008).

VLADIMIR ALEXANDROVICH KANASHEVSKY, МЕЖДУНАРОДНОЕ ЧАСТНОЕ ПРАВО (Private International Law), Moscow (2016).

Vladimir Alekseevich Kartashkin, *Supremacy of International Law and State Sovereignty*, RUSSIAN YEARBOOK OF INTERNATIONAL LAW (2013).

Jesse Kennedy, *Protecting Regulatory Measures in Investment Treaty Law*, CZECH YEARBOOK OF INTERNATIONAL LAW, Volume IV (2013).

EKATERINA IVANOVNA KOZLOVA, OLEG EMELIANOVICH KUTAFIN, КОНСТИТУЦИОННОЕ ПРАВО РОССИИ (Constitutional Law of Russia), Moscow (2003).

IOSIF DAVYDOVICH LEVIN, СУВЕРЕНИТЕТ (Sovereignty), Moscow (2003).

IGOR IVANOVICH LUKASHUK, МЕЖДУНАРОДНОЕ ПРАВО. ОБЩАЯ ЧАСТЬ (International Law. General Part), Moscow (2005).

IGOR IVANOVICH LUKASHUK, ГЛОБАЛИЗАЦИЯ, ГОСУДАРСТВО, ПРАВО, XXI ВЕК (Globalization, State, Law, XXI Century), Moscow (2000).

VLADIMIR MIKHAILOVICH SHUMILOV, МЕЖДУНАРОДНОЕ ЭКОНОМИЧЕСКОЕ ПРАВО (International Economic Law), Rostov-on-Don (2003).

MUTHUCUMARASWAMY SORNARAJAH, THE INTERNATIONAL LAW ON FOREIGN INVESTMENT, Cambridge (2nd ed. 2007*)*.

Czech Yearbook of International Law®

Antonia M. Waltermann

State Sovereignty as a Legal Status

Key words:
*Sovereignty | inferential
analysis | State sovereignty
| territorial sovereignty |
non-intervention | legal status
| legal concepts*

**Antonia M. Waltermann
(PhD.)** is an assistant
Professor at Maastricht
University, Faculty of Law.
E-mail: antonia.
waltermann@
maastrichtuniversity.nl

*Abstract | State sovereignty is a sensitive and
controversial concept in international law that
has been described as 'lacking meaningful specific
content' but also as 'the basic constitutional
doctrine' of international law. One way of
analysing legal concepts is by means of an
inferential analysis: such an analysis looks to the
inferential relationships of a concept in order to
determine its meaning. This contribution offers
a non-exhaustive inferential analysis of State
sovereignty and suggests considering sovereignty
in international law as a legal status that is
independent of the legal consequences attaching
to it. This view of sovereignty reveals a number
of open questions regarding sovereignty and
supports the conclusion that sovereignty is not a
matter of degree (sovereign equality), unlimited or
impervious to change.*

| | |

I.   Introduction

16.01. State sovereignty is a sensitive and controversial concept in international law. It has been described as 'lacking meaningful specific content', as 'the basic constitutional doctrine' of international law, and as many things in between.[1] This contribution seeks to investigate the meaning of State sovereignty, more specifically, State sovereignty as a legal concept that is defined by international law.[2]

16.02. This contribution has the following structure: first, I outline what I mean when I write about *legal* concepts specifically and how it is possible to analyse their meaning (section II). In section III, I apply this means of analysis to State sovereignty in international law, defining it as a legal status. Section IV summarises the findings of section III and briefly touches upon what this picture of State sovereignty means for international law and some of its debates, as well as what the limitations of this view are.

16.03. My purpose in this contribution is to investigate State sovereignty specifically as a legal concept. This by definition excludes more political or rhetorical understandings of State sovereignty from the scope of my inquiry. This contribution pursues two additional objectives: on the one hand, to investigate in how far an inferential analysis of State sovereignty is possible;[3] on the other hand, to demonstrate that although it has limitations as a means of analysis of sovereignty, it nonetheless brings to light some important insights about sovereignty in international law.

II.   Legal concepts and inferential analysis

16.04. The first question that needs to be answered in this context is what it means for a concept to be legal. According to Giovanni Sartor, the meaning of a legal concept is determined by law; in particular, by the legal system that the legal concept is part of.[4] For present purposes, this means that the meaning of State sovereignty is determined by international law. Åke Frändberg calls such concepts 'system-dependent': their meaning depends on the system they are part of.[5] "Ownership" and "murder"

---

[1]   Nico Schrijver, *The Changing Nature of State Sovereignty* 70 THE BRITISH YEARBOOK OF INTERNATIONAL LAW 65 (2000).

[2]   Much of the argument of this contribution is based on ANTONIA WALTERMANN, SOVEREIGNTIES, Maastricht University, Maastricht (2016).

[3]   Section II explains what inferential analysis is.

[4]   Giovanni Sartor, *Legal Concepts and Legal Inferences*, in JAAP HAGE AND DIETMAR VON DER PFORDTEN, CONCEPTS IN LAW, Springer 35 (2009).

[5]   Åke Frändberg, *An Essay on Legal Concept Formation*, in JAAP HAGE AND DIETMAR VON DER

are good examples of this. While property is similar across different legal systems, the rules that determine what one can and cannot do, for example, when one owns something differ per legal system and as such, determine the precise meaning of ownership in that system. "Ownership" or "murder" are part of common parlance, but the precise legal meaning of "ownership" in Germany differs from that of "ownership" in France. The same is true also for murder. Jaap Hage suggests thinking of these different variants of "ownership" (or "murder") as different species within the same genus, or even as different individuals within the same species.[6] How can one distinguish between these species within one genus and how can one know what they mean? With their meaning determined by the legal system they form part of, it is possible to analyse these concepts by means of so-called inferential analyses. In an inferential analysis, one looks at the connection between the legally relevant facts (operative facts) and the legal consequences connected to these facts.[7] The argument here is that many legal rules connect operative facts to legal consequences in an (oftentimes implicit) *if... then...* structure: if conditions a, b, and c are fulfilled, then consequence x occurs.

16.05. Alf Ross (1957) described concepts like "ownership" as having an ordering function in his paper 'Tû-tû':[8] such concepts connect a vast number of operative facts (that is, those facts that match the conditions of a legal rule) to a potentially equally vast number of legal consequences. In other words, "the concept of ownership mediates between the preconditions for becoming the owner of a thing (purchasing it, inheriting it, etc.) and the normative consequences following from owning a thing (having the right to use it, the power to transfer it, etc.)".[9] The following figure visualises this:

PFORDTEN, CONCEPTS IN LAW, Springer Law and Philosophy Library (2009).
[6] Jaap Hage, *The Meaning of Legal Status Words*, in JAAP HAGE AND DIETMAR VON DER PFORDTEN, CONCEPTS IN LAW, Springer 66 (2009).
[7] Giovanni Sartor, *Legal Concepts and Legal Inferences*, in JAAP HAGE AND DIETMAR VON DER PFORDTEN, CONCEPTS IN LAW, Springer (2009), *Ibid.*, at 36 ff.
[8] Alf Ross, *Tû-tû*, 70 HARVARD LAW REVIEW 812 (1957).
[9] Giovanni Sartor, *Legal Validity: An Inferential Analysis*, 21 RATIO JURIS 212, 212-213 (2008).

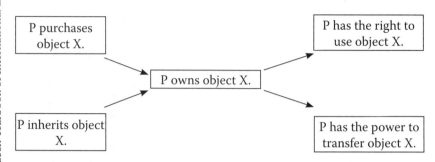

Figure 1: Simplified inferential representation of the concept of property.[10]

16.06. Accordingly, the meaning of legal concepts such as "ownership" – or, for present purposes, "sovereignty" – can be said to be determined by its inferential relationships.[11]

16.07. It is relevant, in this connection, to keep in mind that because a legal concept's meaning is determined by law, whatever intuitions one might have about the concept's meaning do not play a role in determining its meaning. In other words, one needs to forget all one (thinks one) knows about the concept and solely focus on its meaning as determined by the legal system it belongs to.

III. State sovereignty

16.08. In the previous section, I have argued that by means of inferential analysis, one can analyse a legal concept and to grasp its (specifically legal) meaning. In this section, I will sketch out an inferential analysis of State sovereignty in international law.

16.09. When it comes to State sovereignty, the case law of courts, such as that of the International Court of Justice (hereafter: ICJ), provides more information than treaties. This does not mean, however, that State sovereignty is not mentioned in treaties at all.

16.10. The Charter of the United Nations makes mention of sovereignty twice: Article 2(1) states that the United Nations is "based on the principle of the sovereign equality of all its Members" and Article 78 holds that "[t]he trusteeship system shall not apply to territories which have become Members of the United Nations, relationship among which shall be based on respect for the principle of sovereign equality." From this, no inferences can be made about sovereignty or even sovereign equality.

---

[10] This figure is based on the works of Ross and Sartor.

[11] Hage points out that an inferential analysis can furthermore be useful to understanding the function of a legal concept. JAAP HAGE, FOUNDATIONS AND BUILDING BLOCKS OF LAW, Eleven International Publishing 51 (2018).

16.11. A full inferential analysis of sovereignty in international law would far exceed the boundaries of this contribution. For this reason, I will focus on case law of the ICJ and its predecessor, the Permanent Court of International Justice (PCIJ). This places the focus not on sovereignty's long historical background, but instead on the modern concept of sovereignty of the 20th and 21st century.[12] The following can only give a taste of what a full inferential analysis of State sovereignty in international law would look like, but it will nonetheless be possible to draw some conclusions, as well as to consider some implications of this understanding of legal concepts in general and State sovereignty in particular. It bears keeping in mind that this is a glimpse through the window, rather than the full picture.

III.1. The *Wimbledon* case of the PCIJ

16.12. In the *Wimbledon* case, which was brought before the PCIJ in 1923 by France and others, the question arose whether Germany could prohibit the Wimbledon, a British steamship under French charter to pass through the Kiel Canal, or whether the Versailles Peace Treaty (1919) made such a prohibition illegal. Underlying this question was a perceived tension between the contractual obligations a State (in this case Germany) has on the basis of a multilateral treaty and its sovereignty.[13] In this connection, the PCIJ held the following:

> The Court declines to see in the conclusion of any Treaty by which a State undertakes to perform or refrain from performing a particular act an abandonment of its sovereignty. No doubt any convention creating an obligation of this kind places a restriction upon the exercise of the sovereign rights of the State, in the sense that it requires them to be exercised in a certain way. But the right of entering

---

[12]   A search for "sovereignty" in the judgments, advisory opinions and orders of the International Court of Justice yields 157 results for the period of 1946-2018; this does not include any cases of the Permanent Court of International Justice. The selection of cases from PCIJ and ICJ are based on SAMANTHA BESSON, SOVEREIGNTY, Max Planck Encyclopedia of Public International Law, Oxford Public International Law 35-55 (2011), with the exception of Huber's judgement in the *Island of Palmas* case. In the aforementioned paragraphs, Besson also refers to the Advisory Opinion on Reparations for Injuries Suffered in the Service of the United Nations and Advisory Opinion on the Accordance with International Law of the Unilateral Declaration of Independence in Respect of Kosovo. However, these cases are not suitable to an inferential analysis of sovereignty given the fact that they do not mention the term (outside of quotes, in the case of the Kosovo Advisory Opinion). They will therefore be excluded from the scope of this article. The remaining cases will be dealt with in chronological order.
[13]   CLEMENS FEINÄUGLE, WIMBLEDON, The Max Planck Encyclopedia of Public International Law (MPEPIL), Oxford Public International Law (2013).

into international engagements is an attribute of State sovereignty.[14]

16.13. This passage in itself does not give much information about when a State becomes sovereign, what consequences attach to its sovereignty or how it loses its sovereignty. Instead, it gives more fundamental information about the relationship between a State's sovereignty and the obligations it has undertaken. The PCIJ here holds that a consequence of being sovereign (an attribute of State sovereignty) is that a State can change its own legal position. This entails that one sovereign State can have more or fewer obligations than another, equally sovereign State. In my view, the best way to account for this possibility is to view sovereignty as a legal status. When it comes to legal statuses, it is generally possible to distinguish between entrance rules, which determine how to obtain the status, exit rules, which determine how to lose the status, and consequential rules that determine what legal consequences attach to the status.[15] Consequences can be that certain duties attach to the status, such as the prohibition (that is, the duty not to) of intervention, or competences such as that of concluding treaties. Regarding consequential rules, one question is whether the status changes if the consequences attached to it change. What the *Wimbledon* judgement suggests is that sovereignty is better understood as a status which does not change even when its consequences do: instead of assuming that if a State is sovereign, this necessarily entails a, b and c consequence and any State which does not possess a, b and c is not or is less sovereign, this understanding of sovereignty regards it as a status that a State has even in cases where this State has undertaken considerable obligations. Instead of sovereignty meaning that a State necessarily has a, b and c, sovereignty is simply the status of being sovereign, and to this status, consequences a, b and c can be attached – or only consequence a, or consequences a, b, c and d. In other words, a State that has undertaken considerable obligations under human rights treaties, for example, and has thereby limited its own freedom to act, is no less sovereign than a State that has undertaken no such obligations and has thus seemingly unlimited freedom to act. This reading is in line with the idea of sovereign equality and with the phrasing of the PCIJ that the conclusion of treaties can restrict the exercise of the sovereign

---

[14] *Case of the S.S. „Wimbledon"* (Permanent Court of International Justice)
[15] Jaap Hage, *The Meaning of Legal Status Words*, in JAAP HAGE AND DIETMAR VON DER PFORDTEN, CONCEPTS IN LAW, Springer 61 (2009).

Czech Yearbook of International Law®

rights of a State, but this does not constitute an abandonment – or, I would add, a limitation or restriction – of its sovereignty.

16.14. The fact that it is an attribute of State sovereignty that States have the "right of entering into international engagements" implies that one consequence of sovereignty is the competence to enter into international agreements. The PCIJ, however, does not specify whether that is what is meant by "right" in this sentence.[16] Nonetheless, reading "right" as the competence to do so is sensible in that the competence is required to bring about legal obligations by means of a treaty.[17]

III.2.   The *Island of Palmas* case of the Permanent Court of Arbitration

16.15. In the *Island of Palmas* (or Miangas) case, Max Huber sitting as sole arbitrator had to decide over a territorial dispute concerning the question whether the island of Palmas/Miangas was part of the territory of the Netherlands (by way of what was then the Dutch East Indies) or of the United States of America. The island was ceded to the United States by Spain in 1898, but the Netherlands had entered into treaties with local princes and displayed State functions in a peaceful and continuous manner on the island. In order to clarify the rules that would determine this dispute, Huber deemed it necessary to make "some general remarks on *sovereignty in its relation to territory*."[18]

16.16. Following the wording of the Special Agreement concluded between the Netherlands and the United States to the effect that they would submit this dispute to the Permanent Court of Arbitration, he held that

> [i]t appears to follow that sovereignty in relation to a portion of the surface of the globe is the legal condition necessary for the inclusion of such portion in the territory of any particular State.[19]

16.17. He then defined sovereignty as independence:

> Sovereignty in relation to territory is in the present award called "territorial sovereignty". Sovereignty in the relations between States signifies independence. Independence in regard to a portion of the globe is

---

[16]   Rights are ambiguous and it is not always clear what is (or is not) entailed by a right. JAAP HAGE, FOUNDATIONS AND BUILDING BLOCKS OF LAW, Eleven International Publishing 237 (2018).
[17]   ANNE PETERS, TREATY MAKING POWER, Max Planck Encyclopedia of Public International Law, Oxford Public International Law (2009). I mean competence here in a way that largely coincides with Peters' use of "legal capacity".
[18]   *Island of Palmas case (Netherlands, USA)* (Permanent Court of Arbitration,) 838.
[19]   *Ibid.*

the right to exercise therein, to the exclusion of any other State, the functions of a State.[20]

16.18. This indicates that there is a permission to exercise the functions of a State on the given territory, as well as a duty for other States not to do so.

16.19. In Huber's view,

> Territorial sovereignty is, in general, a situation recognized and delimited in space, either by so-called natural frontiers as recognised by international law or by outward signs of delimitation that are undisputed, or else by legal engagements entered into between interested neighbours, such as frontier conventions, or by acts of recognition of States within fixed boundaries.[21]

16.20. This is a first glimpse at an entrance rule of sovereignty. It takes recognition and delimitation either by recognised natural frontiers, undisputed outward signs of delimitation, legal agreements or the recognition of States. Huber elaborates on how to acquire territorial sovereignty at the time the case was decided:

> Titles of acquisition of territorial sovereignty in present-day international law are either based on an act of effective apprehension, such as occupation or conquest, or, like cession, presuppose that the ceding and the cessionary Powers or at least one of them, have the faculty of effectively disposing of the ceded territory.[22]

16.21. In this respect, Huber clarifies that

> practice, as well as doctrine, recognizes—though under different legal formulae and with certain differences as to the conditions required—that the continuous and peaceful display of territorial sovereignty (peaceful in relation to other States) is as good as a title.[23]

16.22. This can be understood as another entrance rule: if an entity continuously and peacefully displays territorial sovereignty over a territory, it is sovereign. This entrance rule is specified as follows:

---

[20] *Ibid.*
[21] *Ibid.*
[22] *Ibid.*, at 839.
[23] *Ibid.*

The principle that continuous and peaceful display of the functions of State within a given region is a constituent element of territorial sovereignty is not only based on the conditions of the formation of independent States and their boundaries (as shown by the experience of political history) as well as on an international jurisprudence and doctrine widely accepted; this principle has further been recognized in more than one federal State, where a jurisdiction is established in order to apply, as need arises, rules of international law to the interstate relations of the States members.[24]

16.23. Accordingly, the entrance rule can be rephrased: if an entity continuously and peacefully displays the functions of a State within a given region, it is sovereign with respect to this region. When it comes to this display of State functions or activities, Huber identifies that this is both a right and a duty:

Territorial sovereignty, as has already been said, involves the exclusive right to display the activities of a State. This right has as corollary a duty: the obligation to protect within the territory the rights of other States, in particular their right to integrity and inviolability in peace and in war, together with the rights which each State may claim for its nationals in foreign territory. Without manifesting its territorial sovereignty in a manner corresponding to circumstances, the State cannot fulfil this duty. Territorial sovereignty cannot limit itself to its negative side, i.e. to excluding the activities of other States; for it serves to divide between nations the space upon which human activities are employed, in order to assure them at all points the minimum of protection of which international law is the guardian.[25]

16.24. Sovereignty entails the permission to exclude all other States from displaying State functions on a given territory and the corresponding duty for all other States not to display State functions on that territory. It also entails the duty for the State in question to protect the integrity and inviolability of other States on its territory and those rights another State may claim for its

---

nationals on its territory. Huber did not specify further what this meant.

III.3. The *Lotus* case of the PCIJ

16.25. The *Lotus* case of the PCIJ ensued when, after a collision of the steamships *Lotus* (French) and the *Boz-Kourt* (Turkish), the Turkish government brought criminal charges against and tried one of the officers of the *Lotus*. France asserted that Turkey did not have jurisdiction, given that the collision happened on the high seas, although the trial took place after both the *Lotus* and the *Boz-Kourt* arrived in Turkey. In this case, the PCIJ found that

> all that can be required of a State is that it should not overstep the limits which international law places upon its jurisdiction; within these limits, its title to exercise jurisdiction rests in its sovereignty.[26]

16.26. Accordingly, one of the consequences of State sovereignty is that within the limits of international law – that is, without violating any of its duties under international law – a State has permission to exercise jurisdiction any which way.

16.27. In conjunction with the *Wimbledon* judgement, this paints a picture of sovereignty as rule-based: there is a general (weak) permission[27] for a State to exercise its jurisdiction as it pleases within its own territorial borders. Moreover, the status of sovereignty is independent of its consequences: a State is not more or less sovereign because it has undertaken obligations.

III.4. The Military and Paramilitary Activities in and against Nicaragua case of the ICJ

16.28. The case of Military and Paramilitary Activities in and against Nicaragua concerns the question whether the United States of America (US) has violated the sovereignty and territorial integrity of Nicaragua by supporting the Contras (paramilitaries) against the Nicaraguan government, overflights and mining Nicaragua's harbours.

16.29. The ICJ made a number of statements regarding sovereignty in this case. One such statement is that the principle of non-intervention "has moreover been presented as a corollary of the

---

[26] *S.S. „Lotus"* Permanent Court of International Justice, (Permanent Court of International Justice,) et 19.

[27] It is possible to distinguish different kind of permissions. A weak permission is one where there is no general prohibition with regard to the permitted kind of action. For example, human beings are weakly permitted to breathe: there is no prohibition on breathing. JAAP HAGE, FOUNDATIONS AND BUILDING BLOCKS OF LAW, Eleven International Publishing 155 (2018).

principle of the sovereign equality of States."[28] Accordingly, non-intervention follows from the principle of sovereign equality of States and statements regarding non-intervention can be linked, directly or indirectly via the principle of sovereign equality, back to sovereignty.

16.30. Regarding non-intervention, the Court held the following:

> A prohibited intervention must accordingly be one bearing on matters in which each State is permitted, by the principle of State sovereignty, to decide freely. One of these is the choice of a political, economic, social and cultural system, and the formulation of foreign policy. Intervention is wrongful when it uses methods of coercion in regard to such choices, which must remain free ones. The element of coercion, which defines, and indeed forms the very essence of, prohibited intervention, is particularly obvious in the case of an intervention which uses force, either in the direct form of military action, or in the indirect form of support for subversive or terrorist armed activities within another State.[29]

16.31. From this statement, it can be derived that sovereignty entails the freedom (presumably in the sense of a weak permission) for a State to choose its political, economic, social and cultural system as well as formulate its foreign policy.

16.32. The Court confirms this freedom to choose the political, social, economic and cultural system again when it holds that

> However the regime in Nicaragua be defined, adherence by a State to any particular doctrine does not constitute a violation of customary international law ; to hold otherwise would make nonsense of the fundamental principle of State sovereignty. on which the whole of international law rests, and the freedom of choice of the political, social, economic and cultural system of a State.[30]

16.33. Equally, it confirms the freedom to formulate its foreign policy when it specifies that

> State sovereignty evidently extends to the area of its foreign policy, and that there is no rule of customary international law to prevent a State from choosing

---

28 *Case Concerning Military and Paramilitary Activities in and Against Nicaragua (Nicaragua v. United States of America)* (International Court of Justice,) et 202.
29 *Ibid.*, at 205.
30 *Ibid.*, at 263.

and conducting a foreign policy in co-ordination with that of another State.[31]

16.34. These freedoms (read: permissions) go hand in hand with prohibitions of intervening in these matters, that is, a duty for all other States not to intervene. This position is affirmed in statements such as this:

> The duty of every State to respect the territorial sovereignty of others is to be considered for the appraisal to be made of the facts relating to the mining which occurred along Nicaragua's coasts.[32]

16.35. Moreover,

> [i]t is also by virtue of its sovereignty that the coastal State may regulate access to its ports.[33]

16.36. The phrasing suggests another (weak) permission here, in this case one to regulate access to ports. While the Court does not explicitly state this, this permission presumably goes hand in hand with a duty for all other States to abide by any access regulations the State in question has created.

16.37. The Court furthermore specified what counts as a violation or infringement of a State's sovereignty:

> The effects of the principle of respect for territorial sovereignty inevitably overlap with those of the principles of the prohibition of the use of force and of non-intervention. Thus the assistance to the contras, as well as the direct attacks on Nicaraguan ports, oil installations, etc., referred to in paragraphs 81 to 86 above, not only amount to an unlawful use of force, but also constitute infringements of the territorial sovereignty of Nicaragua, and incursions into its territorial and internal waters.[34]

16.38. Next to direct attacks,

> [t]he principle of respect for territorial sovereignty is also directly infringed by the unauthorized overflight of a State's territory by aircraft belonging to or under the control of the government of another State.[35]

16.39. Additionally,

> [t]hese violations cannot be justified either by collective self-defence, for which, as the Court

---

[31] *Ibid.*, at 265.
[32] *Ibid.*, at 213.
[33] *Ibid.*
[34] *Ibid.*, at 251.
[35] *Ibid.*

> has recognized, the necessary circumstances are lacking, nor by any right of the United States to take countermeasures involving the use of force in the event of intervention by Nicaragua in El Salvador, since no such right exists under the applicable international law. They cannot be justified by the activities in El Salvador attributed to the Government of Nicaragua. The latter activities, assuming that they did in fact occur, do not bring into effect any right belonging to the United States which would justify the actions in question. Accordingly, such actions constitute violations of Nicaragua's sovereignty under customary international law.[36]

16.40. In paragraph 259, the Court reiterates that accepting limitations in certain areas is an exercise of sovereignty rather than a loss or reduction thereof:

> A State, which is free to decide upon the principle and methods of popular consultation within its domestic order, is sovereign for the purpose of accepting a limitation of its sovereignty in this field. This is a conceivable situation for a State which is bound by institutional links to a confederation of States, or indeed to an international organization.[37]

16.41. This is reminiscent of the PCIJ's understanding of sovereignty in the *Wimbledon* judgement and further affirms that sovereignty can be understood as a status independent of its consequences.

16.42. That States can accept rules that impose obligations on them and thereby limit their freedom to do or refrain from doing something is reiterated also in the following statement:

> [...] in international law there are no rules, other than such rules as may be accepted by the State concerned, by treaty or otherwise, whereby the level of armaments of a sovereign State can be limited, and this principle is valid for all States without exception.[38] (at 269)

16.43. In this judgment, the ICJ furthermore held that the source of the legal concept of sovereignty is customary international law. It defined the scope of sovereignty as extending to "the internal waters and territorial sea of every State and to the air space above its territory."[39]

---

[36] *Ibid.*, at 252.
[37] *Ibid.*, at 259.
[38] *Ibid.*, at 269.
[39] *Ibid.*, at 212.

Czech Yearbook of International Law®

IV.   Implications and limitations

16.44. The previous section analysed the Charter of the United Nations and some of the case law of the International Court of Justice. The UN Charter and the judgements of the ICJ are of course not the full extent of international law, nor the only authoritative sources of it. This means that this contribution is not a full inferential analysis of State sovereignty in international law. Because of this, it can only give a taste of what such a full inferential analysis would look like as it lacks the depth, nuance and complexity of it. Nonetheless, this glimpse into an inferential analysis of State sovereignty in international law demonstrates a number of points about State sovereignty and has a number of implications.

16.45. In the following, I will first describe the conclusions about sovereignty that can be derived from the above analysis, outlining its entrance, consequential and exit rules in as far as possible, before considering the implications of this view.

IV.1.   Entrance Rules

16.46. Entrance rules of sovereignty are those rules that determine how an entity becomes sovereign. In this connection, it is implicit but not made explicit in the analysed material is the entrance rule that *"if an entity is a State, then it is sovereign"* or *"if an entity is a State, then it possesses sovereignty"*.

16.47. In the *Island of Palmas* case, Huber gave more specific entrance rules. These can be paraphrased as follows:
- *"if an entity's sovereignty is recognised and delimited in space by natural frontiers as recognised by international law, it is sovereign"* and
- *"if an entity's sovereignty is recognised and delimited in space by outward signs of delimitation that are undisputed, it is sovereign"* and
- *"if an entity's sovereignty is recognised by legal engagements entered into between interested neighbours"* or *"by acts of recognition of States within fixed boundaries, it is sovereign"* and most notably
- *"if an entity continuously and peacefully displays the functions of a State within a given region, it is sovereign with respect to this region."*

16.48. These entrance rules are not absolute, in that Huber has held that the latter is "as good as title". Accordingly, some of these entrance rules may need to be weighed against other, conflicting entrance rules. The above analysis does not give a clear indication how this is to be done, revealing a potentially vague point.[40]

IV.2.   Consequential Rules

16.49. Consequential rules of sovereignty are those rules that determine the consequences normally attached to the status of sovereignty, that is, the competences, permissions, duties and obligations that a sovereign entity usually possesses. These include the following:

- the competence to enter into international agreements;
- the exclusive (strong) permission to display State functions on a given territory;[41]
- the prohibition (duty not to) display State functions on any territory (except the own)
- the duty to protect the integrity and inviolability of other States on the territory over which a State is sovereign;
- the duty to protect the rights another State may claim for its nationals on its territory;
- the (weak) permission for a State to exercise its jurisdiction as it pleases within its own territorial borders;
- the (weak) permission to choose political, economic, social and cultural system;
- the (weak) permission to formulate foreign policy;
- the (weak) permission to regulate access to its own ports;
- the prohibition (duty not to) intervene in choice of political, economic, social and cultural system of other States;
- the prohibition (duty not to) intervene in the formulation of foreign policy of other States; and
- the duty to respect the territorial sovereignty of other States, which entails a prohibition of direct attacks, a prohibition of unauthorised overflights, and a prohibition of supporting paramilitary actors in conflict with the State's government.

---

[40]   Potentially vague because the analysis of this paper is not exhaustive, meaning that the vagueness could be cleared up elsewhere.
[41]   This is a strong permission in the sense that it is an exception to a general rule if one perceives the prohibition to display State functions on a territory as a general rule and the permission for a State S to display State functions on its territory S as the exception to that general rule.

IV.3.   Exit Rules

16.50.   Exit rules of sovereignty are those rules that determine when an entity loses its sovereignty. None of the analysed material so much as hinted at a possible exit rule regarding sovereignty. This means no conclusions can be drawn regarding the possibility of losing the status of sovereignty and when this might occur.

IV.4.   Implications

16.51.   This understanding of State sovereignty has the implication that the consequences of sovereignty as well as its entrance and exit rules or the entities to which the status is attributed are not inherent to the concept. If sovereignty is a status that is independent of its consequences, this means that the consequences can change (that is, the list of competences, claims, obligations, etc. that usually comes with being sovereign can change) without the status changing, being limited or lessened. Concretely, this means that sovereignty is not an argument against changes in international law: sovereignty is not an obstacle to change, because sovereignty does not change even when international legal rules that relate to sovereignty change. One example would be allowing – or even requiring – humanitarian intervention under specific circumstances, with or without permission of the Security Council. This would not be a violation of sovereignty but simply a change in the consequences that have been, until now, attached to sovereignty.

16.52.   This understanding of sovereignty also entails that States can transfer competences to international organisations and submit themselves to, for example, review by human rights bodies such as the European Court of Human Rights without becoming less sovereign. A last implication of this view is that sovereignty is not a matter of degree, meaning this view fits well with the idea of sovereign equality.

16.53.   The inferential analysis of State sovereignty on the basis of the UN Charter and a number of cases from the PCIJ and ICJ is not extensive and while a more extensive inferential analysis would likely add to the picture of sovereignty, my assumption is that a more extensive or even exhaustive inferential analysis of sovereignty would still leave room for ambiguities. This is both a weakness and strength in my view: it is a weakness in that the lack of clear rules makes the applicability of inferential analysis to State sovereignty questionable; it is a strength in that the inferential analysis demonstrates the imprecision and vagueness of State sovereignty.[42] This in itself is a valuable finding. The most notable example in this connection is the lack of clarity concerning exit rules of sovereignty: how does an entity lose its status?

V. Conclusion

16.54. My purpose in this contribution has been to investigate the concept of State sovereignty in international law by means of an inferential analysis. In doing so, this contribution has served two purposes: on the one hand, it offers a non-exhaustive inferential analysis of State sovereignty in international law; on the other hand, it highlights the vagueness of sovereignty in international law.

16.55. The non-exhaustive inferential analysis outlined in this paper gives the following picture of State sovereignty:

---

[42] However, this finding needs to be relativized in light of the limited number of legal rules (from treaties and case law) that were analysed.

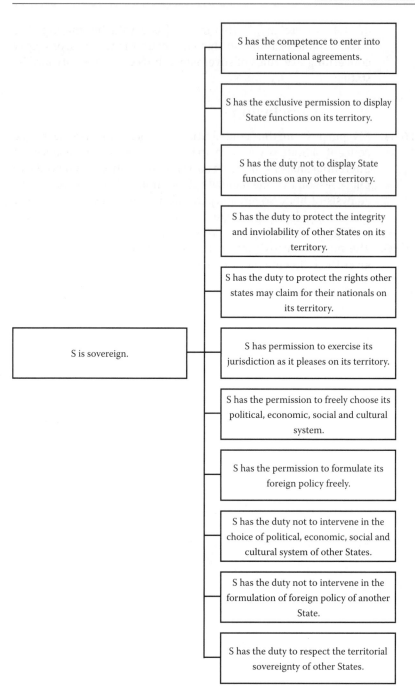

Figure 2: Sovereignty and its consequences

16.56. From this understanding of sovereignty, two conclusions can be drawn: firstly, sovereignty is best understood as a legal status. For this legal status, some entrance rules can be identified, but its exit rules are unclear. Moreover, while there are consequences usually attaching to this status, the status as such is independent from its consequences. This leads to the second conclusion, namely that sovereignty is not unchangeable, unlimited or a matter of degree.

16.57. One final remark regarding possible future inferential analyses of sovereignty: sovereignty finds its basis in customary international law. This does not take away the possibility to find (elements of) it articulated in treaties, but it indicates that case law specifying customary international law on the matter will be an important, if not the main source for any project that seeks to do an inferential analysis of sovereignty.

| | |

Summaries

FRA [*La souveraineté de l'État en tant que statut juridique*]
Au sein du droit international, la souveraineté est une notion sensible et controversée : certains la qualifient de « notion vide de contenu et sans utilité », d'autres estiment qu'il s'agit d'une « doctrine fondamentale du droit constitutionnel » intervenant dans le droit international. Plusieurs méthodes se proposent pour l'analyse des notions de droit, dont l'analyse inférentielle, qui examine les relations impliquées par un concept afin d'en dégager le sens. Le présent article soumet la notion de souveraineté de l'État à ce type d'analyse, sans ambition d'exhaustivité. L'auteur propose de considérer la souveraineté comme un statut juridique indépendant des conséquences juridiques qui en résultent. Cette vision de la souveraineté permet de dégager nombre de questions importantes concernant cette notion, tout en corroborant la conclusion que la souveraineté n'est pas une propriété relative (égalité souveraine), qu'elle a des limites et qu'elle peut évoluer dans le temps.

CZE [*Státní svrchovanost jako právní status*]
Státní svrchovanost je v mezinárodním právu citlivým a kontroverzním pojmem; bývá označována za pojem „postrádající smysluplný konkrétní obsah", ale i za „základní ústavněprávní doktrínu" mezinárodního práva. Právní pojmy je možno, mimo jiné, analyzovat i prostřednictvím inferenční analýzy: tato

analýza zkoumá vztahy vyplývající z určitého pojmu za účelem určení jeho smyslu. Tento příspěvek nabízí nikoli vyčerpávající inferenční analýzu státní svrchovanosti a navrhuje, aby byla svrchovanost v mezinárodním právu chápána jako právní status, který je nezávislý na právních důsledcích s ním spojených. Tento pohled na svrchovanost odhaluje řadu nezodpovězených otázek týkajících se svrchovanosti a podporuje závěr, že svrchovanost není věcí míry (svrchovaná rovnost), není neomezená ani nepřístupná změnám.

| | |

POL [*Suwerenność państwowa jako status prawny*]
Pojęcia prawnicze można m.in analizować w ramach analizy inferencyjnej. W artykule omówiono analizę inferencyjną suwerenności państwowej i zaproponowano, by traktować ją jako status prawny, który nie zależy od związanych z tym skutków prawnych. Takie spojrzenie rodzi szereg otwartych pytań na temat suwerenności i narzuca wniosek, że suwerenność nie jest kwestią stopnia (suwerenna równość), nie jest ograniczona ani zamknięta na zmiany.

DEU [*Die staatliche Hoheit als rechtlicher Status*]
Rechtliche Begriffe lassen sich u.a. auch vermittels Inferenzanalyse deuten. Der vorliegende Beitrag offeriert eine (keineswegs erschöpfende) Inferenzanalyse der staatlichen Hoheit und schlägt vor, Souveränität als rechtlichen Status zu verstehen, der von den mit ihm verbundenen rechtlichen Folgen unabhängig ist. Dieser Ansatz deckt eine Reihe offener Fragen betreffend die Souveränität des Staats auf und stützt den Schluss, dass die Souveränität keine Sache des Grades (im Sinne einer Gleichheit der Souveräne), weder unbegrenzt noch Veränderungen unzugänglich ist.

RUS [*Государственный суверенитет как правовой статус*]
Юридические термины также можно анализировать с помощью анализа инференций. Данная статья представляет отнюдь не исчерпывающий анализ инференций государственного суверенитета и предлагает, чтобы суверенитет воспринимался как правовой статус, который не зависит от правовых последствий, связанных с ним. Этот взгляд раскрывает ряд оставшихся без ответа вопросов о суверенитете и поддерживает вывод о том, что суверенитет не является вопросом степени

(суверенное равенство), не безграничен и открыт для изменений.

ESP [*La soberanía del Estado como un estatuto legal*]
Los conceptos del derecho pueden ser analizados, entre otros métodos, a través del análisis de inferencia. El presente artículo plantea un análisis inferencial de la soberanía del Estado que no pretende ser exhaustivo, y propone que la soberanía sea considerada como un estatuto legal independiente de las consecuencias jurídicas relacionadas con él. Esta perspectiva revela una serie de preguntas relativas a la soberanía que todavía quedan por responder y concluye que la soberanía no reconoce grados (igualdad soberana), no es ni ilimitada ni se encuentra cerrada ante posibles cambios.

Bibliography

SAMANTHA BESSON, SOVEREIGNTY, Max Planck Encyclopedia of Public International Law, Oxford Public International Law (2011).

CLEMENS FEINÄUGLE, WIMBLEDON, The Max Planck Encyclopedia of Public International Law (MPEPIL), Oxford Public International Law (2013).

Åke Frändberg, *An Essay on Legal Concept Formation*, in JAAP HAGE AND DIETMAR VON DER PFORDTEN, CONCEPTS IN LAW, Springer Law and Philosophy Library (2009).

JAAP HAGE, FOUNDATIONS AND BUILDING BLOCKS OF LAW, Eleven International Publishing (2018).

Jaap Hage, *The Meaning of Legal Status Words*, in JAAP HAGE AND DIETMAR VON DER PFORDTEN, CONCEPTS IN LAW, Springer (2009).

ANNE PETERS, TREATY MAKING POWER, Max Planck Encyclopedia of Public International Law, Oxford Public International Law (2009).

Alf Ross, *Tû-tû*, 70 HARVARD LAW REVIEW 812 (1957).

Giovanni Sartor, *Legal Validity: An Inferential Analysis*, 21 RATIO JURIS 212 (2008).

Giovanni Sartor, *Legal Concepts and Legal Inferences*, in JAAP HAGE AND DIETMAR VON DER PFORDTEN, CONCEPTS IN LAW, Springer (2009).

Nico Schrijver, *The Changing Nature of State Sovereignty* 70 THE BRITISH YEARBOOK OF INTERNATIONAL LAW 65 (2000).

xANTONIA WALTERMANN, SOVEREIGNTIES, Maastricht University, Maastricht (2016).

Book Reviews

Květoslav Růžička | Bohumil Poláček | Radek Novák |
Petr Dostalík

The Influence of Roman Law to Selected Institutes of International Commercial Law

Praha: Wolters Kluwer ČR, 220 pages (2018) ISBN: 978-80-7598-143-1

The collective publication that is subject to this review is in many ways remarkable, not only as one of the rare examples of cooperation between legal scholars from (at first sight) rather distant academic fields (international commercial law and Roman law), but mainly because it opens up new research perspectives, not only in Czech legal scholarship. After reading six chapters dedicated to important institutes of contemporary international commercial law, a reader can get the impression that selected institutes and their possible Roman "counterparts" are so close to each other (with one notable exception), that one could wonder, why a similar book was not published (at least for the Czech audience) sooner.

The first chapter is dedicated to the thesis that the contemporary concept of lex mercatoria has its origins not only in its quite known medieval and early modern "ancestors", but also in the classical Roman law concept of ius gentium, because the function of both concepts is very similar: To provide in principle non-state-made law for the regulation of relations between merchants or businessmen from different jurisdictions. This rather introductory chapter is followed by a chapter on the origins of the international sale of goods contract (as elaborated in well-known CISG and the Limitation Convention) in the Roman institute of emptio venditio. Similarly, in the third chapter, Roman contract locatio conductio rei is presented as the origin of various international treaties (and relevant EU regulations too) on international carriage of goods contracts. The famous Lex Rhodia de iactu is the subject of the fourth chapter as an "ancestor" to the particular institute of general average (avarie commune). Bill of laning is the topic of the fifth chapter that in many ways differs from the previous ones because it shows that Roman law did not know a similar institute. The chapter explains the reasons for this absence, traces bill of lading origins to medieval Mediterranean commercial customs and usages and presents the lesser known contribution of the great German scholar Rudolf von Jhering towards development of international commercial law in detail. In my opinion, the fourth and fifth chapters are the most interesting, because they apply closely comparative legal history approach (see below). The book is concluded by a last chapter on the similarities between the Roman iudex privatus, arbiter and recuperator on the one hand and the modern commercial arbitrator on the other. In every chapter we can find many quotations from Roman law materials (in Latin and in translation) supporting the claims of authors.

To review the main idea of influence of Roman law to contemporary international commercial law, however, it is also necessary to identify some problems of this thesis. Since it is in my opinion a general problem, I will try to demonstrate it in the first chapter dealing with general concepts of ius gentium and lex mercatoria. There are in principle two paradigms of contemporary comparative legal scholarship – the dominant functional approach (that compares those institutes of different legal systems that within these systems have the same function) and the comparative legal history approach (popularised mainly by Alan Watson) that tries to "trace back" institutes of one legal system to their historically proven direct "ancestors" in previous legal system, taking into account the fact that in the course of history (driven in private law for a long time by practising lawyers as a distinct professional group, rather than by legislators) the function of the institute can change. In other words, the fact that the "new" institute or concept and "old" institute and concept are similar in their function does not necessarily mean that the "old" institute or concept is a direct "ancestor" of the "new" one. The book in my opinion varies between these two distinct approaches and these "shifts" between paradigms can be demonstrated exactly on its "intellectual history" from ius gentium to contemporary lex mercatoria. While the thesis that Roman ius gentium as a body of rules administered by praetor peregrinus in disputes between two non-Roman aliens, or between a citizen and an alien, gave rise to medieval and early modern lex mercatoria is in general sometimes accepted (e.g. Harald Berman persuasively wrote of the emergence of a common commercial law in medieval Europe that traces its intellectual lineage back to ancient models of ius gentium), there is also an "alternative history" possible that is in my opinion prevalent, at least in the field of history of ideas: Starting from the general "definitions" provided by Roman lawyers connecting ius gentium with natural reason of all humans (quod vero naturalis ratio inter omnes homines constituit - Gaius 1, 1. quoted in the book itself, p. 8, but also Inst. Iust. 1, 2.1.), ius gentium was assimilated to natural law (e.g. in famous lecture De Indis by Francisco de Vitoria ius gentium "either is or derives from natural law") and then (probably for the first time) it was explicitly conceptually distinguished from natural law (in spite of the fact that the content of ius gentium and of natural law is overlapping) and connected with ius inter gentes (as creations of human lawgivers through treaties or customs) by Francisco Suárez (De legibus, chapters XXXV to LXII) and through reception of Suárez's ideas by Grotius (without explicit reference to Suárez, but in general not disputed in contemporary scholarship) ius gentium started its well-known "long march" towards contemporary public international law. This "conceptual lineage" thus shows us that the lasting influence of ius gentium for modern thinking is conceptual rather than practical and rather in line with natural law thinking than in line with lex mercatoria as common commercial customs and usages of merchants. In other words, it is possible that for the intellectual history, a genealogy of concepts (leading through natural law towards public international law) is more important than "genealogy of real-world practices". Similar functions of Roman ius gentium on the one hand and today's lex mercatoria on the other, does not necessarily mean that ius gentium institutes were in general adopted by lex mercatoria. Non-negligible differences between Roman application of ius gentium and medieval application of lex mercatoria probably existed also on the level of practice – e.g. David Bederman (writing on custom as a source of law) points out the rather hegemonic nature of Roman ius gentium (as in fact a state-centred practice) in contrast to pluralistic nature of medieval lex mercatoria.

Nevertheless, this rather critical remark does not at all exclude the hypothesis of authors that many current international commercial law institutes in fact have their origins in Roman law. Rather, this remark shall be understood as an "incentive" for more in-depth search and analysis of origins of particular institutes of international commercial law in Roman law. E.g. Their "genealogy of institute" of general average in the fourth chapter from famous Lex Rhodia through Rolls of Oléron or Book of the Consulate of the Sea, ius commune and Cujas to ABGB and current Czech Civil Code is in my opinion as close as possible to the approach of comparative legal history and their detailed search and analysis should be applauded. A similar conclusion can be made also on the fifth chapter on origins of bill of lading in medieval law. In some other chapters (typically in the second and the third chapter), however, the Roman law institute is first presented (emptio venditio in the first case and locatio conductio rei in the second) and then immediately modern rules established by international treaties are presented without any real "genealogy of institute" through medieval and later times (e.g. without mentioning known immediate modern influences on the content of these treaties). The lack of a conclusion summing up the results of comparison (what is the same like in Roman law and what is different with possible explanation of differences) in every chapter or at least in the end of the book itself is not helpful either.

However, these critiques do not in my opinion diminish the value of the work itself that is both inspiring and innovative (at least in Czech legal scholarship), because trying to find origins of particular institutes is in my opinion more contributing to general knowledge, than some other uses (or sometimes rather misuses) of legal history. I have in mind e.g. the so-called legal origins thesis of a group of American economists (especially La Porta, Lopez-de-Silanes, Shleifer and Vishny) stating (in general without distinctions and detailed analysis) that adoption of common law system leads to higher economic growth for a country than adoption of civil law system (the example of contemporary Chinese economic "giant" is clearly disproving it). If this book inspires more in-depth research in "genealogy of institutes" not only in international commercial law and not only by Czech legal scholars, it must be appreciated as a really pioneering work.

[*JUDr. Michal Šejvl, Ph.D.*]

Institute of State and Law of the Czech Academy of Sciences, Prague

E-mail: sejvl@ilaw.cas.cz

News & Reports

Czech Yearbook of International Law®

News & Reports

State Waivers of Immunity and the Impact on Property Relations and Investments: an Example from the Republic of Belarus

Sovereignty is an inalienable characteristic of any State. However, more often States are beginning to waive a number of aspects of sovereignty, particularly their jurisdictional immunities as regards property relations. The Republic of Belarus is a young and developing State, and is very interested in attracting investments into the Belarusian economy. One of the methods of accomplishing this goal is to provide investors with exceptional guarantees and privileges.

In the Republic of Belarus, an investment contract is frequently concluded with a complex public-private-legal framework. Within the framework of the said contract, the Republic of Belarus takes on a number of additional legal obligations, with both civil-legal and public-law qualities. In return, it demands from the investor an obligation to implement its investments in the territory of Belarus. In connection with these circumstances, disputable legal relations are possible between the parties to such an investment contract.

Before analyzing the issues to consider in of disputes under investment treaties between foreign investors and the Republic of Belarus, it is first of all necessary to point out that the Republic of Belarus, like any other State, has so-called jurisdictional immunities. Generally speaking, there are three types of jurisdictional immunities.

The first is judicial immunity, which is the immunity of a State from jurisdiction of the courts of another State. In other words, as a general rule, a State cannot be a defendant or a third person in court of a foreign

Czech Yearbook of International Law®

State. The second is immunity in relation to the preliminary securing of a claim. So a court of a foreign State cannot secure a claim in relation to another State by applying the measures for securing a claim provided by the procedural law of their court. Finally, there is

immunity in relation to a judicial or arbitral award. This means that a judicial or arbitral award, even if it is rendered against a specific State, can be enforced only if the State concerned voluntarily agrees to implementation of the decision.

Thus, as a general rule, the Republic of Belarus cannot be subject to the courts of a foreign State or foreign arbitration. However, States, including the Republic of Belarus, can waive their jurisdictional immunities.

If the State waives its immunity, any measures related to the protection of the subjective right of a person may be applied as they are to foreign economic activities. In practice, States do not resort to a general. Indeed, this would be impossible in accordance with the principles of public international law. Rather, they do so only when concluding specific transactions, or within certain types of international public-law agreements.

The possibility of waiver by the Republic of Belarus of its jurisdictional immunities under an investment contract is specified in Article 46 of the Investment Code of the Republic of Belarus, which provides that 'an investment contract with foreign investors may provide for the State's waiver of judicial immunity, immunity in relation to the preliminary securing of a claim and execution of a judicial and (or) arbitral award.'

On top of it all, subparagraph 1.4. of paragraph 1 of the Decree of the President of the Republic of Belarus of 6 August 2009 No 10 'On Creation of Additional Conditions for Investment Activity in the Republic of Belarus' provides that any investment contract must necessarily contain rules and a body for the consideration of disputes between the parties related to provisions of the investment contract. The body for the consideration of disputes may be defined in two ways. First, it may be the court of a foreign State. Secondly, it may be an arbitration court established in the territory of a foreign State if the investor is a natural or legal person of a foreign State and the Republic of Belarus has concluded an international treaty that includes the protection of investments, and that such a court is defined as the competent body for the consideration of disputes.

Proceeding from the last statement, it can be concluded that the definition of the body that considers disputes between the parties to the investment contract is not an 'extraordinary condition' of the investment contract, and, consequently, the Republic of Belarus can waive its jurisdictional immunities from itself. However, the appearance in an investment contract of a foreign court or arbitration is possible only if the investor is a subject who is under the jurisdiction of a foreign State and there is already a concluded international public treaty within which the Republic of Belarus has already undertaken to subordinate the investment dispute to the said court.

Included in the above-mentioned international public treaties are more than fifty bilateral international treaties or agreements between the Government of the Republic of Belarus and foreign States on mutual protection of investments. Such treaties provide for arbitration procedures for the consideration of disputes between investors and the relevant State where they invest, as well as between the parties to the relevant international treaty.

The Republic of Belarus has agreements on promotion and mutual protection with Denmark, India, Armenia, Cuba, Moldova, Lithuania, Cyprus, Latvia, Bulgaria, Ukraine, Turkey, the United States of America, Germany, China, Finland, the Czech Republic, Italy, the Netherlands, Sweden, Switzerland, Poland, and others.

There are several typical approaches for such treaties to resolve the issue of the removal of judicial immunity by the State.

For example, Article 9 'Settlement of disputes between a Contracting Party and an investor of the other Contracting Party' of the Agreement between the Government of the Republic of Belarus and the Government of the Kingdom of Denmark on promotion and mutual protection of investments sets out:

> 1. Any dispute concerning an investment between an investor of one Contracting Party and the other Contracting Party shall, if possible, be settled by negotiations.
>
> 2. If any dispute mentioned in paragraph (1) of this Article cannot be settled within six months following the date on which the dispute has been raised by the investor through written notification to the Contracting Party, each Contracting Party hereby consents to the submission of the dispute, at the investor's choice, for resolution to:
>
> a) a competent court of the Contracting Party;
>
> b) the International Centre for Settlement of Investment Disputes (ICSID) for settlement by arbitration under the Washington Convention of 18 March 1965 on the Settlement of Investment Disputes between States and Nationals of Other States. In case of arbitration, each

Contracting Party, by this Agreement irrevocably consents in advance, even in the absence of an individual arbitral agreement between the Contracting Party and the investor, to submit any such dispute to this Centre. This consent implies the renunciation of the requirement that the internal administrative or

judicial remedies should be exhausted;

c) an ad hoc tribunal set up under Arbitration Rules of the United Nations Commission on International Trade Law (UNCITRAL). The appointing authority under the said rules shall be the Secretary General of ICSID. In case of arbitration, each Contracting Party, by this Agreement irrevocably consents in advance, even in the absence of an individual arbitral agreement between the Contracting Party and the investor, to submit any such dispute to the tribunal mentioned;

d) by arbitration in accordance with the Rules of Arbitration of the International Chamber of Commerce (ICC).

3. For the purpose of this Article and the said Washington Convention, any legal person which is constituted in accordance with the legislation of one Contracting Party and which, before a dispute arises, was controlled by an investor of the other Contracting Party, shall be treated as a national of the other Contracting Party.

4. Any arbitration under paragraph 2 (b) – (d) of this Article shall, at the request of either Contracting Party, be held in a State that is a party to the United Nations Convention on the Recognition and Enforcement of Foreign Arbitral Awards, done at New York, 10 June 1958.

5. The consent given by each Contracting Party in paragraph (2) and the submission of the dispute by an investor under the said paragraph shall constitute the written consent and written agreement of the parties to the dispute.

6. In any proceeding involving an investment dispute, a Contracting Party shall not assert, as a defence, counterclaim or for any other reason, that indemnification or other compensation for all or part of the alleged damages has been received pursuant to an insurance or guarantee contract.

7. Any arbitral award rendered pursuant to this Article

shall be final and binding on the parties to the dispute. Each Contracting Party shall ensure the recognition and enforcement of the arbitral award in accordance with its relevant laws and regulations;

Another example can be found in Article 6 of the Agreement between the Republic of Belarus and the United States of America on promotion and mutual protection of investments. The terms set out in that agreement are:

1. For purposes of this Article, an investment dispute is a dispute between a Party and a national or company of the other Party arising out of or relating to:

(a) an investment agreement between that Party and such national or company;

(b) an investment authorization granted by that Party's foreign investment authority to such national or company; or

(c) an alleged breach of any right conferred or created by this Treaty with respect to an investment.

2. In the event of an investment dispute, the parties to the dispute should initially seek a resolution through consultation and negotiation. If the dispute cannot be settled amicably, the national or company concerned may choose to submit the dispute for resolution:

(a) to the courts or administrative tribunals of the Party that is a party to the dispute; or

(b) in accordance with any applicable, previously agreed dispute-settlement procedures; or

(c) in accordance with the terms of paragraph 3.

3. (a) Provided that the national or company concerned has not submitted the dispute for resolution under paragraph 2 (a) or (b) and that six months have elapsed from the date on which the dispute arose, the national or company concerned may choose to consent in writing to the submission of the dispute for settlement by binding arbitration:

(i) to the International Centre for the Settlement of Investment Disputes ("Centre")

established by the convention on the Settlement of Investment Disputes between States and Nationals or other states, done at Washington, 18 March 1965 ("ICSID Convention"), provided that the Party is a Party to such convention; or

(ii) to the Additional Facility of the Centre, if the Centre is not available; or

(iii) in accordance with the Arbitration Rules of the United Nations Commission on International Trade Law (UNCITRAL); or

(iv) to any other arbitration institution, or in accordance with any other arbitration rules, as may be mutually agreed between the parties to the dispute.

(b) Once the national or company concerned has so consented, either party to the dispute may initiate arbitration in accordance with the choice so specified in the consent.

4. Each Party hereby consents to the submission of any investment dispute for settlement by binding arbitration in accordance with the choice specified in the written consent of the national or company under paragraph 3. Such consent, together with the written consent of the national or company when given under paragraph 3 shall satisfy the requirement for:

(a) written consent of the parties to the dispute for purposes of Chapter II of the ICSID Convention (Jurisdiction of the Centre) and for purposes of the Additional Facility Rules; and

(b) an "agreement in writing" for purposes of Article II of the United Nations Convention on the Recognition and Enforcement of Foreign Arbitral Awards, done at New York, 10 June 1958 ("New York Convention").

5. Any arbitration under paragraph 3 (a) (ii), (iii) or (iv) of this Article shall be held in a state that is a party to the New York Convention.

6. Any arbitral award rendered pursuant to this Article shall be final and binding on the parties to the dispute. Each Party undertakes to carry out without delay the provisions of any such award and to provide in its territory for its enforcement.

7. In any proceeding involving an investment dispute, a Party shall not assert, as a defense, counterclaim, right

Czech Yearbook of International Law®

of set-off or otherwise, that the national or company concerned has received or will receive, pursuant to an insurance or guarantee contract, indemnification or other compensation for all or part of its alleged damages.

8. For purposes of an arbitration held under paragraph 3 of this Article, any company legally constituted under the applicable laws and regulations of a Party or a political subdivision thereof but that, immediately before the occurrence of the event or events giving rise to the dispute, was an investment of nationals or companies of the other Party, shall be treated as a national or company of such other Party in accordance with Article 25(2) (b) of the ICSID Convention

Another example is visible in Article 9 of the Agreement between the Government of the Republic of Belarus and the Government of the People's Republic of China on promotion and mutual protection of investments:

1. Dispute between a Contracting Party and an investor of the other Contracting Party about compensation amount in case of expropriation can be submitted to the arbitration tribunal.

2. An arbitration tribunal shall be established for every particular case as follows: each Party appoints an arbitrator; the arbitrators appointed select a citizen of a third State, having diplomatic relations with both Contracting Parties who shall preside over the arbitration tribunal. The two arbitrators are appointed within two months, Chairman is to be selected within four months upon the receipt of a written notification on submitting the dispute to the arbitration tribunal. If within the period stated the arbitration tribunal has not been established, any of the Contracting Parties can apply to Chairman of the Arbitration Institute of the Stockholm Chamber of Commerce to perform all necessary appointments.

3. The arbitration tribunal shall determine its procedure rules. The arbitration tribunal can take the Rules of the Arbitration Institute of the Stockholm Chamber of Commerce as guidance.

4. The Arbitration tribunal takes a decision by majority votes. The decision is final and obligatory for the Contracting Parties. Each Party is obliged to fulfill the

decision in accordance with its State laws.

5. The Arbitration tribunal takes a decision in accordance with the provisions of this Agreement and the laws of the State in whose territory investments were made, including collision norms and universally recognized principles of international law.

6. Each Contracting Party shall bear costs related to arbitrator's activities and his/her participation in the arbitrary proceedings. Expenses related to Chairman activities and other costs shall be covered by the Contracting Parties equally.

These examples show that State parties to a bilateral international public contract waive judicial immunity for themselves. Likewise, they certainly recognize the possibility of considering a dispute between a particular State and a private investor in an arbitration procedure using various types of arbitration. There are several means of realizing this goal. The first is a mechanism for the so-called investment arbitration in the form of the International Centre for the Settlement of Investment Disputes, related to the International Bank for Reconstruction and Development (ICSID) (the convention on the Settlement of Investment Disputes between States and Nationals or other States (Washington, 18 March 1965)). Another method involves institutional or permanently operating international arbitration institutions, created primarily for the consideration of so-called international trade disputes. These include the ICC Arbitration Court (International Chamber of Commerce in Paris), as well as the Arbitration Institute of the Stockholm City Chamber of Commerce. A third method involves ad hoc arbitration which can be formed and enacted on the basis of the provisions of some relevant agreement, or by using the UNCITRAL Arbitration Rules.

A problem has arisen in connection with the above-mentioned agreements in the doctrine of international law. This problem involves the understanding of those jurisdictional immunities waived by the relevant State to which the specific agreement is binding. In the doctrine of international law there is no unity on the issue of whether the reference to the arbitration procedure for resolving disputes in the relevant international public treaty means the waiver of the State from all its jurisdictional immunities. i.e. from judicial immunity, immunity for preliminary securing of a claim and immunity for enforcement of the judgment, or the specified actions of the State are an example of a waiver only solely from judicial immunity, and for the application of preliminary securing, and even more so for the enforcement of the arbitration award, additional special expression of will of the corresponding State is required. Different legal systems have different approaches to this issue. For example, English law proceeds from the premise that the subordination of the State to the jurisdiction of a foreign court does not include subordination to the decision of the court of a foreign State, without the special expression of will of the State. This is also known as a waiver of immunity from executive actions, and is similar to actions for applying measures to secure a claim. Conversely, U.S. law is based on the opposite principle. It proceeds from the premise that the subordination of the State to the jurisdiction of a foreign court means that the State waived immunities in the sphere of execution of the decision and securing the claim. With respect to the previously referenced agreements, we can see a fairly straightforward solution to the question. Let us assume for the sake of argument that it is a decision of the International Center for Settlement of Investment Disputes, related to the International Bank for Reconstruction and Development (ICSID), on the application of the Washington Convention. Currently more than 160 States, including the Republic of Belarus are parties to this Convention. In this case, if the State concerned is a party to this Convention, as well as a party to one of the above-mentioned bilateral international public treaties, then under Article 54 of the Convention, any contracting State recognizes the arbitration award as binding and ensures the fulfillment of monetary obligations imposed by the arbitration award within its territories.

As for the decisions of institutional international arbitration courts, as well as ad hoc arbitrations, their enforcement is based on the United Nations Convention on the Recognition and Enforcement of Foreign Arbitral Awards (New York, 1958) with presently about 150 member-States, including the Republic of Belarus. Most importantly, it is clear that when the relevant State withdraws judicial immunity from itself within the framework of a bilateral international public agreement on mutual protection of investments, the above-mentioned normative provisions specifically stipulate its obligation to enforce the decision of the relevant arbitration court. The State takes on the obligation to take the necessary measures for such enforcement.

Proceeding from the above, the authors believe that the above provisions directly indicate not only the waiver of judicial immunity from the State, but also the waiver of immunity from the enforcement of the arbitral award. Despite the fact that the above agreements do not directly refer to the third jurisdictional immunity of the State, namely, the immunity from the application of measures to secure a claim, the waiver of the State from this immunity is most likely implied, taking into account the State's waiver from immunity associated with the enforcement of the arbitral award. However, it should be noted that, in connection with the latter circumstance, the question of jurisdictional immunity that can be decided depending on the approaches of the respective legal systems cited above, in the absence of a straightforward and direct expression of the will of the State concerned.

We now return to the issues of the procedure for considering disputes under investment contracts between the Republic of Belarus and foreign investors. If one literally follows the provisions of Decree No 10, the subordination of the Republic of Belarus to a foreign court or arbitration should be an infrequent phenomenon. Additionally, Decree No 10 does not legally or actually allow any additional waiver of the Republic of Belarus from its jurisdictional immunities within the framework of a particular investment contract, in comparison with those waivers which have already been made in the framework of relevant international public treaties.

The above conclusion is also confirmed by the Model Form of the Investment Contact, which is an Annex to the Regulation on the Procedure for Concluding or Terminating Investment Contracts with the Republic of Belarus, confirmed by the Decision of the Council of Ministers of the Republic of Belarus No 1449. In accordance with paragraph 15 of this Model Form: 'all disputes, disagreements and claims arising from the contract are subject to settlement in accordance with the act of the legislation of the Republic of Belarus in the International Arbitration Court at the Belarusian Chamber of Commerce and Industry, Minsk, in accordance with its rules.'

In paragraph 16 of the same Model Form it is indicated that, by agreement of the parties, a court of a foreign State, or an arbitration court established in the territory of a foreign State, can be defined as the disputing body, but only if subject to the requirements of subparagraph 1.4 paragraph 1 of the Decree No 10.

Thus, based on the normative material described above, we can make the final conclusion that, as applied to particular investment contracts with the participation of the Republic of Belarus, the Republic of Belarus cannot implement a contract-specific waiver of its jurisdictional immunities and provide for a special foreign court or arbitration as the body considering the dispute under the relevant investment contract.

The maximum that can be applied to the waiver of jurisdictional immunities in a particular investment contract is confirmation in its framework of the already implemented waiver of jurisdictional immunities of the Republic of Belarus. Such frameworks must be defined in the relevant international public agreement, in particular within the framework of the above-mentioned treaties or agreements on mutual protection of investments.

Thus, we note that, contrary to widespread international practice, the Republic of Belarus cannot waive its jurisdictional immunities in relation to a particular investment contract. After all, it is impossible to consider as a specified waiver confirmation of an already made waiver. Such a waiver of jurisdictional immunity is already present due to an international public treaty, and a particular investment contract only gives this waiver the possibility of realization. Otherwise, if we follow the general rule of the Decision of the Council of Ministers of the Republic of Belarus No 1449, then disputes under a particular investment contract should be considered in the International Arbitration Court at the BelCCI, which is a permanently functioning institutional arbitration body formed in the territory of the Republic of Belarus .However, the biggest question in connection with the stated approach of the legislature to the procedure for the settlement of disputes within the framework of a particular investment contract is related to the fact that this approach can lead to a conflict between the provisions of a particular investment contract. This is especially true when the dispute is considered in the International Arbitration Court at the BelCCI and a number of international public obligations of the Republic of Belarus, in particular those mentioned above.

Namely, as described above, within the framework of international public treaties, the Republic of Belarus assumed an unconditional obligation to recognize the possibility of considering the investment dispute in the corresponding arbitration institutions. Let us assume that only the International Arbitration Court at the BelCCI is indicated as the body considering the dispute in the particular investment contract. Does this mean that a foreign investor who is a subject of a State party to an international public treaty or agreement can not apply to the ICC Arbitration Court, or the International Center for Settlement of Investment Disputes (ICSID), or form an ad hoc arbitration, in accordance with the provisions of an international public treaty? In our opinion, at the most basic level, the above question should be solved as follows. The provisions of a particular investment contract, in which only the International Court of Arbitration at the BelCCI is specified as the body considering the dispute, should be adjusted or rather supplemented by the umbrella arbitration clause contained in the international public treaty or agreement with the Republic of Belarus.

In other words, a particular investment contract between a foreign investor and the Republic of Belarus, can supplement the list of arbitration procedures provided by an international public agreement of the Republic of Belarus. The reflection of the International Arbitration Court at the BelCCI in a particular investment contract as the body considering the dispute under this contract does not contradict the specific public legal obligations of the Republic of Belarus, given above in the field of mutual protection of investments. This is especially true since these international public treaties or agreements do not prohibit and cannot prohibit parties of a particular investment contract to provide another body for the resolution of their dispute, in comparison with those specified in an international public treaty.

However, the latter circumstance cannot completely exclude the application of an international public treaty, including the part in question, unless that very treaty or agreement indicates otherwise. If a particular contract specifies a specific procedure for settlement of disputes under this contract, then the provisions of the relevant international public treaty or agreement are not applied.

Consequently, regardless of the indication in a particular investment contract only to the International Arbitration Court at the BelCCI, as the body considering the dispute under this contract, if between the Republic of Belarus with the State of the foreign investor - party of the investment contract there is the international public treaty (agreement), in particular on mutual protection of investments, within the framework of which the Republic of Belarus committed a waiver of jurisdictional immunities in respect of the subjects of the relevant foreign country, indicating other arbitration bodies considering disputes, then the foreign subject in order to protect its rights and property interests, can apply not only to the International Arbitration Court at the BelCCI, but also to any other arbitration institution (or to use any other arbitration procedure), provided by the relevant international public treaty or agreement.

Thus, the consent of specific subjects to the consideration of a dispute in a certain body within the framework of a particular contract does not exclude the previously reached common agreement for the consideration of disputes between any subjects of the respective State and another State. Otherwise, one of the most important principles of international law - the binding nature of the implementation of international treaties - will not be respected. However, the position stated above, if proceeding from the nature of the provisions of the Decree No 10 and the Decision of the Council of Ministers of the Republic of Belarus No 1449, can be questioned. As we have already noted above, subparagraph 1.4. Decree No 10 specifies that for the consideration of a dispute on a particular investment contract in a foreign arbitration, a direct indication must be made in the investment contract itself. This is true despite the existence of relevant international treaties or agreements in the sphere of the mutual protection of investments in the Republic of Belarus. Therefore, it is presumed that without such an indication only by virtue of an international treaty or agreement on mutual protection of investment, a foreign arbitration specified in an international public treaty cannot consider a dispute between the Republic of Belarus and a foreign investor.

In addition, the position stated above is also confirmed directly in the Model Form of the Investment Contract, which is an Annex to the Regulation on the Procedure for Concluding (Terminating) Investment Contracts with the Republic of Belarus, confirmed by the Decision of the Council of Ministers of the Republic of Belarus No 1449. Namely, as noted above, paragraph 15 of this Form is an arbitration clause specifying the International Arbitration Court at the BelCCI as the body considering the dispute under the investment contract. At the same time, the Belarusian legislators, allowing in paragraph 16 of the Model Form an indication of other arbitration procedures for the settlement of disputes under the relevant investment contract, did not provide that in the event of the reflection in a particular investment contract the provisions of paragraph 16 of the Model Form, paragraph 15 of this Model Form should not apply. In other words, Belarusian law stipulates that, when reflecting on a particular investment contract, paragraph 16 and paragraph 15 of the Model Form should also be reflected in the same investment contract. Thus, Belarusian legislators, while using both paragraph 15 and paragraph 16 of the Model Form, allowed for a so-called alternative or broken arbitration clause. I If we are to literally interpret the Belarusian legislators, then it is necessary to specify such procedures in a particular contract for the possibility of applying the arbitration procedures that are alternative to the International Arbitration Court at the BelCCI. According to the Belarusian legislators, the fact that these procedures are already fixed by an international public treaty is not sufficient for their use within the framework of a particular investment contract.

An indirect justification for such a legislative position is that a foreign investor concluding an investment contract and not providing in it a different procedure for the settlement of disputes beyond the International Arbitration Court at the BelCCI, voluntarily renounces the opportunities that are provided by an international public treaty. After all, if a foreign investor did not make this particular investment contract, then they could fully take advantage of the umbrella arbitration clause contained in the international public treaty. In connection with the latter circumstance, one cannot help but recall that the procedure for considering disputes is an obligatory condition for an investment contract with the participation of the Republic of Belarus. A foreign investor can

Czech Yearbook of International Law®

defend their rights based on the provisions of an international public treaty by refusing to regulate an order of settlement of the dispute in an investment contract, if the State of the foreign investor has committed a specific treaty with the Republic of Belarus. But in defense of the position of the Belarusian legislators, no one has interfered and will interfere with the foreign investor's right to provide in a particular investment contract a procedure the for settlement of disputes similar to the procedure for the settlement of investment disputes provided for by an international public treaty or agreement between the State government of a foreign investor and the Republic of Belarus. Thus, we concede a certain variability in relation to the presented problem. Therefore, a solution will heavily depend on the provisions of a particular international public treaty and on the will of a particular arbitration institution, which is named in the relevant international public treaty.

[*Ian Iosifovich Funk, LL.D.*]

is a Professor of BSU, Chairman of the International Arbitration Court at the BelCCI.

E-mail: funk25@mail.ru

[*Inna Vladimirovna Pererva, PhD.*]

is the Head of Information and Consulting Center of the International Arbitration Court at the BelCCI.

E-mail: iac@cci.by

Bibliography, Current Events, CYIL & CYArb® Presentations, Important Web Sites

Alexander J. Bělohlávek

I.   Selected Bibliography for 2018[1]

Opening Remarks:
This overview lists only works published in 2018. The individual chapters into which this overview is divided always cover both substantive and procedural issues.

Titles in translations are indicative.

I.1.   (Public) international law, including constitutional issues and other public-law areas with transnational dimensions and including the legal issues of international business relations, international relationships[2]

I.1.1. [CZE] – [CZECH REPUBLIC] – Titles published within the Czech Republic

<u>Monographs and Collections</u>

LADISLAV CABADA; ŠÁRKA WEISOVÁ, SECURITY, FOREIGN AND EUROPEAN POLICY OF THE VISEGRAD GROUP, Prague: Metropolitní univerzita Praha, ISBN: 978-80-7476-140-9.[3]

JAN ONDŘEJ; PETR MRÁZEK; OTO KUNZ, ZÁKLADY MEZINÁRODNÍHO PRÁVA VEŘEJNÉHO [Title in translation – BASICS OF PUBLIC INTERNATIONAL LAW], Prague: C. H. Beck, ISBN: 978-80-7400-487-2 (2018).[4]

VÁCLAV STEHLÍK; ONDREJ HAMUĽÁK; PETR MICHAL, PRÁVO EVROPSKÉ UNIE. ÚSTAVNÍ ZÁKLADY A VNITŘNÍ TRH [Title in translation - EUROPEAN UNION LAW. CONSTITUTIONAL BASIS AND INTERNAL MARKET], Prague: Leges, ISBN: 978-80-7502-277-6 (2018).[5]

---

[1]   Collected by: Alexander J. BĚLOHLÁVEK, Prague (Czech Republic).
Translations of titles to English are for easy reference only. In certain cases (exceptionally), the translation is not a *literal* translation, but an adapted translation of the title intended to best express the actual contents of the publication in English.
[2]   This sub-chapter includes some publications on selected EU law topics if they cross-boarding another areas of public [international] law and / or constitutional law. Predominantly EU law publications see the separate sub-chapter below.
[3]   Published in English.
[4]   Published in Czech.
[5]   Published in Czech.

ONDŘEJ SVAČEK, MEZINÁRODNÍ TRESTNÍ SOUD (2005-2017) [Title in translation – INTERNATIONAL CRIMINAL COURT (2005-2017], Prague: C. H. Beck, ISBN: 978-80-7400-683-8 (2018). [6]

PAVEL ŠTURMA; ČESTMÍR ČEPELKA, MEZINÁRODNÍ PRÁVO VEŘEJNÉ [Title in translation – PUBLIC INTERNATIONAL LAW], Prague: C. H. Beck, ISBN: 978-80-7400-721-7 (2018). [7]

BARBORA VLACHOVÁ, VYVLASTNĚNÍ A OCHRANA INVESTIC [Title in translation – EXPROPRIATION AND INVESTMENT PROTECTION], Prague: C. H. Beck, ISBN: 978-80-7400-708-8 (2018).[8]

The Lawyer Quarterly, Prague: Ústav státu a práva Akademie věd České republiky [Institute of State and Law of the Academy of Sciences of the Czech Republic], 2018, Vol. VIII, ISSN: 0231-6625[9]

Rastislav Funta, *Extraterritorial application of US-Antitrust law on global cartels from comparative (EU Law) perspective*, No. 3, pp. 214-223.

Jakub Handrlica, *"Exclusivism" in international nuclear law: the concept revisited*, No. 3, pp. 271-283.

Helena Hofmannová, *Comments on the approach to human dignity in case law*, No. 3, pp. 284-294.

Štefan Siskovič; Miriam Laclavíková, *Formation of the Czech Republic and Slovakia*, No. 3, pp. 193-213.

Právní rozhledy [*Law Review*], Prague: C. H. Beck, 2018, Vol. 26, ISSN: 1210-6410[10]

Jana Odehnalová, Řízení *o udělení mezinárodní ochrany z hlediska práva na spravedlivý proces* [Title in translation - *Proceedings for*

[6] Published in Czech.
[7] Published in Czech.
[8] Published in Czech.
[9] A subsidiary title to the monthly periodical Právník [in translation – *The Lawyer*] which will be published by the Institute of State and Law of the Academy of Science of the Czech Republic in Czech. Papers published in *The Lawyer Quarterly* are in English, exceptionally in other languages (German, for instance); abstracts are in English. For papers published in the periodical "*Právník*" [in translation – *The Lawyer*], issued monthly, see the separate excerpt from papers listed under the heading of the respective periodical.
[10] Papers published in Czech.

Granting International Protection from the Perspective of the Right to a Due Process], No. 4, p. 129-134.

Právník [Title in translation - *The Lawyer*], Prague: Ústav státu a práva Akademie věd České republiky [Institute of State and Law of the Academy of Sciences of the Czech Republic], 2018, Vol. 157, ISSN: 0231-6625[11]

Josef Blahož, Ústavněpolitická *koncepce prezidenta W. Wilsona a vznik* Československé *republiky* [Title in translation – *Constitutional and Policital Conceptions of the President Woodrow Wilson and the origin of the Czechoslovak Republic*], No. 10, p. 788-798.

Oldřich Florian, *Proč pouze lidská? Potíž s univerzalitou lidských práv* [Title in translation – *Why Only Human? The Problem with the Universality of Human Rights*], No. 11, p. 956-969.

David Kosař; Ladislav Vyhnánek, Ústavní *identita České republiky* [Title in translation – *Constitutional Identity of the Czech Republic*], No. 10, p. 854-872.

Jiří Malenovský, *Vznik a zánik Československa na pozadí zásady sebeurčení národů* [Title in translation – *Creation and Dissolution of Czechoslovakia against the Background of the Principle of Self-determination of Nations*], No. 10, p. 799-811.

I.1.2. [SVK] – [SLOVAK REPUBLIC] – Selected titles published in the Slovak Republic:

Monographs:

ĽUDMILA ALBERT; ADAM GIERTL; JÁN KLUČKA, REPETITÓRIUM MEDZINÁRODNÉHO PRÁVA VEREJNÉHO [Title in translation – PUBLIC INTERNATIONAL LAW HANDBOOK], Bratislava: Iuris Libri, ISBN: 978-80-89635-38-2 (2018).[12]

PETER LYSINA, MEDZINÁRODNÁ ZMLUVA AKO NÁSTROJ VONKAJŠEJ ČINNOSTI EURÓPSKEJ ÚNIE [Title in translation – INTERNATIONAL TREATY AS AN INSTRUMENT OF EXTERNAL

---

[11]   Papers published in Czech with abstracts in a foreign language. The abstract is most often in English (exceptionally in German or French).
[12]   Published in Slovak.

ACTIVITIES OF THE EUROPEAN UNION], Bratislava: Wolters Kluwer, ISBN: 978-80-8168-890-4 (2018).[13]

PETER VRŠANSKÝ; JOZEF VALUCH; DANIEL BEDNÁR, DOKUMENTY K ŠTÚDIU MEDZINÁRODNÉHO PRÁVA VEŘEJNÉHO. 1. ČÁST [Title in translation – DOCUMENTS FOR PUBLIC INTERNATIONAL LAW STUDIES. PART 1], Bratislava: Wolters Kluwer, ISBN: 978-80-8168-874-4 (2018).[14]

I.2. (Private) international law, European private international law and legal relations in foreign trade relations, including international arbitration and other private-law areas with transnational dimensions

I.2.1. [CZE] – [CZECH REPUBLIC] – Titles published within the Czech Republic

Monographs, Collections and Conference Proceedings

MATĚJ MACHŮ; EVA ADLEROVÁ, OCHRANA DUŠEVNÍHO VLASTNICTVÍ VE STÁTECH ANGLO-AMERICKÉ A SMÍŠENÉ PRÁVNÍ TRADICE [Title in translation – INTELLECTUAL PROPERTY PROTECTION IN THE COUNTRIES OF ANGLO-AMERICAN AND HYBRID LEGAL TRADITIONS], Prague: Wolters Kluwer ČR. ISBN: 978-80-7598-149-3.

ZDENĚK NOVÝ; KLÁRA DRLIČKOVÁ, ROLE VEŘEJNÉHO ZÁJMU V MEZINÁRODNÍ OBCHODNÍ A INVESTIČNÍ ARBITRÁŽI [Title in translation – ROLE OF PUBLIC INTEREST IN INTERNATIONAL COMMERCIAL AND INVESTMENT ARBITRATION], Prague: C. H. Beck, 2018. ISBN: 978-80-7400-687-6.[15]

BOHUMIL POLÁČEK, KAPITOLY Z MEZINÁRODNÍHO DOPRAVNÍHO PRÁVA III – E. SILNIČNÍ PRÁVO ET F. MULTIMODÁLNÍ PRÁVO [Title in translation – CHAPTERS FROM INTERNATIONAL TRANSPORTATION LAW III – E. ROAD TRANSPORT LAW ET F. MULTIMODAL TRANSPORT LAW], Prague: Wolters Kluwer ČR. ISBN: 978-80-7552-789-9.

---

[13] Published in Slovak.
[14] Published in Slovak.
[15] Published in Czech.

Naděžda Rozehnalová; Jiří Valdhans; Klára Drličková; Tereza. Kyselovská. Mezinárodní právo soukromé Evropské unie. [Title in translation – Private International Law of the European Union]. 2nd ed. Prague: Wolters Kluwer ČR. ISBN: 978-80-7598-123-3.

Květoslav Růžička; Bohumil Poláček; Radek Novák; Petr Dostalík, *Vliv římského práva na vybrané instituty práva mezinárodního obchodu* [Title in translation - *Influence of Roman Law on Selected Institutes of International Commercial Law*], Praha [Prague]: Wolters Kluwer ČR, 2018. ISBN 978-80-7598-143-1.

Bulletin advokacie [*Bulletin of the Czech Bar*], **Prague: Česká advokátní komora** [*Czech Bar Association*], **2018, ISSN: 1210-6348**[16]

Alexander J. Bělohlávek, *Notifikační povinnost rozhodců o svých vazbách na strany řízení ve světle mezinárodních standardů* [Title in translation – *Notification Duty of Arbitrators Regarding Their Connections to the Parties in the Light of International Standards*], No. 09, p. 36-39.

Jan Brodec; Helena Skalská; Barbora Vrbíková, *Rozhodné právo pro vypořádání majetkových poměrů manželů a pro dědictví a problémy s jejich koordinací* [Title in translation - *Law Applicable to the Settlement of the Communal Property of Spouses and to Inheritance and Problems with Their Coordination*], on-line edition.[17]

Martin Doleček, *Pravomoc soudů ve vztahu k rozhodčímu řízení* [Title in translation – *Court Jurisdiction in Relation to Arbitration*], No. 09, p. 40-42.

Pavel Horák, *Objektivní arbitrabilita* – **možnosti rozhodčího řízení** [Title in translation – *Objective Arbitrability* – *Courses of Action in Arbitration*], No. 09, p. 25-28.

Milan Kindl, *Na co nezapomínat při sjednávání rozhodčí smlouvy* [Title in translation – *Checklist for Negotiating an Arbitration Agreement*], No. 09, p. 29-32.

---

[16] Papers published in Czech with abstracts in a foreign language. Abstracts in English and in German.
[17] Available on http://www.bulletin-advokacie.cz/rozhodne-pravo-pro-vyporadani-majetkovych-pomeru
-manzelu-a-pro-dedictvi-a-problemy-s-jejich-koordinaci (accessed on 1 February 2019).

Martin Maisner, *Efektivita rozhodčího řízení* [Title in translation – *Effectiveness of Arbitration*], No. 09, p. 46-50.

Robert Němec; Viktor Glatz, *Rozhodčí řízení, jeho specifika a výhody* [Title in translation – *Arbitration, its Specifics and Advantages*], No. 09, p. 18-24.

David Řezníček, *Vykonatelnost a výkon rozhodčích nálezů* [Title in translation – *Enforceability and Enforcement of Arbitral Awards*], No. 09, p. 43-45.

Tomáš Sokol, *Konstituování rozhodčího fóra* [Title in translation – *Constitution of the Arbitration Forum*], No. 09, p. 32-35.

Obchodněprávní revue [Commercial Law Review], Prague: C.H.Beck, 2018, Vol. 10, ISSN: 1211-0558[18]

Alexander J. Bělohlávek, *Investigativní přístup ke zkoumání vlastní příslušnosti soudu jako předpoklad prosazení zásady důvěry v justici jiného členského státu EU: aktivní zkoumání mezinárodní příslušnosti soudem v insolvenčních věcech podle článku 4 nařízení č. 2015/848 revue* [Title in translation – *Inquisitorial Approach to the Examination of the Court's Own Jurisdiction as a Prerequisite for Enforcing the Principle of Trust in the Judiciary of another EU Member State: Active Examination of International Jurisdiction by Court in Insolvency Matters pursuant to Article 4 of Regulation No 2015/848 Rgulation*], Issue No. 3, p. 65-73.

Alexander J. Bělohlávek, *Rozhodčí řízení versus insolvenční řízení z pohledu práva EU – část 1* [Title in translation – *Arbitration versus Insolvency Proceedings from the Perspective of EU Law – Part 1*], Issue No. 6, p. 161-177.

Alexander J. Bělohlávek, *Rozhodčí řízení versus insolvenční řízení z pohledu práva EU – část 2* [Title in translation – *Arbitration versus Insolvency Proceedings from the Perspective of EU Law – Part 2*], Issue No. 7-8, p. 193-209.

[18] Papers published in Czech. Summary in German.

Obchodní právo [Commercial Law], Prague: Wolters Kluwer ČR, a.s., 2018, Vol. X, ISSN: 1210-8278, Reg.No Ministry of Cultural Affairs Czech Republic E 6020 MIČ 46032[19]

Alexander J. Bělohlávek, *Povinnost informovat známé zahraniční věřitele v režimu evropského insolvenčního řízení* [Title in translation – *Duty to Inform Known Foreign Creditors in European Insolvency Proceedings*], OBCHODNÍ PRÁVO [Title in translation – COMMERCIAL LAW], PRAHA [PRAGUE / CZECH REPUBLIC]: KLUWER, 2018, ROČ. [VOL.] XXVII, ČÁST I: [PART I], Č. [ISSUE NO.] 10, S. [P.] 355-368, ČÁST II: [PART II], Č. [ISSUE NO.] 11, S. [P.] 394-404. ISSN: 1210-8278, REG. Č. MK ČR [REG.NO MINISTRY OF CULTURAL AFFAIRS CZECH REPUBLIC] E 6020 MIČ 46032. ORIGINÁLNÍ JAZYK: ČEŠTINA, ABSTRAKT V ANGLIČTINĚ [ORIGINAL LANGUAGE: CZECH, SUMMARY IN ENGLISH].

Právník [Title in translation - *The Lawyer*], Prague: Ústav státu a práva Akademie věd České republiky [Institute of State and Law of the Academy of Sciences of the Czech Republic], 2018, Vol. 157, ISSN: 0231-6625[20]

Magdalena Pfeiffer, *Předběžná otázka v kolizi právních* řádů [Title in translation – *Incidental Question in Conflicts of Laws*], No. 1, p. 65-79.

Monika Pauknerová, *Prostor pro uvážení v českém mezinárodním právu soukromém: ohlédnutí se za mezinárdním právem soukromým k výroční Antnína Hobzy* [Title in translation – *Judicial Discretion in the Czech Private International Law: Looking Back at Czech Private International Law in Honour of Antonín Hobza*], No. 1, p. 12-28.

The Lawyer Quarterly, Prague: Ústav státu a práva Akademie věd České republiky [Institute of State and Law of the Academy of Sciences of the Czech Republic], 2018, Vol. VIII, ISSN: 0231-6625[21]

Alexander J. Bělohlávek, *Anti-suit injunctions in arbitral and judicial*

---

[19]   Papers published in Czech. Summary in English.
[20]   Papers published in Czech with abstracts in a foreign language. The abstract is most often in English (exceptionally in German or French).
[21]   A subsidiary title to the monthly periodical Právník [in translation – *The Lawyer*] which will be published by the Institute of State and Law of the Academy of Science of the Czech Republic in Czech. Papers published in *The Lawyer Quarterly* are primarily in English, exceptionally in other languages (such as German); abstracts are in English. For papers published in the periodical *"Právník"* [in translation – *The Lawyer*], issued monthly, see the separate excerpt from papers listed under the heading of the respective periodical.

procedures in the Czech Republic, No. 4, p. 322-331.

Monika Pauknerová; Magdalena Pfeiffer, *Use of UNIDROIT principles of international commercial contracts to interpret or supplement Czech contract law*, No. 4, p. 452-468.

Monika Pauknerová; Monika Feigerlová, *Private International law for corporate Social Responsibility*, No. 4, p. 379-399.

Other publications

Alexander J. Bělohlávek. *Rozhodčí řízení v mezinárodním obchodním styku podle zákona č. 98/1963 Sb.* [Title in translation - *Arbitration in International Commercial Transactions pursuant to Act No. 98/1963 Coll.*], XI ENCYKLOPEDIE ČESKÝCH PRÁVNÍCH DĚJIN [ENCYCLOPEDIA OF CZECH LEGAL HISTORY / ENZYKLOPÄDIE DER TSCHECHISCHEN RECHTSGESCHICHTE], ŘÍZENÍ [PROCEEDINGS], PLZEŇ [PILSEN / CZECH REPUBLIC] / OSTRAVA [CZECH REPUBLIC]: ALEŠ ČENĚK / KEY PUBLISHING, ISBN: 978-80-7380-715-3 / ISBN: 978-80-7418-282-2, p. 615-620 (Karel Schelle; Jaromír Tauchen eds., 2018).[22]

Monika Pauknerová, *Mezinárodní příslušnost soudu a právo použitelné na smlouvu o převodu obchodního podílu* [Title in translation - *International Court Jurisdiction and Law Applicable to a Share Transfer Agreement*], POCTA ALENĚ WINTEROVÉ K 80. NAROZENINÁM, PRAHA [PRAGUE]: VŠEHRD, p. 218–226 (In Jan Dvořák et Alena Macková eds., 2018).

I.2.2. [CZE] – [CZECH REPUBLIC] – Selected titles of Czech authors published outside the Czech Republic

Alexander J. Bělohlávek, *Interaction between international arbitration and cross-border insolvency – challenges faced by the arbitrators: Effects of Art 18 of the Regulation of the European Parliament and of the Council (EU) No. 2015/848* [Titul v překladu - *Interakce mezi mezinárodním rozhodčím řízením a přeshraniční insolvencí – výzvy rozhodcům: účinky čl. 18 nařízení Evropského parlamentu a Rady (EU) č. 2015/848*], RECENT DEVELOPMENTS IN PRIVATE INTERNATIONAL LAW CHIŞINĂU [CHISINAU –

22 Published in Czech.

REPUBLIC MOLDOVA]: FACULTY OF LAW – MOLDOVA STATE UNIVERSITY [UNIV. DE STAT DIN MOLDOVA], ISBN: 978-9975-108-22-5 (print), p. 234-269 (Mihail Buruiană ed., 2018).[23]

D. KRÁLIK, THIRD PARTY PROTECTION IN PRIVATE INTERNATIONAL LAW. Warszawa: C. H. Beck, p. 37-59. ISBN 978-83-255-9554-8. (Agata Koziol; Paulina Twardoch (eds.) 2018).

Monika Pauknerová, *Réflexions sur la Convention de Bruxelles du point de vue tchèque* – **Reflections on the Brussels Convention from the Czech perspective**, REVUE CRITIQUE DE DROIT INTERNATIONAL PRIVE, issue No 3, p. 529-540 (2018).

MONIKA PAUKNEROVÁ, INTERNATIONAL JURISDICTION OF A COURT AND THE LAW APPLICABLE TO A SHARE TRANSFER AGREEMENT, Europa als Rechts- und Lebensraum, Gieseking Verlag, p. 385-392 (Burkard Hess, Erik Jayme, Heinz-Peter Mansel eds., 2018).

MONIKA PAUKNEROVÁ; HELENA SKALSKÁ, ENFORCEMENT AND EFFECTIVENESS OF CONSUMER LAW IN THE CZECH REPUBLIC, Enforcement and Effectiveness of Consumer Law, Springer Verlag, p. 227-248 (Hans W. Micklitz, Geneviève Saumier eds., 2018).

KVĚTOSLAV RŮŽIČKA; MARKÉTA ČERVENKOVÁ RŮŽIČKOVÁ, ROZHODNÉ PRÁVO V PRACOVNÍM PRÁVU [Title in translation – LAW APPLICABLE IN EMPLOYMENT LAW MATTERS], Pocta Věře *Štangové* [Liber Amicorum *Věra Štangová*]. Plzeň: Aleš Čeněk, p. 291–298, ISBN 978-80-7380-735-1 (Kristina Koldinská ed., 2018).

I.3. EU Law (general, not classified under Chapter I.1. or I.2. above)

I.3.1. [CZE] – [CZECH REPUBLIC] – Titles published within the Czech Republic

Monographs, Collections and Conference Proceedings

VÁCLAV STEHLÍK; ONDREJ HAMUĽÁK; PETR MICHAL, PRÁVO EVROPSKÉ UNIE. ÚSTAVNÍ ZÁKLADY A VNITŘNÍ TRH [Title in translation - EUROPEAN UNION LAW. CONSTITUTIONAL BASIS

---

[23] Published in English.

AND INTERNAL MARKET]. Prague: Leges, ISBN: 978-80-7502-277-6 (2018).

IVA CHVÁTALOVÁ ET AL., PRÁVO SOCIÁLNÍHO ZABEZPEČENÍ V ČESKÉ REPUBLICE A EVROPSKÉ UNII. [Title in translation - SOCIAL SECURITY LAW IN THE CZECH REPUBLIC AND THE EUROPEAN UNION], Plzeň [Pilsen]: Aleš Čeněk, ISBN: 978-80-7380-732-0 (2nd ed., 2018).[24]

MICHAL NULÍČEK; JOSEF DONÁT; FRANTIŠEK NONNEMANN; BOHUSLAV LICHNOVSKÝ; JAN TOMÍŠEK; KRISTÝNA KOVAŘÍKOVÁ, GDPR / OBECNÉ NAŘÍZENÍ O OCHRANĚ OSOBNÍCH ÚDAJŮ. [Title in translation - GDPR / GENERAL DATA PROTECTION REGULATION], Prague: Wolters Kluwer ČR. ISBN: 978-80-7598-068-7 (2nd ed., 2018).[25]

MICHAL PETR, VZTAH ČESKÉHO A UNIJNÍHO SOUTĚŽNÍHO PRÁVA [Title in translation – RELATION BETWEEN CZECH AND EUROPEAN COMPETITION LAW], Prague: C. H. Beck, ISBN: 978-80-7400-669-2 (2018).[26]

NADĚŽDA ROZEHNALOVÁ; JIŘÍ VALDHANS; KLÁRA DRLIČKOVÁ; TEREZA KYSELOVSKÁ, MEZINÁRODNÍ PRÁVO SOUKROMÉ EVROPSKÉ UNIE. [Title in translation – PRIVATE INTERNATIONAL LAW OF THE EUROPEAN UNION]. Prague: Wolters Kluwer ČR. ISBN: 978-80-7598-123-3 (2nd ed., 2018).[27]

VÁCLAV ŠMEJKAL; OLGA FRANCOVÁX MICHAEL KOHAJDA; RICHARD KRÁL; TEREZA KUNERTOVÁ; LENKA PÍTROVÁ; HARALD CHRISTIAN SCHEU; PAVEL SVOBODA; MAGDALÉNA SVOBODOVÁ; ANETA VONDRÁČKOVÁ; ROMAN VYBÍRAL; JIŘÍ ZEMÁNEK, EVROPSKÁ UNIE PO BREXITU. PRÁVNĚ-INSTITUCIONÁLNÍ BUDOUCNOST EVROPSKÉ INTEGRACE [Title in translation – EUROPEAN UNION AFTER BREXIT. LEGAL AND INSTITUTIONAL FUTURE OF EUROPEAN INTEGRATION]. Prague: Wolters Kluwer ČR. ISBN: 978-80-7598-098-4.

LUBOŠ TICHÝ, NAŘÍZENÍ ŘÍM II [Title in translation – ROME II REGULATION]. Prague: C. H. Beck, ISBN: 978-80-7400-713-3 (2018).

---

[24] Published in Czech.
[25] Published in Czech.
[26] Published in Czech.
[27] Published in Czech.

BARBORA VLACHOVÁ, VYVLASTNĚNÍ A OCHRANA INVESTIC [Title in translation – EXPROPRIATION AND INVESTMENT PROTECTION]. Prague: C. H. Beck, ISBN: 978-80-7400-708-8 (2018).

The Lawyer Quarterly, Prague: Ústav státu a práva Akademie věd České republiky [Institute of State and Law of the Academy of Sciences of the Czech Republic], 2018, Vol. VIII, ISSN: 0231-6625[28]

Max Steuer, *Constitutional Pluralism And The Slovak Constitutional Court: The Challenge of European Union Law*, No. 2, p. 108-128.

Právník [Title in translation - *The Lawyer*], Prague: Ústav státu a práva Akademie věd České republiky [Institute of State and Law of the Academy of Sciences of the Czech Republic], 2018, Vol. 157, ISSN: 0231-6625[29]

Tomáš Břicháček, *Evropský pilíř sociálních práv* [Title in translation – *European Pillar of Social Rights*], No. 11, p. 922-944.

Libor Havelka, *Důsledky a limity harmonizace vnitrostátních trestních sankcí prostřednictvím unijního práva: příklad ochrany finančních zájmů Evropské unie* [Title in translation – *The Limits and Consequences of the Harmonization of Criminal Sanctions for the Enforcement of EU Law: the Example of the Fight Against Frau to the Union´s Financial Interests*], No 3, p. 187-199.

David Müller; Ondřej Svoboda, *Právní aspekty investiční politiky Evropské unie* [Title in translation – *Legal Aspects of the EU Investment Policy*], No 3, p. 221-235.

Právní rozhledy [Title in translation – *Law Review*], Prague: C. H. Beck, 2018, Vol. 26, ISSN: 1210-6410[30]

Martina Fojtová, *Členství občanů EU v politických stranách (nejen) v kontextu rovných podmínek výkonu volebního práva* [Title in

---

[28] A subsidiary title to the monthly periodical Právník [in translation – *The Lawyer*] which will be published by the Institute of State and Law of the Academy of Science of the Czech Republic in Czech. Papers published in *The Lawyer Quarterly* are primarily in English, exceptionally in other languages (such as German); abstracts are in English. For papers published in the periodical "*Právník*" [in translation – *The Lawyer*], issued monthly, see the separate excerpt from papers listed under the heading of the respective periodical.

[29] Papers published in Czech with abstracts in a foreign language. The abstract is most often in English (exceptionally in German or French).

[30] Papers published in Czech.

translation - *Membership of EU Citizens in Political Parties (Also) in the Context of Equal Requirements for the Exercise of the Voting Right*], No. 19, p. 665-671.

Helena Pullmannová, *Vztah a limity používání obchodního jména a ochranné známky v judikatuře SDEU* [Title in translation - *Relationship and Limits of Using Company Name and Trade Mark in CJ EU Case Law*], No. 19, p. 649-656.

Právník [Title in translation - *The Lawyer*], Prague: Ústav státu a práva Akademie věd České republiky [Institute of State and Law of the Academy of Sciences of the Czech Republic], 2018, Vol. 157, ISSN: 0231-6625[31]

Magdaléna Svobodová, *Přímý účinek vnějších smluv v konfrontaci s přímým účinkem směrnic EU z pohledu jednotlivce* [Title in translation – *Direct Effect of EU International Agreements in Comparison with Direct Effect of EU Directives from the Perspective of Individuals*], No. 2, p. 115-130.

Pavel Svoboda, *Má EU pravomoci k dosaženícíle sociálně-tržního hospodářství?* [Title in translation – *Does the EU Have the Competences to Achieve the Objective of a Social Market Economy?*], No. 2, p. 143-157.

I.3.2. [SVK] – [SLOVAK REPUBLIC]

Monographs, Collections and Conference Proceedings

ZUZANA ŠIDLOVÁ; ELVÍRA UNGEROVÁ, JUDIKATÚRA SÚDNEHO DVORA EÚ ZA ROK 2017 VO VECIACH DANE Z PRIDANEJ HODNOTY [Title in translation – CASE LAW OF THE COURT OF JUSTICE OF THE EUROPEAN UNION IN 2017 IN VALUE ADDED TAX MATTERS]. Bratislava: Aleš Čeněk, ISBN: 978-80-8168-924-4 (2018).[32]

---

[31] Papers published in Czech with abstracts in a foreign language. The abstract is most often in English (exceptionally in German or French).

[32] Published in Czech.

II.   CURRENT EVENTS

II.1.   Selected scientific conferences, seminars, academic lectures and other professional events in the Czech Republic and in the Slovak Republic[1]

[CZE] Prague, 10 – 11 May 2018
Conference on *Constitutional Continuity between the Czech Republic and the Czechoslovak Tradition*. Organized by the Faculty of Law of the Charles University.

[SVK] Kúpele Nimnica [Spa Nimnica], 12 – 14 October 2018
XIth Slovak – Czech International Law Symposium organized by the Slovak Society for International Law at the Slovak Academy for International Law, supported by the Slovak Ministry of Foreign and European Affairs together with the Czech Society for International Law.[2]

[CZE] Prague, 29 – 30 November 2018
Conference on *Universal Declaration of Human Rights and the Convention on the Prevention and Punishment of the Crime of Genocide: 70th Anniversary*.

---

[1]   Contributions mentioned herein represent a selection from papers related to issues with an international element. CYIL editors hereby apologize to the lecturers for omitting some of them and their topics due to the limited space provided for this section. Editors referred especially to published and other accessible information. Readers are specifically warned that the information about papers presented at the individual conferences and other academic and scientific events is only a selection and definitely does not provide a full report on the entire proceedings and the academic scope of each particular event.

[2]   For more information see http://www.ssmp-ssil.org.

III.   Past CYIL and CYArb® Presentations in 2018

[CZE] Prague, 14 December 2018

First Launch of Prague Rules, Prague [Czech Republic].
Session I - The History and the Spirit of the Prague Rules. Speakers: Alexander J. Bělohlávek and Vladimir Khvalei
Session II – Showing a sphinx face. Limits of the tribunal's role in the managing of arbitration proceedings. Speakers: Duarte Henriques, Hilary Heilbron QC, Beata Gessel-Kalinowska vel Kalisz, Klaus Peter Berger. Topics: Role of the Tribunal in Administering Arbitration Proceedings: the difference between Prague Rules and IBA Rules; Limits of Tribunal's role in managing arbitration; Is there a duty of tribunal to establish facts; The Proactive Facilitation of Settlement by International Arbitrators.
Session III – Let's not decide anything until we decide everything? In-house expectations on the outcome of arbitration and tribunal's role in facilitation of settlement. Speakers: Michael McIlwrath, Dr. Clemens-August Heusch, Susanne Gropp-Stadler.
Session IV – Is the sky the only limit? Scope of discovery and e-discovery in arbitration. Speakers: Andrey Panov (moderator), Michael W. Bühler, Dorothy Murray. Topics: Discovery in Arbitration: Use and Abuse, Tribunal's Role in Document Disclosure, Civil Law vs. Common Law Approach.
Session V – Lie to me. Fact witnesses vs. documentary evidence: can documents lie? Speakers: José Rosell, Olena Perepelinska. Topics: Role of Witness Statements In Evidentiary Process, Tribunal's Role In Managing Witnesses, Weight of Witness Statements In Tribunal's Eyes, Can Witness Lie?

IV. Important Web Sites

http://www.czechyearbook.org; http://www.lexlata.pro

Czech Yearbook of International Law® and Czech (& Central European) Yearbook of Arbitration®

The website is currently available in sixteen languages: English, Bulgarian, Czech, Chinese, Japanese, Korean, Hungarian, German, Polish, Romanian, Russian, Portuguese, Slovenian, Spanish, Ukrainian, Vietnamese. This website allows access to the annotations of all core articles and to information about the authors of these articles as well as to the entire remaining contents (except core articles) of both yearbooks (CYIL and CYArb®).

IV.1.   [CZE] – [CZECH REPUBLIC]

- http://www.cnb.cz. Česká národná banka (Czech National Bank as the Central bank of the Czech Republic).[1]
- http://www.compet.cz. Office for the protection of competition.[2]
- http://www.concourt.cz. The Constitutional Court of the Czech Republic.[3]
- http://www.csesp.cz. Czech Society for European and Comparative Law.[4]
- http://www.csmp-csil.org. The Czech Society Of International Law.[5]
- http://www.czech.cz. Portal „Hello Czech Republic". Basic information about the Czech Republic and news interesting for foreigners. Rather a promotional portal.[6]
- http://www.czso.cz. Czech Statistical Office.[7]
- http://dtjvcnsp.org. Česko-německý spolek právníků. [Czech-German Lawyers Association]. Deutsch-Tschechische Juristenvereinigung e.V.[8]
- http://ekf.vsb.cz. Faculty of Economics, VŠB Technical University

---

[1]   Website available in English and Czech.
[2]   Website available in English and Czech. Basic laws and regulations on the protection of competition in the Czech Republic are also available at the website, both in Czech and in English (unofficial translation).
[3]   Website available in English and Czech. Part of the (significant) case law also available in English.
[4]   Website available in English and Czech.
[5]   Website available in Czech. In English only a brief summary of the webpages.
[6]   Website available in English, Czech, French, German, Russian and Spanish.
[7]   Website available in English and Czech.
[8]   Website available in German.

Czech Yearbook of International Law®

of Ostrava.[9]

- http://www.hrad.cz.[10] Website of the Office of the President of the Czech Republic.
- http://www.icc-cr.cz. ICC National Committee Czech Republic
- http://www.iir.cz. Institute Of International Relations Prague.[11]
- http://www.ilaw.cas.cz. Ústav státu a práva Akademie věd ČR, v.v.i. [Institute of State and Law of the Academy of Sciences of the Czech Republic][12]
- http://www.jednotaceskychpravniku.cz. Jednota českých právníků [Czech Lawyers Union]
- http://justice.cz. Czech justice portal including both courts and the Ministry of Justice, prosecution departments, Judicial Academy, Institute of Criminology and Social Prevention, as well as the Probation and Mediation Service and the Prison Service.[13]
- http://www.law.muni.cz. Faculty of Law, Masaryk University, Brno.[14]
- http://www.mzv.cz. Ministry of Foreign Affairs of the Czech Republic.[15]
- http://www.nsoud.cz. The Supreme Court of the Czech Republic.[16]
- http://www.nssoud.cz. The Supreme Administrative Court of the Czech Republic.[17]
- http://www.ochrance.cz. Public Defender of Rights (Ombudsman).[18]
- http://www.ok.cz/iksp/en/aboutus.html. Institute of Criminology and Social Prevention.[19]
- http://portal.gov.cz. Portal of the Public Administration.[20] This website allows access to the websites of most supreme public administration authorities (including ministries).
- http://www.prf.cuni.cz. Faculty of Law, Charles University in Prague.[21]

---

[9]   Website available in English and Czech. Some information (regarding post-graduate studies) also available in German. Department of Law see http://en.ekf.vsb.cz/information-about/departments/structure/departments/dept-119 (in English).
[10]   Website available in English and Czech. This website also allows access to the personal webpage of the President of the Czech Republic.
[11]   Website available in English and Czech. This Institute was founded by the Ministry of Foreign Affairs of the Czech Republic.
[12]   Website available in English and Czech.
[13]   Website available in Czech. The individual websites of the institutions covered by this portal also contain pages or summary information in English.
[14]   Website available in English and Czech.
[15]   Website available in Czech. Important information from this portal also available in English.
[16]   Website available in Czech. Some basic information also in English and French.
[17]   Website available in English and Czech.
[18]   Website available in English and Czech.
[19]   Website available in English and Czech.
[20]   Website available in English and Czech.
[21]   Website available in Czech. Basic information available in English.

- http://www.psp.cz. Parliament of the Czech Republic. Chamber of Deputies.[22]
- http://www.senat.cz. Parliament of the Czech Republic. Senate.[23]
- http://www.society.cz/wordpress/#awp. Common Law Society.[24]
- http://www.soud.cz. Arbitration Court attached to the Economic Chamber of the Czech Republic and Agricultural Chamber of the Czech Republic.[25]
- http://www.umpod.cz. Office for International Legal Protection of Children.[26]
- http://www.upol.cz/fakulty/pf/. Faculty of Law. Palacký University, Olomouc.
- http://www.vse.cz. The University of Economics, Prague.[27]
- http://www.zcu.cz/fpr/. Faculty of Law, Western Bohemia University in Pilsen.[28]

IV.2.   [SVK] – [SLOVAK REPUBLIC]

- http://www.concourt.sk. Constitutional Court of the Slovak Republic.[29]
- http://www.flaw.uniba.sk. Faculty of Law, Comenius University in Bratislava (SVK).[30]
- http://iuridica.truni.sk. Faculty of Law. Trnava University in Trnava (SVK).[31]
- http://www.justice.gov.sk. Ministry of Justice of the Slovak Republic.[32]
- http://www.nbs.sk. Národná banka Slovenska (National Bank of Slovakia as the Central bank of Slovak Republic).[33]
- http://www.nrsr.sk. National Council of the Slovak Republic (*Slovak Parliament*).[34]
- http://www.prf.umb.sk. Faculty of Law. Matej Bel University, Banská Bystrica (SVK).

---

[22]   Website available in English and Czech.
[23]   Website available in English and Czech.
[24]   Website available in Czech.
[25]   Website available in English, Czech, German and Russian.
[26]   The Office is the Central authority responsible for protection of children in civil matters having cross-border implications. Website available in English and Czech.
[27]   Website available in English and Czech.
[28]   Website available in Czech.
[29]   Website available in English and Slovak.
[30]   Website available in English and Slovak.
[31]   Website available in English and Slovak.
[32]   Website available in English and Slovak. This website also allows access to the following portals: Courts, Slovak Agent before the European Court for Human Rights, Slovak Agent before the Court of Justice of the European Union, The Judicial Academy.
[33]   Website available in English and Slovak.
[34]   Website available in English, French, German and Slovak.

Czech Yearbook of International Law®

- http://www.prezident.sk. President of the Slovak Republic and Office of the President (SVK).[35]
- http://www.uninova.sk/pf_bvsp/src_angl/index.php. Faculty of Law, Pan European University (SVK).[36]
- http://www.upjs.sk/pravnicka-fakulta. Faculty of Law, Pavol Jozef Šafárik University in Košice (SVK).[37]
- http://www.usap.sav.sk. Institute of State and Law, Slovak Academy of Science.[38]

---

[35] Website available in English and Slovak.
[36] Website available in English, German and Slovak.
[37] Website available in English and Slovak.
[38] Website available in Slovak.

Index

A

absolute judicial immunity
13/26, 29

aircraft hijackings
3/15

applicable law
4/29, 30, 39, 40, 41, 46;
5/12, 13, 14; 6/18, 20; 7/30,
31, 34; 9/11, 23; 11/27, 30;
13/4; 14/2; 16/39

arbitration   1/2; 7/10,
15, 22, 25, 32, 33, 34, 35,
36, 43; 9/2, 4, 5, 6, 7, 11,
12, 13, 14, 15, 17, 18, 23,
24, 27, 29, 34, 35; 10/5;
11/3; 13/19, 20; 14/44;
15/12, 27, 31, 32, 33, 35,
37; 16/15, 16

armed forces
1/34; 4/7, 11, 30, 39, 40;
8/12

article 4(2) TEU
4/2, 3, 4, 5, 7, 9, 13, 18, 19,
22, 26, 27, 29, 30, 33, 34,
38, 40, 43, 44

C

civil law   1/3,   28;
3/2, 3, 4, 5, 10, 20, 24; 5/1,
10, 11, 12, 16; 7/15, 16, 22,
30, 36, 43; 8/12, 25; 10/17;
11/26, 27; 12/3, 6, 10, 14,
17, 21, 22, 25, 27; 13/2, 4,
6, 13, 19, 21, 22, 23, 24, 25,
27, 28, 31; 14/36, 37, 44,
46

close connection
3/4, 19, 20, 21, 24, 25, 32;
8/19; 14/45, 46, 49

commercial arbitration
7/10, 22, 25, 32, 33, 34, 35,
36; 9/11, 12; 11/3; 13/19;
14/44

common good
4/32, 37, 47; 10/3, 7, 13,
17; 16/4

competition   3/8,   21,
22; 4/16, 34, 36, 37, 38;
7/31

constitution   2/1, 3, 8;
4/2, 3, 4, 7, 8, 29, 31, 39,
43; 5/2; 6/1, 2, 3, 4, 9, 14,
15, 17, 18, 19, 20, 21, 22,
23, 24, 25, 26, 27, 28, 29,
30, 31, 33, 35; 7/8, 10, 21,
28, 37; 8/6, 7, 8, 9, 12, 19;
9/15, 16; 10/1; 11/2, 3, 4,
5, 6, 7, 9, 10, 11, 12, 13, 14,
15, 17, 18, 20, 21, 22, 23,

7/34; **9**/11; **15**/16, 23

J

judicial immunity

13/1, 5, 7, 15, 17, 19, 20, 21, 23, 26, 29

jurisdiction **2**/2, 3, 5, 6, 10; **3**/1, 2, 3, 4, 5, 6, 7, 8, 9, 10, 12, 13, 14, 15, 16, 17, 18, 19, 20, 21, 22, 23, 24, 25, 26, 27, 28, 29, 30, 32, 34, 35; **4**/23, 24, 47; **5**/3, 4, 10, 14, 15, 18; **7**/31; **8**/11, 12, 13, 20, 21; **9**/16, 24, 25, 26, 27, 28, 30; **10**/3, 5; **11**/1, 8; **12**/25; **13**/5, 6, 7, 14, 15, 16, 19, 20, 21, 23, 29, 31; **14**/1, 3, 4, 5, 6, 7, 8, 10, 12, 13, 15, 16, 17, 18, 20, 21, 22, 23, 24, 27, 31, 35, 36, 37, 38, 39, 40, 41, 42, 43, 44, 45, 46, 48, 49; **15**/21, 27, 29, 31; **16**/22, 25, 26, 27, 49

L

law of bubbles

1/72

legal

- concepts **2**/5; **6**/3; **7**/4, 21, 23; **12**/1, 3, 15, 20, 23, 25, 26, 30; **14**/13; **16**/2, 4, 5, 6, 11, 13

- order of the european union **1**/1, 5, 6, 7, 9, 10, 11, 14, 18, 20, 21, 22, 24, 28, 31, 37, 44, 45, 46, 66, 69, 70, 82; **2**/2, 3, 5, 6, 7, 8, 12, 16, 17, 19, 26; **3**/2, 18, 22, 25, 26, 27, 29, 33; **4**/1, 2, 7, 15, 31; **5**/1, 2, 3, 6, 14, 18; **6**/1, 2, 3, 7, 9, 10, 11, 12, 14, 15, 16, 17, 18, 20, 26, 30, 33, 34, 35; **7**/1, 2, 4, 6, 8, 9, 10, 12, 17, 18, 20, 21, 22, 23, 24, 25, 26, 27, 28, 29, 30, 31, 32, 33, 34, 35, 36, 37, 38, 39, 41, 43; **8**/1, 2, 4, 9, 12, 14, 18, 21, 22, 24, 25, 27, 28, 29, 30, 31, 32, 38; **9**/3, 4, 7, 10, 11, 13, 14, 15, 22, 23, 27, 34, 35; **10**/2, 5, 6, 7, 13; **11**/2, 5, 11, 24, 25, 26, 27, 30, 31, 32; **12**/1, 3, 6, 7, 12, 14, 15, 20, 21, 22, 23, 24, 25, 26, 27, 28, 29, 30, 31, 34, 36, 37; **13**/1, 4, 6, 9, 15, 19, 22, 28, 30, 31; **14**/3, 5, 6, 11, 13, 28, 29, 31, 35, 37, 40, 44, 48; **15**/4, 11, 14, 15, 16; **16**/1, 2, 3, 4, 5, 6, 7, 8, 11, 13, 14, 16, 19, 20, 21, 43, 47, 51, 53, 56

- status **2**/2; **4**/7; **5**/1; **6**/15; **7**/6, 9, 10, 12, 17, 32; **8**/4, 38; **10**/2; **16**/2, 4, 13, 51, 53, 56

legalization of proceeds from

crime   3/18

lex mercatoria

     7/19, 21, 22, 24, 30, 33

local norms   7/6, 38, 40, 43

M

main criminal offence

     3/18; **11**/1

member states

     1/26; **2**/8, 9, 10, 12, 13, 15, 16, 17, 18, 19, 20, 21, 22, 23, 25, 26, 27; **3**/23; **4**/2, 3, 4, 5, 6, 7, 9, 11, 12, 13, 14, 15, 16, 17, 18, 19, 20, 22, 23, 24, 25, 27, 28, 29, 30, 31, 32, 33, 34, 35, 36, 37, 38, 39, 40, 41, 43, 44, 46, 47; **5**/2, 18; **6**/1, 3, 14, 15, 24, 30; **7**/34, 35; **8**/4, 13, 14, 19, 38; **9**/1, 15; **11**/1, 2, 31, 32; **15**/5, 23; **16**/10, 22

money laundering

     3/18; **8**/17; **11**/1

N

national

     - identity   2/15; **4**/2, 7, 43, 44; **7**/4, 11, 40

     - security   1/3, 8, 11; **2**/20, 27; **4**/2, 3, 4, 6, 7, 9, 10, 11, 12, 13, 15, 17, 18, 19, 22, 25, 26, 27, 29, 30, 31, 32, 33, 34, 35, 37, 38, 39, 40, 41, 42, 43, 44,

45, 46, 47; **8**/23, 25; **9**/16; **11**/2; **12**/27; **15**/8, 13, 17, 23, 24

- security organization

     1/8; **4**/10, 11, 12, 29, 30, 31, 32, 35, 38, 39, 40, 41, 43; **8**/25

non-intervention

     2/3, 7; **5**/18; **8**/27, 28; **16**/29, 30, 37

non-state law

     2/3, 7, 12, 20; **3**/6, 8, 24; **4**/34, 40, 46; **5**/13, 16; **7**/10, 11, 25, 31, 34, 35, 38, 43; **8**/1, 28, 37, 38; **9**/1, 15; **10**/3, 13; **13**/31; **16**/14

O

offense   1/17, 83; **11**/9, 10, 13, 18, 21, 23, 27, 29; **12**/15, 23, 27

ordre public   3 / 3 5 ; **8**/24

P

passive personality

     3/13, 14

personality   2 / 1 0 ; **3**/12, 13, 14; **8**/9, 14; **12**/25, 27

police   4/10, 14, 18, 20, 21, 22, 23, 24, 27, 28, 30, 31, 39, 40, 41, 47;

6/15; **8**/36

principle

- of passive personality
3/13, 14; **14**/43, 46

- of personality **2** / 1 0 ;
3/12, 13, 14; **8**/9, 14

- of territoriality **2**/5; **3**/8,
12, 14; **8**/15; **14**/14

- of universality **3**/15

private international law
3/5, 32; **5**/11; **7**/1,
2, 7, 16, 19, 21, 22, 24, 25,
27, 28, 30, 33, 34, 35, 36,
38, 39, 41, 43; **8**/32; **11**/6;
13/7, 8, 19; **14**/15, 36, 37,
38; **15**/13, 31

private law sphere
3/5; **7**/1, 15, 19, 22, 29, 30,
33, 34, 39; **12**/2, 4, 15

prohibition of interference
(non-interference)
3/24

protection   **1**/19; **2**/5,
6, 7, 8, 11, 12, 13, 14, 15,
16, 17, 18, 19, 20, 21, 22,
23, 24, 25, 26, 27; **3**/21, 22,
28, 29, 30; **4**/2, 4, 14, 15,
17, 19, 32, 36, 37, 40, 41,
43, 47; **5**/1, 2, 3, 6, 7, 8, 10,
11, 13, 14, 16; **6**/15; **8**/16,
20, 25, 35, 41; **9**/2, 6, 11,
15, 16, 18, 22, 27, 30, 34;
10/6, 7, 13, 16, 17; **11**/1, 6,
11, 12, 17, 27, 30, 32; **12**/1,

2, 3, 4, 5, 6, 7, 8, 10, 12, 13,
14, 15, 16, 17, 18, 20, 21,
22, 23, 24, 25, 26, 27, 29,
30, 31, 32, 33, 34, 35, 36,
37; **13**/19; **14**/22, 34, 44,
46, 47; **15**/8, 20, 29; **16**/23

public international law
1/9, 70; **2**/2, 8, 9,
10, 12, 15; **3**/1, 2, 3, 4, 5, 6,
8, 12, 13, 16, 19, 21, 23, 24,
28, 35; **5**/2, 10, 11, 16; **6**/2,
3; **7**/2, 7, 10, 11, 16, 19, 21,
27, 28, 34, 37; **8**/2, 9, 24,
31, 32; **9**/7, 11, 13, 14, 34;
10/16; **11**/2, 4, 6, 17, 32;
13/2; **14**/6, 15, 37; **15**/13;
16/11, 12, 14

public policy
2/8; **3**/35; **4**/25, 31, 39;
7/19, 34; **8**/31; **9**/11;
11/27; **14**/3; **15**/23

purpose of sanctions
1/50, 51, 52, 60

R

recognition of a decision
1/22; **3**/20, 31, 34, 35;
6/10; **7**/28, 41; **8**/24, 38;
11/1; **12**/8, 9, 22; **16**/19,
20, 47

reservation of public policy
3/35

restoration   **12**/8, 12,
14, 22, 27, 37

restriction   **1**/35, 41;

21, 34; **16**/10, 12, 44, 53

transnational law

6/4, 5, 35; **7**/1, 6, 8, 10, 16,
17, 19, 21, 22, 23, 25, 27,
28, 32, 41; **8**/19, 22; **11**/23;
14/12, 27

transparency

1/67; **2**/3; **4**/34; **8**/32; **9**/3,
4, 5, 6, 7, 8, 9, 10, 11, 34

U

UNCITRAL model law

7/28

universality   **3**/15

CALL FOR PAPERS FOR VOLUMES 2020/2021

Did you find the articles in the tenth volume of CYIL interesting?
Would you like to react to a current article
or contribute to future volumes?

We are seeking authors for both
the Czech Yearbook on International Law® and the
Czech (& Central European) Yearbook of Arbitration®.

The general topics for the 2020/2021 volumes are following:

CYIL 2020
*Human Rights, Humanity
and Sustainable Development
from the International Law
Perspective*

CYArb® 2020
*Arbitration and International
Treaties, Customs and
Standards*

CYIL 2021
Immunities and Privileges

CYArb® 2021
(Best) Practices in Arbitration

More general and contact information available at:

www.czechyearbook.org
www.lexlata.pro

CYIL – Czech Yearbook of International Law®, 2020
Human Rights, Humanity and Sustainable Development from the International Law Perspective

It is sometimes argued that human rights are an already settled and precisely defined category of imperative standards. Democratic states and international organisations have for decades now attempted to clarify and enforce, as much as possible, human rights and humanity standards, as well as human approaches, to the broadest possible extent. Nonetheless, the contents of even such crucial categories may be susceptible to various changes. The reason is that our present global world is completely different from the world in which the modern standards of human rights came into existence and developed. Globalisation and maximum exploitation of all resources lead the international public, with an ever-increasing urgency, to discuss and adopt measures which ought to secure sustainable development. However, what is the relationship between these measures and fundamental human rights and principles of humanity, and how much can the contents of the latter be influenced by the former? The procedural aspects are another important factor, namely whether the procedural mechanisms of protection and enforcement of human rights are affected as well, and whether perhaps the time has come for a change or, as the case may be, whether the implementation of such changes in our present international environment is possible at all.

CYArb® – Czech (& Central European) Yearbook of Arbitration®, 2020
Arbitration and International Treaties, Customs and Standards

Arbitration is a highly internationalised area. International practice has always influenced the legal development and practice in the individual countries. Conversely, national standards have influenced the creation of international standards and have also significantly influenced the creation and subsequent implementation of international agreements. The 2020 Volume will focus not only on the contents and interpretation of international agreements and international standards, but also on how they change in consequence of an extensive and fast globalisation, new information technologies, how the creation of regional groupings, various political and economic crises bear on or affect their application, etc. The editors wish to point out that fundamental multilateral international agreements are not the only important factors; the often unjustly ignored bilateral international treaties and international agreements limited to a particular region, such as legal assistance treaties, have played their role too as some of them also contain provisions concerning arbitration.

CYIL – Czech Yearbook of International Law®, 2021
Immunities and Privileges

The issues relating to immunities and privileges will be discussed from the public and private law point of view, addressing the immunity of a state, as well as personal and special immunities, their content, and manifestations. The needs of the globalized environment namely suggest that immunities often manifest in situations that international law was previously not concerned with at all, or only marginally. Attention will for example therefore be given to immunities from the perspective of how the Vienna Convention on Diplomatic Relations is applied in practice, immunities in the case of civil and criminal Court proceedings, but also immunities in special situations. Although privileges do not prime facie pose that significant of a question in international law, they cannot be ignored as they are a significant attribute of state representation, diplomatic employees, but also other representatives of the state in international relations.

CYArb® – Czech (& Central European) Yearbook of Arbitration®, 2021
(Best) Practices in Arbitration

Although we are talking about international standards of arbitration, the course of every arbitration is highly influenced by the place (seat) of arbitration. The so called denationalization of arbitration seems to be a debunked idea. Or is this not the case? In any event, despite a high degree of standardization of procedures in arbitration, the influence of national and regional standards cannot be ignored. The standardization of procedures is evident throughout the entire duration of arbitral proceeding. It is evident in commencement of proceedings, in the preparation for hearings, in the hearing themselves, in the burden of proof, as well as in the termination of proceedings. Every state and every region, same as every permanent arbitral institution, has its own "time-tested" procedures through which it influences the culture of arbitration.